# PEACE EDUCATION

## The Concept, Principles, and Practices Around the World

# PEACE EDUCATION
## The Concept, Principles, and Practices Around the World

Edited by

## Gavriel Salomon and Baruch Nevo
*The Stronach Center for Research on
Peace Education
University of Haifa, Israel*

LAWRENCE ERLBAUM ASSOCIATES, PUBLISHERS

2002  Mahwah, New Jersey                    London

| | |
|---|---|
| Senior Editor: | Debra Riegert |
| Editorial Assistant: | Jason Planer |
| Cover Design: | Kathryn Houghtaling Lacey |
| Textbook Production Manager: | Paul Smolenski |
| Full-Service Compositor: | TechBooks |
| Text and Cover Printer: | Sheridan Books, Inc. |

This book was typeset in 10/12 pt. Times, Italic, Bold, Bold Italic.
The heads were typeset in Americana, Americana Italic, and Americana Bold.

Lawrence Erlbaum Associates, Inc., Publishers
10 Industrial Avenue
Mahwah, New Jersey 07430

**Library of Congress Cataloging-in-Publication Data**

Peace education : the concept, principles, and practices around the world / edited by
    Gavriel Salomon and Baruch Nevo.
      p.  cm.
    Includes bibliographical references and index.
    ISBN 0-8058-4193-8 (cloth : alk. paper)
    1. Peace—Study and teaching.   I. Salomon, Gavriel.   II. Nevo, Baruch.
    JZ5534 .P4275   2002
    303.6′6—dc21                                         2001058631

*In memory of André Abraham Salama*

*A humanist and man of vision who managed to combine these qualities with his professional life as an electrical engineer to become a staunch supporter of peace. His last visionary project was to connect all electrical systems in the region, an enterprise that symbolizes his dream for peace in the Middle East.*

*André Abraham Salama was born in 1923 in Alexandria, Egypt and died in 1998 in Haifa, Israel.*

# Contents

## PART IV:  THE RESEARCH

# Preface

The many local wars, conflicts, and intergroup religious, ethnic, and tribal tensions among different groups are said to be the sign of our times. These wars and conflicts have at least two major components—the political–economical and the psychosocial. These two components are in a tight reciprocal relationship, affecting each other and providing meaning for each other. One cannot think of political tensions and conflicts without their psychosocial underpinnings of collective hatred, distrust, fear, and hope. It would be equally difficult to think of the latter without understanding the historical, economical, and political aspects of a conflict, including adversaries' desires to reach independence, claims for land, struggle for self-determination, or fight for equality.

While politicians and civil leaders are struggling, for better or worse, with the political–economical aspects of conflicts, educators, psychologists, clergymen, and other concerned individuals address themselves to the human–psychological sides of conflicts. Employing a variety of means and approaches that range from shared seminars to courses on peace and from collaborative artistic projects to joint soul-searching encounters, they try to cultivate understanding between adversaries, reconciliation, mutual tolerance, skills and dispositions of conflict resolution, and the healing of past wounds. Indeed, the field—often called *Peace Education*—is very active all over the world, involving large numbers of both school children and adults, professionals (teachers, social workers), and political leaders.

However, although very active, particularly in regions of continuous conflict such as Northern Ireland or Israel, the scholarly aspects of the field of peace education lag somewhat behind practice. As Galtung, one of the founders of the field, once commented, there is more research on *peace* than peace *action*, but when it comes to peace *education*, the converse is the case: There is more action, all over the world and under a range of labels, accompanied by what appears to be insufficient scholarship.

This relative paucity of scholarship results, first, in some conceptual confusion: what *is* peace education and how does it differ from its next of kin such as conflict resolution or multicultural education? Second, insufficient scholarship is often reflected in well-intended but not very clear goals for peace education: *What should its attainable goals be?* What can realistically be attained and what conditions have to be met to attain them? What educational and psychological *principles* should be applied to attain effective peace education?

Third, wanting scholarship of the field means insufficient empirical examination of the way it works and—most importantly—the results it does or does not yield. One of the editors of this book, Baruch Nevo, has conducted a survey of recently published works on peace education and has found that only approximately 30% of all relevant programs entail some kind of an evaluation component. Thus, we have only very limited knowledge of how effective the practice of peace education is. Who benefits more from encounter groups, and whose stereotypes become reinforced as a result of involvement in one or another kind of peace education program? Do encounter groups among past enemies lead to a greater mutual acceptance, or do they cause increased divisiveness? When and under what conditions does the former happen and when does the latter? One way to answer such questions is to actually evaluate programs empirically. Another way is to scan existing programs in different parts of the world and search for generalizable lessons that can be learned from them. What could peace educators in, say, Kosovo learn from the experience with the Truth and Reconciliation Commission in South Africa? What lessons can be derived from the day to day contact between Catholic and Protestant neighbors in Northern Ireland that would be of interest to peace educators in Rwanda?

This book is a modest attempt to address these issues and by so doing help to advance the scholarship of the field of peace education. Toward this end, an international group of thirty peace education scholars from a variety of countries—ranging from Rwanda to the USA and from Croatia to the Palestinian Authority—conducted a week-long joint workshop at the University of Haifa, Israel in May of 2000. This book is the result of that workshop—the Andre Salama International Workshop on Peace Education. Based on the workshop's deliberations, we address here four major scholarly issues pertaining to peace education, which constitute the four parts of the book. The first part, the concept of peace education, presents seven views on the nature of peace education, its history, and relationships to neighboring fields. The second part, underlying principles, entails six critical examinations of relevant psychological and pedagogical principles such as the contact experience, conciliation through personal storytelling, reckoning with traumatic memories, body-work, and the socioemotional aspects of reconciliation. The third part, the practice, represents a number of peace education practical approaches in such countries as Northern Ireland, Cyprus, Belgium, Croatia, and Israel, practices from which some generalizable lessons could be learned. Finally, in the fourth part, the research, one study and two reviews of research are presented. The size of this part of the book is a fair representation of the paucity of empirical research in the field.

We owe thanks to many individuals who helped us organize the workshop and edit the book; they are too many to mention them all. However, we are particularly thankful to the Salama family, who found a wonderful way to commemorate Mr. Andre Salama by providing generous support for our international workshop and thus making it possible.

*Gavriel Salomon*
*Baruch Nevo*
Haifa, Israel
June, 2001

# Contributors

**Bar-On, Dan**
PRIME (Peace Research Institute
 in the Middle East)
Ben Gurion University of the Negev
Israel

**Bar-Tal, Daniel**
School of Education
Tel-Aviv University
Israel

**Boninger, David**
Department of Psychology
University of Haifa
Israel

**Cairns, Ed**
Department of Psychology
University of Ulster
North Ireland

**Čorkalo, Dinka**
Department of Psychology
University of Zagreb
Croatia

**Eden, Dvora**
Nothern Galilee College
Israel

**Enslin, Penny**
School of Education
University of Witwatersand
South Africa

**Firer, Ruth**
The Truman Research Institute
 for Advancement of Peace
Hebrew University of Jerusalem
Israel

**Gleicher, Faith**
Department of Communication
University of Haifa
Israel

**Hadjipavlou-Trigeorgis, Maria**
Department of Social and Political
 Science
University of Cyprus
Cyprus

**Harris, Ian**
Department of Educational Policy
 and Community Studies
University of Wisconsin—Milwaukee
USA

**Hertz-Lazarowitz, Rachel**
Faculty of Education
University of Haifa
Israel

**Hewstone, Miles**
Psychology Department
University of Cardiff
Wales

**Kadushin, Charles**
Department of Sociology
Brandeis University
USA

**Leman, Johan**
Federal Center for Equal Opportunities
and Opposition to Racism
Belgium

**Maoz, Ifat**
Department of Communication
Hebrew University
of Jerusalem
Israel

**McCauley, Clark**
Asch Center for Study of
Ethnopolitical Conflict
Psychology Department
University of Pennsylvania
USA

**Mukarubuga, Cecile**
Agency for Cooperation and Research
for Development
Kigali
Rwanda

**Nadler, Arie**
Institute for Diplomacy and Regional
Cooperation
Tel Aviv University
Israel

**Nevo, Baruch**
Department of Psychology and the
Stronach Center for Research
on Peace Education
University of Haifa
Israel

**Ozacky-Lazar, Sarah**
The Jewish-Arab Center
Givat Haviva
Israel

**Perkins, David**
Graduate School of Education
Harvard University
USA

**Salomon, Gavriel**
Faculty of Education and the
Stronach Center for Research
on Peace Education
University of Haifa
Israel

**Shapiro, Sherry**
Dept. of Health, Phisical Education,
and Dance
Meredith College
North Carolina
USA

**Shapiro, Svi**
School of Education
University of North Carolina
USA

**Soudien, Crain**
School of Education
University of Cape Town
South Africa

**Staub, Ervin**
Department of Psychology
University of Massachusetts
USA

**Tal-Or, Nurit**
Department of Psychology
University of Haifa
Israel

# I

# The Concept

# 1

# The Nature of Peace Education: Not All Programs Are Created Equal

## Gavriel Salomon
### University of Haifa

*Imagine that medical practitioners would not distinguish between invasive surgery to remove malignant tumors and surgery to correct one's vision. Imagine also that although different kinds of surgery are practiced, no research and no evaluation of their different effectiveness accompany them. The field would be considered neither very serious nor very trustworthy. Luckily enough, such a state of affairs does not describe the field of medicine, but it comes pretty close to describing the field of peace education. First, too many profoundly different kinds of activities taking place in an exceedingly wide array of contexts are all lumped under the same category of* peace education *as if they belong together. Second, for whatever reason, the field's scholarship in the form of theorizing, research, and program evaluation sadly lags behind practice.*

In this chapter, I wish to offer some basic, conceptual distinctions between different kinds of peace education as they pertain to programs in politically different regions. My argument is that neither scholarly nor practical progress can take place in the absence of clear conceptions of what peace education is and what goals it is to serve. Second, I focus on one class of peace education programs, the class that takes place in regions of intractable conflicts, claiming that other kinds of peace education are subsumed under it; I outline what (in my opinion) its goals and major mission should be.

Peace education has many divergent meanings for different individuals in different places. For some, peace education is mainly a matter of changing mindsets; the general purpose is to promote understanding, respect, and tolerance toward yesterday's enemies (Oppenheimer, Bar-Tal, & Raviv, 1999). A prime example would be peace education programs in regions of intractable conflict such as Northern Ireland, Israel, or Bosnia (e.g., see chapter 19 by Cairns, this volume). For others, peace education is mainly a matter of cultivating a set of skills; the general purpose here is to acquire a nonviolent disposition and conflict resolution skills. Prime examples for such would be school based, violence-prevention programs, peer mediation, and conflict resolution programs (Deutsch, 1993). For still others, particularly in Third World countries, peace education is mainly a matter of promoting human rights (Toh & Floresca-Cawagas, 1996; see also Svi Shapiro, chap. 6, this volume), whereas in more affluent countries it is often a matter of environmentalism, disarmament, and the promotion of a culture of peace (e.g., Harris, chap. 2, this volume).

Is there a common core to all the different varieties of peace education, or is it no more than a loose collection of programs that differ from each other in important ways? Indeed, what is common to schoolyard, violence prevention, multicultural understanding, tolerance toward yesterday's enemy, and the collective striving for dignity and equality? In the absence of clarity of what peace education really is, or how its different varieties relate to each other, it is unclear how experience with one variant of peace education in one region can usefully inform programs in another region. Could experience with peer mediation in a Los Angeles school district enlighten peace educators in Belfast? Would evidence of attitude change as a result of a Swedish program about Peace on Earth inform educators struggling with interethnic tensions in New York? In the absence of conceptual clarity, the benefit of experience and wisdom is unlikely, and the accumulation of a body of scholarship uncertain.

## NOT ALL PROGRAMS ARE CREATED EQUAL

What is peace education? What is the *core* of peace education, its prototypical attributes? What, if anything, distinguishes its most prototypical instantiations from other, similar fields? How does it relate to its relatives—conflict resolution, mediation, democratic education, civil education, multicultural education, and the like—or are all of these to be treated as variants of each other? Given the fact that some programs are designed to cultivate particular skills of interpersonal conflict resolution, whereas others are designed to promote reconciliation with a political adversary, it becomes clear that subsuming all of these programs under one superordinate category of *peace education* harmfully blurs important distinctions. For example, programs designed to cultivate a positive outlook on peace *in general* are profoundly different in their assumptions, the challenges they face, and the goals they hope to attain from programs designed to promote a peaceful disposition toward a *particular* ethnic or racial group.

It is obvious that peace education is not a single entity. A variety of distinctions can be offered. For one, *peace* has more than one meaning, and so does its absence—*violence*. Galtung (1973) distinguished between positive and negative peace, with the former denoting collaboration, integration, and cooperation, and the latter denoting the absence of physical and direct violence between groups. He also coined the construct of "structural violence," denoting societal built-in inequalities and injustices. A second, possible distinction pertains to the sociopolitical context in which peace education takes place: regions of intractable conflict (Rouhana & Bar-Tal, 1998), regions of racial or ethnic tension with no overt actions of hostility (e.g., Leman, chap. 14, this volume), or regions of tranquility and cooperation. A third distinction can be made between desired changes: changes on the local, microlevel, for example, learning to settle conflicts and to cooperate on an interpersonal level, versus desired changes on a more *global*, macrolevel, for example, changing perceptions, stereotypes, and prejudices pertaining to whole collectives. Although in both cases individuals are the targets for change, the change itself pertains to two different levels: more positive ways of handling other *individuals* versus handling other collectives. Still another possible distinction is between the political, economic, and social status of peace education participants: racial or ethnic majority versus minority, conqueror versus conquered, and perpetrator versus victim. Clearly, peace education for the weak and dominated is not the same as for the strong and dominating (for important distinctions, see chapter 3 by Bar-Tal, this volume).

# THREE CATEGORIES
# OF PEACE EDUCATION

Whereas these and other distinctions are of great importance, I think that the sociopolitical context in which peace education takes place supersedes the rest. It is the context that determines to an important extent (a) the challenges faced by peace education, (b) its goals, and (c) its ways of treating the different subgroups of participants. Thus, for example, a rough examination of peace education programs around the world suggests that whereas regions of relative tranquility emphasize education for cooperation and harmony (positive peace), promoting the idea of a general *culture of peace*, regions of conflict and tension emphasize education for violence prevention (negative peace), greater equality, and practical coexistence with real adversaries, enemies, and minorities. Whereas the former are likely to promote individual skills in handling local, interpersonal conflicts, the latter are more likely to address perceptions of and tolerance toward collectives.

With this in mind, I suggest that peace education be classified into three distinctive categories: peace education in regions of intractable conflicts, peace education in regions of interethnic tension, and peace education in regions of experienced tranquility. This distinction is offered mainly for clarification purposes; in the real world, programs are not that well distinguished from each other. Furthermore, no value judgment, importance, or status is implied.

## Peace Education in Intractable Regions

This class of peace education programs takes place in the context of ongoing, violent conflicts between actual adversaries. These are basically conflicts about tangible resources, accompanied and sustained by collectively held national, ethnic, tribal, or religious *narratives* describing (the good) *us* versus (the bad) *them*. These narratives contain a host of collectively held memories of past atrocities and present-day victimhood, and one's own moral superiority over the other (e.g., Rouhana & Bar-Tal, 1998). Peace education in this category attempts mainly to change mindsets that pertain to the collective other, including the other's narrative and one's own group responsibility for the other's suffering. Cases in point are Northern Ireland, Israel–Palestine, Cyprus, and Rwanda.

## Peace Education in Regions of Interethnic Tension

This category of peace education programs takes place in contexts most frequently characterized by interethnic, racial, or tribal tension between a majority and a minority without necessarily entailing either overt acts of aggression or collective memories of a long history of hostilities, humiliation, conquest, or dispossession. Cases in point are Belgium; Blacks, Latinos, and Native Americans in the USA; and guest workers in Germany.

## Peace Education in Regions of Experienced Tranquility

This category of peace education programs takes place in contexts in which there is no specifically identified adversary with whom peace, reconciliation, or coexistence is desired. In such contexts, programs are perhaps best characterized by consisting of education *about* peace rather than education *for* peace, because there is no concrete adversary or outgroup with whom peace is sought. In this respect, education about peace can play a crucial role in cultivating a *bystander concern* for peace such that past indifference to violent acts carried out in other regions of the world (e.g., Rwanda in 1994) will not repeat itself (Staub, chap. 7, this volume).

## FOCUS ON PEACE EDUCATION IN REGIONS OF INTRACTABLE CONFLICTS

Despite the diverse ways in which peace education is operationalized, peace education as designed and practiced in contexts of intractable conflict appears to constitute a superordinate case of peace education as it includes the other kinds of practices and principles. Peace education in regions of intractable conflict often entails elements of antiracism, conflict resolution, multiculturalism, cross-cultural training, and the cultivation of a generally peaceful outlook, but it can neither be equated with these nor reduced to them; it has its residual, unique character that transcends these elements. Relative to these elements, it faces the most difficult obstacles, such as collectively held animosities, shared painful memories, and common national or ethnic views of self and of other, all issues on a collective macrolevel. Such programs are also the least studied and the least conceptually developed ones, relative to those programs that pertain to the microlevel. I thus turn to a more detailed treatment of that category of peace education programs.

Peace education in regions of intractable conflicts *uniquely confronts* what Azar (1990) has described as "ethnic [racial, national, or religious] hostilities crossed with developmental inequities that have a long history and a bleak future." It follows from this conception that this class of peace education faces three important challenges: (a) it faces a conflict that is between collectives, not between individuals; (b) it faces a conflict that is deeply rooted in collective narratives that entail a long and painful shared memory of the past; and (c) it faces a conflict that entails grave inequalities.

The first challenge faced is a conflict, fueled by shared narratives, that is between collectives, not between individuals. In fact, there need not be a personal dimension to the conflict at all: Either there is no contact between individuals on either side of the conflict (Cyprus as a case in point) or, alternatively, daily contact may be accompanied by civilized relationships between individuals (as is the case in the Basque region). Yet, the conflict is alive and kicking. The collective dimension of conflicts is nicely illustrated in a recent newspaper account of the Basque conflict with Spain: "The enemy isn't the Spanish lad next door . . . it's the national state in the form of a central government that responded to the historic cease-fire by arresting the very people with whom it must negotiate" (San Francisco Chronicle, May 24, 1999). In this light, conflict resolution and skills for schoolyard mediation are not of primary relevance for peace education in regions of conflict or tension; the former programs deal with the individual microlevel, whereas the latter has to focus on the collective.

The second challenge facing peace education in contexts of intractable conflict is a collectively held ethos, or narrative, that explains the conflict and each side's role in it, justifies one's own position, and denigrates the other's (Bar-Tal, 2000). Such narratives "generate intense animosity that becomes integrated into the socialization processes in each society and through which conflict-related emotions and cognitions are transmitted to new generations" (Rouhana & Bar-Tal, 1998, p. 762). Of great importance are the collectively cultivated and shared memories providing a historical dimension to the conflict. Collectively held, historical memories are maintained, revived, and promoted by politicians, national historians, textbooks, school curricula, and the media (e.g., Liebes, 1992). Collective, historical memories and narratives affect the views that the individual member of that collective is likely to hold; they affect the way the individual *interprets* the actions of the other, and the way that the individual *relates* to the other. Examples are the memories of the Battle of Little Bighorn held by the Sioux and Cheyenne, as contrasted with its past description in American textbooks, or the memory of the battle of William of Orange in 1690 as it is differently branded into the collective memories of Catholics and Protestants in Northern Ireland. Such memories, as the recent events in Kosovo suggest, have a tremendously strong impact on actual actions, not to mention attitudes and attributions. This is what peace education has to face and to counter.

The third challenge facing peace education is the grave inequalities usually implicated in the conflict—inequalities between conqueror and conquered, between different social or economic statuses, between majority and minority, or between an indigenous population and relative newcomers. Two implications follow from here. One implication is that the two sides would best be served by different kinds of peace education intervention, as they are likely to have different agendas. As a study by Maoz (2000) shows, Palestinians are more concerned with issues of inequalities and past injustices whereas the Israelis are more concerned with the elimination of terror. Similarly, coming to show understanding for the suffering of dispossessed refugees may be an important peace education ingredient for the strong majority, but coming to understand the conqueror's motives or perspective may not be what the conquered would best resonate to. The second implication is that because a feeling of equality among members of contact groups is a major condition for success (Aronson, 1988; Pettigrew, 1998), the absence of equality promises that intergroup contact will fail.

The three challenges just described—facing a conflict fueled by collective narratives entailing a painful, historical dimension and grave inequalities—clearly suggest that peace education in regions of intractable conflict differs to an important extent from the other categories of peace education, particularly peace education in tranquil regions. This does not mean, for example, that the conflict in some high schools between the Jocks and the Goths, or between Puerto Ricans and Blacks, could not entail some of the same characteristics of collectivity and inequality. To the extent that they do, peace education in intractable conflicts would pertain to them, despite the fact that the underlying conflicts are neither as grave nor as deeply anchored in long range, collective memories as those mentioned above.

## THE GOALS OF PEACE EDUCATION IN CONTEXTS OF INTRACTABLE CONFLICTS

It is now possible to offer a conception of peace education in regions of conflict (see Fig. 1.1). We can see peace education, at its best, as an attempt to change the individual's perception of the other's collective narrative, as seen from the latter's point of view, and consequently of one's own social self, as well as to relate practically less hatefully and more trustingly toward that collective other. More specifically, peace education would be expected to yield four kinds of highly interrelated, dispositional outcomes: accepting as legitimate the other's narrative and its specific implications; being willing to critically examine one's own group's actions toward the other group; being ready to experience and show empathy and trust toward the other; and being disposed to engage in nonviolent activities.

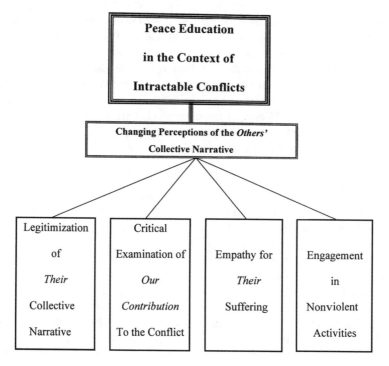

FIG. 1.1. Goals for peace education.

The disposition to accept the other's narrative means in reality the tendency to give that narrative legitimacy and validity. Accepting the other's narrative does not necessarily mean liking it, but it does mean that events, past and present—the ones that constitute the backbone of the collective memory and interpretation—can now be seen from two points of view, rather than defensively rejected, and that both are perceived as right on their own premises. However, such open-minded acceptance cannot remain on the abstract level; it must make contact with real events that are examined afresh. Thus, for example, can the Israeli youngster participating in a peace education program see the flight and plight of the Palestinians in 1948, the *Nakhbah*, from the point of view of a Palestinian? Can "ethnic cleansing" of the Moslems in Bosnia be perceived by a Serb as seen through Moslem eyes? Legitimization of the other's narrative does not necessarily require the adoption of a totally relativistic perspective. One would still be expected to adhere to his or her group's collective narrative.

Tightly intertwined with the legitimization of the other's narrative is the critical examination of one's group's actions toward the other group. Critical examination implies that the pain-inflicting sides in the conflict come to acknowledge their guilt, although, of course, the youngsters participating in the program may have had nothing to do, as individuals, with the atrocities, acts of terror, humiliation, or conquest carried out by their respective groups. Without that acknowledgment, it would be exceedingly difficult to construct a shared reality and establish common grounds (see chapter 7 by Staub, this volume). The Jews would have never shown any conciliatory signs toward the Germans if the latter had not critically and publicly examined their role in the "final solution." The Philippines and Koreans still expect Japan to apologize for its deeds during World War II, something Japan persists in evading. As pointed out by Zhou Xiaizheng, a sociology professor at the People's University, "Germany has been good at making apologies for what it did during World War II. But the Japanese are not good at this, nor are the Chinese. They are always looking for excuses and forgetting misdeeds" (New York Times, January 3, 2001).

This is where the third disposition comes in: empathy and trust. Basically, empathy entails the ability to appreciate the pain suffered by the other side, a willingness to see experiences of the other side from its point of view, to engage in what Cohler and Galatzer-Levy (1992) have called "vicarious introspection." This vicarious introspection, somewhat unlike the more cognitive acceptance of the other's narrative, entails a large emotional component: One comes to feel the agony or the dreams of the other side.

Finally, there remains the goal of adopting a disposition to act in nonviolent ways. I do not mean here actions in the schoolyard, although attaining this would be a desirable side effect. What I mean here would possibly yield two kinds of dispositions: a disposition to forgo the use of force and violence to solve national or ethnic conflicts, and a disposition to actively seek agreement and reconciliation with the other when an appropriate opportunity arises.

# A CAVEAT

The conception of peace education and the goals that emanate from it are both based on an assumption of relative symmetry between the two sides of a conflict. As argued above, both sides are supposed to reach, through one or another kind of peace education program, an empathic perception of the other side's narrative. Would this apply equally to both perpetrator and victim, ruling majority and discriminated minority? Would it be reasonable to expect Black slaves, exiled Palestinians, or persecuted Armenians to accept as legitimate the narratives of slave owners, Israel, or past Turkish governments, respectively? Grave inequalities can become insurmountable barriers to reaching any kind of more positive perception of the oppressor or perpetrator. The greater the social, economic, political, or military inequality between the two sides, the less can peace education, as conceived of here, be a matter of symmetry. When it comes to extreme inequalities, the agenda of the oppressed, conquered, disadvantaged, or discriminated focuses more on the experienced inequality and on the desire to correct it. Inequality easily becomes an energetic force driving feelings of reactance, anger, and frustration that stand in the way of trying to relate positively to an adversary's narrative. Under such conditions, peace education and political action become fused.

# MUTUALITY BETWEEN PEACE EDUCATION PROGRAMS

Does all this then mean that the practice and study of peace education in regions of intractable conflict and tension can neither benefit from its close relatives—conflict resolution, multicultural programs, and such—nor inform them? The differences between the different kinds of peace education, as I have tried to show, are profound. For example, multicultural education, like peace education in regions of conflict, deals with different collective narratives, but there are at least two important differences. First, unlike peace education as explicated here, multicultural education need not entail the kind of traumatic and painful historical components of the other's collective narrative, the one that is laced with hatred, fear, mistrust, humiliation, and bitterness. Second, and most importantly, the narratives that peace education is trying to struggle with are at the very core of a group's sense of identity and collectivity—as is the memory of the holocaust, the defeat of the Serbs by the Turks in the 14th century, and the memories of the Apartheid's humiliation for the Blacks in South Africa. Multicultural education does not usually face such challenges.

Nevertheless, there are both practical and more deep-seated commonalties between the different kinds of programs. Practical commonalties are manifested in educational methods and strategies. Peer mediation and research about it may not appear to have much relevance when perceptions of another group are the target of educational change. However, as a practice, peer mediation may well be a useful ingredient in a program designed to bring each side to accept the legitimacy of the other side's collective narrative through face-to-face encounters. School-based peace curricula may not be the most effective interventions, but they can be quite effective as initial mind openers, precursors to genuine peace education; they can also effectively deal with individual behaviors for local violence prevention such as impulse control, emotional expression, perspective taking, and anger management (Harris & Callender, 1995; Johnson & Johnson, 1996).

Deeper commonalties can be found at the level of basic approaches, or psychological principles, underlying the various practices: the face-to-face contact approach, the mutual exposure approach, the interactive conflict resolution approach (Fisher, 1997), the learning-about-the-other approach, and the like. Thus, to the extent that peace education in regions of conflict or tension is based on underlying principles that have been formulated and studied to serve, for example, conflict resolution or mediation programs, it can benefit from them. Koehler (1990) has studied face-to-face encounters of opposing sides, as part of a conflict resolution program. His findings suggested that when each side presents its arguments, entrenchment rather than understanding often results. Encounters of this kind are popular in peace education programs and findings of this sort are relevant for many program designers. Similarly, findings from research on cross-cultural training for professionals designated for overseas service shows that the expected, positive relationship between participant satisfaction and actual behavioral change are not often obtained. Satisfaction need not be accompanied by actual change while dissatisfaction often does (Brislin & Yoshida, 1996). Despite the dissimilarity between such peace education programs, these findings are of interest as they suggest that self-reports of changes do not necessarily reflect actual changes, a matter of importance when modified dispositions are desired.

In sum, not all peace education programs are alike, as they are designed within different contexts and thus serve different functions. Conceptual clarity as to the basic nature of peace education and its varieties is needed, as only in the light of this is it possible to ascertain how experience and research of one category of programs can usefully inform the design and execution of programs in other categories.

# REFERENCES

Aronson, E. (1988). *The social animal.* New York: Freeman.

Azar, E. E. (1990). *The management of protracted social conflicts.* Hampshire, UK: Dartmouth.

Bar-Tal, D. (2000). *Shared beliefs in a society.* Thousand Oaks, CA: Sage.

Brislin, R., & Yoshida, T. (1996). Intercultural communication training: An introduction. *Journal of Occupational and Organizational Psychology, 69,* 213–215.

Cohler, B. J., & Galatzer-Levy, R. M. (1992). Psychoanalysis and the classroom: Intent and meaning in learning and teaching. In N. M. Szajnberg (Ed.), *Education the emotions* (pp. 41–74). New York: Plenum.

Deutsch, M. (1993). Educating for a peaceful world. *American Psychologist, 48,* 510–517.

Fisher, R. J. (1997). *Interactive conflict resolution.* Syracuse, NY: Syracuse University Press.

Galtung, J. (1973). *Peace: research, education, action.* Copenhagen: Christian Ejlers.

Harris, I., & Callender, A. (1995). Comparative study of peace education approaches and their effectiveness. *The NAMTA Journal, 20*(2), 133–145.

Johnson, D. W., & Johnson, R. T. (1996). Conflict resolution and peer mediation programs in elementary and secondary schools: A review of the research. *Review of Educational Research, 66,* 459–506.

Koehler, D. J. (1990). *Persistence of conflicting views* (Working Paper No. 10). Stanford, CA: Stanford Center for Conflict and Negotiation.

Liebes, T. (1992). Television, parents, and the political socialization of children. *Teachers College Record, 94*(1), 73–86.

Maoz, I. (2000). Multiple conflicts and competing agendas: A framework for conceptualizing structured encounters between groups in conflict—the case of coexistence project of Jews and Palestinians in Israel. *Peace and Conflict: Journal of Peace Psychology, 6*(2), 135–156.

Oppenheimer, L., Bar-Tal, D., & Raviv, A. (1999). Understanding peace, conflict, and war. In A. Raviv, L. Oppenheimer, & D. Bar-Tal (Eds.), *How children understand war and peace.* San Francisco, CA: Jossey-Bass.

Pettigrew, T. F. (1998). Intergroup contact theory. In J. T. Spence, J. M. Darley, & D. J. Foss (Eds.), *Annual Review of Psychology, 49.*

Rouhana, N., & Bar-Tal, D. (1998). Psychological dynamics of interactable ethnonational conflicts. The Israeli–Palestinian case. *American Psychologist, 53*(7), 761–770.

Toh, S. H., & Floresca-Cawagas, V. (1996). Toward a better world? A paradigmatic analysis of development education resources from the World Bank. In R. J. Burns & R. Aspeslagh (Eds.), *Three decades of peace education around the world: An anthology* (pp. 175–210). New York: Garland.

# 2

# Conceptual Underpinnings of Peace Education

## Ian Harris
### University of Wisconsin—Milwaukee

*Every opportunity must be seized to educate people about the horrors of war and the blessings of peace.*
—Daisaku Ikeda (in J. Galtung and D. Ikeda, Choose Peace, Corwin Press, 1995; p. 68)

Over half a century ago, Maria Montessori wrote a book, *Education for a New World* (1946, 1974). Dr. Montessori spent most of her life trying to convince her fellow human beings that they had to use peace education to avert the kind of horror she saw in Italy under the fascist Mussolini. Was she successful in building that New World? Have others, taking a cue from her belief in peace education, learned how to use educational strategies to avoid the terrors of war and violence? For us at the beginning of the twenty-first century, there have been no major world wars since she wrote that book and more people now live under democracy. Millions of citizens are able to communicate instantaneously with each other, bringing to bear Tielhard de Chardin's (1961) concept of a united noosphere. However, millions of people have died from war, also.

Has she convinced people to value peace education?

15

One of the problems in answering that question is figuring out what peace education is. Generally, peace educators warn about the problems of violence and teach about alternatives to violence. However, the problems of violence are so enormous and complex that peace education is practically amorphous, trying like an amoeba to address all the different forms of violence that occur on this planet.

## ADDRESSING DIFFERENT FORMS
## OF VIOLENCE

In a postmodern world, educational reformers adopting the goals of peace education study many different forms of violence, both international and domestic. Violence, in its broadest sense, includes physical, psychological, and structural violence and can be caused by thoughts, words, and deeds—any dehumanizing behavior that intentionally harms another. Physical violence includes direct harm to others—war, ethnic rivalry, juvenile crime, gang attacks, sexual assault, random killing, and physical forms of punishment. Psychological forms of violence occur in places of work, schools, and homes, diminishing a person's sense of worth and security. Structural violence comes from social institutions that deny certain basic rights and freedoms, when citizens cannot get work, health care, water, social security, safe housing, or civil rights. Many problems of violence come from a commitment to militarism to solve problems. Environmental violence caused by pollution threatens people's security, denies them needed resources, and creates fear about the future. Violence at home, in the form of domestic abuse, sexual assault, and child neglect, causes humans to be filled with paranoid fears that make them seek powerful forces to wipe out enemies.

Peace educators adapt their approaches to peace to these different forms of violence within specific, social contexts. In Japan in the 1950s, teachers led a campaign for peace education, where it was known as "a-bomb education," because of their concern about the devastating effects of the atomic bombs dropped on Hiroshima and Nagasaki. In countries of the South, where the problems of poverty and underdevelopment cause violence, this form of education has often been referred to as "development education," in which students learn about the plight of the poor and different strategies to address problems of structural violence. Those concerned with structural violence are often trying to correct actual injustices and discriminations.

In Ireland, peace education is referred to as "education for mutual understanding" (Smith & Robinson, 1992; Whyte, 1991), as Catholics and Protestants try to use educational strategies to undo centuries of enmity. Likewise in Korea, peace education is referred to as "reunification education." Another form of peace education occurs in peace camps in the Middle East with Israeli and Palestinian children, and other places where people are attempting to transform ethnic, religious, and racial hatred. This kind of education hopes to eliminate adversarial mindsets by challenging stereotypes to break down enemy images and by changing perceptions of and ways of relating to the other group.

In the United States and Great Britain, peace education had a focus of "nuclear education," in the decade of 1980s, as teachers and community educators tried to warn citizens, students, and policymakers about the dangers of a nuclear holocaust. Currently, educators in North America and Europe are promoting a form of peace education known as "conflict resolution education." Concerned about interpersonal violence, they provide people with peacemaking skills to manage conflicts non-violently. Teachers pursuing this form of peace education teach alternative dispute resolution methods, as opposed to using their positions of power or rules to settle conflicts. The last half of this century has seen the birth of the field of conflict resolution (Deutsch, 1973; Fisher & Ury, 1981). Within this peace framework fall those encounter educators who use interpersonal dialogue between members of opposing groups to reduce ethnic or religious hatred.

## DIFFERENCE BETWEEN PEACE EDUCATION AND PEACE STUDIES

Peace and violence are dichotomies, somewhat like the Taoist notions of ying and yang. Because of these different forms of violence, peace, peace studies, and peace education also have different meanings. Peace is often referred to as the absence of violence. It is often associated with security. Peace as a positive force implies the process of blessing others, respecting them, cooperating with them, and reducing violence of all kinds.

Peace has different meanings within different cultures as well as different con-notations for the spheres in which peaceful processes are applied. For example, there is a difference between inner and outer peace. Inner peace concerns a state of being and thinking about others, such as holding them in reverence; outer peace processes apply to the natural environment, the culture, international relations, civic communities, families, and individuals. Within each one of these spheres it can have different meanings; for example, within the international sphere, it is often construed to be the balance of power. International relations' experts pursue peace studies in an attempt to avert wars between nations. Sociologists might study cultural peace concerning the norms that legitimize nonviolence and condemn violence. Intercultural peace could imply interreligious and interfaith dialogue, multicultural communication and learning, and so on. Peace within civic society would promote full employment, affordable housing, ready access to health care, quality educational opportunities, and fair legal proceedings. Psychologists concerned with interpersonal conflict would teach about positive interpersonal communication skills used to resolve differences.

There is an important distinction between peace studies and peace education. Peace studies, the study of peace processes, began as a formal discipline in colleges and universities after the Second World War. Peace studies seeks "to analyze human conflicts in order to find the most peaceful (negatively peaceful) ways to turn unjust relationships into more just (positively peaceful)" (Brunk, 2000, p. 25). It often has a geopolitical focus.

Peace education has been practiced by generations of humans who want to live in peace. Peace studies tend to focus on the causes of war, and alternatives to war, whereas peace education is more generic, attempting to draw out of people their natural inclinations to live in peace. Peace researchers identify processes that promote peace, whereas peace educators, educating people about those processes, use teaching skills to build a peace culture. Peace studies' faculties, housed in political science or international relations' university departments, study the causes of wars and ethnic conflict, seeking ways to avoid them. Peace educators, in contrast, are interested in all different aspects of violence from the interpersonal to the geopolitical. They see that education provides an important strategy to achieve peace, because it provides awareness about different peace strategies, including peacekeeping (or peace through strength), peacemaking (or peace through communication), and peacebuilding (or peace through a commitment to nonviolence).

Peace education, focused on peacekeeping strategies, translates the findings of peace researchers about alternative ways the international state system can manage conflict through diplomatic relations (both formal and Track II; see Boulding, 2000). Peace educators try to get students to think of themselves as concerned global citizens willing to transcend national and ethnic differences in order to promote peace. They hope, through the study of security systems, to teach how to construct laws and institutions, like the United Nations, that will help humans avoid the terror of war.

Peace educators teach peacemaking strategies to help children avoid violence by resolving interpersonal conflicts constructively. School personnel bring conflict resolution programs into schools to address aspects of interpersonal violence and to teach peacemaking skills such as mediation, empathy, and alternative dispute resolution methods. School-based peer mediation tries to resolve conflicts between students that may not be overtly violent. Peer mediation programs use a third party, a mediator, to help the parties in conflict resolve their differences. The mediator helps disputants reach a mutually agreed on solution to their conflict. Mediation provides a vehicle for de-escalating violent behavior in schools. One study showed that fights were reduced as much as fifty percent in a school that adopted mediation (Lantieri & Patti, 1996, p. 138).

Peace educators who teach peacebuilding strategies are concerned about building, in children's minds, a desire for peace. Often this type of peace is referred to as *positive peace*, as opposed to *negative peace*, which tries to stop some form of violence. Positive peace education tries to build peaceful communities by promoting an active democratic citizenry interested in equitably sharing the world's resources. These approaches to the problems of violence are controversial because they seek to struggle against injustice and replace structural inequities with institutions that create a more equal world order.

Peace education is not *pacifism education*. The goal is not to make students and citizens quiet, complacent, and content. Peace educators try to point out the problems of violence that exist in society and then instruct their pupils about strategies that can be used to address those problems, hence empowering them to redress the circumstances that lead to violence. Mahatma Gandhi (1958, 1969) used insights he gained from a commitment to nonviolence to overthrow what was at that time the greatest force on earth (the British Empire). Community organizers and Dr. King's use of nonviolence in the Civil Rights struggle (1958) are examples of the legacy peace educators draw upon in teaching youth how to strive nonviolently for their dreams.

## BRIEF HISTORY OF PEACE EDUCATION

Throughout history, humans have taught each other ways to avoid the scourge of violence. The world's religions, following the teaching of such prophets as Moses, Lao Tse, Jesus Christ, Buddha, and Baha'u'llah, have specific scriptures that promote peace. One of the first Europeans who used the written word to espouse peace education was Comenius (1642, 1969) the Czech educator, who in the 17th century saw that the road to peace was through universally shared knowledge. Immanual Kant in his book *Perpetual Peace* (1795, 1970) established the liberal notion that humans could achieve peace by constructing legal and judicial systems. Europeans and Americans, at the beginning of the 20th century, formed peace societies and lobbied their governments against the saber rattling that eventually led to World War I. In the Interbellum period, social studies teachers started teaching international relations so that their students wouldn't want to wage war against foreigners. Peace education became part of a general education reform in which schools were seen as a means to promote social progress. Educators used international studies to help draw citizens of the world together and to contribute toward a more cooperative, peaceful world. Many were convinced that schools had encouraged and enabled war by indoctrinating youth into nationalism at the expense of truth.

At this time, Maria Montessori was traveling through Europe and urging teachers to abandon authoritarian pedagogies, replacing them with a dynamic curriculum from which they could choose what to study. She reasoned that children who didn't automatically follow authoritarian teachers would not necessarily follow rulers urging them to war. She saw that peace depended on an education that would free the children's spirit, promote love of others, and remove the climate of compulsory restriction.

World War II created a new interest in *Education for World Citizenship*. Fifty years ago, Herbert Read (1949) argued for the marriage of art and peace education to help provide images that would motivate people to promote peace. The first academic peace studies program was established in 1948 at Manchester College, Indiana. The Vietnam War stimulated more university and college programs that had a unique, international focus, and the threat of nuclear war stimulated educators, all around the world, to warn of the impending devastation. In 1974 the Quaker Project on Community Conflict in New York published *The Friendly Classroom for a Small Planet* (Prutzman, Stern, Burger, & Bodenheimer, 1988), a curriculum for teachers of young children who wanted to enable students to develop a sense of self-worth, build their community, and acquire the skills of creative conflict resolution. Since that time, the curriculum has gone through 25 editions and has been translated into seven different languages. It is being used extensively in schools in El Salvador, as well as in many other countries. The preface from the first edition sums up its philosophy and states the goals of many modern peace education programs:

> Our particular program has three main goals in the classroom: (1) to promote growth toward a community in which children are capable and desirous of open communication; (2) to help children gain insights into the nature of human feelings and share their own feelings; and (3) to explore with children the unique, personal ways in which they can respond to problems and begin to prevent or solve conflicts. (pp. vi–vii)

This curriculum attempts to deal with the roots of conflict as they exist within the psyches of young children and to teach young children to be open, sharing, and cooperative.

In the 1980s, three books were produced that represent the highlight of an era acutely concerned about the threat of nuclear annihilation. They are *Education for Peace* by a Norwegian, Birgit Brocke-Utne (1985), *Comprehensive Peace Education* by Betty Reardon (1988) and *Peace Education* by Ian Harris (1988), both citizens of the United States. Brocke-Utne pointed out the devastation that militarism, war, and male violence wreaks on females and argued that feminism is the starting point for effective disarmament. She pointed out that societies not at war were not necessarily peaceful societies because they still had considerable domestic violence. Reardon argued that the core values of schooling should be care, concern, and commitment, and the key concepts of peace education should be planetary stewardship, global citizenship, and humane relationships. Harris stated that the ten goals of peace education should be to appreciate the richness of the concept *peace*; to address fears; to provide information about security systems; to understand violent behavior; to develop intercultural understanding; to provide for a future orientation; to teach peace as a process; to promote a concept of peace accompanied by social justice; to stimulate a respect for life; and to end violence. He also emphasized that a peaceful pedagogy must belong to any attempt to teach about peace. The key ingredients of such a pedagogy are cooperative learning, democratic community, moral sensitivity, and critical thinking.

At the beginning of the 1990s, the globalists lost some of their hold on the domain of peace education and the humanists took over. Peace educators became more concerned about civil, domestic, cultural, and ethnic forms of violence. Peace educators try to heal some of the wounds of their pupils who have been raised in violent cultures. Based on the work of Carl Rogers (1942), a popular psychology movement known as *new age healing* has swept throughout the world somewhat on the wings of older, indigenous traditions. This movement has influenced peace educators whose goal is to heal wounds that create huge pools of rage in the psyche.

At the beginning of the new millennium, conflict resolution education is one of the fastest growing school reforms in the West. Conflict resolution educators provide basic communication skills necessary for survival in a postmodern world. Johnson and Johnson (1991) started to teach the skills for peacemaking to teachers, who in turn would instruct their children in some of the more sophisticated aspects of civilized behavior. Lantieri and Patti (1996) build on the work of the resolving conflict creatively approach to school violence to urge teachers to wage peace in the schools. They added to the mix crucial components dealing with antibias and multicultural education. Peace educators are promoting the teaching of affective skills so that children will be more cooperative (Cohen, 1994; Sharan, 1994). Feminists have contributed to the expansion of peaceful approaches to schooling by urging schools to change their curriculum away from a competitive to a caring focus that emphasizes domestic skills (Martin, 1985; Noddings, 1993).

In November 1995, the 186 member states of the 28th General Conference of United Nations Education, Scientific, and Cultural Organization (UNESCO) stated that the major challenge at the close of the 20th century was the transition from a culture of war and violence to a culture of peace. In November 1998, the United Nations General Assembly adopted one resolution promoting the culture of peace and another declaring the year 2000, as the International Year for the Culture of Peace, and the years 2001–2010 to be the *International Decade for a Culture of Peace and Nonviolence for the Children of the World.* From that mandate, UNESCO has developed eight areas of action necessary for the transition from a culture of war to a culture of peace. The first of these is *Culture of Peace through Education.* A manifesto, written by the winners of the Nobel Peace Prize and published in Le Monde on July 2, 1997, states that the only one way to fight violence with nonviolence is education.

## MODERN PEACE EDUCATION

At the end of the 20th century, peace educators provided insights into the origins of violence and the alternatives to violence. At the national level, they deliberate about defense and the effects of militarism. How do countries provide for the security of their citizens? What military arrangements contribute to peace and security? In a postmodern world, peace educators are attempting to supplement concepts of national security, based on peace through strength, with concepts of ecological security, based on reverential relationships to the natural world. At the cultural level, peace educators teach about social norms—such as sexism, ethnic hatred, religious intolerance, and racism—that promote violence. At an interpersonal level, they teach nonviolent skills to resolve conflicts. At the psychic level, they help students understand what patterns exist in their own minds that contribute to violence. Peace educators go right to the core of a person's values—teaching respect for others, open mindedness, empathy, concern for justice, willingness to become involved, commitment to human rights, and environmental sensitivity. A student in a peace education course acquires both theoretical concepts about the dangers of violence and the possibilities for peace, as well as practical skills about how to live nonviolently.

At the beginning of the 21st century, peace education is being used in various parts of the world to challenge stereotypes where there is a long history of humiliation, victimization, and hatred of others perceived as enemies. In Israel, there are "initiatives aimed at eliminating prejudice" and "encounter projects aimed at strengthening Israeli-Palestinian understanding" (Klein, 1997, p. 4). In South Africa, empathy is included among human relations' skills, and workshops on discrimination are being conducted in schools. These approaches to peace education are concerned with the tendency to label others as enemies and oppose or fight them. Peace educators in these contexts attempt to break down enemy images and break through a process of numbing and denial about atrocities committed in intractable conflicts. They promote compassion for the suffering of those in the other group, in the hopes of reducing ethnic and religious hatred, and bringing members of conflicting groups together in a dialogic communication process that searches for common understandings. The key is to accept the other and respect the inherent humanity that resides in all humans.

Peace educators, concerned about the violent behavior of youth, use violence prevention strategies to create street-safe kids, who know how to avoid bullying, weapons, crimes, alcohol, drugs, and pregnancy. There are many risk factors for violent behavior—family patterns of behavior; violent social environments; negative cultural models or peers; alcohol and/or drug abuse; and availability of weapons. Addressing some of these factors directly in school can help inoculate children against risky behaviors. Concern about the impact of these risk factors has led to a form of education known as "resilience education," whose goals are to develop "decision-making and affective skills within each person and connectedness between people in the context of a healthy, democratic learning community" (Brown, D'Emidio-Caston, & Benard, 2001, p. 27). Educators, following the principles of resilience education, encourage the exploration of emotions related to adversity that young people face. This approach to the problems of school violence counteracts peacekeeping strategies used in schools that cause schools to resemble prisons.

Recent concern about escalating levels of civil violence has stimulated a variety of peace education called "conflict resolution education," which helps individuals understand conflict dynamics and empowers them to use communication skills to build and manage peaceful relationships. Conflict resolution educators teach children basic skills such as anger management, impulse control, emotional awareness, empathy development, assertiveness, and problem solving skills. Research studies conducted on conflict resolution education in the United States show that it has a positive impact on school climate. Studies have reported a decrease in aggressiveness, violence, dropout rates, student suspensions, and victimized behavior. Conflict resolution education results include improved academic performance, increased cooperation, and positive attitudes toward school (Bodine & Crawford, 1997). There is a tension in this field between controlling children and teaching values to children. Most of its emphasis is on creating safe schools.

## HOW PEACEFUL ARE WE?

At the end of the 20th century, some who question the cost of technological progress are turning to native belief systems to learn how to care for the natural world. Peace educators who seek a peacebuilding approach to the problems of violence attempt to put in children's minds positive images of peace. Creating a peaceful society involves making those images so attractive that humans will choose to behave nonviolently when faced with conflict. This type of peace education about nonviolence provides young people with an image of a world in which humans work together to resolve differences and live in a way that sustains the planet. Education about nonviolence can help counter a culture of violence that reverberates in the media, entertainment industry, politics, national policy, schools, community, and the family.

However, study does not bring peace. As Johan Galtung has stated, "studies alone do not halt direct violence, dismantle violence, nor do they build structural or cultural peace" (1996, p. 35). Research studies (Eckhardt, 1984; Feltman, 1986) have shown that peace education can change attitudes, but to make the world more peaceful, behavioral change is required. Paulo Freire (1984), the Brazilian adult educator, talked about a type of education that developed what he called "conscientization," a mental process that brings to light the assumptions and contradictions underlying conflicts. Because conscientization helps bring conflicts to the surface, it is a necessary but not a sufficient condition of conflict transformation. Peace education can help people understand the causes of conflict and generate potential solutions, but conflicts must be transformed through a complicated process of agreement, reconciliation, compromise, and forgiveness if they are to be resolved and overcome. Conflict transformation leads to new social structures and self-purification of the actors. Peace education leads to understanding and insight. Action is needed to build direct and structural peace.

Maria Montessori might be pleased with what the human race has achieved through peace education. The people of the world have helped create the United Nations and the International Criminal Court, as well as countless other treaties and conventions meant to regulate in a peaceful way the commerce and behavior of humans. Recently, nations have agreed to a nuclear nonproliferation treaty. A worldwide environmental movement is mobilizing to protest wholesale slaughter of nature. Feminists are tearing away the veil of silence that surrounds domestic abuse. Over 300 colleges and universities have peace studies programs. In schools throughout the world, teachers are using conflict resolution education to help prepare their pupils for a contentious world. The Declaration of Human Rights has been developed to champion the causes of the oppressed. UNESCO, through a worldwide effort, is building cultures of peace in neighborhoods and nations.

But still the slaughter continues.

# REFERENCES

Bodine, R., & Crawford, D. (1998). *The handbook of conflict resolution education: A guide to building quality programs in schools.* San Francisco, CA: Jossey-Bass.

Boulding, E. (2000). *Cultures of peace: The hidden side of history.* Syracuse, NY: Syracuse University Press.

Brock-Utne, B. (1985). *Educating for peace: A feminist perspective.* New York: Pergamon Press.

Brown, J., D'Emidio-Caston, M., & Benard, B. (2001). *Resilience education.* Thousand Oaks, CA: Corwin.

Brunk, C. (2000). Shaping a vision: The nature of peace studies. In L. Fisk & J. Schellenberg (Eds.), *Patterns of conflict: Paths to peace* (pp. 11–34). Ontario, Canada: Broadview.

Cohen, E. (1994). *Designing groupwork strategies for the heterogeneous classroom* (2nd ed.). New York: Teachers College Press.

Comenius, J. (1969). *A reformation of schools* (S. Hartlib, Trans.). Menston (Yorks.) Scholar Press. (original work published in Latin in 1642)

de Chardin, T. (1961). *Phenomenon of man.* New York: Harper & Row.

Deutsch, M. (1973). *The resolution of conflict.* New Haven, CT: Yale University Press.

Eckhardt, W. (1984). Peace studies and attitude change: a value theory of peace studies. *Peace and Change, X*(2), 79–85.

Feltman, R. (1986). Change in peaceful attitude: a controlled attitude change study of internationalism. *Peace Research, 18*(1), 66–71.

Fisher, R., & Ury, W. (1981). *Getting to yes.* Boston: Houghton Mifflin.

Freire, P. (1984). *Pedagogy of the oppressed.* New York: Continuum.

Galtung, J. (1996). *Peace by peaceful means.* Oslo, Norway: The International Peace Research Institute.

Gandhi, M. (1958, 1969). *All men are brothers: Life and thoughts of Mahatma Gandhi as told in his own words.* (Ed.), Krishna Kripalani, introd. by Sarvepalli Radhakrishnan. Paris: UNESCO.

Harris, I. (1988). *Peace education.* Jefferson, NC: McFarland.

Johnson, D., & Johnson, R. (1991). *Teaching students to be peacemakers.* Edina, MN: Interaction Book Company.

Kant, I. (1975, 1970). Perpetual peace: a philosophic sketch. In Hans Reiss (Ed.), *Kant's political writings* (2nd ed.). Cambridge: Cambridge University Press.

King, M. L. (1958). *Stride toward freedom: The Montgomery story.* New York: Harper.

Klein, U. (1997). Peace research and peace education in Israel. *AFB-INFO: Newsletter of the Peace Research Information Unit, (2)*, Bonn: Arbeitsstelle Friedensforschung Bonn.

Lantieri, L., & Patti, J. (1996). *Waging peace in our schools*. Boston: Beacon.

Martin, J. (1985). *Reclaiming a conversation: The ideal of an educated woman*. New Haven: Yale University Press.

Noddings, N. (1993). *The challenge to care in schools: An alternative approach to education*. New York: Teachers College Press.

Montessori, M. (1946, 1974). *Education for a new world*. Thiruvanmiyur, India: Kalakshetra.

Prutzman, P., Stern, L., Burger, M., & Bodenheimer, G. (1988). *The friendly classroom for a small planet*. Gabriola Island, Canada: New Society Publishers.

Read, H. (1949). *Education for peace*. New York: C. Scribner's Sons.

Reardon, B. (1988). *Comprehensive peace education: Educating for global responsibility*. New York: Teachers College Press.

Rogers, C. (1942). *Counseling and psychotherapy: Newer concepts in practice*. New York: Houghton Mifflin.

Sharan, S. (Ed.). (1994). *Handbook of cooperative learning methods*. Westport, CT: Greenwood.

Smith, A., & Robinson, A. (1992). *Education for mutual understanding: Perceptions and policy*. University of Ulster: Centre for the Study of Conflict.

Whyte, J. (1991). *Interpreting Northern Ireland*. Oxford: Clarendon.

# 3

# The Elusive Nature of Peace Education

## Daniel Bar-Tal
### *Tel-Aviv University School of Education*

Peace, together with freedom, equality, and justice, is one of the most desirable values in almost every society. It has become a universal symbol—a master concept that connotes a general, positive state that includes all the positive qualities that are cherished and aspired to by human beings. This meaning becomes evident in our time when we look at the volumes of documents on peace produced by international institutions and organizations including the United Nations and United Nations Educational, Scientific, and Cultural Organization (UNESCO). Thus, it is not surprising that many societies decide to educate the younger generation in the light of this symbol. The educational system fulfills this mission for society through the schools, which have the authority, the legitimacy, the means, and the conditions to carry it out. Schools are often the only institution that society can formally, intentionally, and extensively use to achieve this mission. In other words, through its agencies (e.g., the Ministry of Education) a society can set its objectives for peace education, prepare the curriculum, delineate the contents of the textbooks and instructional materials, set guidelines for organizing the political climate in the schools, add extracurricular programs, train teachers, instruct schools to show initiative, and oblige students to participate in this learning (see Bar-Tal, in press-a). However, peace education is very different from most subjects given in schools. Because groups and individuals project onto the concept *peace education* their own particular vision of a desirable society, the means to achieve it, and the school's role in this mission, the consequence is the very multifaceted state of peace education we see at the present time. Thus, in comparison with other domains of education, peace education is by nature elusive.

## THE UNIQUE NATURE OF THE OBJECTIVES OF PEACE EDUCATION

Different educational systems in various states around the world have provided peace education throughout the twentieth century up until today (see reviews by Aspeslagh & Burns, 1996; Hermon, 1988). A review of the programs of education for peace in different states indicates that they differ considerably in terms of ideology, objectives, emphasis, curricula, contents, and practices (see, e.g., Bjerstedt, 1988, 1993a; Haavelsrud, 1974; Wulf, 1974). For example, in Australia, peace education focuses on challenging ethnocentrism, cultural chauvinism, and violence, on the one hand, and promoting cultural diversity, nuclear disarmament, and conflict resolution, on the other (Burns, 1985; Lawson & Hutchinson, 1992). In Japan, peace education mostly targets issues of nuclear disarmament, militarism, and the nature of responsibility for acts of violence performed in the past (Murakami, 1992). In South America, peace education is preoccupied with structural violence, human rights, and economic inequality (Garcia, 1984; Rivera, 1978). In the United States, peace education programs often concern prejudice, violence, and environmental issues (Harris, 1996; Stomfay-Stitz, 1993).

Within the wide range of different peace education programs, a common general objective can be found. They all aim to foster changes that will make the world a better, more humane place. The goal is to diminish, or even to eradicate, a variety of human ills ranging from injustice, inequality, prejudice, and intolerance to abuse of human rights, environmental destruction, violent conflict, war, and other evils in order to create a world of justice, equality, tolerance, human rights, environmental quality, peace, and other positive features (see Bjerstedt, 1993b; Burns & Aspeslagh, 1996; Harris, 1988; Reardon, 1988). The different outlines of the objectives reflect the degree of dissatisfaction with the present situation. Therefore, it is possible to see peace education as a mirror of the political–societal–economic agenda for a given society, because peace objectives often contain a direct challenge to the present state of a society within the suggestions for change (Vriens, 1990). In effect, peace education mobilizes pupils and teachers to take part in a campaign for change. They are to raise their banner toward an alternative vision of society with the aim of counteracting the beliefs, attitudes, and actions that contradict the objectives of peace education. The objectives of peace education can only be achieved by imparting specific values, attitudes, beliefs, skills, and behavioral tendencies that correspond with the objectives. Imparting values of peace is of particular importance as these values influence specific beliefs, attitudes, and behavior. In addition, peace education emphasizes the acquisition of peaceful behavioral patterns, as changes in behavior ultimately signal the achievement of peace education's objectives. Thus, peace education can be seen as a type of socialization process because its objectives are concerned with the internalization of specific worldviews, as defined by the society in question.

These unique objectives have a number of societal and pedagogical implications, which amplify the elusive nature of peace education. These two groups of implications are discussed as follows.

## SOCIETAL IMPLICATIONS

Three main societal implications are discussed: the condition-dependent nature of peace education, its dependence on social agreements, and its function as a social platform.

## Peace Education Is Condition Dependent

Peace education is always related to the particular conditions prevailing in the society that carries out this educational mission. These conditions produce the specific needs, goals, and concerns of a society, which are reflected in a particular peace education program. Different conditions can affect various aspects of society. For example, societies differ in terms of the nature of intergroup relationships: some are at war or involved in an intractable conflict, whereas others live in relative peace with cooperative intergroup relationships; societies differ in structure: some are multicultural, whereas others are relatively homogeneous; societies differ in economic equality: some are economically polarized, whereas others live in relative equality; societies differ in their civic culture: some are democratic, tolerant, and open, whereas others are relatively autocratic, intolerant, and closed. The different conditions just described pose particular needs, goals, and concerns, which are expressed in the issues that preoccupy a specific society. Issues raised by the conditions in a society may pertain to war, intractable conflict, violence, intolerance, prejudice, inequality, or other problems. The nature of peace education is dictated by the issues that preoccupy a specific society, because it has to be perceived as being relevant and functional to the societal needs, goals, and concerns. This is an important requirement for the initiation and realization of peace education in any society. Nevertheless, it is inevitable that such a requirement contributes to the elusive nature of peace education, because different societies strive to achieve a wide variety of objectives and also because each society views peace education differently. The overall result is that different societies have different definitions of the nature of peace education and its scope, and therefore set different objectives, propose different curricula, and write different texts (see, e.g., Bjerstedt, 1986, 1988, 1990). Moreover, societies differ with regard to their commitment to peace education. Whereas some see it as an important mechanism to change society for the better, others may avoid reference to controversial issues and restrict it to particular objectives or even ban it altogether. Indeed, different political, economic, and societal conditions inevitably influence whether peace education is implemented in schools, what kind it is, and how it is carried out.

## Peace Education Is Based on Societal Agreement

The objectives of peace education propose a vision for a particular society by specifying the desired direction that society should take, and sometimes offering alternatives to the present state of affairs. This implies that, in democratic societies, members of society have to agree with the objectives and contents of peace education. Without legitimization, peace education would be difficult to implement successfully. Clearly, it is relatively simple and easy to develop peace education when it contains those values that society cherishes, proposes goals that society embraces, and suggests a framework of solutions and courses of action that society accepts. However, in reality, such situations are rare and it is more common that certain sections of society do not support the objectives of peace education. The objectives may be perceived as posing a threat to a particular group, several groups, or even society as a whole (see examples provided by Cairns, 1987; Collinge, 1993). Some groups may be afraid of losing power, status, privilege, or wealth. Other groups may perceive the objectives of peace education as negating their ideological beliefs. Some groups may perceive that the objectives of peace education threaten traditional cultural values, or even the order of the social system.

Thus, peace education is a special challenge, based, as it is, on the need for societal agreement in order to implement it successfully in schools. That is, at least a significant part of society has to accept the objectives propagated by peace education and its principles in order to legitimize its institution in the educational system. Agreement should be achieved through public debate, which reflects societal negotiation in democratic societies. The outcome of societal agreement is that the objectives of peace education (content, curricula, and projects) will be the result of consideration, compromise, and adaptation to the constraints of a particular society. It can be said that each society develops a particular peace education that is responsive to its own political dictates. This aspect of the development of peace education is another factor contributing to its elusiveness.

## Peace Education Serves as Societal Platform

The objectives of peace education do not only relate to pupils in schools but also concern the whole of society. They suggest directions for all members of society and propose desirable values, beliefs, attitudes, and patterns of behavior. Therefore, if objectives are to be achieved, peace education cannot merely be an isolated venture in schools. A society that places peace education on its agenda has to spread its messages through other social institutions and channels of communication in order to show the pupils that they are part of a general effort to change society.

Peace education in schools without a wider social campaign is fruitless and disconnected from social reality. Pupils soon feel that it is irrelevant to their life experience and view it as an insignificant endeavor. Thus, although the term *peace education* is often restricted to educational practices in schools, there is also the need for peace education on a wider scale that applies to the whole of society (Bar-Tal, in press-b). Societal peace education is related to society's peace culture and is supposed to reach members of society through the channels of the mass media, literature, television programs, films, and the like. Each society has its own ways and means to express the values propagated by peace education. Because societies differ so greatly with regard to the manifestation of peace values by means of institutions and the available channels of communication, this adds another factor to the elusiveness of peace education.

## PEDAGOGICAL IMPLICATIONS

In addition to societal there are also pedagogical implications that derive from the unique characteristics of peace education objectives, which also contribute to its elusiveness. The objectives of peace education differ remarkably from the objectives of traditional, educational subjects. Their unique nature requires the development of special methods to achieve them. An innovative and creative approach is needed to carry out the educational mission of peace education. The pedagogical implications are elaborated as follows.

### Peace Education Is an Orientation

Peace education can be regarded neither as a separate subject matter nor as a project, but must be seen as an educational orientation that provides the objectives and the instructional framework for learning in schools. It must be incorporated into the objectives and curricula of other subjects and be interwoven into their instruction (Harris, 1988). Peace education provides a prism through which the pupils learn to view and evaluate topics and issues raised in the various subjects, and through this process they learn to view and evaluate current issues in society. History, geography, the social sciences, literature, and languages are the most salient examples of subjects that should include suitable themes for peace education (e.g., the causes of war, its cost, the causes of discrimination, peacemaking, different types of peace, the meaning of justice, and the importance of equality). Teaching these subjects, using peace education orientations, and keeping its objectives in mind is the best way to implement peace education in schools. In addition, particular courses focusing specifically on different themes of peace education should be developed and offered in schools to complement the themes of traditional subjects (see suggestions by Harris, 1988; Merryfield & Remy, 1995).

It is assumed that such an approach requires an engagement with current concerns in society. However, this requirement means that peace education is subject to ambiguity. This is because deciding how much peace education should be incorporated into subjects, which special courses should be developed, and how all these measures can be accomplished are complex decisions determined by political and pedagogical constraints.

## Peace Education Has To Be Open Minded

It is essential that peace education be open minded and should avoid becoming simple indoctrination. This means that it has to remain open to alternative views, with an emphasis on skepticism, critical thinking, and creativity (Harris, 1988; Reardon, 1988). These characteristics are necessary in peace education in view of the objectives, which are supposed to prepare the students to function in society. Thus, pupils have to learn to weigh and evaluate issues, to consider alternatives, to voice criticism, to originate creative ideas, and to make rational decisions. It is the openness of peace education that develops pupils psychologically and specifically prepares them to adhere to the values of peace education while providing them with tools for coping with real-life issues in accordance with these values. It also equips them to solve dilemmas of contradicting values that are encountered in real-life situations, but perhaps most important of all it facilitates the internalization of peace values and inoculates against adopting nonpeaceful alternatives.

The pedagogical implications of peace education make it a most demanding task for educators. It contradicts the principles of traditional education and sets standards that schools often find hard to achieve. Such standards are not new and have been set in the past, but they are of special importance in achieving the objectives of peace education. They challenge the educators to develop new programs and methods of teaching within the framework of peace education.

## Peace Education Has To Be Relevant

Peace education, by nature, deals with the problems that concern a society. These problems are high on the public agenda and often the focus of public controversies. It is thus imperative that peace education be related to concrete, current concerns and social issues. Peace education must not only deal with values and behavioral principles on a general level but should also relate them to specific issues and cases that arise in a society. A relevant approach will show students that they are dealing with real-life issues that concern society. In this way they will be encouraged to apply general values to specific instances taking place. Because each society has its own specific concerns and issues to which peace education has to refer, the content of peace education must reflect this and programs should be tailored to address the relevant themes.

## Peace Education Requires Experiential Learning

Because peace education aims to form a state of mind, its principal modes of instruction target experience. Experiential learning is the key method for the acquisition of values, attitudes, perceptions, skills, and behavioral tendencies, in other words, their internalization. Internalization cannot be achieved by merely preaching; its main acquisition mechanism is practice. Students need to live under the conditions described in peace education in order to internalize its objectives, and they must put into practice the ways of life prescribed for society by peace education for the achievement of its goals. Such a learning climate should include conditions that reflect the objectives of peace education, such as, for instance, tolerance, cooperation, peaceful conflict resolution, multiculturalism, a nonviolent environment, social sensitivity, respect for human rights, and the like (see examples by Bey & Turner, 1995; Deutsch, 1993; Hall, 1999; Hicks, 1988). Setting up experiential learning in schools is a difficult task for educators. It not only requires pedagogical expertise but also, more importantly, demands that teachers have the skill and ability to manage the learning environment while serving as role models for the students.

## Peace Education Is Teacher Dependent

The success of peace education is more dependent on the views, motivations, and abilities of teachers than traditional subjects are. This is so, first, because it refers mainly to the acquisition of values, attitudes, skills, and behavioral tendencies by pupils. This means that the teachers who teach peace education must themselves be in line with its objectives. Teachers who carry out peace education have to cherish its values, hold comparable attitudes, and exhibit similar behavioral tendencies. This precondition is problematic because most teachers do not enter the teaching profession because they hold peace education objectives; some may even have opinions that contradict the values of peace education.

In addition, a special level of pedagogical skills and expertise is required to implement peace education in schools, because it requires the internalization of values, attitudes, and beliefs as well as the use of experiential learning and dedication to causes that may be controversial in that society. In order to implement peace education, teachers have to possess these skills and knowledge and be motivated to carry it out (Reardon, 1988). Educational systems will first have to set up training programs to impart these skills and knowledge, as without them peace education cannot achieve its objectives.

## Difficulties in Evaluating Peace Education

It is difficult to evaluate the achievements of peace education, because its objectives pertain mainly to the internalization of values, attitudes, skills, and patterns of behaviors (see Nevo, chap. 24, this volume). The tests and exams normally used in schools are unsuitable for the evaluation of peace education outcomes, because they do not usually evaluate a state of mind but rather the level of acquired knowledge. The evaluation of peace education requires special techniques adapted to measuring a different kind of outcome. This implies a special call to educators to come up with a creative and original solution because evaluation is an essential aspect of peace education implementation. Evaluation allows the selection of those programs and methods that are effective and have proved capable of achieving the special objectives of peace education.

## SUMMARY

The present analysis explains why peace education is elusive, that is equivocal, openly defined, conditional, disputable, and controvertible. First, the elusiveness of peace education is related to the social, political, and economic implications of the objectives. The objectives, in contrast to those of traditional subjects, suggest an agenda for societal change. They concern the existing norms, ideologies, structures, and institutions in society, and they often propose alternatives to them. Peace education is thus a societal program that concerns society. Its objectives are relevant to society's ideas about its well being. However, ideas differ from one society to another, even though each hopes to achieve the same goal, which is a more peaceful society. Each society constructs its own ideas of peace and sets objectives accordingly. Moreover, ideas of peace often instigate debate, controversy, and even conflict. Therefore, the programs of peace education implemented in democratic societies are the outcome of societal negotiation.

Peace education is also elusive because it is more about attempting to develop a particular frame of mind rather than transmitting a body of knowledge, as is the case of the traditional subjects of education in schools. In other words, the implicit objective of traditional subjects in schools, such as mathematics, biology, or even the social sciences, is the transmission of knowledge. In contrast, in peace education, the objectives imply not only the transmission of knowledge but, more importantly, also the change of the affective, attitudinal, and behavioral repertoire of the pupils. These objectives dictate a variety of pedagogical practices requiring an innovative and creative approach. Educators need to develop new curricula, programs, and modes of instruction to implement peace education in schools.

In addition, the objectives of peace education imply that its content differs considerably from traditional subjects. Whereas the content of traditional subjects is well defined (i.e., pupils in every part of the world can identify the subject from its content), the content of peace education is of a wider scope and is less defined. Even though their objectives may be similar, each society will set up a different form of peace education that is dependent on the issues at large, conditions, and culture, as well as the views and creativity of the educators.

This chapter points out those unique features of peace education that determine its development. Peace education, therefore, poses a special challenge to society and its agents, the educators. Though it is often viewed as *mission impossible*, in my view it serves a momentous and indispensable function in any society. Peace education provides hope for a better future for the younger members of society, because it indicates that their society is aware of its ills and is striving to remedy them in order to build a better place to live. Such hope is essential as it provides goals toward a better future and places it within their grasp; for without such goals, society is doomed to decline and decay.

## REFERENCES

Aspeslagh, R., & Burns, R. J. (1996). Approaching peace through education: Background, concepts and theoretical issues. In R. J. Burns & R. Aspeslagh (Eds.), *Three decades of peace education around the world* (pp. 25–69). New York: Garland.

Bar-Tal, D. (in press-a). Thoughts about a desirable policy of peace education in the state of Israel. In Y. Door, D. Nevo, & R. Shapira (Eds.), *Educational policy in Israel in 2000*. Tel Aviv: Ramot (in Hebrew).

Bar-Tal, D. (in press-b). The nature, the rationale and the effectiveness of Education for Co-Existence. *Journal of Social Issues*.

Bey, T. M., & Turner, G. Y. (1995). *Making school a place of peace*. Thousand Oaks, CA: Corwin.

Bjerstedt, A. (1986). *Peace education today and tomorrow*. Malmö: Educational Information and Debate.

Bjerstedt, A. (1988). *Peace Education in Different Countries*. Malmö: Educational Information and Debate No. 81.

Bjerstedt, A. (1990). Towards a rationale and a didactics of peace education. In A. Bjerstedt (Ed.), *Education for peace in the nineties* (pp. 45–72 ). Groningen: PEC/IPRA.

Bjerstedt, A. (Ed.). (1993a). *Peace education: Global perspective*. Malmo: Almqvist & Wiksell.

Bjerstedt, A. (1993b). Peace education in schools around the world at the beginning of the 1990s. In A. Bjerstedt (Ed.), *Peace education: Global perspectives* (pp. 149–169). Malmo: Almqvist & Wiksell.

Burns, R. J. (1985). Teachers and peace education in Australia: Whose task? In C. Alger & J. Balazs (Eds.), *Conflict and crisis of international order* (pp. 467–476). Budapest: Centre for Peace Research Coordination at The Hungarian Academy of Sciences.

Burns, R. J., Aspeslagh, R. (Eds.). (1996). *Three decades of peace education around the world*. New York: Garland.

Cairns, E. (1987). *Caught in crossfire: Children in the Northern Ireland conflict*. Belfast: Appletree.

Collinge, J. (1993). Peace education in New Zealand. In A. Bjerstedt (Ed.), *Peace education: Global perspectives* (pp. 11–18). Malmo: Almqvist & Wiksell.

Deutsch, M. (1993). Educating for a peaceful world. *American Psychologist, 48*, 510–517.

Garcia, C. (1984). Latin America traditions and perspectives. *International Review of Education, 29*(3), 369–390.

Haavelsrud, M. (Ed.). (1974). *Education for peace: Reflection and action*. Surrey, England: IPC Science and Technology.

Hall, R. (1999). Learning conflict management through peer mediation. In A. Raviv, L. Oppenheimer, & D. Bar-Tal (Eds.), *How children understand war and peace: A call for international peace education* (pp. 281–298). San Francisco: Jossey-Bass.

Harris, I. M. (1988). *Peace education.* Jefferson, NC: McFarland.

Harris, I. M. (1996). From world peace to peace in the 'hood. *Journal for a Just and Caring Education, 2,* 378–398.

Hermon, E. (1988). The international peace education movement, 1919–1939. In C. Chatfield & P. van der Dungen (Eds.), *Peace movements and political cultures* (pp. 127–142). Knoxville: University of Tennessee Press.

Hicks, D. W. (Ed.). (1988). *Education for peace: Issues, principles and practices in the classroom.* London: Routledge.

Lawson, M., & Hutchinson, F. (1992). Peace education in Australia: the legacy of the 1980s. *Peace, Environment and Education, 3*(1), 22–32.

Merryfield, M. M., & Remy, R. C. (Eds.). (1995). *Teaching about international conflict and peace.* Albany, New York: State University of New York Press.

Murakami, T. (1992). *Peace education in Britain and Japan.* Kyoto: Office of Sociology of Education, University of Education.

Reardon, B. A. (1988). *Comprehensive peace education: Educating for global responsibility.* New York: Teachers College Press.

Rivera, D. (1978). A brief approach to the violence of knowledge. *International Peace Research Newsletter, 16*(3), 38–48.

Stomfay-Stitz, A. (1993). Peace education in America, 1828–1990. Metuchen, NJ: Scarecrow.

Vriens, L. (1990). Peace education in the nineties: A reappraisal of values and options. In A. Bjerstedt (Ed.), *Education for peace in the nineties* (pp. 7–23). Groningen: PEC/IPRA.

Wulf, C. (Ed.). (1974). *Handbook of peace education.* Frankfurt: International Peace Research Association.

# 4

# Paradoxes of Peace and the Prospects of Peace Education

## David Perkins
*Harvard Graduate School of Education*

## PRISONERS OF WAR

We are all prisoners of war. Most of us do not spend months or years behind barbed wire, staring up at guard posts situated at the four corners of a filthy enclosure. Nonetheless, we are all prisoners of war. We partake in that long and persistent legacy, that pernicious bustle of activity, that recurrent menace. Human history so far argues that war lies deep in human nature. Periods of peace have sometimes fostered the illusion that the human race had matured to the point where war would forever be left behind. In its own time, World War I was called the Great War, and some said that such a thing could never happen again. But it did. Armed conflicts of modest scope pepper the world today in the first years of the new millennium.

No wonder that peace education is such an attractive notion. No wonder that research to find out how peace education might best function seems to fall among the most important kinds of research one could imagine. We have learned to educate tolerably well for literacy and numeracy. The World Bank and other international institutions have recognized the power of basic education to help lift whole populations to higher standards of economic productivity and health.

Surely peace education and research on peace education deserve equal if not greater investments.

It is encouraging that peace education has been a concern of a large number of people for some time. However, as the rich contributions in this volume show, it has not proved to be a simple or easy enterprise. One factor contributing to the complexity is the very range of what peace, and peace education, can mean. For instance, Galtung (1969) offers a distinction between positive peace—collaborative and integrative in style—and negative peace—the absence of violence. Salomon (chap. 1, this volume) suggests recognizing three categories of peace education, briefly describable as peace education in regions of intractable, violent conflict; in regions of interethnic tension; and in regions of tranquility. This chapter concerns Galtung's negative peace more than positive peace, and it addresses the first and to some extent the second of Salomon's categories. In other words, the focus falls on violence between peoples and what peace education can do to help.

Although the character of war has changed somewhat in recent years, the problems appear as troubling as ever. The age of imperialism appears to be over. No longer can one nation hope to secure a vast empire by force of arms. The threat of nuclear Armageddon seems considerably less than half a century ago, which is the result of a mix of political and economic factors. However, armed conflict and its threat persist in many parts of the world. People in Africa and numerous other settings have learned to fight cheap wars, based on small arms and guerilla tactics (Boutwell & Klare, 2000; Musser & Nemecek, 2000). Ethnic rivalries with long historical roots underlie many of these, sustained by a history of victimization on both sides, with each side demonizing the other (Rouhana & Bar-Tal, 1998).

The beginning observation, that we are all prisoners of war, remains all too true of the world today. Educational issues aside, why does peace prove so often so hard to attain and sustain? Why, when most of us would rather be at peace, do we so often find ourselves at war? Unless we can understand the dynamics of the processes that nudge populations toward peace or war and incorporate such understandings into peace education, the latter seems unlikely to succeed. An analogy might be drawn between peace education and early medical practice. Before the germ theory of disease, physicians certainly acquired some tricks of the trade that could help some people some of the time. However, only the foundation of understanding provided by the germ theory of disease could lift medical practice from a craft to a science. Likewise, only a deep understanding of the dynamic processes that generate peace and war is likely to enable genuinely and consistently effective peace education.

Such an understanding certainly lies beyond the scope of this chapter or even this book. Nonetheless, gestures in that direction are imperative. Thus the present examination of the problem has a dual mission: on the one hand, to understand somewhat better the persistence of war in human history; on the other, to ponder the implications for effective peace education.

## PRODUCTIVE PEACE

To understand the prospects of peace education, we must understand the prospects of peace. Peace education only makes sense when peace makes sense as a way of relating to others. We tend to identify peace with matters such as respect for others' rights and tolerance of others' faiths, skin colors, ethnic and national identities, and so on. These are indeed worthy and important factors. However, they can obscure an important point: Peace thrives when it is adaptive, when it is not just nice but advantageous, when people are better off in a tolerant, collaborative relationship than an adversarial relationship.

Regrettably, this is not always the case. Peace—and peace education—make little sense with Nazi Germany or some other strong aggressor looming on your borders. Wars of aggression are no great mystery. One group or nation wants to possess or dominate on a large scale something the other group or nation has: wealth, land, a strategic position, and even from time to time a supposedly mis-guided religion. One party attacks; the other defends. Such wars are certainly regrettable but also understandable. As a corollary, peace, and peace education, also make little sense under conditions of severely limited resources, where it's you or me, your tribe or my tribe, your nation or my nation that will survive. Under such conditions, conflict is almost inevitable.

It is when peace is seen as productive by both parties that it has a reasonable chance. Fortunately, today in the world this is very often the case. War being as destructive as it is, and the prospects for trade and other collaborations being as generous as they are, the opportunities for productive peace are great and the prospects for education toward such peace are many.

## FIVE PARADOXES OF PEACE

However, then one must ask, "Why do we not see more peace?" When peace is productive, it would seem that nations, tribes, and other groups should fall into stable, peaceful relationships, simply for adaptive reasons. Now certainly such relationships occur, but history and experience suggest that such relationships are unstable. They easily degenerate into rivalries where there need be no rivalry, greed where there is enough to go around, violence where all parties suffer. Such phenomena can be captured in at least five paradoxes of peace.

## Paradox 1: We Often Get War When Peace Seems To Be Mutually Productive

Nations or groups within nations often find themselves at war, or close to war, with neither party particularly interested in a war of aggression, with both parties preferring a peaceful resolution of disagreements. Instead, events get out of hand.

An arms race, fueled by spiraling mistrust, creates a situation in which a single event can tip the situation into armed conflict.

The basic reason for paradox 1 is not difficult to understand. I prefer peace, and you prefer peace. However, I want peace on my terms and you want peace on your terms. Perhaps there is a contested plot of land to which we both lay claim. Neither of us will surrender it to the other. William Shakespeare, in *Hamlet*, Act IV, scene iv, has Hamlet himself speak out about this paradox of war. Hamlet chastises himself for not having taken decisive action much earlier, when to his shame, he observes at a battle

> The imminent death of twenty thousand men,
> That for a fantasy and trick of fame
> Go to their graves like beds, fight for a plot
> Whereon the numbers cannot try the cause.

In other words, the plot of land at stake does not even provide enough room on which to fight the battle for it. What is important is not the land itself but its symbolic significance to the warring parties. Jerusalem, a very small city "wherein the numbers cannot try the cause," offers an apt example.

## Paradox 2: Productive Peace Is Less Stable Than War and Cold War

It is interesting that we speak of wars escalating, but not peace escalating. One might think of warlike (including cold war) and peaceful states of affairs as equals and opposites, but the systems of relationships between groups and nations do not behave symmetrically in this respect. History suggests that relationships slide toward hot or cold war more readily than they slide toward peace. To put this in terms palatable to the contemporary theory of complexity, both peace and war–cold war are attractors in the unfolding dynamics of complex social systems (e.g., Gell-Mann, 1994). However, war appears to be a strong attractor, in the sense that when conditions are mixed, with some events markedly peaceful and others markedly warlike, the situation tends to shift toward war. To put the matter another way, peace more readily deteriorates into war–cold war than war–cold war evolves into peace. This paradox does not mean that all peaceful relationships eventually falter. Some prove robust, depending on history, the character of those involved, and so on. The point, rather, is that productive peace is less stable than it should be, given that by definition productive peace is advantageous.

How can we understand this paradox of peace? For one factor, the fragility of peace has to do with the fragility of trust. Recurrent strife around the world demonstrates that groups can develop profound mistrust easily and that such distrust persists within individuals and cultures, as between Israelis and Palestinians, the factions in Northern Ireland, or the Turkish and Greek Cypriots. Social science research on mental models helps to understand why (Rouhana & Bar-Tal, 1998). Extreme models tend to constitute self-fulfilling prophecies. People process new information in selective ways that confirm the existing model. Even positive actions toward the other party can be read as negative—deliberately deceptive or forced by circumstances. For instance, when the authorities undertake an investigation of police brutality toward minorities, "it's only because of public opinion."

Furthermore, the existing model elicits behavior that tends to confirm it. Not trusting you, I behave in ways that display that mistrust, and this quickly leads to your recognizing that you do not have my good will and therefore behaving in ways that display mistrust of me, which in turn confirms my initial misgivings. Consider, for example, how the refusal to decommission weapons has stalled the peace process in Northern Ireland after the Good Friday accord of 1998 (Duffy, 2000).

## Paradox 3: Peacekeeping Mechanisms Often Generate Another, Different War

From time to time, societies respond to the threat of war between groups within them or war across societies by creating peacekeeping mechanisms. Examples include police forces that temper gang warfare within urban areas, along with international peacekeeping forces and world courts.

Although certainly such mechanisms can be valuable, they also have a somewhat paradoxical quality. Peacekeeping mechanisms generally require a power structure to prevent aggressive action and punish transgressors. This power structure can take many forms—an authority figure such as the head of a tribe or a dictator, a system of courts and formal punishment, or the collective acts of people against a transgressor, as with stoning.

The trouble is, such a power structure can itself come to be seen as a threat by one or another party, provoking a warlike posture toward the structure. Likewise, members of the power structure tend to adopt a warlike posture toward those regulated. For example, relations between the police and African Americans in many U.S. communities have this character. Recognition of this dilemma is very old. When the Roman senate was about to organize a police force, Cato the Elder warned, "quis custodiet ipsos custodes?"—"who polices the policemen?"

This paradox appears difficult to escape from. Yet, from time to time, peaceful societies exist and function in a fairly orderly way within themselves. How can this be? Two possibilities occur: (1) These happy situations happen but they are unstable. Sooner or later, they will degenerate, through a war between the enforcers and those they regulate. (2) There are sophisticated configurations that partially resolve the third paradox. Fortunately, the second seems to be closer to the truth. Societies have invented configurations that introduce enforcing power structures with sharply restricted roles. Some typical characteristics include the following.

*Due Process and Ritualized Punishment.*   The enforcers are allowed to do only harm of specified kinds (fines, jail sentences, or executions) as a result of due process by decision-makers (for instance, judges and juries).

*Decision Makers Are not the Enforcers and Cannot Easily Form Coalitions with the Enforcers.*   Keeping the enforcers and the decision makers separate and out of communication can help with this. Jury trials do so by randomly selecting the juries and keeping them away from the police except in the formal context of the court.

*Enforcers and Decision Makers Are Subject to Enforcement by the Same Mechanism (Although Perhaps a Specialized Branch of It).*   To discourage enforcers and decision makers from doing harm with impunity, they must be subject to sanctions. However, the mechanism for this cannot be another completely different set of enforcers and decision makers, because this simply recreates the third paradox at another level. Thus, the same system of police, courts, and jails that regulates theft and murder also must regulate jury tampering and bribery of judges.

It must be acknowledged that these mechanisms are not perfect, but they do help ameliorate the third paradox of peace.

## Paradox 4: Peace Between Two Parties Generally Has To Involve Many Parties

Although it would seem that only two parties need agree to peace between them, stable peace generally involves a network of interested parties, policies, mechanisms, and so on that surround the two parties in question and help to sustain peace.

Suppose in the entire world there were just two nations. They might be at peace, but each might seem a threat to the other, making this peace unstable. What is needed is an enforcer to eliminate safe harm. So let us add a third nation to be the enforcer. However, this is not enough: We also need a decision maker separate from the enforcer, or the power structure risks falling into the third paradox. Thus we will add a fourth nation to the world. But what is to prevent the third and the fourth from forming a dangerous coalition? We need other nations in the mix, participating in the decision making and power. However, adding one or two more will not change things that much. We need many participating nations. In other words, the social constructions that deal with the third paradox do not work very well for small numbers of participating nations or other groups. This observation yields the fourth paradox of peace.

# Paradox 5: Movement Toward Peace Often Generates Acts of War

Finally, although movement of antagonistic parties toward peace certainly is to be sought, it often generates acts of war designed to sabotage the peace. For example, Duffy (2000) points out how Northern Ireland's Good Friday agreement of 1998 offended hardliners and led to violence designed to sabotage the decommissioning of arms, a critical ingredient of the peace process.

Again, reasons are not hard to find. Members of either camp can easily see movement toward peace as an unacceptable abrogation of principle. As Rouhana and Bar-Tal (1998) point out, each camp sustains a perception of exclusive legitimacy. Compromise accordingly is a loss for both. Or as Duffy (2000) emphasizes, quoting John Whyte, "Questions of religion and national identity are largely non-bargainable." Thus, for some, the very act of reaching for peace on mutually acceptable terms amounts to an intolerable surrender.

## THE TRAGEDY OF SAFE HARM

Why do the paradoxes of peace arise? To be sure, answers have already been offered, paradox by paradox. They included factors such as rival groups wanting peace but insisting on peace without ceding something they want; spiraling mistrust that drives groups toward war or cold war; peacekeeping mechanisms backfiring by themselves becoming *the enemy*; the difficulty of maintaining a truly just peace-keeping mechanism if there are only three or four participating groups; and the sabotage by hardliners of movements toward peace. Although the particulars are different, every one of the five paradoxes shows people reacting as though deeply threatened. How can we account for the force of this reaction?

It is hypothesized that a core part of human psychological makeup is a *safe harm* schema, a schema that warns us against leaving ourselves in positions where another can harm us safely. The basic structure of a safe harm situation occurs when A (an individual or group) fears harm from B without substantial repercussions for B. A might develop such a fear when B's weapons or numbers are stronger and there is no civil mechanism to protect A, for instance when there is no effective law between rival gangs in the inner city or no international law that can moderate between nations. A might develop such a fear when there is something A and B both want and A anticipates that B could easily seize and hold it and otherwise avoid retaliation.

Safe harm can be physical—my property is taken and I am imprisoned, tortured, or killed, without any mechanism of reprisal. Safe harm can also be symbolic. I may be required to ride in the back of a bus, or I may be depicted through vicious stereotypes, again with little that I can do about it.

Safe harm can involve the past, the present, the future, or some combination of these. For instance, situations of safe harm encountered in the past, when your ancestors slaughtered or enslaved my ancestors, may fester and fuel present conflicts. Fear of being put in a position of safe harm tomorrow may promote escalation today.

Why does the safe harm schema exercise such power? Why do we strive so hard to avoid situations of safe harm? Plausibly, aversion to safe harm and the traumatic qualities of being subjected to it have a basis in psychobiology and evolutionary psychology.

In general, evolutionary psychology proposes that important aspects of human behavior have evolutionary roots, for instance, rationality and altruism (e.g., Barkow, Cosmides, & Tooby, 1992). The evolutionary basis of such traits argues that they do not take forms as general as one might think. Altruism is more likely with relatives or within the tribe. People prove to be much more able reasoners in detecting violations of social accords than in detecting general logical shortfalls. Concerning competition and social structure, Pierce and White (1999) propose that material and symbolic localized resources, clearly visible to all, trigger social schemata involving strong competition and hierarchy, whereas distributed and less visible resources trigger social schemata involving less competition, more foraging, and loose friendly affiliations. Consider for instance how a conspicuous, symbolic locale such as Jerusalem, or a conspicuous, localized resource such as the Panama Canal invite efforts to dominate and possess.

In the same spirit, it is suggested that the safe harm schema involves a compulsion with an evolutionary basis. Such a compulsion is highly adaptive in many situations. Allowing oneself to be in a situation in which one is subject to safe harm is risky! The safe harm scheme says, "No, don't tolerate such a position. Escape, or arm yourself, or strike first."

The tragedy of safe harm is that sometimes the safe harm schema works too hard. Fear of safe harm leads to self-defeating actions, as when two parties conduct an arms race toward an ultimate conflict that neither party wants, simply because each fears safe harm from the other.

The underlying logic of this tragedy is well illustrated by the classic prisoner's dilemma (e.g., Axelrod, 1984; *The Prisoner's Dilemma*, 1995). In this dilemma, two prisoners are interrogated separately from one another for a major crime they might have committed. Each can certainly be convicted of minor charges with a sentence of 1 year, but not the major crime. Seeking a conviction, the police tell each prisoner, "We value the evidence you can give. You face 10 years in jail if convicted. However, if you testify against the other prisoner, even if he testifies against you, we'll cut that sentence in half. And if he doesn't testify against you, we'll even waive the minor charges." If neither prisoner testified, each would only be imprisoned for 1 year. However—and here lies the dilemma—without knowing what the other prisoner is going to do, it's always to the advantage of each prisoner to testify, as illustrated in the diagram below.

To spell out the dilemma, suppose I am prisoner $A$. I say to myself, "Well, suppose $B$ testifies. Then I'll be convicted for sure. But if I testify against him, at least my sentence will be cut in half. On the other hand, suppose $B$ does not testify. Then I may as well testify anyway, because then I won't even have to serve the 1-year sentence." Of course, $B$ reasons in the same way. So both testify and both serve 5 years that they might have avoided.

|  | I testify | I don't |
|---|---|---|
| **You testify** | I serve 5 years | I serve 10 years |
| **You don't** | I go free | I serve 1 year |

The safe harm schema reflects the same kind of situation in individual or group conflict situations. Here is an example for situations involving only two parties that invite escalation. Note its similarity to the example for the prisoner's dilemma. As the example notes, escalation has a cost.

|  | I escalate | I don't escalate |
|---|---|---|
| **You escalate** | Balance of power: I'm not safe, but I'm not subject to safe harm, though I had to pay for the escalation. | I am exposed to destruction, a safe harm situation. |
| **You don't escalate** | I'm safe, because I can retaliate overwhelmingly, though I had to pay for the escalation. | Balance of power: I'm not safe, but I'm not subject to safe harm. |

Indeed, the safe harm schema explains the force that generates the paradoxes of peace. People are strongly motivated to avoid situations that subject them to safe harm. This means that they tend not to trust others when betrayal might subject them to safe harm. They escalate rather than risk being caught in a weak position.

It is important to emphasize that the safe harm schema is not a war schema. It does not program people for war. It does not correspond to some aggressive imperative built into the human genes. Instead, it is basically a defensive schema that drives people to avoid situations of potential or actual victimhood. Under certain conditions, the effect of the safe harm schema pushes people toward warlike relationships, but this happens because of an escalation of defensive stances that tips into war.

## MODELS OF PEACE, SAFE HARM, AND UNIVERSALITY

The analysis so far argues that even productive peace—peace perceived as desirable by both sides—is not so easily attained and sustained. The five paradoxes of peace elaborate the difficulties involved. The concepts of safe harm and the biologically rooted safe harm schema explain the force behind the paradoxes. With all this working against productive peace, it is reasonable to ask what prospects for peace are left.

Here it is important recognize different models of peace. There are at least five: friendly peace, ethical peace, interdependent peace, civil peace, and retaliatory peace. Each deserves a brief definition.

### Friendly Peace

This model of peace depends on mutual friendship and trust. When individuals, members of two groups, or members of two nations by and large feel on friendly terms with one another and trust one another, general harmony abides between the two, even if there are occasional squabbles and irritations. Consider, for example, political relations between such countries as the United States and England, who once during the American Revolution were deeply at odds. These countries have been allies for a long time and have fundamentally friendly relations, with an expectation of mutual support. Of course, more is involved than this—networks of trade relationships, for example—but the friendliness factor seems important.

### Ethical Peace

An ethical model of peace has quite a different character. It does not depend on friendship but rather the commitment of both parties to an ethics of rights and justice, often including empathy and even elements of spirituality. Although two parties (whether individuals, groups, or nations) may not be friends, and may even be rivals, peace abides because of the ethical commitments of each. Trust plays a role, but not the same sort of trust as in friendly peace. Trust rests not in the good will of the other party, as in the case of friendship, but in the ethical commitments of the other party. Although this sounds immensely attractive, it is not easy to find examples of large groups with reason for antagonism toward one another that have been held in check solely by ethical considerations. The clearest examples might arise in groups with strong, religious commitments that specifically and centrally restrain violence, as among Quakers. However, religions with a few peaceful precepts offer no guarantee, as a world history littered with episodes of religious conflict demonstrates.

## Interdependent Peace

This names yet a third model of peace, based on interdependence with equitable roles for both parties. Suppose, for example, that two nations sustain a thriving trade relationship. Each benefits from the energetic productivity of the other (a productivity that could not be expected if one took over the other), and together they enhance the quality of life in each. Peace between the two becomes a necessary condition for the well-being of both. For an example in the making, United States–mainland China trade relations are in part motivated by the recognition that economic interactions help to keep the peace, by making war unprofitable.

## Civil Peace

This fourth model of peace again displays a very different style. Civil peace depends on civil mechanisms: accords, laws, justice, courts, and so on. Within nations, conventional systems of justice foster peace between individuals, groups, and corporations. Among nations, analogs of such systems of justice—world courts and United Nations peacekeeping actions, for example—attempt the same.

## Retaliatory Peace

This final model skirts the border of war. Retaliatory peace depends on a balance of retaliatory powers, those that cannot be eliminated by a preemptive strike. A classic example of this model was the concept of MAD—Mutual Assured Destruction—from the cold war that dominated the latter half of the 20th century.

These various models of peace involve a number of contrasts and trade-offs. Two factors in particular invite close examination. First, these models of peace do not speak equally to the problem of safe harm. Some protect the parties involved against safe harm much better than do others. This is important because, as argued earlier, safe harm is the troll under the bridge of peace, the potent fear that makes productive peace unstable. Second, these models of peace are not all universal. "Universal" in this instance means applicable in principle to any situation, regardless of other circumstances, such as the relative power of the parties involved. Universality is important because a model of limited scope cannot serve the needs of peace in diverse situations.

How then do the five models of peace score relative to protection against safe harm and universality? The following example sums up the character of each; a commentary follows.

| | Protects against safe harm | Universal, independent of power, etc. |
|---|---|---|
| **Friendly peace** | No, friendship can deteriorate. | No, can't be friends with everyone. |
| **Ethical peace** | No, ethics easily abandoned or reframed. This has happened over and over again historically. | Yes, in principle, but beware of how easily ethics are reframed. |
| **Interdependent peace** | Yes, to harm the other is to harm oneself. | No, interdependencies vary widely among groups and over time. |
| **Civil peace** | Yes, to harm the other prompts punishment and/or reparation (if the civil mechanism works well!). | Yes, equity in civil mechanism (if the mechanism works well). |
| **Retaliatory peace** | Yes, to harm the other is to prompt retaliation. | No, depends on having a balance of power, which may well be upset. |

Consider how each model of peace addresses safe harm. Friendly peace is an attractive and enjoyable state of affairs between individuals, groups, or nations. However, in itself it offers no protection against safe harm, because either side can violate the friendship and do serious harm without suffering for it, for instance through a preemptive strike. Indeed, if anything, friendship leads us to expose ourselves to safe harm at the hands of the other party, because we trust the other party out of friendship. However, friendships between individuals often deteriorate, as everyday experience shows, and so do friendships between peoples and nations, as history shows.

Ethical peace suffers from a similar shortcoming with respect to safe harm. Either party can overstep the bounds of ethics and, potentially, do harm without repercussions. Moreover, ethical commitments offer a rather flimsy barrier. The history of prejudice teaches that people rather easily adjust their ethical principles to exclude outright enemies and many other groups, such as slaves or recent immigrants of a different ethnicity. Rouhana and Bar-Tal (1998) underscore how such rivalries typically involve perceptions that one's side has the only legitimate position as well as dehumanization of the other side. In addition, the politicization of religion tends to remove religious restraints. Staub (chapter ?, this volume) elaborates how differentiation from and devaluation of the other are systematic parts of the human condition, fundamental in the formation of our social networks and rivalries. Thus, those on the other side have no right to rights.

In contrast, interdependent peace, civil peace, and retaliatory peace all protect against safe harm through repercussions, albeit by quite different mechanisms. In interdependent peace, by harming the other I harm myself. In civil peace, if I harm the other, the civil mechanism harms me. In retaliatory peace, if I harm the other, the other harms me back.

Now consider the generality of each model of peace. Friendly peace, like friendship, is bound to be limited. One cannot be a friend with everyone. Interdependent peace and retaliatory peace are similarly limited, interdependent peace because it depends on a genuine relationship of interdependence, which may not be present, and retaliatory peace because it depends on a genuine balance of power, which may not be present. In contrast, ethical peace and civil peace are universally applicable in principle, although each has its caveats—ethical peace because ethics can so easily be adjusted, as already noted; and civil peace because the civil mechanism is a delicate machine with many parts and may not work that well.

## THE SUBTLE ART OF CIVIL PEACE

With these points in mind, it's notable that civil peace is the only model of peace that both protects against safe harm and has some claim to universality. No wonder civil mechanisms have arisen over and over again in human civilization. Certainly friendship, ethics, interdependence, and even retaliation are important to peace in various circumstances. However, arguably it is naive to imagine that sustained peace on a wide scale is possible without a clear presence of civil peace.

However, this does not mean that civil peace offers an easy path to peace—far from it. Civil peace is a challenging and complex enterprise in several respects. A system of civil peace has to be established before it can accomplish anything, yet, as paradox 5 points out, hard liners may effectively sabotage the accords required for civil peace. Furthermore, the power structure required for civil peace can itself become a focus of conflict, unless it functions within a relatively elaborate and equitable decision-making structure with many participants—paradoxes 3 and 4. Beyond simply being fair, such a system has to operate with reasonable efficiency and reliability to protect against safe harm. For instance, when a judicial system becomes overburdened with cases and cannot deal with the caseload effectively, it stops protecting against safe harm even though every case it actually processes may be handled in an entirely fair way.

Nor is fairness for today enough. Systems of civil peace must take into account not only current transgressions but also historical ones. There are certainly ethical arguments for this, but the point of the moment is that attending to historical transgressions is necessary to protect against safe harm as it is in fact perceived.

Groups who feel that they have suffered safe harm in the past are still looking for the balance to be righted. They are not likely to participate actively and with trust in a civil system that says, "That was then, this is now: Let's start with a clean slate." The safe harm schema will drive them away.

One systematic effort to attend to this dilemma is the Truth and Reconciliation Commission of South Africa, designed to recognize the crimes done in the name of Apartheid, reconcile the rival groups, and build national unity. In return for frank testimony, the commission offered absolution, whereas those who did not reveal their crimes in the name of Apartheid remain subject to legal action. Soudien (chap. 13, this volume) argues persuasively that the commission does not accomplish the reconciliation that it ideally would, for one reason, because its procedures address specific acts of violence with identifiable perpetrators and victims rather than the broad pattern of oppression and violation of human rights under Apartheid. Nonetheless, the commission offers a clear example of an endeavor to recognize and exorcise the ghosts of past safe harm.

In the same spirit, it is important that the civil system in the United States be respectful of the difficult histories of groups such as African Americans or Native Americans. This does not typically mean treating injuries from previous generations as though they occurred today, for instance by turning most of the North American continent over to Native Americans. Standing in the way are both political realities and complex issues of who possesses the original right to what. After all, Native Americans fought wars among themselves and took over one another's territories too. But it does mean making certain allowances. The same applies to civil systems that operate internationally. They could not practically be expected to treat long histories of injury in the same manner as war crimes that happened yesterday. However, to succeed as civil systems, to achieve the commitment of the participants so essential to their functioning, they must make allowances for the past.

Finally, recalling the third paradox again, civil mechanisms cannot themselves become so powerful that there is no way to impugn them. There must be room for civil protest, even civil disobedience. An understanding of civil peace must make room for protesting against the system itself, to protect against its own corruption. This is what makes principles of free speech so fundamental to effective civil systems. Again, although there are, no doubt, ethical arguments, there is a strong pragmatic argument: Without free speech and other avenues of protest, civil systems will not be—and should not be—trusted, because they will not be able to protect their constituencies from safe harm at their own hands.

## NOT JUST FOR POLITICIANS

All this has a very political character. It might be suggested that civil peace is a specialized matter for politicians, diplomats, police, international police forces, lawyers, judges, and so on. Let them establish the system, make the laws, identify the possible transgressors, decide who's guilty, and levy justice. Peace education can dodge these intricacies and dwell instead on mutual understanding, on ethics, on working together, and perhaps ultimately on friendship across the many historical and contemporary boundaries that separate various groups.

Certainly mutual understanding and the ethical stances, interdependence, and even friendship that may grow out of mutual understanding are to be sought through peace education. However, according to the present argument, it will not be enough. Peace education cannot neglect civil mechanisms, because the other mechanisms either lack sufficient generality or do not protect against safe harm. Thus, stable peace depends critically on civil mechanisms as part of the mix.

Moreover, politicians, diplomats, and other specialists cannot carry the burden of civil peace by themselves. Although most people may not be involved in setting up civil systems, civil peace has to be respected by most of the participants or it will not work. This is more likely if people understand it and its role, which in turn means that peace education should address it. Further, individuals who are not professional politicians may well be in situations in which they can labor to set up systems of civil peace in their immediate locale. For this to happen, people need to understand how and why civil peace helps. Finally, individuals who are not professional politicians can promote the cause of civil peace, even when they are not involved personally in setting up civil systems. This again requires understanding how and why civil peace helps.

One way of summarizing the thrust of this chapter is to draw out some implications for a curriculum for peace education. Such a curriculum should include, among other things, the following matters:

- Peace and war, a *complex, dynamic system.*
- The specter of safe harm, a powerful, biologically based force.
- Multiple kinds of peace, some of them speaking better to the problem of safe harm, and some of them more widely applicable.
- Civil peace, the only one that both addresses safe harm strongly and has universal applicability in principle.
- The art and craft of civil peace, which, in light of the aforementioned, has special importance.
- But of course, due attention to mutual understanding, friendship, ethical peace, and interdependent peace.

Another way of summarizing the thrust of this chapter recognizes some serious problems of pedagogy posed by the curriculum content mentioned earlier, along the following lines.

## Conceptual Challenges

Complex dynamic systems are hard to understand and it is hard to understand how to redirect them, because of their odd behavior, as in the paradoxes of peace.

## Emotional Challenges

Peaceful and warlike relationships involve deeply rooted, biologically based feelings and motives around harm, security, and identity.

## Challenges of Action

Conceptual understanding is not understanding in action. For peace education to do its job, learners need to do more than master ideas conceptually. They need to become civil and ethical activists, at least within their immediate contexts. Peace education should in many respects be *feet first* rather than *head first*, cultivating practical behaviors along with understanding rather than expecting appropriate behaviors to flow from cerebral understanding (cf. McCauley, chap. 22, this volume).

To return to the opening image of this essay, we are all prisoners of war. One thing that can help us to get out of the prison camp built into the human condition is an understanding of how that prison camp is constructed. It has been argued here that the plan of construction involves the safe harm schema and its consequences, the paradoxes of peace, the several kinds of peace, and their respective strengths and weaknesses. Remedies must respect the nature of this prison camp and include critical ingredients such as civil peace. Although the war against war must be fought on many fronts from diplomacy to education, certainly peace education has a responsibility to address the deeply paradoxical nature of war from a systemic perspective and prepare learners with a realistic and action-oriented understanding toward likely solutions.

## ACKNOWLEDGMENTS

I thank two scholars, educators, friends, and colleagues of many years, Gavriel Salomon of Israel and Carlos Vasco of Colombia, for conversations that helped me to develop the ideas outlined here. Comments from Ramzi Soleiman were particularly valuable.

## REFERENCES

Axelrod, R. (1984). *The evolution of cooperation*. New York: Basic Books.
Barkow, J., Cosmides, L., & Tooby, J. (1992). *Evolutionary psychology and the generation of culture*. New York: Oxford University Press.
Boutwell, J., & Klare, M. (2000). A scourge of small arms. *Scientific American, 282*(6), 48–53.
Duffy, T. (May 21–26, 2000). Fragile steps: Forging a culture of peace in Northern Ireland. Presented at the AnDré Salama International Workshop for Research on Peace Education. Haifa, Israel.
Galtung, J. (1969). Violence, peace, and peace research. *Journal of Peace Research, 6*(3), 167–191.
Gell-Mann, M. (1994). *The quark and the jaguar: Adventures in the simple and the complex*. New York: W. H. Freeman.

Musser, G., & Nemecek, S. (2000). Waging a new kind of war. *Scientific American, 282*(6), 47.

Pierce, B. D., & White, R. (1999). The evolution of social structure: Why biology matters. *The Academy of Management Review, 24*, 843–853.

Rouhana, N., & Bar-Tal, D. (1998). Psychological dynamics of intractable conflicts: The Israelic-Palestinian case. *American Psychologist, 53*, 761–770.

The Prisoner's Dilemma (1995). Special issue. *The Ethical Spectacle* [online]. Available: http://www.spectacle.org/995/

# 5

# The Gordian Knot
# Between Peace Education
# and War Education

## Ruth Firer
### The Hebrew University of Jerusalem

Why is *peace education* such a difficult task? This is the main question posed in this chapter. I would like to argue that one of the answers to this question lies in the continuous *war education* that youngsters and adults have been receiving since the beginning of mankind, and I also argue that war studies can be converted into a catalyst of peace education.

Wars, conflicts, and terrorism serve as the main topics of the stories, paintings, and other artifacts of the human past. These are still the most exciting subjects in the present mass media and culture. War education is both a product of *war culture* and the means of its perpetuation. According to many socio-biologist scholars, it constitutes the essence of the human being, as it did for Darwin (Laszlo & Jong, 1986), and Freud (Smoker et al., 1990). Scholars who follow such a line refer to war as the catalyst of human progress and a natural part of its character. They emphasize the collective values that are encouraged by conflicts and aggression, such as love of the patria and nation, brotherhood, loyalty, courage, self-sacrifice, and obedience to God. Some would even include in this list the love of peace and justice (Lamm, 1976). Howard (1983, pp. 7–23), who describes the history of wars, states that until World War II, wars were accepted by many as a normal way of human life.

*War culture*, especially in totalitarian regimes, is of a holistic nature. It is reflected in and influences all realms of life, including the personal. Also in Western, democratic culture and economy, aggression and Zero sum games form the basis of the competitive struggle. They rule the lives of the individuals involved; from early childhood the individual learns to fight for his or her space and to defend him- or herself against the aggression of others ("Lebensraum," Rutzel, 1941, can be used as metaphor in a different context).

The systematic research of wars and their impact on human lives that developed mainly after World War II is characterized by its interdisciplinary methods. The researchers reevaluate ancient texts, such as the Bible, and Greek and Roman descriptions of wars, to trace their influence on the culture of their times and their impact on later history until the present time. They are certainly in agreement (even without acknowledging it) that "You may not be interested in war, but war is interested in you" (Trotsky's aphorism in Walzer, 1977, p. 29). Therefore, these researchers, like many laymen, understand that only by learning about the characteristics of wars and their impact can they grasp the nature of peace and of *peace culture* and try alternative ways to transform conflicts from aggression to negotiation, or as Howard (1983, p. 8) concludes, this need to understand the "interaction between power and constant, freedom and obligation, state and community."

Education is part of any hegemonic culture, very often reflecting and reproducing it; therefore, the political and practical effects of such research are obvious. The public debate in Israel, over the place of an ideological, Zionist education in history textbooks, and national curriculum 1999–2001, is a very good example of such cultural turning shift (see references–articles in Israeli newspapers). Usually when war and peace cultures are compared, they are held as contradictions; while the contradictory elements are obvious, I would offer another way to compare these two kinds of cultures. Scholars have to be attuned to the similar principles, such as patriotism, justice, and other motivations, which both cultures claim to be theirs. The same principle applies to teaching methods, in which, unfortunately, the method of indoctrination can be practiced by both sides. This usage of similar elements has to be traced and analyzed in spite of the obvious differences in the historical narratives and goals.

It goes without saying that in reality *war culture* and *peace culture* are interwoven, in spite of being inherently in contradiction to one another. Such an incoherent and disharmonic situation creates endless dilemmas that, on one hand, confuse individuals and communities, but, on the other hand, when a society is prepared for them, enhances humankind's self-awareness and autonomous, decision-making abilities. Whenever a characterization is needed, however, the strongest typologies of a given society, against the background of the real situation it faces determine the nature of the culture. Therefore, it is legitimate to speak about theoretical holistic cultures, wherein a particular context dominates and determines, for the most part, the collective and individual lives of the nation.

Following the same logic, *peace culture* can also be holistic (dominating), and by the same rule, so must peace education (both as a condition and as a result). It has its own set of values and interests, and it claims superiority over other national aims and goals as the only viable situation for the continuation of the community. Aware of the need to avoid a categorical approach, I would argue that understanding the importance of the role of *peace culture* in education could suffice for a start in replacing with it *the culture* of war. It is a self-evident truth that the quickest and most important way to shift from *war culture* to *peace culture* is by stopping wars, terrorism, and aggressive conflicts known as "Negative Peace". So it is a fact that peace education can be implemented during a reconciliation process (post-conflict)—or at any other point—in "intractable conflicts" (Bar-Tal, 1996), as a preparatory or preventive means within peaceful societies ("Positive Peace" based on human rights). In such a cases, the goal includes revising textbooks, national curriculum, and mass media in order to incline the political and the cultural atmosphere toward a peace orientation. The new, legitimized content of knowledge must now address issues of widespread education about conflict, including questions such as: How many people know that 150 to 160 wars and civil clashes have broken out around the world between 1945 and 1994, in which 33 to 40 million people were killed? How many individuals know that out of 200 United Nations member states (in 1994), about 60 were involved in these wars and clashes? During the 50 years following the end of World War II, there were only three weeks of peace around the globe. Names such as Burundi, Cyprus, Morocco, Angola, Pakistan, Israel, and Palestinian Territories and Authority are only a few out of the many conflict zones all over the world. In all these places, men, women, and children have been bombed, poisoned, tortured, raped, and massacred (Topler, 1994). And recently, after September 11, 2001, it is obvious that every place can be a "conflict zone." When we teach about wars and conflicts, these sometimes hidden, yet present facts about the global impact of war have to be emphasized. The "myth making" of wars within a national collective that legitimizes mythical memories have to be replaced by the real data (Howard, 1983, pp. 188–195).

My second argument is that *peace culture*, as well as peace education, has to produce new narratives that will be as exciting as the traditional epics of wars. That means introducing new heroes into historiography, literature, the mass media, and other reflectors of culture, such as heros and heroines who rescue people in distress. We must change plots and compose stories of men and women fighting against the hardships of nature in order to improve lives. This goal includes changing the definition of fundamental values such as courage and patriotism in context of war waging, which should be presented as the fear to make peace and as an expression of aggressiveness that originates from cowardice. Killing terrorism of all kinds should be included in the list of negatives and clear, red lines should be drawn for justified self-defense. Human rights education has to be enhanced, and non-violent civil disobedience topics have to be included in every civics education class (Firer, 2000).

It is not by coincidence that the news relayed by the mass media always deals with catastrophes, conflicts, and aggression. These events have what I call *war appeal.* The main challenge in changing this situation is to create *peace appeal* as suggested earlier. Peace activists and educators can learn a few tricks from the opposite side.

I would like to demonstrate my argument by looking at the following case study: It is the story of the War of 1967, as described in six history textbooks that have been in use in Israeli, Hebrew speaking, junior high and secondary state schools from 1987 on. The chapter on the War of 1967 is included in Firer and Adwan (2002), *The Narrative of the Israeli Palestinian Conflict in History and Civic Textbooks of Both Nations*. (George Eckert Institute, in press)

The War of 1967 is seen as one link in the chain of events in the Israeli–Arab–Palestinian conflict that started in the late 19th century when the first Zionist waves of immigrants started to arrive in the land and build Jewish settlements on it. Like all the other Arab–Jewish clashes, the War of 1967 is described in five out of six textbooks as a direct result of Arab–Palestinian provocation. The main reasons for the war, as presented in these textbooks (with merely slight differences when compared with each other), are Egyptian President Nasser's anti-Israel policy, the refusal of the Arabs to reach an agreement concerning sharing the Jordan and Yarmuk water, Syria's attempt to divert water at its origin, the Palestinian–PLO declarations to destroy Israel and the Fatah (the main PLO military faction) attacks against Israeli civilians (as encouraged by Syria and launched primarily from Jordanian territory) the closure of Israel by the Egyptian, Syrian and Jordanian treaty, and the stationing of Egyptian armies in the Sinai desert reinforced the siege laid on Israel before the war broke out.

On May 16, Egyptian President Nasser ordered a withdrawal of the United Nations Emergency Forces (UNEF) from the Egyptian–Israeli border, and on May 22, he announced a blockade of all goods bound to and from Israel through the Strait of Tiran. The Syrians, on their part, increased border clashes with Israel and mobilized their troops, supported by the USSR (as were the Egyptian military forces).

After this description, it is emphasized that the Israeli politicians did their best to get international help in avoiding the war, but to no avail. Only when Israel learned, unhappily, that although they had done everything possible to avoid conflict, they were actually left alone to defend themselves against the Arab enemies, did they start the *war of defense* that became known as *The Six-Day War*. This war is described as a battle of the few, betrayed by the rest of the world, and standing up to the many and the mighty. The quantitative comparison of the Israeli and Arab soldiers and their weapons enhances this image.

The explicit or implicit conclusion in the textbooks is that Israel is neither guilty nor responsible for the outcome of the War of 1967, and that the Arabs brought the calamity upon themselves. The Israeli victory in the North, Center, and South of the country is described in texts that are concise (one to two pages at most), using short sentences, and the clipped, no-nonsense language of military maneuvers. One can almost hear in the background the strains of a Victory Parade.

The discourse referring to the enemy includes words such as *destruction, wiping out, defeats, collapses*, and so on, yet when alluding to the IDF (Israeli Defense

Forces), the words are *conquering, triumph, controlling the skies*, and the like. The human price of war is mentioned at random, and it mostly relates to the high cost of enemy losses. With the exception of the Jordanians, the enemy countries are portrayed as the losers.

The central hero of Jewish history textbooks is the Israeli nation and state. Everything therefore, is, described and evaluated in relation to this protagonist. This principle is also in operation when the results of the War of 1967 are described and weighed. These are stated both for short term and long term, but they are always evaluated in the light of the benefits accrued to Israel. According to this differentiation, they are categorized as positive and negative results; sometimes the same result has both positive and negative sides—such as, on the one hand, gaining the territories that gave Israel strategic depth and a trump card for future peace negotiation, but, on the other hand, creating, in the long run, a problem with the growing Palestinian nationality. The main, negative result is the continuation and escalation of Israeli–Arab–Palestinian conflict.

In general, the more contemporary these books are, the more negatively are the results presented, with the war narrative undergoing change, as reflected in works by Barnavi (1998) and Naveh (1999), and reaching a peak in Yacobi's textbook (1999).

Nevertheless, the story of the war still remains generally the Biblical story of David, who single-handedly defeated the giant Goliath. Only the war of 1948 (*the Israeli War of Independence*) has been described in the textbooks until lately in similar, heroic-military terms. As mentioned earlier, the new textbooks that are influenced by the revisionist. Post-Zionist, new historians in Israel (Pappe, 1995, Moris, 2000), set a different tone and therefore aroused fierce, public debate that ended recently in political intervention. The Educational Committee of the Israeli parliament postponed the use of Yacobi's textbook (composed by him within the Ministry of Education, 1999) because of its "lack of Zionism." Indeed, from both ends of the political spectrum, members of this Committee voted against this history textbook for use in regular, Hebrew speaking, junior high schools. Their arguments included the fact that according to this textbook, the War of 1967 started with the Israeli bombarding of Syria and not as a consequence of the conventional causes cited in the textbooks described earlier (Ha'Aretz, in Sar, November 20, 2000). However, when weighing the pros and cons of the Six-Day War in the Israeli textbooks, one has to look at the whole story of the conflict—from 1967 until the late 1990s. In spite of the glorious combat and magnificent victory that it represented, all authors continue to describe the War of Attrition, the Yom Kippur War (1973), the endless security problems on and within the borders, the Lebanon War (1982), and the First Palestinian Intifada (1987), thereby emphasizing the heavy toll this warring environment has taken on Israeli history. What they refrain from stating clearly is that this whole, continuous conflict constitutes proof that the War of 1967 did not achieve its purpose. In a word, the Israelis did not attain their long wished for goal of peace and security.

Even the latest developments in the presentation of the War of 1967 have little to do with *peace education*. I would argue that had the result for Israel been different—meaning that the Palestinians accepted the Israelis as their rulers—and that as a result of the War of 1967, the Arab–Israeli conflict came to an end, the war would be presented even in the new textbooks as a great achievement, regardless of the loss of life.

Anyway, the central point of this and the problem of human rights regarding the Palestinian population is to demonstrate the possibility of using war stories as tools of peace education and as of means reducing the positivistic and ethnocentric description and evaluation attributed to them. I would, therefore, recommend integrating into the teaching of history and political science in schools some general reflections about the nature of war. In such a case, it must be demonstrated that wars and terrorism reflect problems that cannot be solved by aggression, and they rather constitute a human tragedy for all sides involved. Included in the textbooks, beside the maps of *victory*, should also be photos and stories of Israeli, Egyptian, Jordanian, and Palestinian youth and men crippled for life; included also should be photos and stories of the families who lost their sons, brothers, husbands, and fathers; included also should be the number of Palestinian villages that were destroyed and their names, photos, and stories of the newly created Palestinian refugees who now join their kin from the War of Independence (1948) and Israeli and Palestinian victims of the intractable conflict from 1967 on. Furthermore, what should be incorporated into the story of the War of 1967 is the responsibility of the winning side to head the efforts of peacemaking and to compensate the victims of the war in order to start a healing process between the sides involved in an animosity more than 100 years old. For it is my strongest belief that the change in Israeli textbooks led to such a revision and it was my hope that the new, Palestinian textbooks would begin a similar process, in their own way. In the meanwhile, the El Aqsa Intifada erupted in September 2000, and on both sides the extremist, anti-peace powers have prevailed. It appears that more blood must be shed before the people of the Middle East area will be ready to switch from a *culture of war* to *a culture of peace*.

## REFERENCES

Bar-Tal, D. (1996). *Michsholim badereh el hashalom.* [Obstacles on the way to peace] Jerusalem: Hamachon Letipuach Bechinuch. The Hebrew University of Jerusalem, (in Hebrew).

Firer, R. (1985). *The agents of the Zionist education.* Ramat Gan: Sifriat Poalim, Ha'Kibbutz Ha'Meuhad, (in Hebrew).

Firer, R. (1996). "Shalom" education through the peace process. *Citizenship, 4*(2), 5–19, London.

Firer, R. (2002) in Firer, R. & Adwan, S. "The narrative of the Israeli Palestinian Conflict in History and civic Textbooks of Both Nations": Georg Eckert Institute, Germany.

Freud, S. (1990). Why war? A reply to a letter from Einstein. In Smoker et al. (Eds.), *A reader in peace studies* (pp. 161–617). New York: Pergamon Press.

Howard, M. (1983). *The Causes of Wars.* Harvard University Press. Cambridge, MA.

Lamm, Z. (1976). *War and education.* Sifriat Meen Ha'Moked, Tarbut Ve'Chinuch. Tel Aviv, (in Hebrew).

Laszlo, E., & Jong, Y. Y. (c. 1986). War. In *World encyclopedia of peace* (Vol. II, pp. 533–556). New York: Pergamon Press.

Moris, B. (2000). *Tikun taut* [Correcting a mistake]. Tel Aviv: Am Oved, (in Hebrew).

Pappe, I. (1995). Ha'historia ha'chadasha shel ha'Tsionut: Ha'imut ha'akademi veha'pumbi [The new history of Zionism: the academic and public debate]. *Kivunim, 8,* 39–47, (in Hebrew).

Saburo-Jenaga, X. (1993/1994). The glorification of war in Japanese education. *International Security, 18*(3), 113–133.

Topler A. (1976). *War and anti war.* Sifriat Ma' Ariv. Tel Aviv, (in Hebrew).

Walzer, M. (1977). *Just and unjust wars.* New York: Basic Books.

# ADDITIONAL RESOURCES

Barnavi, E. (1998). *The 20th century: A contemporary history of the Jewish people.* City: Tel Aviv Books. (For secondary schools and matriculation, in Hebrew)

Golan, A. (2000, November 30). Shiur Behamassat Ha'Zionut [A lesson in how to make Zionism unappealing]. *Ha'Aretz.*

Naveh, E. (1999). *The 20th century.* Tel Aviv Books. Junior high school, (in Hebrew).

Kedem, M. (1987). *Toldot ha'Zionut 1939–73* [The history of Zionism 1939–1973]. Or Am. Secondary matriculation, (in Hebrew).

Naveh, E. (1994). *The 20th century.* City: Tel Aviv. Tel Aviv Books. Secondary school matriculation, (in Hebrew).

Oren, A. (1990). *The Jewish people, the land of Israel and the state of Israel.* Jerusalem: Zalman Shazar Center, Keter Publishing House. Vocational secondary schools, (in Hebrew).

Sar, R. (2000a, November 20). Vaadat ha'chinuch pasla pe echad sepher historia [The Education Committee unanimously rejected a history book]. *Ha'Aretz.*

Sar, R. (2000b, December 1). Mabat chadash al ha'Zionut blimudai ha'historia [A new look at Zionism in the study of history]. *Ha'Aretz.*

Yacobi, Dani (Ed.). (1999). *Olam shel tmurot. (A changing world).* Ministry of Education, Curriculum Department. Junior high school, (in Hebrew).

# 6

# Toward a Critical Pedagogy of Peace Education

## Svi Shapiro
### University of North Carolina at Greensboro

### VIOLENCE AND HATE IN THE NEW
### GLOBAL CULTURE

In the past year, events in every continent have brought home to us again the horrifying and painful consequences of human hatred, as this is mobilized around ethnic and national divisions. Even as we begin a new millennium with all of the talk about globalization, it feels as if we are awash in such bitter conflicts: Bosnia, Northern Ireland, Indonesia, Turkey, Iraq, Sierra Leone, Rwanda, Fiji, the Russian republics, and Israel, to name but a few of them. To these struggles we can add the internal forms of division and hatred in relatively homogeneous societies—ones in which people are hurt and brutalized because of their race, language, gender, disability, religion, sexual identity, and migrant status. In a world with so many hate-filled social conflicts, what might it mean to talk about an education that attempts to teach for a more peaceful, less violent, civic, and global culture? What do we know about the practice of such teaching? Can such an education alter the all-too-frequent human tendency toward demonizing, dehumanizing, and brutalizing the other? On the edge of the new millenium, it is hard to imagine a more important task than the struggle for what Jewish tradition calls *Tikkun Olam*—the repair and healing of our world.

Hopes that the pain unleashed by these social divisions is somehow the smoldering embers of ancient, human behaviors—aggression, intolerance, irrational discrimination against others—seem to find little support in the ever-present human propensity to hate and kill those in some way different from oneself. These seem to be not the residues of an earlier, more violent, and intolerant world, but an apparently much more intractable dimension of the human condition. This does not mean, however, that behind the irrational demonizing and stereotypical fantasies about others are not real grievances and injustices; there is indeed validity to the claim that before there can be peace there must be justice. Human history, with all of its miseries, suffering, exploitation, genocide, and brutalizing of one group of people by another, ensures that the degree of stored up pain and anger is, unfortunately, abundant. The demand for justice, if not vengeance, is not easily satisfied. It is because of this that the process of peacemaking—the bargaining between aggrieved parties—is often a glacial process, full of heart-breaking misunderstandings, difficulties, and failures. Yet there is no alternative to it short of endless war and enmity. Ultimately, breaking the cycle of violence, hatred, and injustice depends on some kind of politics of negotiation and reconciliation. "Blessed are the peacemakers" is more than empty cant.

Yet this is a time when we can see more clearly than ever that peaceful understanding and coexistence between human beings depends on something more than the deal-making between political leaders. It requires a transformative process more deeply rooted; a profound change in our cultural attitudes, beliefs, and behavior—indeed, in the psychological dispositions that shape how human beings react and relate to the others who share our world. Political agreements and treaties are necessary but not sufficient moments in the making of a world where difference is tolerated if not respected, and violence gives way to a reciprocal vision of life's preciousness. I do, however, believe that it is possible to draw on what we have learned from our century's extraordinary barbarism so as to begin to construct an education for our children that might lead them away from its endemic violence, dangerous stereotypes, and conformity to intolerant behavior. The overriding challenge of an education for the new millenium is surely to be found in this struggle for some kind of genuine peace education.

Despite what our political and corporate leaders want us to believe, the educational bridge to the 21st century will not ultimately be found in the ever-increasing technological cleverness of school graduates. The quality of life in the new millenium will depend much more on the capacity of human beings to find ways to resist the draw of victimizing and brutalizing others, and the seduction of joining those who build their sense of identity and value on the indignity of others. Amidst the present clutter of educational talk that is so bereft of human vision and social imagination, one that is obsessed by test scores and technical competencies and the ability of one nation's kids to outperform the children of other nations, a call for another kind of vision for education is beginning to be heard around the world. Among parents, teachers, and citizens, there is a growing recognition that the economic and political globalization of the planet is increasing, not lessening, bitter, ethnic rivalries, social animosities, violence, and intolerance. Globalization, with its corrosion of traditional cultures, destabilization of communities, polarization of wealth (a recent United Nations report noted that the combined wealth of the world's three richest families is greater than the annual income of 600 million people in the least developed countries) carries with it an increased likelihood of human frustration, anger, and violence. More than ever we need an education that will address why we make wars, destroy lives, brutalize and devalue others, and follow those who lead us into the blind rage of ethnocentrism or other forms of hatred and bigotry. At the very least, globalization will require a more balanced vision of education for our children—one that concerns itself not just with the capacity to work in the postindustrial economy. It will demand also the ability and will to contribute to the making of a pluralistic culture in which there is tolerance and respect for difference, and in which conflicts are resolved through democratic means. In the New World order of both growing, global integration *and* intensifying, communal strife, educating for a less violent, more peaceful world must be seen as an urgent priority of public policy. We do not know just how many lives will depend on it, but based on recent experience we may surely expect that it will be many. Of course any attempt to mitigate the violence in our world through education faces extraordinary obstacles. In the United States, for example, the *culture* of guns (latest estimates put the number of firearms in circulation at over 190 million) and the glorified pervasiveness of violent images throughout the society can leave little doubt as to its influence in shaping the outlooks of young males. Across the globe, recent surveys have shown the appalling numbers of children (estimated at over 2 million) now actively mobilized as combatants in wars. Such bloody experience, quite apart from its terrible effects in maiming and killing the young, is also psychologically traumatic. Any educational efforts pale before such realities.

## RESISTING AUTHORITY: EDUCATING FOR DEMOCRACY

What might such an education look like? Forty years after Hannah Arendt described what she called the "banality of evil" and its place in the Nazi genocide machine, we continue to be reminded of the power of unquestioning conformity to authority in the making of human beings ready and willing to commit atrocities against others. Again and again we see young men (it is usually men) recruited to become part of armies or paramilitary organizations trained to unthinkingly obey orders to humiliate, terrorize, and kill those designated as the enemy. Again and again we hear the voices of those who have maimed and murdered plead that they did no more than follow the orders given to them. Whether in Nazi Germany or Bosnia, My Lai or Serbia, South Africa or Israel, we are witness to the effects of teaching individuals that the meaning of being good citizens or soldiers is to unreflexively accept the decisions and commands of others. Yet educators (and generals) know that acting without consciousness or conscience is a *taught* response. Brought up and educated in democratic environments, individuals can just as surely respond to authority with critical attitudes and a readiness to resist inhuman commands. Those who commit themselves to teaching for freedom know the influence on young people of schools and classrooms where there is a constant emphasis on the development of a *critical imagination*. They know the liberating consequences of environments where kids are constantly encouraged to question assumptions, challenge the *taken-for-granted* dimensions of reality, and approach knowledge and truth as the stuff of human invention. Teachers committed to democratic education know that such places nurture autonomy and a radical disposition to resist the imposition of oppressive dogmas or dehumanizing demands.

Teachers in the Federal German Republic understood this when they pushed for classrooms that nurtured the independent, questioning spirit of students; critically minded individuals are antithetical to fascism and mindless authoritarianism. In the United States, since the 1960s, we have learned that students who are encouraged to question and challenge cultural assumptions are unlikely to accept racism, anti-Semitism, homophobia, sexism, or other ideologies of hate. Of course, I know from years of experience just how difficult such pedagogy can sometimes be. Students, used to classrooms and schools where the hidden curriculum teaches them that to be successful one follows blindly the dictates of teachers or administrators, often resist the demand that they begin to think for themselves and question what they hear. It can be profoundly disorienting after years of what Paolo Freire called "banking education" to be expected to overcome the mental passivity that authoritarian teaching instills in people. Democratic environments not only mean a readiness to challenge the taken-for-granted reality, they also mean a willingness to assume more responsibility for deciding what one believes and how one will act. It is often easier to go on believing and acting as one has been told to do. There is nothing natural about democratic citizenship; it requires a sustained and persistent education that cultivates the appropriate moral, existential, and emotional ways of being.

## MULTICULTURAL EDUCATION: HEARING
## THE VOICES OF THE EXCLUDED

If a more peaceful world is necessarily a more just one, then it is certainly easy to see the importance of cultural changes that give dignity and recognition to all those hitherto suppressed or invalidated, human voices. Despite those who would sneeringly deride such changes with comments about *political correctness*, the multicultural movement in schools in North America, Europe, Australia, New Zealand, and elsewhere is an expression of hope and celebration for many people worldwide.

This is the authentic human face of globalism—a witnessing of the diversity of human experience, and a recognition of the complex, multifaceted range of human expression and creativity. Multiculturalism gives voice to all those identities that have been denied, effaced, or despised by those whose visibility and acceptance are underscored by their economic and political power. It means an education, in which the history and experience of those who have been marginalized or ignored because of their language, religion, sexuality, ethnicity, race, age, disability, or nationality, becomes part of *all* our awareness and understanding. To the extent that education has begun to grapple with the full meaning of *inclusion*—whether in terms of curriculum that more fully reflects the range of human knowledge and creativity, or of classrooms that begin to address the diversity of human experience and history that is present in them—the anger and resentment that come from people's exclusion and invisibility give way to a sense of hope and possibility.

What is, however, ultimately at issue in the matter of inclusive classrooms and multicultural learning is the question of social justice. This means that an education concerned with peace must teach students how societies create hierarchies that privilege the experience, culture, and humanity of some and devalue that of others. Such teaching must show students the pain, and frequently anger, that follow when people's lives are stunted and exploited and their cultures denied or destroyed. Through this *pedagogy of justice*, students begin to grasp how much of the bitterness and violence in the world is the stored up frustration of those who have been deprived both of dignity and opportunity. We know that even quite simple experiences with the young, like the well-known classroom experiments where children were divided into the groups of privileged blue eyes and despised brown eyes, can powerfully evoke the sense of anger and frustration of those condemned to a lesser category. The effects of such lessons can be lifelong. Unfortunately, it is still the case that struggles for justice are dealt with in schools often only in the most sanitized and blandest of ways. Studies of textbooks typically used in American classrooms, for example, show just how watered down such historical experience becomes, leaving little sense of the passion, commitment, and courage needed to battle systems of oppression and inequality, or of the capacity and willingness of ordinary people to challenge these worlds of pain. For many students, as I have found in my own teaching, the absence of such knowledge is only a part of the problem. After all, there is the profoundly troubling recognition that often students' own privileges in school and in the world are the result of persistent economic, political, and cultural inequalities. One's own success or advantages are related to the way the world has privileged *your* knowledge, experience, and resources over others. This means that serious consideration of social justice requires one to confront one's own advantages rather than blaming those who are disadvantaged or oppressed. None of this is comfortable or easy. It requires honesty and courage by students in looking at their own lives and circumstances. It demands a readiness to open their eyes and hearts to the reality of those who may have been invisible to them before, and a willingness to see their own role in a system of exclusion and hierarchy. My experience in this kind of work is that education of this sort necessitates classrooms that insist on the difficult process of looking at the world from the viewpoint of the other, with a sense of compassion for the painful renegotiation of who *we* are in the world.

## CONFLICT AND THE INVIDIOUS CONSTRUCTION OF IDENTITY

We have to admit here that the relationship between an education that acknowledges and celebrates cultural identities and the possibility for a less violent, more peaceful world is not a simple one. The opportunity to vigorously assert one's identity is often a two-edged sword allowing those who have been condemned to a prison house of silence to finally speak, but also permitting us to see just how much we define ourselves through the negation of others. In the language of postmodern thought, we have come to see how identity is the construct of discursive or cultural *relations*; what one is, is always defined in relationship to someone else—and usually someone who is seen negatively. Being Black is the obverse of being White; being Arab the negation of being European; female the opposite of male, and so on. The former in each case becomes little more than the denied or devalued qualities of the latter projected onto a despised or excluded group. Such thinking has powerfully upset those dangerous, racist, misogynist, sexist, or homophobic categories that paint human beings into seemingly fixed (or *essential*) spaces. It has opened up the possibility of seeing who we are as fundamentally fluid and always in *connection* to those who we might prefer to view as entirely separate and distinct from us. Yet it also points to how much we weave our identity from threads of invidious distinctions in which we put down or scorn the characteristics of the other. It is easy to see how the freedom to assert one's identity becomes not the road to less violence and more peace, but the vehicle for all kinds of hate-filled intolerance. It is certainly possible to understand the wariness of Zygmunt Bauman toward the new politics of identity in which, he says, the "imagined communities" of nation and ethnicity provide the language for all kinds of intolerance, chauvinism, and separatism. These "neo-tribes," as he calls them, offer the possibility of escape from the anxiety and uncertainty of modern existence, with their promise of reassuring traditions and secure identity. Yet they do so at a steep price, for they are frequently a flight into parochialism and authoritarianism.

It is hard to deny that the struggle for justice and dignity does so often carry with it bitterness and scorn for others as well as a turning inwards. In the process of educating for peace, this must certainly be faced. There is no easy answer to this conundrum. Creating spaces where voices can be heard does mean, sometimes, listening to words of anger, hostility, and resentment. In spite of, or, perhaps, because of this we need educational spaces where there is a persistent effort to bridge differences, to create compassionate connections among people, notwithstanding the divisiveness and disaffection. The feminist, educational philosopher Jane Roland Martin has written eloquently about the need for schools and classrooms to be places where not simply the *productive* values of achievement and mastery are taught, but where the *reproductive* values of connection, relationship, and caring are emphasized. Where schools are so much about success and getting ahead—true just about everywhere in the world—it is hard to imagine creating the kind of compassionate and caring communities that make possible honest and open dialogue. Such places are ones where individuals learn to really struggle with the painful issues of difference and injustice in a pluralistic culture. Unlike the hollow, institutional integration typically practiced around race or disability or language, where students coexist but remain largely strangers to one another, real, educational communities would make possible human encounters with genuine dialogue and interaction. Such places would enable individuals to learn how to face and deal with issues of anger, distrust, and intolerance. In the shadow of the brutality and murder of students by their peers at schools in the United States and elsewhere, it would seem that large, impersonal, competitively oriented schools are probably incapable of creating this kind of dialogic, educational community. This would require learning communities that are smaller and more intimate, and where the curriculum emphasizes cooperation, mutual support, and critical reflection on the purpose and meaning of students' lives. I know from my own work that truly dialogic communities require the safety, trust, and opportunity to speak that can only emerge in small, face-to-face situations. It is not possible to confront our fears and prejudices unless the educational space allows individuals to know each other not as stereotypes, but as real, flesh and blood human beings with the full range of human fears, hopes, dreams, and desires. Such more intimate spaces do not guarantee progress in social harmony, but they do make much more likely the capacity to recognize the other as a human being of equal worth and value to oneself.

## EMPHASIZING SIMILARITY AND DIFFERENCE IN PEACE EDUCATION

Although educating for peace does seem to require continuing the effort to recognize and value our differences, I am left believing that this is only half the story. Certainly justice and democracy, now inseparable from the vision of civic and global peace, do imply the full recognition of our living in a pluralistic world—a world of multiplicity and complex differences. Yet I believe that to educate for peace means also to teach about that which connects us across cultural borders: our shared humanity. Although there are those who are dismissive of the more transcendent vision of our humanness, it is hard to see how we can live without some version of this. It speaks, after all, to that profound quality that connects and unites human beings while, or after, all our distinctions have been given their due recognition. For some, humanity is a philosophical invention, whereas for others it is the ineffable expression of God's creation.

However we see it, it is hard to deny just how powerful and transformative is the notion of the precious and unique quality of human life. It drives the extraordinary and expanding movement for granting human rights throughout the world. It nurtures the deep sense that human life is something sacred, a matter of incalculable value. It unleashes the radical vision that only loving communities can truly and fully honor the infinite worth and dignity of each person. Such profound notions offer not only inspiring possibility but also revolutionary critique of the world we live in. To see in every person the *face* of God, as the French–Jewish philosopher Emanuel Levinas has described it, is to grasp just how ethically desensitized we become when this face is turned into the *other*. The latter is the dehumanized being of our world that we may now be permitted to exploit, violate, dominate, or murder. In our grossly desensitized world this is, indeed, the everyday reality for so many human beings. Educating for peace means, I believe, teaching students to recognize this precious or sacred quality of life, and its inseparability from the loving communities that are needed to nourish and develop it. It means too, teaching our students just how much the values that drive our society, and increasingly our world, are antithetical to this. The terrible confluence of masculinity and capitalism, with their relentless emphasis on competition, control, aggression, separation, and a ruinous attitude toward nature, thwarts and destroys our ability to see the sacred faces of all who share our world. As teachers we need to seek those aspects of our students' moral or spiritual traditions that speak to the extraordinary value of human life—whether that is found in their religious values, political convictions, or cultural beliefs. My own experience has taught me that somewhere in their worldview most students will find such a view of human life, albeit often in competition with views that are racist, ethnocentric, or that in some other way draw negative distinctions between themselves and others. Teaching for peace means eliciting and affirming that part of our worldview that sees life as of inestimable and transcendent value. Nothing in my teaching experience has been more powerful than witnessing the transformation that occurs when individuals are encouraged to acknowledge the other as human—beings of sacred worth *just like they are.*

## A PEDAGOGY OF LOVE
## AND COMPASSION

When talking in class about the importance of the vision of a loving community to the repair and healing of our world, I am sometimes asked if we can teach love. I confess this is a difficult question. In jest I sometimes reply that Gandhi, when asked what he thought about Western Civilization, answered that he thought it *would be* a good idea! Perhaps there is something more than irony in his response.

When wisdom cries out for change in human behavior, the arbiter of what we teach cannot be simply what is empirically most evident or predictable. The vision of loving connections between human beings not only stirs our imagination to the sense of possibility; it also forces us to confront the hateful and violent character of so much of our world. It compels us to recognize how far we are from what Daniel Landes and Sheryl Robbin call "ethical mindfulness," which is the demand that in all of our human contacts and relationships we consider the sensitivities and imagine the pain of others. For many of those I teach, this terrible dissonance appears to nourish a yearning for change. A pedagogy for peace does not in itself produce peace, but it does encourage what Herbert Marcuse called "immanent critique"; a deeper appreciation of the contradiction between this world of so much unnecessary suffering and the ageless dream of a mutually caring and just, human community. If only for the short time we are together with our students, the classroom might become a place where we name this intolerable schism.

## ACKNOWLEDGMENT

An earlier, abbreviated version of this paper appeared in *Tikkun* magazine.

## REFERENCES

Bauman, Zygmunt. Modernity and Ambivalence. Ithaca: Cornell University Press 1991.
Levinas, Emmanuel. "God and Philosophy." translated by Richard A. Cohen, *Philosophy Today* 22. no. 2 (Pummer 1978).
Marcuse, Herbert. *One Dimensional Man*. Boston: Beacon 1964.

# 7

# From Healing Past Wounds To the Development of Inclusive Caring: Contents and Processes of Peace Education

## Ervin Staub
*University of Massachusetts at Amherst*

I see peace education as having several aims. All are important in helping to develop peaceful individuals and creating a peaceful world, even if practical considerations may prevent a focus on all of them in a specific instance. If these aims are taken seriously, peace education will concern itself with the total life experience of children and adults. These aims are:

to help with the development of caring and nonaggressive children and adults who are able to relate to people in their own lives in peaceful ways;

as an extension of this, to help children as well as adults develop into people concerned about and able and willing to promote others' welfare—as people who fulfill their needs in constructive, nonaggressive ways, and respond to others' needs;

to help raise children who become adults and to help adults become people who take action to prevent violence both in their own society and in the world. This includes working to create structures and institutions that inhibit violence and promote peace, such as *caring schools*; an effective but humane justice system that promotes peace—a system that advances justice in their society and the world; and an international system that responds to and helps prevent discrimination and violence against groups of people.

For peace education to be effective, it has to combine conceptual and experiential learning. What children need to learn in the conceptual and experiential realms overlaps, but conceptual learning by itself does not help children to develop in ways that fulfills the aims I described. I refer here to *children*, because that is where peace education has to start. However, adults need peace education as well and require some of the same knowledge and experience, even if some of the methods may differ. In the course of peace education, children or adults need to develop emotional orientations, values, and skills that are required for peaceful conduct and for committed actions to promote peace. Although one can identify universal elements that are important in peace education, these have to be appropriately applied to particular contexts. The immediate requirements of peace education will be different for Jewish and for Palestinian children and adults; for children in Angola who had been recruited or forced into fighting and have now become free again (Wessels & Montiero, 2001); for children in a peaceful midwestern community in the United States; or for members of military forces in countries with widely differing circumstances, such as Colombia or Denmark.

## CONCEPTUAL ELEMENTS OF PEACE EDUCATION

I describe next some important elements of what people need to learn in the conceptual realm.

## The Devaluation of Them

People need to learn about the human tendency to differentiate between *us* and *them* and to devalue and harm *them*. This is often the most basic source, a cornerstone of violence, especially group violence.

Much work has been done on the roots of differentiation and devaluation. These roots include the tendency of the human mind to categorize, into tall and short, many and few, as well as us and them. They include the way stereotyping provides people with expectations about others, thereby simplifying human relations, offering ready ways to perceive and act in relation to people belonging to particular groups. They include the importance of one's own people and group in providing security. The rudiments of this can be seen in infants, who around the age of 6 months begin to show attachment to caretakers, as well as fear of strangers.

Once differentiation between them and us evolves, people begin to favor the ingroup. According to social identity theory, because their identity is invested in a group, people can protect their sense of self and enhance themselves by elevating their group over other groups (Tajfel, 1982; Tajfel & Turner, 1979).

How a whole group comes to be devalued and how this devaluation becomes part of a culture has been less of a focus of study. Starting points for cultural devaluation include, in my view, reactions to great differentness; the need to create a separate identity (e.g., Christians as they separated themselves from Jews); justifying putting others in a lower status (making Blacks into slaves) or justifying having others in a lower status or treating them badly (members of ethnic groups or poor people in general); and the need for a scapegoat or ideological enemy when there are severe economic problems in a society, or persistent political and social chaos (Staub, 1996b).

Once groups are devalued, many forces will be at work to maintain the devaluation. Members of the group are likely to experience discrimination, negative images of them will be spread through literature and the media, and children will be taught to devalue them. Under certain circumstances they can become scapegoats and selected as ideological enemies. When a society faces intense economic problems, political disorganization and chaos, or other difficulties, already devalued groups are likely to be blamed for these problems. In such difficult times, new ideologies are frequently created or adopted—new visions of better social arrangements. People need such visions to gain hope in difficult times. Unfortunately, these ideologies are usually destructive in that they identify enemies who stand in the way of the ideology's fulfillment (Staub, 1989b).

In the case of conflict between groups, a past history of devaluation of the other makes it more difficult to resolve the conflict without violence. Negative views of the other, and mistrust, can make conflict intractable and lead to violence.

Devaluation can vary in content as well as (in part associated with content) intensity. The other can be seen as less intelligent and lazy; or as morally bad—people who will lie and cheat and do other bad things; or as people who are out to exploit *us*, harm us, and even to destroy us. Devaluation is more likely to give rise to violence when it is more intense, or when a group that is viewed negatively and is disliked does relatively well in society by having decent jobs, good material conditions, and reasonable status in society. The latter was true of Jews in Germany, the Armenians in Turkey (Staub, 1989b), the Tutsis in Rwanda (des Forges, 1999; Staub, 1999) and the Baha'i in Iran (Bigelow, 1993).

It is very important for peace education to show that a negative view of the other is often devaluation rather than a correct representation of the other. It is also very important for children and adults to come to notice and objectively look at the negative views propagated in their society about others who are potentially at risk to be harmed (and also about their own group, if they are a member of a group at risk). Peace education should also help people become aware of how they themselves devalue others.

In summary, peace education has to help people learn about and become aware of the importance of the devaluation of groups of people (and at times of individuals—for example, a devalued child who is the object of bullying in school) in creating violence. It must identify and help overcome the devaluation people themselves hold. It should aim to move people to try to diminish the devaluation of others in their society or group. All this requires, in addition to conceptual education, experiential education as well.

What I call a *functional approach* may be valuable in correcting devaluation. This is a perspective to understanding the evolution of cultures, how special characteristics of each group evolve, and where the differences between one's own group and other groups originate. In this perspective, when groups face particular environmental conditions, they respond to them in ways that may be partly accidental, in that they are the result of decisions by leaders at the time. Past decisions, however, shape new reactions to environmental conditions—such as scarcity, or threat by other groups.

The function or purpose of responses to particular conditions is to deal with those conditions. In turn, however, they shape and create culture and social organization. A history of different conditions or choices made in response to them may result in great divergence and variation. For example, in the face of scarcity, in some simple societies, people share everything; in others, they are extremely selfish (Staub, 1978).

As children and adults gain such a functional understanding, they may come to see, not only other societies, but also their own, as the result of this kind of evolution. They may come to see it not as the God-given way of life, but the outcome of a history of events and responses to them. This may lead to greater acceptance of others.

## Destructive Versus Peaceful Ways of Resolving Conflict

Conflict is inevitable. Two children want to play with the same toys; two groups want the same territory as living space, or rely on the same, scarce water supplies. What leads us to resolve conflict in aggressive ways and how can it be resolved peacefully?

There are emotional elements that lead to destructive versus peaceful conflict resolution. One of these is past history that has led to the perception of others in general, or some specific group, as threatening. Devaluation, fear, anger, and hostility may have developed as a result of a culture that teaches or indoctrinates people, or as a result of real experiences of antagonism and violence in interaction with the other (Staub, 1989b). Difficult past experiences can also lead to the projection of hostility on to some group, that is, the assumption that they are hostile toward oneself. In addition to conceptual learning about all this becoming aware of one's own and one's group's devaluation of others and of tendencies to project hostility is extremely important.

In addition to these perceptual and emotional elements, there can also be value elements contributing to aggression. A culture may lead children and adults to hold personal or group gain so important that it justifies aggression. A related finding, in the personal realm, is that individuals who highly value financial success are less likely to engage in helpful or generous acts on behalf of others (Staub, 1995). In the case of conflict involving gain or loss for the group, such values, combined with devaluation of the other, can lead to aggression. In contrast, cultures can promote the value and recognize the satisfaction inherent in positive connection and peace.

## Understanding the Origins of Violence Between Individuals and Groups

Violence by groups is a result of multiple influences and how they join. Devaluation is only one of them. An important aspect of peace education is to help people understand how violence between groups originates. As people we trained in a project in Rwanda on healing, forgiveness, and reconciliation told us, after they had heard about and discussed the influences that lead to genocide, if people know how such violence comes about, they can also take preventive action (Staub, 2000; Staub & Pearlman, 2001).

In addition, as people come to see what the role is of each member of a society in the creation and evolution of such violence, they can begin to act differently. Frequently, this role is that of the passive bystander, whose passivity encourages perpetrators. Consideration of the importance of passive bystanders in violence by groups can motivate people to become active bystanders, exerting influence against the societal processes that lead to harm inflicted on groups, whether these are simply discrimination, or progressively increasing levels of violence.

In the project in Rwanda, we trained people who worked for local Non Governmental Organizations (NGOs) that worked with groups in the community (Staub, 2000; Staub & Pearlman, 2001). We later evaluated the effects of the work with community groups of some of the people we trained, as they used our training integrated with their usual approach.

An aspect of the training was to describe to participants how genocide and mass killing usually originate (see Staub, 1989b, 1999) and discuss how this applies to Rwanda. Coming to see the horrible violence that took place in Rwanda, more than 700,000 thousand people killed in 3 months, most of them Tutsis (des Forges, 1999), as not incomprehensible evil, but the result of understandable forces (Staub, 1999), seemed to have powerful positive effects.

In the course of the discussion of the origins of genocide, participants seemed to feel humanized, reincluded in the realm of humanity. In addition to forming impressions, we also formally evaluated, using elaborate questionnaires, the effects of the *integrated* training on members of community groups, in comparison with traditional training in which trainers used the approach their organization normally used, or control groups that received no training. The integrated training also included brief lectures on and discussions of the effects of the trauma created by such violence on survivors: in terms of interpersonal relations, specific symptoms, and the deep frustration of basic human needs. It included discussion of avenues to healing from trauma. It also included people thinking about and describing the very painful, horrible things that happened to them during the genocide, in small groups, in which other members offered empathy, often crying as their fellow participants told their stories.

Those in the integrated group reported in questionnaires fewer trauma symptoms 2 months after the end of the training. They also demonstrated more positive orientation to the other group, by which we mean a combination of greater awareness that genocide had complex origins, expressing willingness to work with the other group for important goals (the welfare of children, a better future), and expressing willingness to forgive the other group if its members acknowledged what they did and apologized for the group's actions. The latter we think of as *conditional forgiveness*.

The exploration of the origins of the genocide seemed to some degree also to humanize perpetrators in the victims' eyes. We worked with an ethnically mixed group, and it seemed that members of the perpetrator group also felt humanized (those present were, presumably, not perpetrators but bystanders to the genocide).

Understanding origins may also help members of a group that has perpetrated violence to empathize with those who suffered from it. In turn, this can open them to reconciliation. Without understanding the origins of their own actions, and without some healing by perpetrators and other members of a perpetrator group from the effects on them of they themselves or their group perpetrating great violence, they are likely to continue to justify their actions by blaming their victims.

## Influences That Lead To Group Violence

Peace education has to help people consider the important sources of violence by groups against others (see Staub, 1989b, 1999). These include instigators, or starting points. One of these is difficult conditions of life in a society. Another is conflict between groups, including conflict between privileged, powerful groups in a society and those with little power or privilege (Fein, 1993). Violence usually evolves, step by step. Inflicting limited harm on a group changes perpetrators, bystanders, social norms, and institutions, making greater harm more likely. Bystanders, or witnesses, can exert powerful influence by their inaction or action.

Whether members of the society or outside groups and nations, bystanders often do nothing, thereby encouraging perpetrators. Peace education will have special value if its recipients, when they are in the position of witnessing the evolution of violence in their own or in other societies, come to recognize early that this is happening and act in response to it. Instead of remaining passive, going on with business as usual and thereby supporting perpetrators, or becoming complicit, bystanders can exert positive influence and act to inhibit the further evolution of harmdoing. Or they can take preventive action before violence begins, in situations in which the building blocks for violence exist. Ideally, peace education will include an exploration of and training in actions people might take, ways they might find, join, or recruit like-minded others, as well as identification of the circumstances that require action.

Education about the origins of individual violence can also be important. Many people who are the recipients of peace education may have been harshly or violently treated in their families, neighborhoods, schools, or as members of a devalued group in their society. Understanding the influences that led harmdoers to act as they did can have positive effects on people who suffered as individuals, similar to the consequences I just discussed for people who were badly treated as members of a group.

Understanding the origins of violence led, among the people we trained, to the thought that violence can be prevented. This was a hope-generating realization. People said over and over again: If we know how this comes about, we can do something to prevent it.

## Understanding Bystanders

A further important aspect of conceptual learning is to understand the reasons for the passivity of bystanders, the potential power of bystanders, and the effects on bystanders of both passivity and action. Bystanders are passive for many reasons. One of these is diffusion of responsibility. Because many people know about the events in question, such as discrimination against people, each feels less responsible to act. Another reason is what I have called a *cultural tilt*. Bystanders are part of the same culture as perpetrators. They have been exposed to devaluation of the victims; they may have experienced conflict and hostility between their own group and the victims' group; they may have experienced societal upheavals that led to self-focus; and they may be exposed to ideology and propaganda that makes the *other* a scapegoat and ideological enemy. Bystanders may also fear ostracism or worse if they oppose the direction their society is taking (Staub, 1989a, 1989b). Finally, individual bystanders may feel helpless, because in order to have a significant effect on a societal process, people need to join and act together.

However, passivity changes bystanders. It is very difficult to see the continuing victimization of people, to remain passive, and not to distance oneself from those who are suffering. To reduce their feelings of empathy, which creates distress, and to reduce guilt, bystanders often distance themselves from victims. Like perpetrators, they justify the harm, they devalue the victims more, and they exclude them from the moral realm. The victims become people to whom moral considerations do not apply. Changes in bystanders can lead some of them to join perpetrators (Lifton, 1986; Staub, 1989a).

Although passivity by bystanders encourages perpetrators, the power of bystanders to exert positive influence is great. By what they say, individuals can influence how other individuals act in the face of an emergency, when someone suddenly needs help (Staub, 1974). They can even influence perpetrators, as the actions of people in the village of La Chambon in France showed. Their courageous actions in helping Jewish refugees affected the local police, and even officers in a German SS unit (Hallie, 1979). The efforts by the Bahai' communities around the world led the United Nations, as well as individual nations, to protest the persecution of Bahai' in Iran. This resulted in halting the ongoing executions of Bahai' and possibly inhibited the evolution toward mass killing (Bigelow, 1993).

Learning about different aspects of bystandership can lead individuals to make everyday decisions that lead them to become active, positive bystanders. It can lead them to exert influence on their nations, on appropriate organizations, and on other bystanders. Nations, when they act at all, and especially if they act early and in a thoughtful, psychologically appropriate manner, can have an especially powerful influence.

## EXPERIENTIAL ELEMENTS
## OF PEACE EDUCATION

In the experiential realm, peace education has varied responsibilities.

## Fulfilling Children's Basic Psychological Needs

This is the most general and diffuse aspect of peace education. All human beings have fundamental, shared psychological needs (Kelman, 1990; Maslow, 1968). These include needs for security, for a positive identity, for positive connection to other people, for autonomy, for feelings of effectiveness and control, and for a meaningful comprehension of the world (Staub, 1989b, 1996a, 1996b, 1998a).

To fulfill these needs, children (and adults) require affection and nurturance. They also require guidance, offered in a positive manner. They need rules that are based on and explained in terms of comprehensible values. Children also need discipline, but this ought to be positive rather than punitive—discipline that does not diminish the child and does not break connection to other people. When basic needs are fulfilled, the building blocks for caring about others' welfare will be present. When they are frustrated to a significant extent, the building blocks for hostility and aggression will develop—insecurity, disconnection and mistrust, and so on.

## Learning By Doing

An aspect of positive guidance is to lead children to engage in action on others' behalf. Just as violence evolves, so do caring and helping. Children and adults *learn by doing*, through the actions they themselves engage in. Children who taught younger children, or made toys for poor, hospitalized children, were later more helpful (Staub, 1979). Adults in Nazi Europe who acted to rescue Jews often agreed, at the start, to help in a limited way. However, many of them became engaged in and committed to helping and continued to help (Oliner & Oliner, 1988; Staub, 1989b). As people help others, with some positive effects, they are likely to come to value other people and their welfare more and to see themselves as helpful people.

## Crosscutting Relations: From Devaluation To Inclusive Caring

It is possible to develop caring for people but to receive instruction and have experiences that limit this caring to those in one's own group. For effective peace education, the caring people develop has to be inclusive, ideally extending to all human beings. Children and adults need to engage in *action* on behalf of not only people in their group, but also *others* outside their group, whether otherness is defined by ethnicity, religion, nation, or, more restrictively, family and neighborhood.

Many rescuers of Jews grew up in families that did not draw as sharp a line between their own group, however that was defined—as Poles, or Germans, or Christians—and people in other groups. Many of these families accepted and engaged with outsiders, including Jews, more so than the average person in their society—for example, people who did not help Jews (Oliner & Oliner, 1988). Seeing important people in one's life behave in this way, and having experiences and engagement with people belonging to different groups, has tremendous value. Connections to and deep engagement with people outside one's group can help one to overcome devaluation and develop inclusive caring. Rescuers also tended to have parents who treated them in positive ways, as discussed earlier.

The deeper the connections to members of other groups, the greater their positive effect. Superficial connections, such as members of different groups living in the same neighborhood, do not overcome prejudice. Tourists, having seen how others live without any real engagement with them, may come home with enhanced prejudice (Stroebe, Lenkert, & Jonas, 1988). In contrast, cooperative learning procedures in schools have had positive effects. In cooperative learning, children have to work together to fulfill tasks. In such procedures, children from different groups may be put together. In one such practice, the *jigsaw technique* (Aronson et al., 1978), each of six children learns some material that he or she has to teach the others. To fulfill the task set for them, in the end each child needs to know all the material. Teaching and learning from each other requires significant engagement with each other. Joint tasks that require significant engagement are also important for adults to overcome devaluation and develop inclusive caring. Having shared goals, which have been referred to as *superordinate goals*, is important (Sherif et al., 1961).

This discussion is consistent with the contact hypothesis, as proposed by Allport (1954) and as extended by many others. However, social psychologists have found that contact has variable success in creating positive attitudes. Allport himself suggested that certain conditions must be fulfilled for contact to be effective: equality on the part of the participants, those in authority supporting the contact, and others. Further conditions were added later (Cook, 1970).

With many such conditions, the usefulness of the concept, the possibility of the kind of contact that has positive effects, becomes limited. It is difficult to find circumstances in which all these conditions are fulfilled. Perhaps, however, one problem is that often, in research, the contact itself is quite limited. Without deep engagement and a reasonable degree of interdependence in fulfilling shared goals, contact is likely to be ineffective. Contact may also be counterproductive if one party or side in the contact does not truly cooperate. In cooperative learning, a child who does not do his or her share is likely to generate resentment and may increase negative feelings toward the group he or she represents.

Prior orientation may greatly enhance the effectiveness of contact (Staub, 1989b). People coming from different groups often have different modes of communication, including nonverbal communication, and different modes of engagement with tasks. Understanding the other can enable people to accept these differences rather than to react negatively to them and become unable to cooperate because of them. Such guidance may help children, for example, to value a child who in a cooperative learning situation exerts effort, accepts information from others, and tries to use it, even if this child may be less effective and contribute less than others. Information may help peers and teachers understand and accept, for example, that children coming from some collectivist cultures, such as Native Americans, learn to consult each other, give shared responses to questions, and have difficulty standing out as individuals.

Depending on the task people engage in, very different contributions are required. In one case a child needs to learn some material and to be able to teach it to others. In another, a person has to be able to share painful experience. In still another, it may be the willingness and ability to acknowledge harm that one's group has done to the other. In each case, people's capacity to do this at a particular time will vary. Orienting participants to accept *where the other is*, whether in knowledge, skills or psychological state, can have powerful effects on the process that follows.

These points suggest that we must focus on the underlying processes required for contact to be effective. These may include understanding and empathy with the other; respect and acceptance, which may mean fairness and equality in the current situation even when there is substantial asymmetry in the outside world; and everybody contributing according to his or her ability. It may be that only a few of such process requirements must be fulfilled for contact to be effective.

Two important conditions that have been proposed, authorities supporting contact and equality, have not been fulfilled in the early problem-solving workshops between Palestinians and Israelis conducted by Kelman (1990) and his associates (Rouhana & Kelman, 1994). In the larger society there was asymmetry in Palestinian–Jewish relations, and authorities and the society in general were sufficiently hostile to such engagement that participation in the meetings was held confidentially. Although within the meetings the authorities, Kelman, and his coworkers supported the engagement, and presumably equal relations prevailed, the conditions in the larger world were not fulfilled. Still, based on the reports, positive relations developed between participants. These later extended to the larger world in that former participants later became involved in the peace process.

## Helping People Heal From Victimization and Woundedness

Our project in Rwanda has aimed, more than anything, at helping people heal after the tremendous trauma of the genocide. Without such healing, feeling vulnerable and seeing the world as dangerous, survivors of violence may feel that they need to defend themselves from threat and danger. As they engage in what they see as self-defense, they can become perpetrators.

Even in groups that have not been so victimized, many children and adults are psychologically wounded. Many people experience bad treatment in their families, neighborhoods, or in other ways. Such people need to heal, through connections to caring people (which help them develop resilience), engagement with their experience under supporting conditions, and other avenues. Healing lessens self-focus and creates the possibility of caring about other people. It can lead to altruism born of suffering (Staub, 1998a), that is, people helping others, working for the welfare of other people, and working for peace, so that others won't suffer in similar ways.

One avenue to healing is engagement with painful past experience, under circumstances that help to change the emotional force and meaning of the experience (Herman, 1992; Pearlman & Saakvitne, 1995). Usually, this involves talking about or sharing the experience, with one other person, a therapist, and/or with members of a small group who have had similar experiences and are empathic and supportive (Bar-On, this volume; Staub & Pearlman, 2001), or in some other safe context. Writing about a painful experience (Pearlman & Staub, 1996; Pennebaker & Beall, 1986; Pennebaker, Hughes, & O'Heeron, 1987; Staub & Pearlman, 2001), or even talking about it into a tape recorder, can, in certain cultures, help in healing.

However, in Rwanda, a verbally oriented society, writing about painful experience was not easy for people, even literate ones. In the project we conducted there, we ended up having people simply think about their painful experiences during the genocide and then proceed to talk about these experiences with others, in small groups. They were able to talk about intensely painful experiences and received caring support from others (Staub & Pearlman, 2001).

A result of such sharing is often the creation of some meaning, a *story* that lessens the pain (Herman, 1992). Meaning about victimization and pain is not easy to create. One type of meaning that healing makes possible is the vision of a world in which people will not be harmed and the belief that one can help create such a world.

## Moral Courage and Constructive Loyalty

Engaging children in decision making about important matters and in the give and take around decisions can contribute to the development of moral courage. This refers to the ability and willingness to speak out and act in support of important values, in the face of opposition, specifically on behalf of the welfare of other people and peace. It is lack of such courage that often results in passivity by bystanders. When children learn to express their views, to speak out for what they believe, at home and in school, they may develop moral courage that will stay with them later in life.

People differ in the nature of their connection to their group. For example, blind patriots show an uncritical acceptance of and support for anything their nation does. They do not question. They gather less political information than constructive patriots. The latter, in contrast, feel that because they love their country, it is their obligation to try to improve it when it acts contrary to important values or to the country's own honorable traditions (Staub, 1997; Schatz & Staub, 1997). It is important to identify other important dimensions of people's relationship to their group that affect the likelihood that they participate in destructive processes, passively stand by, or oppose an evolution of increasing destructiveness.

## A Sense of Effectiveness and Principled Action

Many people have no idea how to act on behalf of peace, even if they are deeply concerned and have a strong desire to promote a peaceful world. A very important element of peace education must be to help people learn how to find or create avenues of action for peace. Effective action requires that people act jointly with others. Although at times a single voice can make a difference, usually many voices are required for people to be heard.

Creating peace is a slow and difficult process. It is easy to be discouraged. It is important for people to develop commitment to principled action on behalf of peace, so that they will continue to act when they can see no immediate result. Thus there is a contradiction here. Often, people will express their motivation to act, or even will feel motivated, when they believe they can be effective. However, it is also essential for people to act when change is slow. Both learning to maximize one's effectiveness and principled engagement in working for peace are important outcomes that peace education must aim to promote.

# REFERENCES

Allport, G. W. (1954). *The nature of prejudice*. Reading, MA: Addison-Wesley.

Aronson, E., Stephan, C., Sikes, J., Blaney, N., & Snapp, M. (1978). *The jigsaw classroom*. Beverly Hills, CA: Sage.

Bigelow, K. R. (1993). A campaign to deter genocide: The Baha'l experience. In H. Fein (Ed.), *Genocide watch*. New Haven, CT: Yale University Press.

Cook, S. W. (1970). Motives in conceptual analysis of attitude-related behavior. In W. J. Arnold & D. Levine (Eds.), *Nebraska symposium on motivation*. Lincoln: University of Nebraska Press.

des Forges, A. (1999). *Leave none to tell the story: Genocide in Rwanda*. New York: Human Rights Watch.

Fein, H. (1993). Accounting for genocide after 1945: Theories and some findings. *International Journal of Group Rights, 1*, 79–106.

Hallie, P. P. (1979). *Lest innocent blood be shed. The story of the village of Le Chambon, and how goodness happened there*. New York: Harper & Row.

Herman, J. (1992). *Trauma and recovery*. New York: Basic Books.

Kelman, H. C. (1990). Applying a human needs perspective to the practice of conflict resolution: The Israeli-Palestinian case. In J. Burton (Ed.), *Conflict: Human needs theory*. New York: St. Martin's Press.

Lifton, R. J. (1986). *The Nazi doctors: Medical killing and the psychology of genocide*. New York: Basic Books.

Maslow, A. H. (1968). *Toward a psychology of being* (2nd ed). New York: Van Nostrand.

Oliner, S. B., & Oliner, P. (1988). *The altruistic personality: Rescuers of Jews in Nazi Europe*. New York: Free Press.

Pearlman, L. A., & Saakvitne, K. (1995). *Trauma and the therapist*. New York: Norton.

Pearlman, L. A., & Staub, E. (1996, November). *Trauma and the fulfillment of the human potential*. Workshop presented at the meetings of the International Society for Traumatic Stress Studies, San Francisco, CA.

Pennebaker, J. W., & Beall, S. K. (1986). Confronting a traumatic event: Toward an understanding of inhibition and disease. *Journal of Abnormal Psychology, 95*, 274–281.

Pennebaker, J. W., Hughes, C. F., & O'Heeron, R. C. (1987). The psychophysiology of confession: Linking inhibitory and psychosomatic processes. *Journal of Personality and Social Psychology, 52*, 781–793.

Rouhana, N. N., & Kelman, H. C. (1994). Promoting joint thinking in international conflicts: An Israeli-Palestinian continuing workshop. *Journal of Social Issues, 50*, 157–178.

Schatz, R., & Staub, E. (1997). Manifestations of blind and constructive patriotism. In D. Bar-Tal & E. Staub (Eds.), *Patriotism in the lives of individuals and groups*. Chicago: Nelson-Hall.

Sherif, M., Harvey, D. J., White, B. J., Hood, W. K., & Sherif, C. W. (1961). *Intergroup conflict and cooperation: The Robber's Cave experiment*. Norman, OK: University of Oklahoma Book Exchange.

Staub, E. (1974). Helping a distressed person: Social, personality and stimulus determinants. In L. Berkowitz (Ed.), *Advances in experimental social psychology* (Vol. 7, pp. 203–342). New York: Academic.

Staub, E. (1978). *Positive social behavior and morality: Vol. 1. Social and personal influences*. New York: Academic.

Staub, E. (1979). *Positive social behavior and morality: Vol. 2. Socialization and development*. New York: Academic.

Staub, E. (1989a). Steps along the continuum of destruction: The evolution of bystanders: German psychoanalysts and lessons for today. *Political Psychology, 10*, 39–53.

Staub, E. (1989b). *The roots of evil: The origins of genocide and other group violence*. New York: Cambridge University Press.

Staub, E. (1995). How people learn to care. In P. G. Schervish, V. A. Hodgkinson, M. Gates, & Associates (Eds.), *Care and community in modern society: Passing on the tradition of service to future generations*. San Francisco: Jossey-Bass.

Staub, E. (1996a). Altruism and aggression in children and youth: Origins and cures. In R. Feldman (Ed.), *The psychology of adversity*. Amherst: University of Massachusetts Press.

Staub, E. (1996b). Cultural-societal roots of violence: The examples of genocidal violence and of contemporary youth violence in the United States. *American Psychologist, 51*, 117–132.

Staub, E. (1997). Blind versus constructive patriotism: Moving from embeddedness in the group to critical loyalty and action. In D. Bar-Tal & E. Staub (Eds.), *Patriotism*. Chicago: Nelson-Hall.

Staub, E. (1998a). *Basic human needs and their role in altruism and aggression*. Unpublished manuscript, Department of Psychology, University of Massachusetts at Amherst.

Staub, E. (1998b). Breaking the cycle of genocidal violence: Healing and reconciliation. In J. Harvey (Ed.), *Perspectives on loss: A sourcebook*. Philadelphia: Taylor & Francis.

Staub, E. (1999). The origins and prevention of genocide, mass killing, and other collective violence. *Peace and Conflict: Journal of Peace Psychology, 5*(4), 303–336.

Staub, E. (2000). Genocide and mass killing: Origins, prevention, healing, and reconciliation. *Political Psychology, 21*(2), 367–382.

Staub, E., & Pearlman, L. A. (2001). Healing, reconciliation and forgiving after genocide and other collective violence. In name of editor (Ed.), *Forgiveness and reconciliation*. Radnor, PA: Templeton Foundation.

Stroebe, W., Lenkert, A., & Jonas, K. (1988). Familiarity may breed contempt: The impact of student exchange on national stereotypes and attitudes. In W. Stroebe, A. W. Kruglanski, D. Bar-Tal, & M. Hewstone (Eds.), *The social psychology of intergroup conflict: Theory, research and application*. New York: Springer-Verlag.

Tajfel, H. (1982). Social psychology of intergroup relations. *Annual Review of Psychology, 33*, 1–39.

Tajfel, H., & Turner, J. C. (1979). An integrative theory of intergroup conflict. In W. G. Austin & S. Worchel (Eds.), *The social psychology of intergroup relations*. Monterey, CA: Brooks-Cole.

Wessels, M., & Montiero, C. (2001). Psychological intervention and post-conflict reconstruction in Angola: Interweaving western and traditional approaches. In D. Christie, R. V. Wagner, & D. Winter (Eds.), *Peace, conflict and violence: Peace psychology for the 21st century*. Englewood Cliffs, NJ: Prentice-Hall.

# II

# Underlying Principles

# 8

# Understanding the Conditions and Processes Necessary for Intergroup Contact to Reduce Prejudice

## Nurit Tal-Or, David Boninger, and Faith Gleicher
### University of Haifa

*It is easier, someone has said, to smash an atom than a prejudice.*
—Gordon W. Allport (1954, p. XVII)

Simple solutions to complex problems can often be a mirage. Since the debut of the *contact hypothesis* put forth by Gordon Allport in 1954, practitioners and laypeople alike have hung on to the seemingly simple promise that, if we could just get people together, we could solve the conflict. Unfortunately, this simple solution is, in fact, a misinterpretation of the contact hypothesis, and it is an overly simplistic approach to an overwhelmingly complex problem. Not surprisingly, just getting people together does not work. Allport (1954) did not argue that contact, in and of itself, would reduce prejudice. On the contrary, he and others (e.g., Amir, 1969; Pettigrew, 1998) recognized that contact under some conditions may actually accentuate hostilities. As is often the case, the interesting question is not whether or not contact reduces intergroup hostility; it is *under what conditions* contact will reduce intergroup hostility. To answer this question, we also need to ask what the underlying *processes* are that are responsible for that reduction.

Our goal in this chapter is to provide a snapshot of what social psychologists have learned about the conditions and processes that are responsible for a reduction in prejudice and hostility following intergroup contact. The literature in this area is enormous and we will make no attempt to provide a comprehensive summary of that literature (for those interested in more comprehensive coverage of these topics, see Brewer & Brown, 1998; Oskamp, 2000; or Pettigrew, 1998). First, we present the original formulation of the contact hypothesis and the critical conditions that Allport (1954) specified. Second, we present more recent models of the process by which contact may reduce stereotypes and prejudice. Third, we review recent theory and research that has more generally (not specifically within a contact setting) examined the cognitive processes underlying stereotype maintenance and change. We then return to the contact hypothesis to demonstrate how a unique integration of our understanding of these underlying, cognitive processes and of the models of intergroup contact may best enable us to make effective use of contact in peace education. We will conclude with a concrete example of a program of intergroup contact in the Arab–Israeli conflict.

## THE CONTACT HYPOTHESIS

Allport (1954) referred to a group in which an individual is a member as an *ingroup*, and to a group in which an individual is not a member as an *outgroup*. Allport assumed, and it has since been widely demonstrated (for a recent review, see Fiske, 1998), that people typically have a favorable view of their ingroup while maintaining more negative (and often disparaging) stereotypes and prejudices toward outgroups. This tendency plants the seeds for intergroup hostility and conflict.

In an effort to provide an antidote to these resulting prejudices and intergroup conflicts, Allport proposed the contact hypothesis, which is based on the notion that interaction between members of opposing groups can lead to a reduction in prejudice and hostility (Allport, 1954; Amir, 1969). Allport took pains, however, to point out that we should not expect that contact, under all conditions, reduces prejudice. Instead, Allport's writings clearly pointed to a set of conditions that were necessary for intergroup contact to be effective: environmental support for intergroup contact, equal status between groups, close contact, and cooperation (See also Amir, 1969; Pettigrew, 1998).

## Supportive Environment

Institutional and social support for intergroup contact creates a more fertile environment for the development of more positive, intergroup attitudes and behaviors. The classic study by Deutsch and Collins (1951) of segregated versus integrated housing provides strong support for the significance of social and institutional support. This study examined the attitudes of White subjects toward contact with Blacks. Deutsch and Collins found that the type of housing in which they lived seemed to affect the attitudes that subjects *expressed* about contact with Blacks. Tenants in segregated housing expressed more negative attitudes toward contact with Blacks than did tenants in integrated housing. In many cases, however, it was found that the tenants in segregated housing did not actually object to such contact, but feared public response to it. They thought that contact was not considered conventional behavior and so would be perceived negatively by society. Tenants in integrated housing units, in contrast, felt more comfortable making contact with Blacks, because they perceived social and institutional support for such contact.

## Equal Status

Also important to the success of contact is equal status between the ingroup and outgroup (Allport, 1954; Amir, 1969). Generally, in the world outside of the contact situation, the ingroup and outgroup do not have equal status. However, contact between majority and minority groups when the minority holds inferior status, for instance, is not likely to reduce prejudice (e.g., Stephan & Rosenfield, 1978). Conditions that promote equal status (which, in and of itself, is a violation of commonly held stereotypes about differences between the groups) help to create an environment in which other components of commonly held stereotypes and prejudices are more vulnerable and thereby more susceptible to change.

Perhaps the most well-known demonstration of the effectiveness of intergroup contact under conditions of equal status is reported by Aronson and Bridgeman (1979). In their seminal work on the use of the *jigsaw technique* in integrated classrooms, equal status and cooperation were induced in the classroom by using small group, learning tasks between white pupils and pupils from other, ethnic minorities (e.g., Blacks or Latinos). In these learning tasks, each member of the group was responsible for one segment of the lesson (i.e., he or she had to become an expert on that specific material). Each expert then had to share his or her knowledge with the rest of the group. In this way, each pupil was dependent on his or her fellow pupils in order to succeed. This interdependence fostered perceptions of equal status and in turn strengthened the pupil's self-esteem, created more, positive attitudes toward school, and increased liking for other, ethnic groups. Interestingly, the jigsaw technique even enhanced the minority pupils' scholastic level without jeopardizing the level of the majority group.

Aronson and Bridgeman (1979) do point out, however, that equal status can be a problematic concept. For example, at first glance, pupils in an integrated (e.g., Blacks and Whites) classroom have equal status: they are all the same age. However, if the teacher is biased against Blacks, or if White students show scholastic superiority, then the groups are no longer equal. Thus, in order to truly create equal status, it may be necessary in some contexts to switch roles between the majority and minority groups (e.g., Cohen & Roper, 1972).

## Close Contact

For intergroup contact to succeed, that contact must also be close, prolonged, and frequent (Deutsch & Collins, 1951; Stephan & Rosenfield, 1978; Wilner, Walkley, & Cook, 1952). For example, Stephan and Rosenfield (1978) found that the variable that best predicted positive change in White pupils' attitudes towards Mexicans in the United States was the frequency of their contact with Mexicans. Several explanations have been proposed for importance of close and prolonged contact (Brewer & Brown, 1998). First, to the extent that close contact is pleasant and satisfying, that pleasant feeling may be generalized to the group as a whole (Cook, 1962). Second, when contact is close, prolonged, and frequent, it maximizes the opportunity for stereotype disconfirmation, and it provides for reminders and reinforcement of those disconfirmations. Finally, close contact increases familiarity between groups and allows for the recognition of similarities between groups. These mechanisms provide a powerful counterweight to the way in which outgroups are typically perceived.

## Cooperation

In addition to equal status and close contact, the interaction between groups must also be in an environment of cooperation and not competition (Allport, 1954). That is, the benefits of contact will be maximized when groups share a common goal that fosters cooperation. The importance of this condition was nicely demonstrated by Sherif and his colleagues (Sherif, Harvey, White, Hood, & Sherif, 1961) in a well-known study of children at summer camp. The boys at camp were divided into two groups that faced off against each other in various, competitive situations. This competition quickly led to negative attitudes toward the opposing group, attitudes that were manifest in clear acts of intergroup hostility. Sherif and his colleagues managed to reverse the harsh rivalry only by introducing new superordinate goals that forced cooperation between the groups. Aronson and Bridgeman's (1979) jigsaw classroom that we described earlier is also an excellent demonstration of the importance of cooperation and superordinate goals. Importantly, the results of the cooperative effort have to be positive in order for intergroup hostilities to diminish (Worchel, Andreoli, & Folger, 1977).

## Summing Up

Institutional support, equal status, close contact, and cooperation represent a tall order of conditions necessary for intergroup contact to reduce intergroup prejudice and hostility. Thus, it is very clear that intergroup contact, in and of itself, will *not* necessarily reduce prejudice. In fact, when Allport's conditions are absent, contact may be more likely to worsen prejudices (e.g. Sherif et al., 1961). Although

Allport's stipulation of these conditions was an important step in understanding when intergroup hostilities may be reduced, his formulation of contact theory said little about the underlying psychological processes by which change occurs *following* intergroup contact. More recent research in social cognition and intergroup relations addresses these issues. It is to this research that we turn now.

## COGNITIVE PROCESSES AND RECENT MODELS FOR EFFECTIVE INTERGROUP CONTACT

In focusing on the cognitive processes that may help to explain the influence of intergroup contact on stereotypes and prejudice, there are two distinct contexts (or stages) in which these processes may occur (Wilder, 1986). The first context is during the actual contact between individuals of opposing groups, whereas the second context is after the intergroup contact has taken place. Although in the first context it is possible that people may have experiences that challenge their stereotypes, this does not necessarily ensure that the ensuing cognitive processes (after intergroup contact) will lead to the generalization of this stereotype-inconsistent information to the group as a whole, and to a reduction in prejudice toward the group. Therefore, if contact between members of two groups does not bring about the expected reduction in prejudice, it may be because of a failure within either the context of the contact itself or a failure in the process of generalization after the contact.

The conditions suggested by Allport for effective contact between groups primarily relate to the first aspect of the process, the contact encounter itself (Rothbart & Lewis, 1994). To the extent that conditions are right and a new positive perception is formed during the interaction, a question remains regarding the conditions that would ensure that this perception is generalized and maintained. A number of models have attempted to address this question and to specify additional conditions that may optimize the results of intergroup contact (e.g., Brewer, 2000; Brewer & Miller, 1984; Dovidio & Gaertner, 1999; Gaertner, Dovidio, Anastasio, Bachman, & Rust, 1993; Hewstone & Brown, 1986). These models emphasize the importance of the cognitive representation of the contact situation as a crucial factor in determining the outcome of the interaction (Brewer & Brown, 1998). These models contrast an interpersonal focus on others as individuals (e.g., Joe, Bob, and Sam) and an intergroup or category-based focus on others as members of a group (e.g., the Black guys and the White guys). The continuum from an interpersonal to an intergroup focus stems directly from the writings of Tajfel and Turner on social identity theory (e.g., Tajfel & Turner, 1986). Although these models share a focus on the continuum on which others are perceived, they differ in their recommendations of how best to focus contact participants in order to ensure that contact leads to stereotype and prejudice reduction. The following brief review of these models is largely based on the more comprehensive review by Brewer and Brown (1998).

## Decategorization Versus Mutual Differentiation

According to the decategorization model (Brewer & Miller, 1984), participants in an interaction should be encouraged to make contact between individuals and not between groups and to direct their attention toward information at the individual level and not at the categorical level. Brewer and Miller (1984) assert that a focus on the individual reduces the salience of the ingroup–outgroup category distinction, enables the reduction of the importance of category boundaries, the reduction of the perception of the outgroup as homogenous, and the reduction of the strength of the group stereotype. In short, a focus on the individual reduces the power of group distinctions.

In support of this model, Bettencourt, Brewer, Croak, and Miller (1992) examined the role of interpersonal relationships (i.e., between individuals) in contact situations. In order to accomplish this, they used the minimal group paradigm (e.g., Tajfel, 1970) in which they divided their experimental participants into two groups based on a minimal difference between them.[1] After this, they formed a number of smaller groups that included within them an equal number of members from the two original, meaningful groups, and instructed these small groups to engage in an interaction. All the groups were asked to perform a task; however, for some of the groups, the instructions for the interaction focused on the interpersonal relationships within the group, whereas for the other groups, the instructions focused on the task the group was to accomplish. The researchers found that the interpersonal focus reduced the bias in favor of the ingroup, compared with the task-focused condition.

The decategorization model has been criticized because although it suggests conditions for effective contact in the context of the contact encounter itself, it does not address the issue of the generalization from the contact encounter to stereotypes and prejudices toward the group as a whole. Studies have shown that even if positive relations between the individuals are achieved through contact, generalization of these relations does not take place unless these individuals are perceived as representative cases of the group as a whole (e.g., Johnson & Hewstone, 1992). Ironically, then, the individualizing focus may be effective during contact because

---

[1] For those not familiar with the minimal group paradigm, it is important to note that this methodology of creating groups in the laboratory has proven to be very effective in a vast array of empirical studies over the past 30 years, starting with Tajfel (1970). That is, even when participants are separated into groups that are arbitrarily defined, they exhibit biases in thought and behavior that favor their own group at the expense of the outgroup.

it deemphasizes the contact participants' connection to their group, but it may be ineffective after contact for the same reason.

In taking a contrasting approach, Hewstone and Brown (1986) proposed the mutual differentiation model. This model suggests that contact should take place at the intergroup or category level and not at the interpersonal level, in order to foster a generalization of the attitudes to the group as a whole and not only toward some of its individual members. Hewstone and Brown (1986) claim that fruitful contact is best created by giving members of the different groups separate yet complementary roles, so that category differences are maintained in the context of mutual interdependence. Deschamps and Brown (1983) found that contact in which members of the different groups were assigned different roles led to more positive attitudes between the groups than contact in which no such separation took place. The mutual differentiation model thus facilitates generalization because of its focus on the category level. Some interpersonal focus is certainly occurring (interdependence encourages this), but in contrast with decategorization, the focus on the category or group level is primary.

## Bridging the Gap: Dual Identification and Cross-Categorization

Two additional models suggest intermediate possibilities that try to bridge the gap between these competing approaches. These models focus on additional types of category membership in order to draw focus away from the problematic ingroup–outgroup distinction. Dovidio and Gaertner and their colleagues propose a Common Ingroup Identity Model that emphasizes processes of recategorization (into a category inclusive of the outgroup) and the acquiring of dual identities (identity with an ingroup *and* with an inclusive superordinate group). These processes are hypothesized to occur as consequences of intergroup contact when Allport's conditions are present (Dovidio & Gaertner, 1999; Dovidio, Kawakami, & Gaertner, 2000). That is, instead of a focus on the category distinction that separates between the two opposing groups, intergroup contact may lead to a focus on a superordinate category that includes *both* groups. For example, Black and White Americans are, at the superordinate level, both Americans. Catholic and Protestant Irish are, similarly, both Irish. A focus on the superordinate level category allows members of both groups to think of themselves as one unit, and it maximizes the likelihood of pleasant contact, of reduced salience of the ingroup–outgroup distinction, and of generalization of stereotype reduction to the group as a whole.

Dovidio and Gaertner and their colleagues have gathered both experimental and correlational evidence to support their model (e.g., Gaertner, Mann, Dovidio, Murrell, & Pomare, 1990; Gaertner, Rust, Dovidio, Bachman, & Anastasio, 1994). For example, in a correlational study, Gaertner et al. (1994) examined the perceptions of students in a multiethnic high school in the United States. Results indicated that favorable perceptions of intergroup contact predicted stronger perceptions of the student body as one group (recategorization into the superordinate category) and stronger perceptions of the student body as made up of different groups *on the same team* (dual identities). Importantly, this recategorization and recognition of dual identities also predicted less hostility in intergroup attitudes and feelings.

The Common Ingroup Identity Model relies on a hierarchical representation of categories: The personal identity is contained within a social identity, which is also contained within a more global, social identity. Alternatively, Brewer's recent work (e.g., Brewer, 2000) points to an alternative possibility of cross-categorization, which is concurrent membership in different categories at the same level. For instance, a person can belong simultaneously to the *male* category, *teacher* category, and *Palestinian* category. These categories are not contained one within the other, so that there are males who are neither teachers nor Palestinians, and there are Palestinian teachers who are not male, and so on. According to Brewer, these crosscutting distinctions make social categorization more complex and reduce both the magnitude and implications of ingroup–outgroup distinctions. They also may lead, by means of principles of cognitive balance (Heider, 1958), to greater liking for others who are outgroup on one dimension but ingroup on another dimension.

In a laboratory experiment examining cross-categorization, Marcus-Newhall, Miller, Holtz, and Brewer (1993) separated participants by means of the minimal group paradigm into two categories: overestimators and underestimators. They were then divided into mixed groups that included two members from each category. The groups were asked to perform a problem-solving task, in which each group member received a specific role. The assignment of roles to group members allowed for a manipulation of cross-categorization (i.e., assigned roles either did or did not cut across categories). An examination of participants' perceptions of one another found that cross-categorization of roles (as compared with no cross-categorization) caused less bias in favor of the ingroup following contact.

## Summary and Critique

Both Dovidio and his colleagues (Dovidio et al., 2000) and Brewer (2000) attempt to locate an intermediate possibility between contact at the interpersonal level and contact at the intergroup level. These models not only help to explain why contact under the right conditions may reduce prejudice (because of a focus on superordinate or crosscutting categories), they also suggest that these representations may serve, practically, as cognitive guides for how participants should perceive the contact encounter. In other words, there is likely to be a bidirectional relationship between intergroup contact and how we represent others. On the one hand, positive interactions between groups, when contact takes place under the right conditions, will increase the likelihood that recategorization or cross-categorization will take place. On the other hand, at the same time, inducing participants to focus on superordinate categories or on crosscutting categories prior to a contact situation may also help to maximize the likelihood of positive interactions.

Unfortunately, however, practical application presents a problem for both of these models and the intermediate representations they emphasize. In the world beyond the contact encounter, crosscutting categories and superordinate categories are often less salient and less powerful than the primary, outgroup–ingroup distinction upon which prejudices originated. For example, there is evidence that people naturally tend to use more specific or base categories rather than higher level, superordinate categories (Brewer, Dull, & Lui, 1981; Devine & Baker, 1991). Thus, even if the superordinate category is emphasized during the contact encounter, it is most likely not dominant in the real world. Brewer (1996) suggests that participants' unstable identification with the superordinate category is a result of its relative inability, compared with lower-level categories, to maximize people's concurrent and opposing needs for distinctiveness and belonging (see also Brewer, 1991).

A classic study of Black and White miners from West Virginia (Minard, 1952) demonstrates the potentially transient nature of categories made salient by intergroup contact. The miners worked harmoniously together in the mine, with complete integration between Blacks and Whites. However, once they emerged from the mine, they functioned in complete separation. Apparently, during the contact situation, the category of *miners* was most salient, whereas as soon as they left the mine, the basic, more chronically salient, racial category immediately returned and separated the miners. Thus, contact participants may tend, upon returning to their regular lives, to ignore the common denominator of a crosscutting or superordinate category and return to the more accessible, base level category distinction.

The more general point here is that even if a category is successfully triggered by intergroup contact, its strength may still be overwhelmed by the strength of the competing, ingroup–outgroup distinction. In situations in which real groups are at odds, the distinction between them is likely to be important, salient, and automatically accessed. It might be difficult, then, to find categories that matter as much to the contact participants as the basic, ingroup–outgroup distinction. If so, a reduction in prejudice will be hard to achieve. If both superordinate categories and cross-categories are at a disadvantage compared with the basic, ingroup–outgroup distinction, then only *repeated and prolonged social contact* that emphasizes the superordinate or cross-category can truly begin to make up this disadvantage.

Our review and critique of these models may once again make us wonder if, indeed, it is easier to smash an atom than a prejudice. Yet, these models and the empirical support that has accompanied them have provided some important validations and some critical insights. The empirical research has validated the importance of the conditions for beneficial, social contact that Allport specified almost 50 years ago. However, in addition to this validation, these models also suggest that to truly understand and maximize the effectiveness of contact, it is essential to take into account what is going on in the heads of contact participants.

How are they thinking about the other group, in what categories are they placing members of the opposing group, and are they finding common categories between themselves and the others? These are all questions that are brought into focus by the models just presented.

For practitioners, this means that, in a contact encounter, by providing the conditions that Allport specified *and* by attempting to drive the categorizations that contact participants make, you will be simultaneously influencing both the individuation of contact participants and generalization toward the group. Recent research in social cognition is relevant to this dual focus because it has addressed both the *how* and the *why* of processing others as individuals or as members of groups. Although this research did not examine intergroup contact per se, it has examined techniques that focus people on individuals or on group memberships, and the cognitive implications of these different focuses for stereotype formation, maintenance, and change. It is to this research that we turn now.

# INFORMATION PROCESSING APPROACHES

## Individuating Versus Category-Based Impression Formation

Fiske and Neuberg and their colleagues (Fiske, 2000; Fiske & Neuberg, 1990; Fiske, Neuberg, Beattie, & Milberg, 1987; Neuberg & Fiske, 1987), in their work on how people form impressions of others, refer to a continuum that ranges from impressions based on the individuating characteristics of the individual in question to impressions based on that individual's membership in some category or group. This distinction in how we form impressions of others closely parallels a distinction we have already drawn between interpersonal and intergroup focus in contact situations (e.g., Tajfel & Turner, 1986). Fiske and Neuberg (1990) have identified several factors that influence where on this continuum impressions will be formed. One factor is the extent to which the individual's characteristics seem to match the perceiver's perception of the category (i.e., the stereotype). A second is the perceiver's motivation to arrive at an accurate impression. We address each of these in turn, after which we discuss their implications for the contact hypothesis.

## Match Between Characteristics and Categories

Fiske and her colleagues (Fiske et al., 1987) manipulated the type of information about target individuals that they gave to experimental participants. Participants received information about the target individuals' personality characteristics and their professions. However, sometimes an individual's profession seemed to match his or her characteristics (e.g., an artist is creative), sometimes it seemed to contrast with them (e.g., a construction worker is an intellectual), sometimes the profession was accompanied by a neutral descriptor (e.g., medium height), and sometimes the profession was absent (i.e., the target was labeled as a *person*) but was accompanied by meaningful characteristics that did provide information. After they received this information about each of the target individuals, participants were asked to form impressions of them.

Fiske et al. (1987) found that participants relied more on the category information (the target's profession) when the characteristics matched the category and when the characteristics were not informative. In contrast, they tended to rely more on the individuating information (the target's characteristics) when the category was not informative and when the individuating characteristics were inconsistent with the category. These results suggest that when forming impressions of others, people are practical. They reserve cognitive resources by ignoring information that is not meaningful and by favoring the type of information that appears, at least at first glance, to be more informative and more easily applied. So if a cursory survey of the information seems to suggest that the category information is applicable, people, as perceivers, rely on it as the primary source of their impression about the target individual. In contrast, if the initial information people receive about a person suggests that he or she does not match the category to which he or she belongs, they tend to rely more on the person's characteristics as a source of their impression of him or her.

## Motivation To Be Accurate

Fiske and Neuberg (1990) also point to motivation as an important factor in determining how people form impressions of others. Because basing impressions on a person's individuating characteristics is more effortful than basing impressions on category membership, motivation is an important antecedent of individuated processing. Although it requires more effort, individuated processing is more accurate. Interestingly, people appear to be aware of this trade-off between category-based processing (less work, but less accurate) and individuated processing (more work, but more accurate). As such, they will expend the cognitive effort to work with specific information about a person when the stakes are high. An experiment conducted by Neuberg and Fiske (1987) showed that experimental participants who were dependent on the performance of another person based their impression of her or him more on her or his individuating characteristics than on the category information that they received about him (that he or she was schizophrenic).

How is this research relevant to the contact hypothesis? Both the conditions described earlier (the mismatch between characteristics and the category, and the motivation that stems from dependence) will most likely be present in intergroup contact situations that satisfy Allport's conditions. Superordinate goals and the need to cooperate will certainly maximize one's motivation to accurately perceive others in the contact situation. And where is the mismatch between individual characteristics and the stereotype? Stereotypes of outgroups typically do *not* include characteristics such as open-minded, willingness to positively interact with opposing groups, peace loving, and the like. In other words, the participation in a contact encounter, may, in and of itself, be inconsistent with the stereotype. This inconsistency or mismatch will, along with the heightened motivation that comes with interdependence, encourage individuated processing. Put simply, Fiske and Neuberg's accumulated research (Erber & Fiske, 1984; Fiske et al., 1987; Neuberg & Fiske, 1987) explains how the conditions (e.g., cooperation) of the intergroup contact situation help to reduce the power of stereotypes. These conditions encourage contact participants to form individuated impressions of members of the opposing group.

We saw earlier, however, that individuated impressions are only part of what is necessary to begin to fully breakdown prejudices. For individuated information to exert a meaningful influence on existing stereotypes, the individuated information must be translated into well learned, personal beliefs about the outgroup as a whole. And even when these personal beliefs are in direct conflict with the stereotype, there are still additional conditions that must be present for these personal beliefs to successfully reduce the influence of the dominant, automatically activated stereotype.

## Minimizing the Influence of Automatically Activated Stereotypes

In a series of three studies, Patricia Devine (1989) measured individual differences in levels of prejudice toward Blacks in the United States (the level of prejudice was measured by using the Modern Racism Scale developed by McConahay, Hardee, & Batts, 1981). Devine also measured knowledge of the commonly held, cultural stereotype, use of that stereotype, and personal beliefs toward Blacks. This research demonstrated several important points: (1) People both high *and* low in prejudice were *equally* knowledgeable of the cultural stereotype. (2) When given the chance to think carefully about what they personally believed, only people high in prejudice wrote down beliefs that were consistent with the cultural stereotype (e.g., that Blacks are aggressive). In contrast, people low in prejudice successfully ignored their knowledge of the cultural stereotype and, instead, expressed personal beliefs that were inconsistent with the cultural stereotype. (3) When people were *unaware* that their knowledge of the cultural stereotype had been activated in memory, the stereotype biased their perception of ambiguous events, and this was the case for people both high and low in prejudice. Activation of the cultural stereotype without awareness was accomplished by using a priming paradigm in which words associated with Blacks (Negroes) and with the Black stereotype (e.g., lazy) were preconsciously displayed to participants (see Devine, 1989 for a more detailed description). After the stereotype was activated, participants were asked to evaluate the ambiguous behavior of a person whose race was unspecified. People both high and low in prejudice were influenced by the priming manipulation and rated the ambiguous behavior as hostile, which was consistent with the primed stereotype for Blacks.

Devine (1989) interpreted her results across these studies as suggesting that when people change their beliefs toward an outgroup, it does not lead to the disappearance of the commonly held, cultural stereotype. The stereotype remains in memory as a well-organized and easily activated, cognitive structure. For people low in prejudice, the influence of the stereotype is likely to be minimized when the ability to engage in effortful processing is high. In contrast, when the ability to engage in effortful processing is low (or there is no awareness that the stereotype has even been activated), then the influence of the automatically activated stereotype is likely to be significant. In other words, it is only under conditions that allow for controlled processes that people will succeed in reducing the influence of the cultural stereotypes in favor of more particularized, personal beliefs about others (Devine, 1989).

Devine argues that the extinction of a stereotype is the same as the extinction of a bad habit: It is not enough to decide to get rid of the bad habit. There is a need for persistent effort to control it. In order to make the stereotype extinct, each time it is activated, the person needs to think of his or her new belief system until the new beliefs are so well learned that they replace the automatic activation of the stereotype. In returning to the contact hypothesis, here again we see clear evidence for the importance of repeated and prolonged contact. Although isolated incidents of contact may create new beliefs about the opposing group, it is unlikely that these beliefs will compete with the automatically activated stereotype.

## THE CONTACT HYPOTHESIS—NOW WITH COGNITION AND PERSEVERANCE

Allport's ideal contact situation consisted of institutionally supported, close contact between individuals of equal status, in which these individuals work cooperatively to reach a superordinate goal. Fiske and Neuberg's research (Fiske et al., 1987; Fiske & Neuberg, 1990; Neuberg & Fiske, 1987) indicates that this situation contains the critical elements that provide for the perception of *the other* as an individual rather than as simply *one of them*. This contact situation increases the motivation to carefully process information and is likely to create a mismatch between the content of existing stereotypes and the characteristics of the people in the contact encounter. This mismatch and the increased motivation work together to encourage contact participants to go beyond the stereotype and to form individuated impressions of members of the opposing group. Once we perceive others as individuals, we are more likely to recognize the *heterogeneity* of the opposing group. This is the beginning of the breakdown of stereotypes and prejudice.

The perception of others as individuals is the focus of the decategorization model (Brewer & Miller, 1984) that we reviewed earlier. Although this model has been criticized (e.g., Johnson & Hewstone, 1992), perhaps it may be most useful to view this model as representing a first and necessary stage in the breakdown of prejudice. As in any staged approach, earlier stages facilitate the onset of later stages: Seeing people as individuals (and thus reducing the salience of the disliked category) may set the stage for the kind of recategorization emphasized in the Common Ingroup Identity Model (Dovidio & Gaertner, 1999; Dovidio et al., 2000; Gaertner et al., 1990, 1994) and in the cross-categorization approach (Brewer, 2000). In turn, positive interactions that facilitate the perception of outgroup members as individuals and as members of categories to which the perceiver also belongs may eventually allow for a return to the original outgroup distinction, but now in the context of the kind of positive, mutual differentiation that Hewstone and Brown (1986) envisioned. This approach is consistent with research and theory that has suggested that when intergroup conflict is extreme, the contact situation should focus first on the interpersonal level and only at a later stage move to an intergroup level (Hewstone, 1996; Pettigrew, 1998).

Thus, individuated processing that results from contact under Allport's conditions may be viewed as a necessary, but not sufficient, step in the reduction of stereotypes and prejudice (Hewstone & Greenland, 2000). The subsequent stage of generalization must also occur but is not so easily achieved. Generalization is inhibited by mechanisms that cause the individuated contact participants to be perceived as exceptions to the rule of the stereotype, or as members of a subgroup that does not represent the outgroup as a whole (Johnson & Hewstone, 1992; Rothbart & John, 1985). Generalization is also inhibited by the spontaneous activation of the stereotype and by its subsequent use in the interpretation and evaluation of the behavior of outgroup members (Devine, 1989). Clearly, the bridge from the stage of individuated processing to the stage of generalization (e.g., actual changes in stereotypes toward the outgroup) is not an easy bridge to cross. Devine's depiction (1989) of automatically activated stereotypes as bad habits reinforces this view—bad habits are broken only by way of perseverance and hard work.

Prolonged contact, although hard to achieve, may be the most important determinant of whether or not the more advanced stages of generalization are successfully reached. It is only through prolonged contact that positive and non-stereotypical associations to the outgroup can become more accessible and more competitive in the face of the commonly held, cultural stereotype. Prolonged contact also allows for feelings of empathy to develop toward the outgroup (see also Pettigrew, 1997). Empathy, in turn, may lead to the generation of alternative explanations for the characteristics that comprise the outgroup stereotype. For example, Israeli Jews might see Palestinian unrest as a function of the Palestinians' violent nature. To the extent that the Jews can be brought to attribute the unrest to

Palestinians' frustration with an untenable living situation, the stereotype of violent Arabs may be diminished. Because a person's attitude toward a member of a stereotyped group is dependent on the attributions she or he makes (Weiner, 1980, 1990), these alternative explanations can serve an important function in the breakdown of stereotypes and prejudice.

Interestingly, this gradual, staged approach is also consistent with the theory of social judgment by Sherif and Hovland (1961), which stipulates that for any given attitude object (e.g., the outgroup), our attitudes consist of a latitude of acceptance and a latitude of rejection. Positions that fall in our latitude of acceptance (even if they fall on the edge of that latitude) are assimilated, whereas positions that fall in our latitude of rejection are disregarded. The theory of social judgment suggests a gradual process of persuasion, with each stage an attempt to expand the latitude of acceptance regarding the attitude object. In intergroup contact, a critical, first step in expanding one's latitude of acceptance may be the removal of the category label (and the clear boundaries it delineates). This is the step that the decategorization model emphasizes. Once this expansion has taken place, then recategorization and mutual differentiation may be more likely to fall within one's latitude of acceptance.

In practical terms, this suggests a gradual approach in constructing contact encounters in which full-fledged cooperation may emerge over time. In the first encounter, participants from opposing groups may simply sit together in the same room to hear a lecture (which is likely to fall within everyone's latitude of acceptance). In subsequent encounters, however, participants may be asked to engage in small, group discussions. Then, in later encounters, superordinate goals can be introduced to set the stage for more, full-fledged cooperation. Role-playing and exercises that promote empathy may also be emphasized in later encounters, along with a focus on common, ingroup identities and crosscutting categories. Finally, a return to the original, ingroup–outgroup distinction may allow for a healthy, mutual differentiation in the context of more positive, group stereotypes. Although this gradual, staged approach is a promising recipe for intergroup contact to reduce prejudice, it also drives home the conclusion that a single or limited number of contact encounters will be insufficient to achieve these goals.

## A CONTACT ENCOUNTER IN THE ARAB–ISRAELI CONFLICT

We now describe a program of contact encounters between Israeli Jews, Palestinians living in the Palestinian Authority, and Jordanians. Although this program of contact encounters has not been systematically evaluated, we present it because we view it as an excellent example of an intergroup contact encounter in which many, if not all, of the critical conditions for success have been met. The encounters, in Israel and Jordan, began in the summer of 1998 with participants of high school age. The program is called the NIR School of the Heart, and it brings together approximately 60 high school students (20 from each cultural group) who have a scientific orientation toward medicine and health-related fields (the program is sponsored by a medical technologies company). Participants must also be proficient in English, which is the neutral language of discourse during the encounters. The participants come for an intensive, 2-week course (1 week in Israel and 1 week in Jordan), during which time they live together in dormitories in which there are people in a room (one from each cultural group). The staff of the NIR School is also made up of Israelis, Palestinians, and Jordanians.

The goal of the program is to learn about medicine and advances in medical technology. In addition to this abstract goal, there is also a concrete goal of completing a final project that addresses and proposes potential solutions to a particular problem in medicine or in medical technologies. The final project is conducted in groups of six (two from each cultural group) and requires a final, oral presentation. During the 2-week course, time is split among classroom instruction, group discussions, study time, work on the group projects, and informal, free time. In addition to the 2-week, summer courses, participants also attend an interim session for 4–5 days during the winter in which they review material.

Why do we view this as an excellent example of intergroup contact? First, it is clear that the superordinate goals of learning and completing the final projects will help to create interdependence and cooperation. Second, participants also live together—which further promotes close and cooperative contact. Third, the contact encounter is also intensive—it is not a 1-day, one-time shot, but rather a prolonged, 2-week encounter that then repeats itself in the winter (for a shorter time period) and then again in the summer. This kind of prolonged, intensive contact will maximize the power of newly learned information. Fourth, perceptions of equal status are maximized not only by having similar ages and equal numbers of participants and staff from each group, but also by using English as the language of discourse. In the eyes of this neutral language, all participants are equal. Moreover, the interdependent nature of the final project will also help to foster perceptions of equal status.

What about a supportive environment? Since 1993, there has been growing, regional support for the peace process and for programs that promote coexistence. Thus, until recently, institutional support, both locally and more broadly, was quite strong. As such, the NIR School seems to have had every critical ingredient of successful intergroup contact. As we have seen, these are ingredients that are likely to encourage seeing the *other* as an individual rather than as simply *one of them* and to realizing that the opposing group is not homogenous but actually contains people not all that different from us.

Although systematic, evaluation research has yet to be conducted, three summer sessions (1998, 1999, 2000) have, at least on the face of it, been a success. Meaningful friendships have developed and participants continue to return for subsequent encounters. Certainly participants see each other more as individuals than as members of the opposing group, the first stage on the path toward prejudice reduction. The remaining challenge, of course, is the achievement of the more advanced stages of generalization. Yet, it would appear that the repeated and prolonged nature of the program places these advanced stages within reach, provided that the contact encounters extend their focus to those factors that are critical for generalization (e.g., common ingroup identities, crosscutting categories, and a return to the original ingroup–outgroup distinction).

Unfortunately, as we write these words, the program is faced with enormous obstacles because the supportive environment in which it once existed has fallen apart. In September of last year (2000), unrest again returned to the area, leading to a breakdown in the peace process and a nearly complete loss of public enthusiasm for programs such as this one. Nevertheless, the sponsor of the NIR School of the Heart has continued to support the program, and at present, the staff is still working toward holding a successful session in the summer of 2001. Sadly, this example shows that even the most promising of programs can still run into seemingly insurmountable barriers. This brings us back to where we began: Perhaps it is easier, as Allport suggested, to smash an atom than a prejudice. Still, that should not stop us from trying.

## ACKNOWLEDGMENTS

The authors thank Uri Gopher for his comments on an earlier draft of this manuscript. We acknowledge the hard work of the entire staff of the NIR School of the Heart.

## REFERENCES

Allport, G. W. (1954). *The nature of prejudice.* Cambridge, MA: Addison-Wesley.

Amir, Y. (1969). Contact hypothesis in ethnic relations. *Psychological Bulletin, 71,* 319–342.

Aronson, E., & Bridgeman, D. (1979). Jigsaw groups and the segregated classroom: In pursuit of common goals. *Personality and Social Psychology Bulletin, 5,* 438–466.

Bettencourt, B. A., Brewer, M. B., Croak, M. R., & Miller, N. (1992). Cooperation and the reduction of intergroup bias: The role of reward structure and social orientation. *Journal of Experimental Social Psychology, 28,* 301–309.

Brewer, M. B. (1991). The social self: On being the same and different at the same time. *Personality and Social Psychology Bulletin, 17,* 475–482.

Brewer, M. B. (1996). When contact is not enough: Social identity and intergroup cooperation. *International Journal of Intercultural relations, 20,* 291–303.

Brewer, M. B. (2000). Reducing prejudice though cross-categorization: Effects of multiple social identities. In S. Oskamp (Ed.), *Reducing prejudice and discrimination* (pp. 165–184). Mahwah, NJ: Lawrence Erlbaum Associates.

Brewer, M. B., & Brown, R. J. (1998). Intergroup relations. In D. Gilbert, S. Fiske, & G. Lindzey (Eds.), *Handbook of social psychology* (Vol. 2, pp. 554–594). Boston: McGraw-Hill.

Brewer, M. B., Dull, V., & Lui, L. (1981). Perceptions of the elderly: Stereotypes and prototypes. *Journal of Personality and Social psychology, 41*, 656–670.

Brewer, M. B., & Miller, N. (1984). Beyond the contact hypothesis: Theoretical perspectives on desegregation. In N. Miller & M. B. Brewer (Eds.), *Groups in contact: The psychology of desegregation* (pp. 281–302). New York: Academic.

Cohen, E., & Roper, S. (1972). Modification of interracial, interaction disability: An application of status characteristics' theory. *American Sociological Review, 6*, 643–657.

Cook, S. W. (1962). The systematic analysis of socially significant events. *Journal of Social Issues, 18*, 66–84.

Deschamps, J. C., & Brown, R. J. (1983). Superordinate goals and intergroup conflict. *British Journal of Social Psychology, 22*, 189–195.

Deutsch, M., & Collins, M. E. (1951). *Interracial housing*. Minneapolis, MN: University of Minneapolis Press.

Devine, P. G. (1989). Stereotypes and prejudice: Their automatic and controlled components. *Journal of Personality and Social Psychology, 56*, 5–18.

Devine, P. G., & Baker, S. M. (1991). Measurement of racial stereotype subtyping. *Personality and Social Psychology Bulletin, 17*, 44–50.

Dovidio, J. F. & Gaertner, S. L. (1999). Reducing prejudice: Combating intergroup biases. *Current Directions in Psychological Science, 8*, 101–105.

Dovidio, J. F., Kawakami, K., & Gaertner, S. L. (2000). Reducing contemporary prejudice: Combating explicit and implicit bias at the individual and intergroup level. In S. Oskamp (Ed.), *Reducing prejudice and discrimination* (pp. 137–164). Mahwah, NJ: Lawrence Erlbaum Associates.

Erber, R., & Fiske, S. T. (1984). Outcome dependency and attention to inconsistent information. *Journal of Personality and Social Psychology, 47*, 709–726.

Fiske, S. T. (1998). Stereotyping, prejudice and discrimination. In D. Gilbert, S. Fiske, & G. Lindzey (Eds.), *Handbook of social psychology* (Vol. 2, pp. 554–594). Boston: McGraw-Hill.

Fiske, S. T. (2000). Interdependence and the reduction of prejudice. In S. Oskamp (Ed.), *Reducing prejudice and discrimination* (pp. 115–136). Mahwah, NJ: Lawrence Erlbaum Associates.

Fiske, S. T., & Neuberg, S. L. (1990). A continuum model of impression formation: From category-based to individuating processes as a function of information, motivation, and attention. In M. P. Zanna (Ed.), *Advances in experimental social psychology* (Vol. 23, pp. 1–108). San Diego, CA: Academic.

Fiske, S. T., Neuberg, S. L., Beattie, A. E., & Milberg, S. J. (1987). Category-based and attribute-based reactions to others: Some informational conditions of stereotyping and individuating processes. *Journal of Experimental Social Psychology, 23*, 399–427.

Gaertner, S. L., Dividio, J. F., Anastasio, P., Bachman, B. A., & Rust, M. (1993). The common ingroup identity model: Recategorization and the reduction of intergroup bias. In W. Stroebe & M. Hewstone (Eds.), *European review of social psychology* (Vol. 4, pp. 1–26). London: Wiley.

Gaertner, S. L., Mann, J. A., Dividio, J. P., Murrell, A. J., & Pomare, M. (1990). How does cooperation reduce intergroup bias? *Journal of Personality and Social Psychology, 59*, 692–704.

Gaertner, S. L., Rust, M., Dividio, J. F., Bachman, B. A., & Anastasio, P. (1994). The contact hypothesis: The role of a common ingroup identity on reducing intergroup bias. *Small Groups Research, 25*, 224–249.

Heider, F. (1958). The psychology of interpersonal relations. New York: Wiley.

Hewstone, M. (1996). Contact and categorization: Social psychological interventions to change intergroup relations. In C. N. Macrae, C. Stangor, & M. Hewstone (Eds.), *Stereotypes and stereotyping* (pp. 323–368). New York: Guilford.

Hewstone, M., & Brown, R. J. (1986). Contact is not enough: An intergroup perspective on the contact hypothesis. In M. Hewstone & R. Brown (Eds.), *Contact and conflict in intergroup encounters* (pp. 1–44). Oxford: Blackwell.

Hewstone, M., & Greenland, K. (2000). Intergroup conflict. *International Journal of Psychology, (35)*, 136–144.

Johnson, L., & Hewstone, M. (1992). Cognitive models of stereotype change: Subtyping and the perceived typicality of disconfirming group members. *Journal of Experimental Social Psychology, 28*, 360–386.

Marcus-Newhall, A., Miller, N., Holtz, R., & Brewer, M. B. (1993). Crosscutting category membership with role assignment: A means of reducing intergroup bias. *British Journal of Social Psychology, 32*, 125–146.

McConahay, J. B., Hardee, B. B., & Batts, V. (1981). Has racism declined? It depends upon who's asking and what is asked. *Journal of Conflict Resolution, 25*, 563–579.

Minard, R. D. (1952). Race relationships in the Pocahontas coal field. *Journal of Social Issues, 8*, 29–44.

Neuberg, S. L., & Fiske, S. T. (1987). Motivational influences on impression formation: Outcome dependency, accuracy-driven attention, and individuating processes. *Journal of Personality and Social Psychology, 53*, 431–444.

Oskamp, S. (2000). *Reducing prejudice and discrimination.* Mahwah, NJ: Lawrence Erlbaum Associates.

Pettigrew, T. F. (1997). Generalized intergroup contact effects on prejudice. *Personality and Social Psychology Bulletin, 23*, 173–185.

Pettigrew, T. F. (1998). Intergroup contact theory. *Annual Review of Psychology, 49*, 65–85.

Rothbart, M., & John, O. P. (1985). Social categorization and behavioral episodes: A cognitive analysis of the effects of intergroup contact. *Journal of Social Issues, 41*, 81–104.

Rothbart, M., & Lewis, S. (1994). Cognitive processes and intergroup relations: A historical perspective. In P. G. Devine, D. L. Hamilton, & T. M. Ostrom (Eds.), *Social cognition: Impact on social psychology* (pp. 347–382). San Diego, CA: Academic.

Sherif, M., Harvey, O. J., White, J., Hood, W., & Sherif, C. (1961). *Intergroup conflict and cooperation: The Robber's Cave experiment.* Norman, OK: University of Oklahoma Institute of Intergroup Relations.

Sherif, M., & Hovland, C. I. (1961). *Social judgement: Assimilation and contrast effects in communication and attitude change.* New Haven, CT: Yale University Press.

Stephan, W. G., & Rosenfield, D. (1978). Effects of desegregation on racial attitudes. *Journal of Personality and Social Psychology, 36*, 795–804.

Tajfel, H. (1970). Experiments in intergroup discrimination. *Scientific American, 223*, 96–102.

Tajfel, H., & Turner, J. (1986). The social identity theory of intergroup behavior. In S. Worchel & W. G. Austin (Eds.), *Psychology of intergroup relations* (pp. 7–24). Chicago, IL: Nelson-Hall.

Weiner, B. (1980). May I borrow your class notes? An attributional analysis of judgement of help-giving in an achievement-related context. *Journal of Educational Psychology, 72*, 676–681.

Weiner, B. (1990). On perceiving the other as responsible. *Nebraska Symposium on Motivation, 38*, 165–198.

Wilder, D. A. (1984). Intergroup contact: The typical member and the exception to the rule. *Journal of Experimental Social Psychology, 20*, 177–194.

Wilder, D. A. (1986). Cognitive factors affecting the success of intergroup contact. In S. Worchel & W. G. Austin (Eds.), *Psychology of intergroup relations* (pp. 49–66). Chicago, IL: Nelson-Hall.

Wilner, D. M., Walkley, R. P., & Cook, S. W. (1952). Residential proximity and intergroup relations in public housing projects. *Journal of Social Issues, 8*, 45–69.

Wolfe, C. T., Spencer, S. J., & Fein, S. (1995). Influence of motivation on implicit stereotyping. Paper presented at the 103rd Annual Convention of the American Psychological Association, New York; mentioned in J. L. Hilton & W. von Hippel (1996), *Stereotypes: Annual Review of Psychology, 47*, 237–271.

Worchel, S., Andreoli, V. A., & Folger, R. (1977). Intergroup co-operation and intergroup attraction: The effect of previous interaction and outcome of combined effort. *Journal of Experimental Social Psychology, 13*, 131–140.

# 9

# Conciliation Through Storytelling: Beyond Victimhood

Dan Bar-On

*Ben Gurion University of the Negev*

Israelis and Palestinians are still deeply rooted in their self-perceptions and feelings of being victims of their conflict and viewing the other party as victimizers (Rohana & Bar-Tal, 1998). In addition, over the past 30 years, the Israelis, perceived as the more powerful party in the conflict, have developed sophisticated strategies of exclusion of the "other" as part of their collective identity. These strategies of exclusion hinder their ability to accept Palestinian feelings and perspectives, and, in particular, cause the Israelis to refrain from relating to the Palestinians as a people equal to them in moral stature. This is an example of asymmetrical relations within conflicts that put into question the validity of our concepts of reconciliation, conflict resolution, and coexistence, based as they are on the assumption of symmetry. The psychological concept of victimhood is presented here (relating both to victim and victimizer) as an energy-draining mechanism of collective and individual identity that hinders peacebuilding efforts and processes.

# THE CONCEPTUAL
# CONFUSION CONCERNING
# PEACEBUILDING PROCESSES

The strategy of bringing parties of ethnic conflicts together is only part of the problem of peacebuilding. A critical view of the literature that discusses psychosocial processes between parties involved in ethnic conflicts suggests that this new field suffers from a lack of conceptual clarity. Usually, these processes are discussed within the concepts of conflict resolution, forgiveness, and reconciliation. They lack, however, clarity in terms of their underlying assumptions (Azar, 1990; Bar-On, 1999; Enright of North, 1998; Staub, 1998).

One can look at bottom-up peacebuilding processes of resolving ethnic conflicts as sufficient processes that complement necessary, top-down processes. The latter should include the following components.

First, a preliminary political solution has been established.

Second, legal measures have been undertaken against the perpetrators of inhuman atrocities committed during the conflict. These could take the form of the Nuremberg Trials after World War II, an international tribunal as in the case of Rwanda and Bosnia, an international tribunal as in the case of Northern Ireland, or the TRC and Amnesty as was the case in Latin America and South Africa (Hamber & Kibble, 1999).

Third, financial compensation has been proposed or provided for the victims of those atrocities.

After these processes have been implemented, one could stress the need to look for ways of complementing the above with a bottom-up process of reconciliation that could take different symbolic, educational, or interpersonal forms. Usually the concept of psychosocial reconciliation is based on several a priori assumptions.

First, the parties involved have reached a new stage in which the motives for maintaining their conflict have lessened considerably or become irrelevant. Second, an earlier stage of conciliation and trust had existed between the parties, which preceded the outburst of the violent conflict, and this could now be reestablished. Third, an economic, legal, social, and political symmetry has developed between the parties involved in the ethnic conflict, enabling them to become equal partners in the reconciliatory effort. Fourth, the concepts of conflict resolution, forgiveness, and reconciliation have a similar meaning within the cultures of the parties of the conflict. Fifth, the conflict is defined as a polarized, one-dimensional situation of a dispute between two defined groups. These assumptions, however, do not apply to conflicts of a more violent and long-term nature. First, conflicts may change on the manifest level but this does not necessarily mean a decrease in motive or the prevention of a new outburst in the future. The best example of this unrecognized tension is the ethnic conflict in Bosnia and more recently in Kosovo. At first, one assumed that earlier ethnic tensions had been resolved under the Communist regime of Yugoslavia (with an intermarriage rate of 46%). However, the disintegration of that regime caused the tensions stemming from World Wars I and II that had not been worked through to surface and escalate into atrocities and extreme bloodshed, including relations toward neighbors and long-term acquaintances. This example demonstrates that a conflict can be suppressed on the manifest level, but if it is not worked through psychosocially, it may still be present in some hidden form. It is this hidden aspect that psychosocial working through strategies have to address before one can expect successful peacebuilding.

Second, some conflicts did not have a previous phase of conciliation or trust. The 100-year-old Israeli–Palestinian conflict is an example of a harsh dispute over territories (Bar-Tal, in press). In this social context, there was no initial stage of harmony, unless one goes back to Biblical times or to Medieval Spain. Similarly, the South African scene originated in severe colonial oppression and wars between the parties. A further example is Northern Ireland, where the bitter rivalry goes back to centuries of bloodshed and violence between the parties. Such a lack of initial conciliation may require special creative procedures in which this fact will be acknowledged rather than ignored or suppressed.

Third, rarely do violent conflicts ignite or persist between equals. They usually happen between parties that have a built-in asymmetry, in terms of economic, legal, or social power. This may be the case between a majority and a minority within one nation, or between a suppressed (Black) majority and a dominant (White) minority as in the case of South Africa, or between two parties that view each other as threatening, as in the Palestinian–Israeli conflict (Maoz, 2000a). Therefore, conciliation may require a political and socioeconomic empowerment of the weaker side before a new social context of mutual respect can be formed.

Fourth, reconciliatory activity may be interpreted differently within separate cultural or religious belief systems (Azar, 1990). For example, asking for forgiveness after the atrocities of the Holocaust is perceived differently by Jews and by Christians. Whereas within the Christian tradition this is a necessary and sufficient act for reconciliation, one that any representative of the community may initiate, within the Jewish tradition no one but the victims themselves are *entitled* to receive a request for forgiveness from the victimizers (Dorff, 1992). In many cases, this discrepancy creates new sources of tension because one side assumes it did what it had to do, while the other side feels humiliated in addition to the primary feelings of pain and suffering.

Fifth, many of the ethnic conflicts are multiple conflicts rather than one single, polarized conflict. The major parties of the ethnic conflict may be subdivided within themselves into further subdivisions on the basis of differences that include ethnic, economic, secular versus religious, or center versus periphery. In addition, present tensions may elicit unresolved past conflicts. All these tensions may interact in various ways and also reinforce one another. Therefore, the image of a single, polarized conflict that can be rationally resolved may be a counterproductive, oversimplified image.

# STORYTELLING AMONG SMALL GROUPS PROCESSES RELATIONS TO ETHNIC CONFLICTS

Bar-Tal (in press) writes:

> Resolution of intractable conflicts pertains to elimination of perceived incompati-
> bility between opposing parties through negotiations by their representatives (peace
> making). But formal termination of a conflict, through conflict resolution, is only
> part of a long-term reconciliation process (peace building), which requires formation
> of peaceful relations based on trust and acceptance, cooperation and consideration
> of mutual needs. Psychological aspects of reconciliation require societal, cultural
> change of the conflictive ethos, especially of beliefs about goals, about the adversary
> group, about one's own group, about inter group relations with the former adversary,
> about the nature of peace. (p. 1)

The question is, How can one achieve these goals? What can help transform the
hatred, the negative attitudes toward the former enemy, and one's own investment
in the conflict-based identity into the openness necessary for peacebuilding? We
know that small group processes are used to try to bring together the two sides to
establish a different kind of relationship between the former adversary collectives.
There are two known methods that make use of small group processes while trying
to resolve current ethnic conflicts.

A here-and-now approach, based on a sealed off safe space, disconnected from
the hostile environment, tries to create good, personal relationships between the
participants while disregarding the history of the conflict and its current asymmetric power relations (Maoz, 2000b). It is largely based on the "contact theory"
(Allport, 1954; Pettigrew, 1998). Though it may have advantages in the short run,
it usually has little long-term effect, as external power relations and the still hostile
environment may overrun the positive effect created by the small group process.

The collective identity approach tries to introduce into the group context the
social power relations and the history of the ethnic conflict, usually at the price of
creating a close, personal relationship of trust and friendship among the participants
of the group (Suleiman, 1997). Based my our experience,[1] though the members
of the minority group are empowered through this strategy while the dominant
group develops new insights into its own ambivalence and power orientation, the
lack of personal relations often does not enable the groups to move beyond their
rigid, collective perspectives. Therefore, it is not clear if the learning process in
the groups has lasting effects beyond the meeting room.

---

[1] The author observed an Israeli and Palestinian group process at a seminar at Ben Gurion University
of the Negev during the years 1995–1998. Jewish and Palestinian facilitators from Nveh Shalom Peace
School led these seminars.

The TRT (To Reflect and Trust)[2] storytelling approach suggests another way. This method enabled members of Jewish and German groups to reflect on their personal and collective history and the extreme asymmetry between their parents during the Holocaust. At the same time, it let members of the group develop trust and create personal relations, helping each other reflect on their earlier prejudices (Bar-On, 1999). This approach of sharing personal narratives facilitated participants' ability to develop empathy toward the others and understand their experience (McNamee & Gergen, 1999). Still, even the TRT group was faced, from its early stages, with the dilemma of inside–outside commitment: How could they maintain their new comradeship without betraying their original collective affiliation? One way to resolve this tension was to initiate activities outside the group setting that helped disseminate the process. In addition, the group worked within a format of short, intensive encounters over a long enough sequence of time (6 years). Perhaps this slow pace helped integrate the group process into daily life events, absorbing changes that took place in the personal and social environment over that time.[3]

One should, however, not forget that a lot of preparation and working through took place among the German and the Jewish individuals and groups separately prior to the encounter of both sides in 1992. This happened mainly through the German self-help group, on the one hand, and, on the other, through individual therapy and a German–Jewish Dialogue group that worked in Boston for 4 years prior to the first TRT encounter.[4] Probably, this preparation could not have taken place without the self-selection process both on the German side and on the Jewish side prior to the German self-help group and the TRT group formation. Only twelve out of about 90 German interviewees showed up for the initial encounter, and only five out of many members of One Generation After from Boston chose to join the first TRT meeting.

After working for 5 years within this format of storytelling, the TRT group decided to organize a seminar with practitioners from current conflicts to test whether its method of storytelling was relevant for peacebuilding processes in

---

[2]This group of descendants of Nazi perpetrators has met as a self-help group since 1988, as a by-product of the interviews the author carried out in Germany (Bar-On, 1989). After following their work with admiration, as they were the only such self-help group who confronted these issues in Germany, the author asked the group if they would now be ready to meet a group from "the other side." After they answered positively, he approached a few of his students from Ben Gurion University of the Negev, who took a seminar with him on the Psychosocial Aftereffects of the Holocaust on Second and Third Generations. He also approached a few members of One Generation After, the organization of descendants of Holocaust survivors in Boston and New York, whom he met during his Sabbatical at Harvard and MIT in 1991–1992. These three subgroups constituted the first Wuppertal encounter of the group, later known as the TRT group.

[3]One should note that, during these years, more openness and demand for such encounters could be identified within both certain Jewish as well as German communities (Bar-On, 1995).

[4]Analyzing family history through interviews and storytelling was part of Israeli and German student seminars on the aftereffects of the Holocaust on second and third generations, before they encountered each other in Israel and in Germany (Bar-On, Ostrovsky, & Fromer, 1997).

these sites as well. It chose three conflict sites: Northern Ireland, South Africa, and the Middle East—Palestinians and Israelis. Members of the TRT initiated contacts and traveled to the three relevant conflict sites and interviewed potential participants for its 1998 Hamburg Seminar. It was proposed that all participants in the seminar be practitioners or "multipliers" in their own settings, working on issues of long-range aftereffects of the conflict within families of victims and victimizers. Preferably, they had already formed teams in their own setting. The TRT could absorb up to six people from each country, three from each side of the conflict, thereby matching the total number of the TRT membership.

For the following reasons, it became obvious that the Jewish–German dialogue on the Holocaust was very different from current ethnic conflicts. First, it had happened in the distant past. Second, only the descendants could encounter each other, especially because of the enormity and totality of the planned and industrially executed genocide by the Nazis. Third, the parties are today territorially separate (excluding the Germans Jews who did not take part in the TRT process). Fourth, a global consensus was established after World War II that the parties are clearly divided into two sides, that of the victims and that of the victimizers.

In some of the current ethnic conflicts, the psychosocial working through is taking place while the necessary legal and territorial aspects have not yet been finalized. Practitioners, who try to help the working through take place, belong to the generation of the victims and the victimizers, and the boundaries between these categories are somewhat blurred. In contrast, they do not have to deal with the kind of massive destruction the Holocaust imprinted on the minds of its survivors.

## SUMMARY OF THE HAMBURG SEMINAR

I wish to highlight several points regarding the relevance of the TRT storytelling process to coping with current conflicts.

First, the responses of the participants from the current conflict groups emphasize the importance of the storytelling process led by the TRT group and of the emotional atmosphere of support provided by this group and by the other participants of the seminar. These two components of the seminar are described by participants as crucial elements that helped them to work through their own current conflicts.

The Hamburg experience was a meaningful experience also for the members of the TRT group themselves. Their accounts describe how they felt they could transmit what they had learned and experienced earlier, and try to make it relevant for people who came from extremely diverse and unstable settings. They found out, through the Hamburg seminar, that they had developed a kind of a method that they used to work through their own traumas. Learning to listen and retain within themselves the stories of their previous enemies gave them the power and energy to help others do the same. Instead of feeling somehow on the margin of their own societies, they could now feel at the center of a socially useful and complex, new experience (Bar-On, 1999).

Second, with regard to the specific focus on the German—Jewish–Israeli—Palestinian triangle, our analysis leads me to believe that a meaningful link can be seen between the German–Jewish TRT work and the Palestinian–Israeli context. One can see this link in terms of method (storytelling) but even more so in terms of content (the relevance of working through issues of victimhood and victimization in the Holocaust to working through these issues in the current Israeli–Palestinian conflict). Probably the acknowledgment and working through process of the Holocaust that took place in the original TRT group enabled the Jewish–Israeli members to acknowledge and start to work through their role in relation to the Palestinian–Israeli conflict.

Results of the evaluation questionnaires[5] show that members of the Palestinian group came into the seminar setting with suspicion and expressed the lowest expectations compared with the other guest conflict groups (probably related to the Holocaust context that would create a Jewish dominance). Yet, after their participation in the seminar, they highly valued the Palestinian–Israeli conflict group and the TRT-led storytelling process. I read a reflection of this change in the account of a Jewish member of the group, who tells me how specifically the Palestinian–Israeli group, which she initially tried to avoid, became an illuminating experience for her own identity construction.

The evaluation of the Hamburg seminar suggests in what ways the TRT group process could become relevant also for practitioners of other current, ethnic conflicts. Further, the storytelling and the trust and reflection that followed became especially helpful in the Palestinian–Israeli context, still suffering from the lack of previous, conciliatory memories, and from severely asymmetric power relations between the parties. These caused deep mistrust, strong, emotional separateness, and identity investment in maintaining the conflict. It seems that of all the aspects that Bar-Tal (in press) mentioned as steps for psychological reconciliation, it was the storytelling combined with the emotional support that created the necessary openness for moving beyond victimhood. We learn from the Jewish TRT member's narrative how difficult it was for her, as a Jew that identifies with the Israeli side, to give up this strong self-defining aspect of her identity. How can one ignore, through a victim's identity construction, that one's group members also became victimizers of other people? The advantage of storytelling that was an essential part of the process in Hamburg was in recognizing the avoided feelings of the other.

There are still many conceptually and methodologically open questions raised during the seminar that will have to be addressed by future ones. What in the TRT experience was so crucial for the positive outcome of the invited participants? Was it the method of storytelling, the supportive emotional environment, the level of empathy reached by the TRT members (McNamee & Gergen, 1999), or the combination of all these elements together? What are the right pace and format for reaching out to each of these contemporary conflicts, representing distinct

---

[5]Again, in interest of relevance and space, only the summary of those results is presented here. The full results appear in Maoz (2000c).

cultures, religions, and traditions? How can the TRT method be translated from the microlevel into the macrolevel? How can it be implemented in different conflict sites? An initial link was formed in Hamburg between a traumatic past and several, painful, current realities, but we are still at the beginning of a long journey of creating a genuine process of peacebuilding.

## ACKNOWLEDGMENT

This chapter is based on an article submitted to *Group*, written together with Dr. I. Maoz, who was the evaluator and observer at the Hamburg 1998 seminar.

## REFERENCES

Allport, G. W. (1954). *The Nature of Prejudice.* Reading, MA: Addison-Wesley.

Azar, E. E. (1990). *The management of protracted conflict.* Hampshire, England: Dartmouth Publishing Company.

Bar-On, D. (1989). *Legacy of silence: Encounters with children of the Third Reich.* Cambridge: Harvard University Press.

Bar-On, D. (1995). Encounters between descendants of Nazi perpetrators and descendants of Holocaust survivors. *Psychiatry, 58*(3), 225–245.

Bar-On, D. (1999). *The "Other" Within Us: Changes in the Israeli Identity from a Psychosocial Perspective.* Jerusalem: Mosad Bialik (in Hebrew).

Bar-On, D., Ostrovsky, T., & Fromer, D. (1997). "Who am I in relation to the other?": German and Israeli students confront the Holocaust and each other. In Y. Danieli (Ed.), *International Handbook of Multigenerational Legacies of Trauma.* New York: Plenum.

Bar-Tal, D. (in press). From intractable conflicts through conflict resolution to reconciliation. *Journal of Political Psychology.*

Dorff, E. N. (1992). Individual and communal forgiveness. In D. Frank (Ed.), *Autonomy and Judaism.* (pp. 193–217). New York: State University of New York Press.

Enright, R., & North, J. (1998). *Exploring Forgiveness.* Madison: University of Wisconsin Press.

Hamber, B. E., & Kibble, S. (1999). *From truth to transformation: The truth and reconciliation commission in South Africa.* London: Catholic Institute for International Relations.

Maoz, I. (2000a). Power relations in intergroup encounters: A case study of Jewish-Arab encounters in Israel. *International Journal of Intercultural Relations, 24*(4), 259–277.

Maoz, I. (2000b). Multiple conflicts and competing agendas: A framework for conceptualizing structured encounters between groups in conflict—the case of a coexistence project of Jews and Palestinians in Israel. *Peace and Conflict: Journal Peace Psychology, 6*(2), 135–156.

Maoz, I. (2000c). Expectations, results, and perspectives. In D. Bar-On (Ed.), *Bridging the Gap.* Hamburg: Koerber Foundation, 135–164.

McNamee, S., & Gergen, K. (1999). Relational responsibility. In S. McNamee, & K. Gergen, et al., *Relational Responsibility: Resources for Sustainable Dialogue (3–48).* Thousand Oaks, CA: Sage.

Pettigrew, T. F. (1998). Intergroup contact theory. *Annual Review of Psychology, 49,* 65–85.

Rouhana, N. N., & Bar-Tal, D. (1998). Psychological dynamics of ethnonational conflict: The Israeli-Palestinian case. *American Psychologist, 53,* 761–770.

Staub, E. (1998). Breaking the cycle of genocidal violence: Healing and reconciliation. In J. H. Harvey (Ed.), *Perspectives on loss: A sourcebook* (pp. 231–238). New York: Bruner/Mazel.

Suleiman, R. (1997). The planned encounter between Israeli Jews and Palestinians as a microcosm: A social-psychological perspective. *Iyunim Bechinuch, 1*(2), 71–85. (in Hebrew)

# 10

# Friendship, Contact, and Peace Education

## Charles Kadushin
*Brandeis University*

## David Livert
*City University of New York*

*I have devoted many years of my life to the promotion of conversation between Arabs and Jews in Israel. These days, however, I have noticed a new tendency on my part; avoiding Jewish-Arab encounters, and finding myself obsessed with the question, "How many meetings between Jews and Arabs are necessary before the Jews are convinced that peace and conquest do not go together?" Will another encounter with them or some additional explanation help the situation? ... Also, as to relationships between the Jews and Arabs of Israel, it is difficult to convince the Jews that discrimination and co-existence do not go together. [Our translation].*
—Daviri (2000, p. 1)

This paper explores the relationship among contact, friendship, and peace education. The context is contemporary Israel, but the theory is universally applicable. The conventional view of the topic is that peace educators can set up situations such as those alluded to by Daviri that foster contact and conversation between groups that begin with hostile views of one another. These situations then lead to better understanding and possibly to friendship, which in turn leads to the possibility of lessening of tension between the groups, and of perhaps eventually establishing peace between them. Daviri now despairs of reaching understanding even among his friends in the academy. Other Arabs and Palestinians who developed

117

friendships with Israelis as a result of organized encounters or joint work on peace negotiations now publicly declare that they cannot face their former friends. Perhaps this is a good time for hand-wringing and cynicism. However, it is also an opportunity to carefully review the literature on friendships and social networks on the one hand, and the Allport (1954) "contact hypothesis" on the other to glean some insights into these phenomena.

Curiously, the sociological literature on friendship (see Adams & Allan, 1998, for a convenient review and bibliography) and the social psychological literature on the contact hypothesis (see Pettigrew, 1998, for a review and bibliographies) seem largely unaware of one another, despite the fact that a major outcome of contact is friendship. Indeed, both literatures seek to define the conditions under which intergroup contact occurs and when such contact can lead to intergroup friendship. This essay seeks to repair this lack of correspondence between the two literatures in the hope that a greater understanding of intergroup contact and friendship will provide new possibilities for peace education. Although the contact hypothesis literature deals with many possible outcomes, the emphasis here will be on friendship, from the point of view of a peace process: Friendship is perhaps the most fragile yet most far reaching consequence of contact.

## FRIENDSHIP

We begin with friendship, which despite its ubiquity is much misunderstood as a social phenomenon. Though friendship is frequently thought of as dyadic, an understanding of friendship "acknowledges the fact that personal relationships do not operate independently of one another, but instead are influenced by social communication patterns and interactions taking place between the relationship participants and important others in their lives" (Sarason, Sarason, & Pierce, 1995, p. 616). That is, an entire network is involved even in seemingly isolated relationships (Wellman, Carrington, & Hall, 1988). This network tugs and pulls on the friendship dyad. Networks influence friendships "because the large majority of friendships are derived from some sort of ongoing, focused activities (Feld & Carter, 1998, p. 137). This "embeddedness" (Granovetter, 1985) stems from the fact that all informal networks such as friendship relationships are pegged to, or draped around, formal, institutional arrangements (Kadushin, 1976). These formal arrangements can be organized foci of activities "including families, work places, voluntary organizations and neighborhoods" (Feld & Carter, 1998, p. 136) and importantly, for present purposes, schools. These "all have the common effect of bringing a relatively limited set of individuals together in repeated interactions" (Feld & Carter, 1998). Repeated interaction leads to the creation of a dense network of relationships, some of which are friendship relations but some of which can be mandated by the formal, institutional structure such as doing reports or papers together or formal work relationships. This dense network of embedded relations leads to solidarity (Bleiszer & Adams, 1992; Fischer, 1982) or intensity

(Milardo, 1986): Individuals are influenced by the opinions of others within their network and thus develop common opinions and common norms. As a result, highly embedded, personal relationships tend to follow the norms of the group in which they are embedded (Feld & Carter, 1998, p. 139). Further consequences of dense networks are high levels of mutual support (Hall & Wellman, 1985) but also social pressures that limit free choice (Festinger, Schacter, & Back, 1950). On the one hand, dense, embedded relationships provide the means for resolving seemingly irreconcilable conflicts between friendship dyads. Conversely, friends with few, mutually overlapping networks often have their conflicts escalate because their separate networks of friends tend to hear only one side of the story, and thus their differences are reinforced rather than diffused. Further, because the networks are separate, their members have little stake in the maintenance of a relationship with a person they do not know (Feld & Carter, 1998, pp. 39–140). We have obviously reached the point of *deriving* from a series of propositions the very quotation with which this chapter began.

A further, critical point about friendships is the tendency for people to form friendships with those who are like them in some way. This quality has been termed *homophily* (Lazarsfeld & Merton, 1955/1978). Homophily is defined statistically as a greater than expected chance of a network having a higher proportion of units with a similar characteristic than would be expected from the distribution of that characteristic in a particular population (Verbrugge, 1977). Pairs can also be said to be homophilous if their characteristics match in a proportion greater than expected by the population from which they are drawn. Lazarsfeld and Merton distinguished between status-homophily, which can be ascribed (e.g., age, race, sex) or acquired (e.g., marital status, education, occupation), and value-homophily (e.g., attitudes, stereotypes), which has also been termed *homogeneity* (Hall & Wellman, 1985). Numerous studies have documented the tendency toward homophily in a variety of social networks (Fischer, 1982; Huckfeldt, 1983; Lauman, 1973; Moore, 1990; Verbrugge, 1977). Most studies document only one or two forms of homophily, with a few exceptions (Verbrugge, 1977).

There are two reasons for a virtually universal tendency toward homophily. First, psychologically, people tend to prefer relationships with others who are like them (Byrne, 1971; Condon & Crano, 1988). Second, as we saw, people tend to form friendships with those with whom they have had contact, but this contact occurs either in situations of "focused activity" (Feld & Carter, 1998) or in situations of geographic proximity such as neighborhoods or housing developments (Festinger et al., 1950; Huckfeldt, 1983; Lazarsfeld & Merton, 1955/1978). Indeed, intergroup friendships are more likely to be formed in situations of close proximity and easy access (Nahemow & Lawton, 1975): as daily access increases, homophilous friendships are more likely.

Focused activities are socially structured to involve people of both similar statuses and similar attitudes and values. For example, work groups in the occupational sphere tend to bring together people with common qualifications who usually share common backgrounds (Fernandez & Weinberg, 1997; Lin, Ensel, & Vaughn, 1981).

Schools tend to be segregated by race, class, ability, and formerly by gender. The findings of Black–White relationships in American schools are uniformly that cross-race friendships are extremely rare (Epstein & Karweit, 1983). Members of voluntary organizations are self-selected to have common interests and social backgrounds (McPherson & Smith-Lovin, 1987).

In all modern societies, neighborhoods and housing tend to be segregated by class and ethnicity. This has been well documented for the United States (Massey & Denton, 1993). In Israel, "90 percent of Arab Israelis reside in exclusively Arab towns or villages. Even the 10 percent who do live in mixed cities occupy separate, residential areas" (Ben-Ari & Amir, 1986, p. 45). Thus, homophily is the result not only of individual preference but also of social structures and pressures.

Finally, the very idea of friendship and what it entails depends on the cultural and historical context (Adams & Allan, 1998). Male sociability, especially in working class culture, tends to revolve on sports activities, drinking in bars, and other masculine interests. Feminine sociability, in Western societies, has traditionally been focused on more intimate interests and the sharing of confidences. As Western society becomes more oriented to professions, information, and psychological awareness, male friendship tends to acquire more attributes of female friendships (Adams & Allan, 1998).

## CONTACT

We now review the contact hypothesis, though our summary of the friendship literature suggests that because of the tendency toward homophily, social contact is far from being a random event. Rather, contact with others follows social, structural rules. The social contact hypothesis has been claimed as social science's major contribution to reducing intergroup bias and conflict (Gaertner, Dovidio, & Bachman, 1996), representing a union of both social science research and social activism (Stephan & Stephan, 1996). In its simplest form, the contact hypothesis states that one avenue to reducing prejudice and intergroup hostility is through the creation of situations in which members of an ingroup have positive interactions with members of an outgroup. The earliest formulations of the contact hypothesis were framed during the post-World War II period in which social scientists were reacting to the horrible consequences of racism embodied by the Holocaust and to segregation and racial prejudice in the United States. Unquestionably the most influential conceptualization was provided by Gordon Allport in *The Nature of Prejudice* (1954), although similar ideas were proffered by other researchers and interventionists seeking to understand how to ameliorate discrimination (Deutsch & Collins, 1951; Williams, 1947). A belief in the positive effects of social contact became part of the debates and evidence culminating in the *Brown v. Board of Education* (1954) decision to desegregate public schools.

The majority of empirical studies testing the contact hypothesis have been conducted in field settings, such as schools, summer camps, and residential housing, but a good number have been conducted in laboratory settings. It is well accepted in the social contact research that contact does not invariably lead to friendship or, consequently, to attitude or behavior change. Allport in fact (1954) identified four necessary conditions for intergroup contact to result in positive, attitude change. First, the individuals from the two groups in the contact situation must be of equal status. If members of one group have an inferior role or status, then it is likely that existing ingroup stereotypes will be reinforced. Although equal status between participants can be created in laboratory or field experiments, the homophily principle suggests that unequal status distinctions outside of the contact situation may exist, thus attenuating the effects of positive, intergroup contact. This is a particular concern when group membership is associated with socioeconomic status, education, or privilege. Subtler but perhaps even more important are status differences caused by unequal access to networked resources, thus multiplying the gaps caused by contact biases in the first place. These networked resources have been called "social capital," and there are considerable differences between Arabs and Jewish Israelis even of the same nominal status. As Nan Lin (Lin, 2000, p. 793) summarizes the matter, "Social groups (gender, race) have different access to social capital because of their advantaged or disadvantaged, structural positions and associated social networks ... Inequality in social capital, therefore, can be accounted for largely by structural constraints and the normative dynamics of social interactions." Daviri, quoted earlier, complains about Israelis' discriminating against Arabs and essentially "not getting it." Individuals who have equal status prior to entering the contact situation are more attuned to similarities between one another, which can strengthen social contact effects (Stephan & Stephan, 1996). Conversely, the less visible but important differences in social capital can exacerbate relations even when there is contact.

A second condition is normative support by respected authorities. For example, the decades since Civil Rights' legislation have witnessed the establishment of normative support for intergroup contact between Blacks and Whites in the U.S. military, business, and religious institutions. Such support can be problematic, however, when the authority figures do not include members of both the ingroup and the outgroup (Stephan & Stephan, 1996). Again, Daviri's complaint is germane.

The two remaining conditions concern the presence of a common task for contact situation participants. Participants should share a common goal and tasks in the contact situation should be cooperative. Instances such as participating on an athletic team or in study groups for school can potentially provide these conditions. Task situations have also been contrived for studying social contact effects, such as running a simulated railroad (Cook, 1978, 1985) or a winter survival task (Pettigrew, 1997). A considerable body of research supports the relationship between intergroup cooperation and improved, intergroup relations, particularly in educational settings (see review by Johnson, Johnson, & Maruyama, 1984). Aspects of the task such as the competence of each member, role within the task, and success in achieving the task also can affect perceptions of outgroup members (Cook, 1978, 1985).

Research within both laboratory and field settings has generally supported the effectiveness of Allport's four conditions. Some studies have found a positive effect for contact despite the absence of one or two of the prerequisite conditions (Cook, 1985; Pettigrew, 1998; Stephan & Stephan, 1996); other studies have been offered as disconfirmation of Allport's hypothesis, although they often lack one or two of these conditions.

In addition to the *Allport four*, researchers have since suggested a number of other conditions required for social contact to achieve its desired effects. As a result, some researchers have argued that the growing list of conditions may render the contact hypothesis untestable: The creation of situations that embody all of the proposed conditions would require considerable effort (Pettigrew, 1998). However, one of these additional conditions, acquaintance potential, requires further consideration. In Pettigrew's view, contact that leads to cross-group friendship is mostly likely to have positive effects. "The contact situation must provide the participants with the opportunity to become friends" (italics in original; Pettigrew, 1998, p. 76).

In various formulations (Amir, 1976; Cook, 1978, 1985), researchers have argued that individuals in the contact situation must have sufficient time and opportunity to learn informally more about each other and to become potential friends. Acquaintance potential may be important for several reasons (Brewer & Brown, 1994). First, such opportunities provide the chance for participants to acquire more information about one another and to get to know one another as individuals. Cook (1978, 1985) suggests that social contact situations must promote association of a sort that will reveal enough detail about members of the disliked group to encourage the seeing of them as individuals rather than as persons with stereotyped group characteristics. Such individualizing information also may disconfirm existing, negative stereotypes about outgroups. The positive reactions engendered by forming new acquaintances and friendships may generalize to the outgroup as a whole. Finally, and perhaps more importantly, acquaintances formed within a contact situation may lead to the formation of friendships that transcend the contact situation. Rather than treat acquaintance formation as a requisite condition of social contact situations, we consider the formation of friendships a key consequence of contact. Cross-group friendship can materially aid in the creation of conditions for peace.

# CONCLUSION: FRIENDSHIP, CONTACT, AND THE PROSPECTS FOR PEACE EDUCATION

We are now in a position to summarize the conditions under which contact might produce friendship. We further explore the implications of the Allport hypothesis and the implications of the network literature for peace education.

First, in naturally occurring contacts—in situations that are not specifically manipulated to promote intergroup relations—homophily reduces the chance for positive contact. That is, contact between groups such as Arabs and Israelis is unlikely in the first place, and if it does occur, contact is unlikely to lead to friendship. Geographic colocation or propinquity is rare, although Falah (1996) found that urban, Israeli Jews and Arabs often shared functional proximity—that is, they had contact in their daily life. In contrast, acquaintances and friendships were highly homophilous. Although proximity is present, this situation lacks the other requisite conditions for social contact (e.g., equal status, cooperative task) to lead to positive outcomes. Further, networks that link Israeli Arabs to each other and Israeli Jews to one another have very few cross-links bridging Arabs and Jews. The result is that the existing, informal, social networks in which people are naturally embedded produce centripetal forces rather than centrifugal ones, thus pulling Arabs and Jews even further apart.

The situation with formal networks is if anything even more circumscribing. Voluntary associations and situations that might bring Arab and Jews together are almost entirely lacking. Although employment is putatively voluntary, in terms of the goal of bringing outgroups together, the workplace can be considered an involuntary contact situation. Most Arab–Israeli, workplace relations are those in which Israelis far outrank the Arabs, thus violating one of Allport's conditions for contact to be effective. Another involuntary contact situation is school, but at the elementary and high school levels, geographic segregation as well as the ethnic–religious tracking systems of the Israeli education system largely preclude any contact at all. The one exception is the Israeli university system in which both Jewish and Arab Israelis participate on a relatively equal footing, though Jewish students are said to complain that Arab students are ill prepared.

Haifa University has 20% Arab students, the largest proportion of Arab students in Israel. This high proportion is due to the university's location in Northern Israel, the area of the highest density of Arab population within Israel. Because students stay at a university for a relatively long time period, there is a chance for acquaintance to develop into friendship. However, homophily and network structure principles seem to operate here as well, best captured by a recent tendency of Arab students to call themselves Palestinian and to refrain from voluntary association with Israeli Jews.

Because natural occasions for contact in Israel as well as elsewhere seem to doom the creation of cross-group friendships to the rare occasion, the conscious manipulation of contact seems to offer the only choice. Mindful of the barriers to the conversion of contact into friendship that are noted in this chapter, we can still suggest some network principles that might increase the probability of contact developing into friendship. The most hopeful aspect is the tendency of modern society to be composed of crosscutting social circles (Kadushin, 1966; Simmel, 1922/1955). This means that unlike rural society in which statuses are highly clustered—ethnicity, geographic location, social rank, occupational statuses, and the like are highly related to one another—in contemporary, urban society the link between statuses that might form homophilous relationships is much weaker. Thus contacts between academic Arabs and Jews in Israel can be (and have been) constructed to emphasize their common, professional statuses and deemphasize other status as being less relevant to the contact situation. A circle of professionals or academics interested in peace can be (and has been) formed that ignores other statuses the participants might not have in common. Whether the common status and task is expertise in health, water supply, energy, political polling, or sociology, for example, in the past it has been possible to emphasize these commonalities rather than the ethnic differences and the record shows that substantial friendships have been made. Peace education has tended to capitalize on this strategy that flows directly from the principles of network theory and the contact hypothesis.

This strategy has, however, run into difficulties as suggested by the quote from Daviri, an Arab psychologist, with which we began. It is obvious that another status, nationality, not shared by friends, has become more salient, swamping the shared statuses. What may be less obvious is the strong support such swamping has from the network structure of Arabs and Jews in Israel. First, the precondition of crosscutting circles of modern societies is largely true only for secular Jews, the overwhelming majority of whom live in urban settings. Arabs in Northern Israel tend to live in rural villages where their networks can exert concerted pulls away from their professional and modern statuses. To the extent that their reference is village society, then friendship too has different meanings from the ones more common in modern Israeli society (Adams & Allan, 1998). Interestingly, the radical, religious right among Jews shares many of the village network characteristics we have attributed to Arab, rural society in Israel. Not surprisingly, these Jews are not in the forefront of attempts to create dialogue and contact between Arabs and Jews.

Peace education always begins at home. Despite the strong, environmental situation pulling Jews and Arabs apart, more can be done in Haifa University to create support for the four Allport factors proven to be conducive to transforming casual contact into friendship. Because the Jews are the majority and the management of the university is exclusively Jewish, it falls upon Jews to change the situation, however recalcitrant the Arab minority might appear to them to be. To repeat: Equality, normative support (at least in the university context), common goals, and cooperative projects are less common in the university than the Allport contact hypothesis calls for. The best empirical source for testing the prevalence of these factors is obviously the minority, Arab student body, not the majority, Jewish administration, which almost by definition is less motivated to address these issues and probably less sensitive as well. We do not, however, underestimate the pulling apart created by existing Jewish and Arab networks. To counter them, the university might consider embarking on a radical solution that empirical studies (Newcomb, 1961) have demonstrated might work: subsidized, integrated, Arab–Jewish, student living facilities in Haifa.

Nonetheless, there is a need for more research regarding the environmental effects on friendship dyads. The Newcomb College experiment has not been repeated and the housing project studied by Deutsch and Collins (1951) has in fact been razed. A survey of the literature pertaining to intergroup friendship formation as it relates to social contact indicates that relationships are strongly shaped by their social environment. Relatively little research, especially longitudinal, is available on how these influences play out across the phases of friendship formation and what network properties may be most important. The present impasse in Arab–Jewish relations is also an opportunity to explore this topic both to the benefit of research on peace education but also to the benefit of social science generally.

# REFERENCES

Adams, R. G., & Allan, G. (Eds.). (1998). *Structural analysis in the Social Sciences: Placing friendship in context*. Cambridge, UK: Cambridge University Press.

Allport, G. W. (1954). *The nature of prejudice*. Reading, MA: Addison-Wesley.

Amir, Y. (1976). The role of intergroup contact in change of prejudice and race relations. In P. A. Katz (Ed.), *Towards the elimination of racism* (pp. 245–280). New York: Pergamon.

Ben-Ari, R., & Amir, Y. (1986). Contact between Arab and Jewish youth in Israel: Reality and potential. In M. Hewstone & R. Brown (Eds.), *Contact and conflict in intergroup encounters* (pp. 45–58). Oxford: Basil Blackwell.

Bleiszer, R., & Adams, R. G. (1992). *Adult friendships*. Newbury Park, CA: Sage.

Brewer, M. A., & Brown, P. J. (1994). Intergroup relations. In S. F. Gilbert, S. F. Fiske, & G. Lindzey (Eds.), *Handbook of social psychology* (4th ed., Vol. 2, pp. 554–594). Boston: McGraw-Hill.

Brown, V. (1954). Board of Educ., 347 U.S. 483.

Byrne, D. (1971). *The attraction paradigm*. New York: Academic.

Condon, J. W., & Crano, W. D. (1988). Inferred evaluation and the relation between attitude similarity and interpersonal attraction. *Journal of Personality and Social Psychology, 54*, 789–797.

Cook, S. W. (1978). Interpersonal and attitudinal outcomes in cooperating interracial groups. *Journal of Research and Development, 12*, 97–113.

Cook, S. W. (1985). Experimenting on social issues: The case of school desegregation. *American Psychologist, 40*, 452–460.

Daviri, M. (2000). How is it possible to convince? Haaretz, Hebrew Internet Edition, December 4. (in Hebrew)

Deutsch, M., & Collins, M. (1951). *Interracial housing: A psychological evaluation of a social experiment*. Minneapolis, MN: University of Minnesota Press.

Epstein, J. L., & Karweit, N. (Eds.). (1983). *Friends in school: Patterns of selection and influence in secondary schools*. New York: Academic.

Falah, G. (1996). Living together apart: Residential segregation in mixed Arab-Jewish cities in Israel. *Urban Studies, 33*, 823–857.

Feld, S., & Carter, W. C. (1998). Foci of activities as changing contexts for friendship. In R. G. Adams & G. Allan (Eds.), *Structural analysis in the Social Sciences: Placing friendship in context* (pp. 136–152). Cambridge, UK: Cambridge University Press.

Fernandez, R. M., & Weinberg, N. (1997). Sifting and sorting: Personal contacts and hiring in a retail bank. *American Sociological Review, 62*, 883–902.

Festinger, L., Schacter, S., & Back, K. (1950). *Social pressures in informal groups: A study of human factors in housing*. Stanford, CA: Stanford University Press.

Fischer, C. S. (1982). *To dwell among friends*. Chicago: University of Chicago Press.

Gaertner, S. L., Dovidio, J. F., & Bachman, B. A. (1996). Revisiting the contact hypothesis: The role of a common ingroup identity. *International Journal of Intercultural Relations, 20*(3–4), 271–290.

Granovetter, M. (1985). Economic action and social structure: The problem of embeddedness. *American Journal of Sociology, 91*, 481–510.

Hall, A., & Wellman, B. (1985). Social networks and social support. In S. Cohen & S. L. Syme (Eds.), *Social support and health* (pp. 23–41). Orlando, FL: Academic.

Huckfeldt, R. R. (1983). Social contexts, social networks, and urban neighborhoods: Environmental constraints on friendship choice. *American Journal of Sociology, 89*, 651–669.

Johnson, D. W., Johnson, R. T., & Maruyama, G. (1984). Goal interdependence and interpersonal-personal attraction in heterogeneous classrooms: A meta-analysis. In N. Miller & M. B. Brewer (Eds.), *Groups in contact: The psychology of desegregation*. Orlando, FL: Academic.

Kadushin, C. (1966). The friends and supporters of psychotherapy: On social circles in urban life. *American Sociological Review, 31*, 786–802.

Kadushin, C. (1976). Networks and circles in the production of culture. *American Behavioral Scientist, 19*, 769–784.

Lauman, E. O. (1973). *Bonds of pluralism*. New York: Wiley.

Lazarsfeld, P. F., & Merton, R. K. (1978). Friendship as a social process: A substantive and methodological analysis. In M. Berger, T. Abel, & C. H. Page (Eds.), *Freedom and control in modern society* (pp. 18–66). New York: Octagon Books. (Original work published 1955)

Lin, N. (2000). Inequality in social capital. *Contemporary Sociology, 29*, 785–795.

Lin, N., Ensel, W. M., & Vaughn, J. C. (1981). Social resources and strength of ties: Structural factors in occupational status attainment. *American Sociological Review, 46*, 393–405.

Massey, D. S., & Denton, N. A. (1993). *American apartheid: Segregation and the making of the underclass*. Cambridge, MA: Harvard University Press.

McPherson, J. M., & Smith-Lovin, L. (1987). Homophily in voluntary organizations: Status distance and the composition of face-to-face groups. *American Sociological Review, 52*, 370–379.

Milardo, R. M. (1986). Personal choice and constraint in close relationships: Applications of network analysis. In V. J. Derlega & B. A. Winstead (Eds.), *Friendship and social interaction* (pp. 145–166). New York: Springer-Verlag.

Moore, G. (1990). Structural determinates of men's and women's personal networks. *American Sociological Review, 55*, 726–735.

Nahemow, L., & Lawton, M. P. (1975). Similarity and propinquity in friendship formation. *Journal of Personality and social psychology, 32*, 205–213.

Newcomb, T. M. (1961). *The acquaintance process*. New York: Holt, Rinehart, & Winston.

Pettigrew, T. F. (1997). Generalized intergroup contact effects on prejudice. *Personality and Social Psychology Bulletin, 23*, 173–185.

Pettigrew, T. F. (1998). Intergroup contact theory. *Annual Review of Psychology, 49*, 65–85.

Sarason, I. G., Sarason, B. R., & Pierce, G. R. (1995). Social and personal relationships: Current issues, future directions. *Journal of Social and Personal Relationships, 12*, 613–619.

Simmel, G. (1955). Conflict and the web of group affiliations (R. Bendix, Trans.). Glencoe, IL: Free Press. (Original work published 1922)

Stephan, W. G., & Stephan, C. W. (1996). *Intergroup relations*. Boulder, CO: Westview Press.

Verbrugge, L. M. (1977). The structure of adult friendship choices. *Social Forces, 56*, 576–597.

Wellman, B., Carrington, P. J., & Hall, A. (1988). Networks as personal communities. In B. Wellman & S. D. Berkowitz (Eds.), *Social structures: A network approach* (pp. 130–184). New York: Cambridge University Press.

Williams, R. M. (1947). *The reduction of intergroup tensions*. New York: Social Science Research Council.

# 11

# Postresolution Processes: Instrumental and Socioemotional Routes to Reconciliation

## Arie Nadler

*Argentina Chair for Research in the Social Psychology of Conflict and Cooperation, Tel Aviv University*

## INTRODUCTION: THE PROBLEM OF RECONCILIATION IN PERSPECTIVE

Commonly, conflict between groups begins from a social reality of coexistence. In most if not all cases, after the conflict has taken its toll of suffering, the parties begin to negotiate their disagreements with the aim of concluding a deal to reestablish coexistence. If negotiations are successful the conflict is said to be resolved and peaceful coexistence is expected to prevail again. Yet, events in Northern Ireland, South Africa, and most notably the Middle East tell us postagreement reality is mixed. Together with hopes for peaceful coexistence, there is always the danger of violence that threatens to undo what had been achieved. Even in the postresolution period, relations between former enemies continue to be characterized by mistrust, stereotypes, and implicit animosity. All this serves to remind us that coexistence is the outcome of long processes of peacebuilding and reconciliation rather the result of a single stroke of a pen on an agreement. These processes of postresolution (i.e., peacebuilding and reconciliation) are at the center of the present contribution.

Most psychological research on conflict has ignored these postresolution processes and has focused instead on studying the reasons behind intergroup conflict

(Brewer & Brown, 1998), negotiations, and the variables that predict its successful outcome (Pruitt & Carnevale, 1993). One reason for this relative neglect of research and theory on postagreement processes is the prevailing view that conflict is rooted in reality-based disagreements over resources, and once the parties have agreed on a formula on how to divide these contested resources, conflict is replaced by coexistence (Sherif, Harvey, White, Hood, & Sherif, 1961). This view of conflict is shared by other disciplines in the social sciences. This rational perspective on conflict and its resolution, in general, heavily influences the analyses of conflict by social scientists. This outlook disregards the role of emotional processes that continue to threaten the viability of the newly gained agreements. This is especially true in cases of protracted conflicts in which the parties have learned to distrust the *other*, see themselves as the victims of the other's brutality, and are motivated by a desire to avenge past wrongdoing (Frijda, 1993).

The present discussion views coexistence as predicated on the parties' willingness to address the emotional barriers that separated them. For coexistence to prevail, the parties must learn to overcome the gulf of mutual hatred and mistrust and free themselves from the destructive, emotional forces that emanate from a history of conflict and victimization. To illustrate these processes of reconciliation and peace building, I refer to examples taken from the Palestinian–Israeli context. Before moving to a more detailed analysis of postresolution processes of reconciliation, I find it necessary to comment on the time and place at which these words are written.

As I am writing these words, the deadly clashes between Israelis and Palestinians are making the headlines once more. This is very different from what prevailed in this region only a short time ago. When I began putting my thoughts to paper, in the middle of summer 2000, it seemed like Israelis and Palestinians were heading toward the signing of a permanent peace agreement. At present, this forward movement has come to a screeching halt. Although I hope that by the time these words are read by others, the forward movement toward a peaceful coexistence will have resumed, these recent events remind us that signatures on agreements create the possibility of coexistence rather than ensuring it. Without the transformation of social reality from one that is governed by mistrust and animosity to one that rests on foundations of mutual acceptance and trust, the conflict remains ready to be reignited.

Turning to social psychology for relevant insights on postresolution processes reveals a lacuna of knowledge on reconciliation between groups. The research that exists has centered on interpersonal relations (e.g., McCullough, 2000). Although the findings of this research are relevant to the intergroup level, they are not immediately applicable to it. Processes of reconciliation between estranged, romantic partners may be similar, but they are not identical to processes of reconciliation between groups that have emerged from years of protracted and bloody conflict. This theoretical void calls for a development of research and theory on psychological processes of reconciliation and peacebuilding between adversarial groups. Moreover, we need to gain an understanding on postagreement processes of reconciliation and peacebuilding and learn how to implement these understandings on the ground. Otherwise, the smoldering embers of conflict will continue to glow red and hot. The present contribution is one step in this direction.

## THE TRC PROCESS: TRUTH TELLING, THE PHILOSOPHER'S STONE OF RECONCILIATION?

A relevant example of promoting intergroup reconciliation in the era of postagreement is the Truth and Reconciliation Commission (TRC) in South Africa. This process began *after* a political agreement ended minority rule in South Africa, and it represents a bold attempt to build trust and mutual acceptance by healing the emotional wounds that were created by past wrongdoing. In essence, the process consisted of inviting the perpetrators of atrocities to come forward and tell their story to their victims. If they did that, they would be forgiven and free from punishment. In broad terms, the TRC represents a "social exchange between perpetrator and victim: The perpetrator receives forgiveness and the victim in turn is empowered by the ability to grant or withhold forgiveness." In fact, in the older Apartheid system, the White South African was all powerful and the Black South African a helpless victim. As they exchange admission of guilt with forgiveness, the power relations between the former victim and perpetrator are transformed. The two parties become more equal to each other and more ready to embark on a road of building coexistence between equals. The practice of furthering coexistence through truth telling has not been confined to post-Apartheid South Africa. Similar truth-finding commissions have done work in South America (e.g., Argentina, Chile), and calls to emulate the process are heard in other areas of conflict such as the Balkans and the Middle East.

Other expressions of the same process represent attempts by leaders to further reconciliation with former, adversarial groups by apologizing for past wrongdoing committed by their group. Political life in the last years of the 20th century seems to be permeated with the politics of apology and forgiveness. To cite a few examples, Willy Brandt, the former Chancellor of Germany, fell to his knees on the ground of a former, Nazi, death camp and asked forgiveness from victims of Nazism; president Alwyn of Chile apologized for the crimes of the Pinochet regime on nationwide television; and in April, 2000 during a visit to Israel, Pope John Paul apologized to the Jewish people for two millennia of persecutions. These and similar examples share a common thread with the truth commissions. All are efforts that suggest that the road to reconciliation is paved with the emotional processes of healing through truth telling.

In the present contribution, I suggest that this view may be somewhat simplistic and that there are at least two major paths, rather than one, toward reconciliation. One path, exemplified by the TRC, asserts that reconciliation between former adversaries occurs through socioemotional processes such as truth telling by the perpetrator and forgiveness by the victim. The other path to reconciliation underscores the incremental, positive changes in relations between former enemies that result from the cooperation between the two parties in numerous projects in which the parties gradually learn to trust each other. The first path toward reconciliation suggests that reconciliation occurs almost instantaneously after the emotional wounds of the past have been healed. The second approach underscores the slow and gradual changes that will eventually yield coexistence between former adversaries. I label the first path *socioemotional reconciliation*, and the second *instrumental reconciliation*. Although both are important, each is differentially applicable in different contexts. This differential applicability depends on the kind of conflict, the circumstances of conflict resolution, and the goal of reconciliation. In the next section, I propose to consider these three layers of conflict and later analyze how they determine the applicability of socioemotional and instrumental reconciliation.

# THE THREE LAYERS OF CONFLICT AND ITS RESOLUTION: CHARACTERISTICS OF CONFLICT, CONFLICT RESOLUTION, AND GOALS OF RECONCILIATION

To analyze postagreement processes of reconciliation and peacebuilding, one needs to consider the characteristics of the conflict, the circumstances surrounding the resolution of the conflict, and the goals of reconciliation. For the sake of clarity, I describe these three layers of conflict and its resolution against the background of two examples: The conflict in the Middle East and the conflict in South Africa.

## Type of Conflict: Intragroup or Intergroup Conflict

Parties to conflict can be two groups within the same society or two different groups or nations. The South African example represents a case in which two communities within the same nation were in adversarial relations. The White South Africans dominated the Black South Africans and created the Apartheid regime to preserve their dominance. This was the background for intrasocietal conflict. This is very different from the internation conflict between Israelis and Palestinians in the Middle East. For the past 100 years the conflict between Israelis and Palestinians has been between two nations that are struggling for the same piece of land.

## Circumstances of Conflict Resolution

Is there a clear victor? Is there a consensus on who is victim and who is perpetrator? The end of conflict may see one party victorious and the other vanquished.

The South African example represents the first case. Resolution occurred when the prevailing Apartheid regime was abolished and replaced by a different political system, that is, democracy. Under these circumstances there was a consensus between the two parties, and others, on who was the victim and who was the perpetrator. In the South African example, all shared the view that the Black South Africans were the innocent victims of the evil, Apartheid regime. Alternatively, conflict may end when the parties prefer the costs of compromise to the costs of continued struggle and not because one system was defeated and destroyed. In the Middle East, conflict resolution has not meant the replacement of one evil system with a more benevolent system. Rather, resolution occurred when the two adversaries decided to coexist. Under these circumstances, the distinction between victims and perpetrators is not clear cut. Both Israelis and Palestinians view themselves as the sole legitimate victim (Rouhana & Bar-Tal, 1998). Israeli identity is permeated with associations to Jewish victimization during the Holocaust (Nadler & Liviatan, 2001), and Israelis view themselves as the targets of unjustified aggression and hostility from their Arab neighbors. The Palestinians see themselves as the victims of Zionist settlement in pre-1948 Palestine that resulted in the loss of their homes in pre-1948 Palestine. Since 1967 Palestinians in the Gaza strip and the West Bank have seen themselves, and actually are, the victims of military occupation.

## The Goal of Reconciliation: Integration and Inclusion or Separation?

The goal of reconciliation may be harmony between the former adversaries in a single, unified society, or peaceful coexistence in two separate societies. The purpose of reconciliation in South Africa was social integration: White and Black South Africans realized that the existence of South Africa was predicated on the ability of the former foes to find a common ground that would enable them to live together in the same country. To accomplish this goal, all social energies had to be harnessed to facilitate a future in which both past tormentors and past victims could be included in the same South Africa. Processes such as the TRC were meant to heal a torn society. This is an inclusive goal of reconciliation. The goal of reconciliation in the Israeli–Palestinian case is very different than in the South African case. The Israelis and Palestinians do not have an inclusive goal. The desired end state of reconciliation is autonomous, mutually accepting coexistence between Israel and a Palestinian state. The goal of reconciliation is separation and mutual acceptance. This distinction between inclusion and separation as the goal of reconciliation is not unique to intergroup relations and is relevant for interpersonal relations as well. In most cases, reconciliation within a family (e.g., husband and wife; child and parent) has an inclusive goal. Family members work to heal their differences and become one again. With two neighbors or two spouses that have decided to break up their family and pursue divorce, the story is different. Like two separate nations their goal is separation that will enable interdependent coexistence.

This analysis suggests two modal types of circumstances as far as postresolution processes are concerned. In the first, conflict is an intragroup or intranation, the resolution consists of eradicating an old and unjust social system, and the goal of reconciliation is social harmony within a single, unified society. In the second, conflict is intergroup or internation, its resolution reflects a compromise between the two entities rather than a replacement of one by the other, and the goal of reconciliation is peaceful coexistence between separate entities.[1] As already implied, the path to reconciliation is different in each of these modal cases. In the first case, social integration between former victim and perpetrator will be facilitated through socioemotional reconciliation. In the second case, separate coexistence will be facilitated by instrumental reconciliation. I now address these two paths toward reconciliation in some more detail.

## THE SOCIOEMOTIONAL PATH TO RECONCILIATION: REMOVING EMOTIONAL BARRIERS

Socioemotional reconciliation aims at dealing with the conflict-related emotions that block the road to social integration. Chief among these emotional blocks is the need for revenge. When conflict ends, the victimized party is likely to be motivated to seek revenge against its former tormentor. One relevant feature of this intense, human emotion is its cyclical nature. When victims take revenge on their tormentors, they become the new tormentors. The new victim, the former tormentor, is now preoccupied with his or her own quest for revenge. Put differently, the never-ending cycle of revenge is the best antidote to reconciliation in the era of postresolution.

It has been suggested that one major, psychological function of revenge is to restore to the helpless victim his or her sense of control and empowerment (Frijda, 1993; Kim, Smith, & Brigham, 1998). As noted previously, the truth and reconciliation processes in South Africa seem to have done exactly that. When the White policeman of the Apartheid regime admitted guilt over past wrongdoing, the power relations between him, the former tormentor, and his Black victim were reversed. From the former situation where the helpless, Black victim was at the mercy of his or her White tormentor, the TRC created a situation in which the power to forgive or withhold forgiveness for past wrongdoing was in the

---

[1] Although these two modal combinations may be the common ones, in actuality these three characteristics may appear in other combinations. For example, the end of the Second World War (i.e., an international conflict) saw the eradication of an evil system (i.e., the Nazi regime) that was consensually defined by all as the cruel perpetrator.

hands of the former victim. What emerges, then, is that through confession by the tormentors and the granting of forgiveness by the victims, the two parties become phenomenologically more equal to each other, and thereby more likely to pursue a common future in a society where both intend to become integral parts.

An important aspect of socioemotional reconciliation processes is that they are assumed to produce a psychological revolution in the collective psyche of the two parties. There is an implicit assumption about an almost instantaneous, emotional healing that results from the candid telling of truth by the wrongdoer and genuine forgiving by the victim. The basic idea in socioemotional reconciliation is that the past is the key to the future. Dealing with the past by confessing to crimes and granting forgiveness transforms the present and enables a better future.

Conceptually, research and theory on apologies as the way to mend severed social bonds is relevant to the present discussion of socioemotional reconciliation. In his book entitled *Mea Culpa*, Tavuchis (1991) notes that apology is a risky behavior. It exposes the party making the apology to the possibility that the offended party will withhold its forgiveness. This view underscores the role of trust as a prerequisite for apology to positively affect relations between adversaries. The wrongdoer that apologizes must trust that the victim will reciprocate with expressions of forgiveness and willingness to open a new slate in the relationships. The victim must also trust the perpetrator who apologizes. The former victim must trust that the adversary's apology and request for forgiveness are a genuine expression rather than another manipulative ploy. Existing social–psychological research indicates that when there is a high degree of mistrust between interactants, the apology may be misinterpreted and result in even worse relations between them than had it not been made (Darby & Schlenker, 1982).

The research by McCullough and his colleagues on forgiveness in close relations echoes this emphasis on the role of trust as a prerequisite for effective apology (McCullough, 2000; McCullough et al., 1998; McCullough & Worthington, 1994; McCullough, Worthington, & Rachal, 1997). This research examined the variables that explain the willingness of a person to forgive the transgression of his or her intimate partners (e.g., marital infidelity). The results of these studies indicate that forgiving is a turning point in severed, interpersonal relations and after it has occurred, the motivation to aggress against the transgressor is replaced by relationship-constructive behaviors. However, congruent with the emphasis on the role of trust in this context, the data indicate that forgiving is dependent on whether or not there is empathy between victim and transgressor. The victim's empathy with the feelings of distress that are associated with the perpetrator's expressions of remorse and apology predict his or her willingness to forgive.

Applied to the present context of socioemotional reconciliation between former adversary groups, these results indicate that admitting wrongdoing in exchange for forgiveness will lead to reconciliation only against a background of trust between the parties. A recent experimental study has supported this hypothesis (Nadler &

Liviatan, 2001). In this study Israeli–Jewish respondents read a speech that was attributed to a high-ranking Palestinian statesman. Half of the respondents read a speech that ended with the speaker's expression of empathy toward Israelis' conflict-related sufferings, whereas the remaining half read a speech that did not include an expression of empathy. Further, for half of the respondents the speech included the speaker's acceptance of Palestinian responsibility for having caused these sufferings, and for the other half such statements were missing. Finally, Israeli Jewish respondents were divided on a basis of premeasurement into groups having relatively high or low trust in Palestinians. In line with the assertion regarding the role of trust in this context, the Palestinian speaker's expression of empathy and willingness to accept responsibility for the other party's suffering had a positive effect only on the perceptions and feelings of high-trust Israeli Jews.

These points tell us that the effectiveness of socioemotional reconciliation in removing emotional barriers to reconciliation is predicated on the existence of enough mutual trust between the former adversaries. Such basic trust is more likely when conflict ends with a consensual agreement on who is the victim and who is the perpetrator. Under these conditions, there is no competition for the role of legitimate victim and the transgressor can expect that admission of guilt will be reciprocated with forgiveness and readiness to turn over a new leaf in the relations, rather than be the first link in a renewed chain of incriminations. Under these conditions, apologizing and telling the truth about past transgressions is less risky and socioemotional reconciliation can be effective in furthering a more harmonious future between victim and perpetrator.

Socioemotional reconciliation is more risky in a situation in which each party feels itself the only legitimate victim. For example, Israelis and Palestinians can agree on facts, but they are bitterly opposed on the meaning of these facts. Both agree that 1948 was a year of turning point in their history. But each views itself as the legitimate victim and the other as the perpetrator. The Israeli Jews remember that in 1948 the young nation was attacked in an unprovoked way by its Arab neighbors. The Palestinians call this same event the Naqba and view it as a national disaster in which they lost their homes. The psychological role of victimhood in blocking reconciliation is that a self-declared, sole and legitimate victim is absolved from the responsibility of examining the possibility that the self or one's group is also perpetrator and that the other side is also a victim. Being preoccupied with one's own victimhood detracts from one's ability to empathize with the *other*. Victims empathize with the only legitimate victims they know: themselves. Because of this, socioemotional reconciliation between two self-proclaimed legitimate victims is extremely difficult. Both sides feel that it is the responsibility of the other side, which by definition is the tormentor, to make amends. There is no place, when two victims are involved, for any story but their own story of victimhood and righteousness. Under such conditions one's acceptance of responsibility for the other side's suffering may be met with more demands rather than reciprocated with forgiveness.

Under these conditions socioemotional reconciliation may do more harm than good. Truth telling may turn into a reciprocal cycle of accusations, reinforce stereotypes, and deepen mistrust, rather than be reciprocated with forgiveness. To accept the other's pains, and one's responsibility for causing them, requires empathy and trust that simply do not exist between the two former enemies who are preoccupied with their own pains and victimization.

The goal of reconciliation efforts in this case is to gradually build trust between the parties, which will enable them to address the thorny issues that socioemotional reconciliation deals with: blame and forgiveness. To arrive at this stage, the two parties must first learn to trust the other to the degree necessary to allow such a process to move forward. For this to be accomplished, a slow process of instrumental reconciliation has to be put into motion.

# INSTRUMENTAL RECONCILIATION: THE EVOLUTIONARY PROCESS OF PEACEBUILDING

Instrumental reconciliation views reconciliation as the product of a slow and gradual process that is made up of many small instances of one party assisting the other, seeking the other's assistance, and cooperating with its past enemy to achieve common goals. Such gradual changes on the ground are assumed to slowly build a psychological reality of greater trust and lesser animosity between the former adversaries. To use a classic example from social–psychological research, one is reminded that the animosity between the *rattlers* and the *eagles* in Sherif et al., Robber's Cave experiment (Sherif et al., 1961) occurred gradually and only after these two groups cooperated on a number of consecutive events to obtain superordinate goals.

The importance of cooperating for the building of trust between adversaries is echoed in much social–psychological research and theory (Brewer, 1999). Yet, research within the framework of the contact hypothesis (Amir, 1976; Pettigrew, 1998) tells us that such cooperative ventures will increase trust only when the two parties cooperate as equals to achieve common goals. This emphasis on equality underscores a major difficulty in the process of instrumental reconciliation between former adversaries. Commonly, at the conflict's end, one side is more powerful and more advanced than the other. Under such conditions, the other may view what is equal cooperation to one side as degrading dependency.

This reality of inequality and the difficulties that it poses for instrumental reconciliation is most evident in the Middle East, where Israel is perceived as being technologically and economically more powerful than its Palestinian neighbors. These are not only perceptions. Gross National Product figures and other economic indices tell the same story. However, although this more advanced Israeli economy and technology can be viewed as a resource that the whole region could benefit from, it is often perceived as representing the danger of Israeli economic domination. These perceptions are a source of increased mistrust between Arabs and Israelis. Almost paradoxically: instrumental reconciliation can lead to greater trust only when there is equal cooperation between unequal parties.

Social–psychological research on reactions to receiving help and willingness to seek help from others is relevant here. This research focuses on interpersonal assistance and indicates that receiving (Nadler & Fisher, 1986) or seeking assistance can, under certain conditions, have self-threatening implications for the recipient of help (Nadler, 1991, 1997, 1998). The recipient may view assistance as a sign of inferiority and this can lead to negative reactions to receiving help and unwillingness to seek it. Recent research has also demonstrated this to be the case when intergroup rather than interpersonal helping relations is the focus. Schneider, Major, Luthanen, and Crocker (1996) found that African Americans who had received help from a White helper suffered a decrease in their feelings of esteem. Prataksis and his colleagues (Pratakanis, 1999; Pratakanis & Turner, 1996) applied the threat to self-esteem conception (Nadler & Fisher, 1986) to the educational field and analyzed affirmative action programs in terms of the stigmatic effects of such assistance for its recipients. Halabi and Nadler (2001) found that Arab children who had received assistance from a Jewish teacher were more threatened than Arab children who received similar assistance from an Arab teacher. This was especially so when recipients' group affiliation was primed prior to the receipt of help. In a similar vein, Peleg and Nadler (2001) found that Arab women were less willing to seek assistance from an Israeli Jew than an Israeli Arab. Finally, and in the same line, Nadler (1999) has recently conceptualized intergroup helping relations as ways in which groups challenge or maintain power relations between them.

This social–psychological body of knowledge serves to illuminate the complex nature of assistance and cooperation between adversaries. It tells us that if cooperation preserves the inequality between the parties in which the one more powerful or having more resources gives and the one with fewer resources or less powerful receives, cooperative projects may exacerbate feelings of mistrust rather than diffuse them. All this indicates that in creating an optimal process of instrumental reconciliation, one needs to attend to the psychological implications of helping relations between those who are unequal.

## Some Conditions for Effective Programs of Instrumental Reconciliation

In the final section I highlight some principles that are relevant to an optimal design of instrumental reconciliation. These observations are not based on a systematic body of social–psychological research and theory on peacebuilding between former adversaries. Such a body of knowledge simply does not exist. My comments in this section are based instead on interviews that were conducted with professionals who have done this work of peacebuilding between Israelis and

Palestinians. Most of these projects have been conducted under the auspices of the Peres Center for Peace in Tel Aviv, Israel, and all my interviewees were Israeli professionals doing that work. In a second stage of our work we plan to extend the interviews to Palestinian as well as Israeli interviewees.

*Equality has to be Deliberately Designed and Maintained.* First of all, one has to be reminded of the almost obvious: Equality must be cultivated purposefully and deliberately. The events that surrounded the 1995 Casablanca meeting, when a Middle East economic summit was organized in Casablanca, exemplify this point. It was the first of its kind and aroused much excitement among Israelis and others. In Israel, teams were working around the clock to prepare fancy, computer presentations proposing joint projects between Arabs and Israelis. The Israeli delegation arrived in Casablanca in full force. This impressive and costly event did not prove to be the success all had hoped for. Some Arab delegates perceived the Israeli delegation as trying to flex its technological muscle to embarrass the Arabs. In some sense it did more harm than good. This event reinforced fears of being dependent on Israeli technology rather than promoting instrumental reconciliation. The Israeli side was guilty of not designing equality in a deliberate and meaningful manner. It was guilty of not being sensitive and empathic enough with the concerns about dependency of the other side.

What are the ways to build equality between unequal, former adversaries? My interviews indicate that one important principle is that of equal and continuous involvement. Joint projects should involve all concerned parties from the design through implementation of the projects. Another vehicle to solve the equality paradox in instrumental reconciliation is to use the equalizing effect of third parties that are viewed as an impartial, valuable resource by the two former adversaries. When the project involves a third party that is more knowledgeable or resourceful than the two adversaries, the power structure of the cooperative project is transformed. It is no longer a social interaction in which one party is dependent on, or feels inferior to, its former adversary. Rather, both parties have something to learn or receive from the more resourceful, third party. The presence of such a powerful, third party equalizes the two former adversaries and the dependency of one over the other is diluted. In the context of building instrumental reconciliation between Israelis and Palestinians, such a third party can be an international organization (e.g., United Nations Educational, Scientific and Cultural Organization (UNESCO)), or another body that is acceptable to both sides (e.g., a major European or American research center or university).

*Interpersonal Trust: The Safety Net.* My interviews have highlighted the importance of interpersonal trust as a safety net in building projects of international reconciliation. Joint projects of peacebuilding are often riddled with crises and setbacks. The situation in the Middle East, as I am writing these words, is a painful reminder of this. It seems that if there is a core group of individuals who trust each other, are with the project from its inception, and care about its success, they may be able to save the day when everything else threatens to collapse. There are numerous tales of joint Israeli–Palestinian projects that threatened to fold because of a string of misperceptions and misunderstandings. Fortunately, the people who were with these projects from the start also had enough trust in each other to get things back on course. This means that a sustainable peacebuilding project will benefit from a gradual buildup. The first step should consist of building a trusting and committed inner circle of partners. This inner circle will act as a buffer in the crises that must follow.

*Cultural Differences can Derail Instrumental Reconciliation.*    Another important potential impediment to instrumental reconciliation emanates from cultural differences. Using the Israeli–Palestinian context as an example, the respondents in my interviews have brought many examples of the cross-cultural differences between Israelis and Palestinians and their effects on peacebuilding projects. In meetings, Israelis seemed to have been guided by the questions of how to get from here to there in the shortest and fastest way. Palestinians, in contrast, seemed to be more concerned with first establishing personal acquaintance and trust in the other side. Israelis were described by my interviewees as commonly beginning a meeting by asserting their views, whereas Palestinians were described as beginning by inquiring about the other side's opinions. Palestinians were viewed as more attentive and less directive than Israelis. There are other important differences, such as the respect for age and seniority that is more characteristic of Arab than Israeli society. I do not propose to present a complete list of all the differences, nor do I suggest a deterministic view of culture. Differences between people in the same culture are often greater than differences between people from different cultures. Yet, cultural background matters and one has to be cautious in building peace across cultures. For example, the meaning of cancellation of meetings, or coming late to meetings, may be very different across cultures. Misunderstandings attributable to such differences may cause projects to falter and even collapse. Recent social–psychological theorizing on the self (e.g., Markus & Kitayama, 1991) in a cultural context may be useful to formulate theoretically driven hypotheses in this context.

*Content Matters: Addressing Real, Pressing, and Common Problems.* My interviews suggest that the success of instrumental reconciliation is dependent on the content area in which it takes place. One of the most successful areas of peacebuilding between Israelis and Arabs has been agriculture. For example, the agricultural cooperation between Israelis and Egyptians withstood the most turbulent political times. Even during the war in Lebanon and the Intifada, Israeli and Egyptian farmers continued to cooperate in experimental farms on the Nile Delta. Agriculture seems to have been the first solid bridge of peace among Israelis, Palestinians, Jordanians, and Moroccans. Why? Is it because agriculture deals with the most common and basic human need—food? Is it because farmers have a common identity that transcends divisive national identities? The complete answer is probably made up of these two answers and more. However, this tells us that the content of instrumental reconciliation projects matters. It has to be made up of projects that respond to real and pressing human needs. Growing food is a good example in many areas of the world. So are issues such as scarce water, polluted environment, adequate medical care, or the preservation of wildlife. In the Middle East, water may be a more pressing and real problem, and in the former Yugoslavia, the clearing of old minefields may be the pressing issue. Regardless of the specific issue, peacebuilding projects have focus on areas that represent real problems and concrete solutions within a reasonable time frame.

## SUMMARY AND A CONCLUDING COMMENT

In this contribution I made some observations on the processes of peacebuilding and reconciliation. To enable a clearer presentation, I focused on specific examples, chief among these the examples drawn from the Israeli–Palestinian context. However, I suggest that the principles that I focused on are applicable to many other contexts of socioemotional and instrumental reconciliation in the era of postagreement.

The reader may find a summary diagram of the central distinctions and hypotheses that were proposed in the preceding sections in Table 11.1. As a final

**TABLE 11.1**
Conflict Types, Resolution Contexts, and Reconciliation Goals and Routes

| Parameter | Type | Type |
|---|---|---|
| | Intranation[a] | Internation[b] |
| I  Context of resolution | Consensus on victim and aggressor | Both parties view themselves as victims |
| | One system is branded *evil* and is uprooted | Neither system–group is uprooted or defeated |
| II  Goal of reconciliation | Social integration | Separation; independent coexistence |
| V  Two routes to reconciliation | Socioemotional | Instrumental |
| | Replacement of revenge cycle by apology–forgiveness cycle | Projects of equal cooperation between former enemies |
| | Empathy and assuming responsibility | What the *strong* views as cooperation the *weak* views as degrading dependency |
| | Trade-off between assuming responsibility and granting forgiveness | Need to purposefully–deliberately plan equal cooperation |
| | Revolutionary change of social reality | Evolutionary change of social reality |

[a] South Africa, Chile, and Argentina.
[b] Israelis and Palestinians.

statement, let me reiterate the hope that I expressed at the beginning of this chapter. As I am writing these concluding comments, Israelis and Palestinians are fighting once again. My hope is that when these words are read by others, issues of peacebuilding and reconciliation will once again be on everyone's mind.

# REFERENCES

Amir, Y. (1976). The role of intergroup contact in change of prejudice and ethnic relations. In P. A. Katz (Ed.), *Towards the elimination of racism*. New York: Pergamon.

Brewer, M. B. (1999). The psychology of prejudice: Ingroup love or outgroup hate? *Journal of Social Issues, 55*(3), 429–444.

Brewer, M. B., & Brown, R. J. (1998). Intergroup relations. In D. T. Gilbert, S. T. Fiske, & G. Lindzey (Eds.), *Handbook of social psychology* (4th ed.). New York: McGraw-Hill.

Darby, B. W., & Schlenker, B. R. (1982). Children's reactions to apologies. *Journal of Personality and Social Psychology, 43*(4), 742–753.

Frijda, N. H. (1993). The lex talionis: On vengeance. In S. H. M. Van Goozen, N. E. Van de Poll, & J. A. Sergeant (Eds.), *Emotions: Essays on emotion theory* (pp. 269–283). Hillsdale, NJ: Lawrence Erlbaum Associates.

Halabi, S., & Nadler, A. (2001). *Intergroup helping: The effects of receiving assumptive help from outgroup member*. Ramat-Aviv: Tel Aviv University.

Kim, S. H., Smith, R. H., & Brigham, N. L. (1998). Effects of power imbalance and the presence of third parties on reactions to harm: Upward and downward revenge. *Personality and Social Psychology Review, 24*(4), 353–361.

Markus, H., & Kitayama, S. (1991). Culture and the self: Implications for cognition, emotion, and motivation. *Psychological Review, 98*, 224–253.

McCullough, M. E., & Worthington, E. L. J. (1994). Models of interpersonal forgiving and their applications to counseling: Review and critique. *Counseling and Values, 39*(1), 2–14.

McCullough, M. E., Worthington, E. L. J., & Rachal, K. C. (1997). Interpersonal forgiving in close relationships. *Journal of Personality and Social Psychology, 73*(2), 321–336.

McCullough, M. E., Rachal, K., Snadage, S. J., Worthington, E. L. J., Brown, S. W., & Hight, T. L. (1998). Interpersonal forgiving in close relationships: II. Theoretical elaboration and measurement. *Journal of Personality and Social Psychology, 75*(6), 1586–1603.

McCullough, M. E. (2000). Forgiveness as human strength: Theory, measurement and links to well being. *Journal of Social and Clinical Psychology, 19*(1), 43–55.

Nadler, A. (1991). Help seeking behavior: Psychological costs and instrumental benefits. In M. S. Clark (Ed.), *Review of personality and social psychology* (Vol. 12). New York: Plenum.

Nadler, A. (1997). Personality and help seeking: Autonomous versus dependent seeking of help. In G. Pierce, B. Lakey, I. Sarason, & B. Sarason (Eds.), *Sourcebook of social support and personality* (pp. 379–407). New York: Plenum.

Nadler, A. (1998). Esteem, relationships and achievement explanations of help seeking behavior. In S. A. Karabenick (Ed.), *Strategic help seeking: Implications for learning and teaching* (pp. 61–96). Hillsdale, NJ: Lawrence Erlbaum Associates.

Nadler, A. (1999, July). *Intergroup Helping Relations: Helping and Group Identity*. Paper presented at the Annual Meeting of the European Association of Experimental Social Psychology, Oxford, England.

Nadler, A., & Fisher, J. D. (1986). The role of threat to self-esteem and perceived control in recipient reaction to help: Theory development and empirical validation. In L. Berkowitz (Ed.), *Advances in experimental social psychology* (pp. 81–121). New York: Academic Press.

Nadler, A., & Liviatan, I. (2001). *The effects of acceptance of responsibility and expressed empathy towards adversary's suffering on conflict-related perceptions.* Ramat-Aviv: Tel Aviv University.

Peleg, G., & Nalder, A. (2001). Inter-group help seeking: Willingness of Arab and Jewish women to seek help as affected by the national identity of the help giver. Unpublished Manuscript, Tel Aviv University.

Pettigrew, T. F. (1998). Intergroup contact theory. *Annual Review of Psychology, 49,* 65–85.

Pratakanis, A. R. (1999). The significance of affirmative action for the souls of white folk: Further implications of a helping model. *Journal of Social Issues, 55*(4), 787–815.

Pratakanis, A. R., & Turner, M. E. (1996). The proactive removal of discriminatory barriers: Affirmative action as effective help. *Journal of Social Issues, 52,* 111–132.

Pruitt, D. G., & Carnevale, P. J. (1993). *Negotiation in social conflict.* Buckingham, UK: Open University Press.

Rouhana, N. N., & Bar-Tal, D. (1998). Psychological dynamics of intractable ethnonational conflicts: The Israeli-Palestinian case. *American Psychologist, 53*(7), 761–770.

Schneider, M., Major, B., Luthanen, R., & Crocker, J. (1996). Social stigma and the potential costs of assumptive help. *Personality and Social Psychology Bulletin, 22*(2), 201–209.

Sherif, M., Harvey, O. J., White, B. J., Hood, W. R., & Sherif, C. W. (1961). *Intergroup conflict and cooperation: The Robber's Cave experiment.* Norman, OK: University of Oklahoma Press.

Tavuchis, N. (1991). *Mea culpa: A sociology of apology and reconciliation.* Stanford, CA: Stanford University Press.

# 12

# The Commonality
# of the Body: Pedagogy
# and Peace Culture

## Sherry B. Shapiro
### *Meredith College*

*There is nothing in particular about being Jewish that makes incarceration in a concentration camp cruel. There is nothing in particular about being a Bosnian woman that makes rape degrading. There is nothing in particular about being African-American that makes beatings or socially constructed poverty afflictions. Recognizing these wrongs requires the recognition of the humanity of their victims.*
—Farley (1958, pp. 174–175)

Recent feminist and postmodern scholarship has posed a sharp challenge to our traditional approaches to learning and knowing. In particular, it has brought to light the way in which the emotions and feelings have been excised from critical rationality. In this chapter, I draw on these findings as a way of reconceptualizing what it means to educate for human change in general, and peace education in particular. This work also draws on my own considerable experience as an educator who has focused on art, the aesthetic, and the body as the medium for self and social change.

Modernity brought to the fore several changes in human existence, including an assumption that everyone has the right to take part in the struggle for betterment: being better, doing better, getting better (Smith, 1999). Dennis Smith, a British sociologist, described the modern sensibility as where "every group claims *that right* (doing better) for its own members." However, he further suggests that the enfranchised group may wish to deny that same right to certain other groups whom they regard as "inhuman"or "uncivilized" (p. 7). This promise of modernity was also tied to three larger molding forces including the following: the national state, science, and capitalism. My project here is to focus on this promise of modernity and how rationality or reasoned thinking became valued with the rise of modern science, and further, how that valuing has shaped education and therefore the ways in which we conceptualize learning and teaching. In this context, my chapter sets out to critique an educational philosophy that relies disproportionately upon rationality as the vehicle for pursuing education. Further, I seek to offer a vision and a practice for peace education that develops our ability to be compassionate human beings. The Dalai Lama defines compassion in terms of a state of mind "that is nonviolent, nonharming, and nonaggressive. It is a mental attitude based on the wish for others to be free of their suffering and is associated with a sense of commitment, responsibility, and respect for others" (Lama & Cutler, 1998, p. 114).

   Foundational to my belief about any pedagogy concerned with peace is the need to address not simply how we think and cognitively know the world but the extent to which we develop our capacity for feeling, empathy, and emotional connection to ourselves and to others. This state of being holds within it the willingness and courage to share a common humanity, transforming rational knowledge into the capacity and desire to address the suffering of others. In his work as a voice for world peace, the Dalai Lama has noted that it is the general experience of suffering that acts as a unifying force that connects us with others. As he says, "perhaps this is the ultimate meaning behind our suffering. It is our suffering that is the most basic element that we share with others, the factor that unifies us with all other living creatures" (p. 211).

## EDUCATION AND MODERNITY: THE PROMISE OF RATIONAL THOUGHT

Education for modernity implied the confluence of reasoned, abstract thinking with the lethal competitiveness of capitalism. Within modernity, freedom became the ability to separate and distance oneself from others and the natural world, as well as having the desire to *get ahead* of others. However, the promises of rationality in the service of free market ideology to bring about a freer, happier, more meaningful, human existence seem to have lost their power. It appears increasingly that the globalization of capitalism and the technocratic state seem to have spawned profoundly negative consequences for the human condition. Increasing social inequalities between peoples and countries exacerbate human frustrations, envy, unfulfilled desire, and bitterness. Even within the rich countries, large numbers of people, albeit endowed with unparalleled degrees of choice, feel adrift morally, spiritually, and existentially. There is growing anger at the way corporate or state institutions objectify and administer our personal lives. The combination of modernity and capitalism has produced a world in which many people feel more alone, disconnected, and emotionally bereft. It is easy to see this in the levels of social anxiety, depression, and the abuse directed at self and others. If we are to find the seeds of a culture of peace, we surely cannot seek them among the ruins of enlightenment thinking and practices. Rationality, with its obsession for objectifying and controlling people and situations, is incapable of moving us toward a world of compassion and human connectedness. And Capitalism, which knows the price of everything and the value of nothing, can succeed only in turning the warmth of human bonds into the iciness of market relationships. An education concerned with peace will have to extract itself from the dehumanizing grip of modernity.

## TOWARDS AN EMBODIED LANGUAGE FOR EDUCATION

Martin Heidegger's work (1968) brings our attention to the dialectical relationship between how we think and how we live. Institutions of learning and the educational experiences of our children can greatly affect how we think and, therefore, how we live. Yet our educational systems have remained caught in modernity—that is, in a way of thinking that separates objective knowing from subjective experience, mind from body, the rational from the emotional—a philosophical separation between thinking and being. What results from this kind of education? What role does the human body take on in our struggle for control, for freedom? What kind of world is created? This kind of dualism between the rational and the sensual, the individual and the social, and control and freedom have become deeply embedded in our educational systems. The pervasiveness of the absolute monarch of reason in our schools has lead to a culture of domination in which students learn to value competition over community, self over other, and disconnected information over connected knowing. Here we come to question the wisdom of abstracting the mind from the body, the intellectual from the hermeneutic. It has been through this abstraction that we have come to believe that reasoning occurs outside the circumstances of our experiences and our life-world. The opposite is true.

Thinking and understanding are inseparable from the language, experience, and culture of historically and socially situated human beings. This insight is surely one of the most significant in recent, postmodern, and postpositivist scholarship. What human beings come to say or believe about their world is always a situated kind of knowing—one in which the materiality of life experiences shapes, organizes, and selects the structures of our meaning and reason. It is within this epistemological context that the works of thinkers such as Michel Foucault have been so important. They have made clear that at the core of the materiality of our life experiences *is the body*. It is this body inscribed by culture and history that determines so much about who we are, how others see us, and the sense that we give to our world. For us as educators to take seriously this insight would mean nothing less than a paradigm shift in how we view pedagogy and the process of learning. No longer can we suggest that the ability to rationally apprehend a situation is enough. Desire, feeling, sensitivity, empathy, compassion, and a sense of justice become the focus for our pedagogy. The life energies—what Herbert Marcuse calls the erotic—are central to a kind of knowing that transcends what Paulo Freire (1988) called the "banking method" of education. Instead of the usual, cold, unfeeling, disconnected knowing of our classrooms, we may insist on an education whose practice is shaped by sensibility and sensuality, by feeling, connection, and caring, as well as moral outrage and ethical responsibility. Put more simply, education that is concerned with peace must touch and trigger among students a passion for love and justice. This passion for others also implies a visceral sense of a life with greater meaning, possibility, and fullness for oneself. It is this erotically alive classroom that I refer to when I speak of an embodied education.

## THE COMMONALITY OF THE BODY

In education we have taught, as we have believed, that the body must be overcome— that it must be transcended if one is to see things as they really are. In this way, it has been asserted, we can come to know without the distortion of human ex- perience or perception: where knowledge is unsullied by the human passions, feeling, emotion, and the presence of the body (Shapiro & Shapiro, 1995). An excision of embodied education, as a way of subjective knowledge from the edu- cational process, is at the same time an excision of the body–subject's experiences, emotions, and passions from the ground of reason. All this points to a philosoph- ical and educational tradition that seeks objective knowledge and understanding, and that seeks to transcend time and place in its attempt to reach what is truth. Of course the body, or embodied knowing, represents an entirely antithetical language (Eagleton, 1990). It is one of place, temporality, particularity, and ineffability. It is a place of engagement with life's pains, suffering, desire, and ecstasies. It is also the place of commonality between human beings. Though the body offers a knowledge or knowing that does not claim to be fully the truth or fully recover- able or assessable, there can be no doubt about its power to evoke and to resonate with all that is most gut wrenching and visceral in our existence (Shapiro, 1999). Postmodern critique, as well as feminist critique, has opposed the idea of disem- bodied knowledge, which it sees as both an impossibility and a mystification. In fact there is no escape, despite our rationalist illusions, from human presence and engagement in the world. From this perspective there can be no escape from the body. Indeed, the body, far from being an obstacle for knowing, "is seen instead as the vehicle of human making and remaking of the world, constantly shifting location, capable of revealing endless points of view" (Bordo, 1993). Coming to know through our bodies means to understand how our desires, beliefs, values, and attitudes have been shaped and instilled in us. To know through our bodies means to recognize how our deepest loves and hates, loyalties and prejudices become part of us. Knowing through our bodies means, too, understanding critically the way our deepest feelings and passions have been structured by the culture in which we live. No peace education aimed at human transformation of our beliefs and attitudes can ignore this deep substratum of embodied knowledge.

To begin to include an embodied language in education would mean a pedagogy that involves the student in critical reflection of her or his world in terms of issues of power, control, and moral or ethical sensitivity—much of these understood as mediated through the somatic lives of individuals. Human beings form their identities with and through somatic messages transmitted by the culture, and especially today, through the mass-mediated forms of popular culture. One can think of the pulsating rhythms of rock music, the sexuality of youth styles, the body posturing of rap and hip-hop, or the macho aggressiveness of street corner kids. However, traditional and local cultures are also transmitted through and with the body. Here images of kneeling or swaying bodies in prayer come to mind, as well as patriarchal relationships expressed in the way men occupy physical space or women diminish their presence through low voices and veiled appearances. One thinks too of soldiers whose power is enhanced by heavy boots, unwavering stance, and weapons thrown over the shoulder. A society's values are expressed in how citizens occupy street space, or line up or push their way to the front of a queue, or in their eating habits. Of course folk and artistic traditions too are conveyed through our embodied ways of being with all that they say about freedom, community, and aesthetic values.

Our studies of the hidden curriculum have revealed much about how schools transmit somatically the dominant, frequently authoritarian values of society. One can think here of the commands teachers direct at the child's body: sit still, face front, stand up straight. These provide powerful ways in which educational institutions instruct students in acceptable ways of behaving: boys don't cry, swallow your anger, keep a stiff upper lip, act like a lady. These directions, sometimes seen as harmless, shape our feelings and responsiveness to others in the most intimate and powerful of ways. What constitutes acceptable ways of being in the culture is transmitted through a precognitive process that is sedimented in our body tissues, muscles, and skeletal posture.

A language that emerges from our embodied existence speaks to a kind of knowing that erases our typical, Western dualities of mind and body. This knowing demands that we listen to our bodies, feel our emotions, release our passions, and reunite our critical powers of thinking with our feelings, in the hope of grasping more fully the nature of our human subjectivity. It is symptomatic of the emergence of this kind of knowing that modern medicine is increasingly challenged by forms of therapy that insist on treating the whole person—both mind and body. More and more, we see how the intense drivenness of contemporary societies inflicts itself on the muscles and immune processes of the body. Body frailty mediates oppressive economic and social institutions. The popularity of homeopathic and holistic medicine testifies to the significant shift in how citizens are moving toward more embodied ways of knowing.

## TRANSFORMATIONAL PEDAGOGY: PROMISES AND DEFEATS

This concreteness of embodied existence has been a significant factor in feminist scholarship. Here, the concreteness is connected to the clarification of the actualities of the determining factors of human existence. The body becomes the sign of both promises and defeats, of oppression and possible liberation. What women know is that their bodies carry the stigmata of their societies; whether because of race, gender, class, ethnicity, nationality, or sexuality. Bodies, too, are utilized to mark us as consumers and to separate us through the invidious comparisons of our looks and appearances. Our bodies may ultimately designate us for rape, torture, or genocide. It is the body in this historical epoch that so often determines the truth of our lives. More hopefully it is the body that feels compassion, or the compulsion to act with ethical responsibility. Wendy Farley (1996) argues that this ethical dimension is housed in our erotic being. The erotic, as explained by Farley, "is first of all a capacity for joy, which connects us to others. . . ." She continues:

> By connecting us to others, Eros functions as a profound teacher; it allows us to draw near others in ways that do not harm them. This nondominating proximity permits an understanding of others to emerge that would otherwise not be possible. Rooted in joy, the erotic empowers human beings for the work of world-transformation. The joy of Eros is deeply ethical in quality and effect. It is through Eros, which is drawn out of itself by the wonder of existence, that orientation toward reality becomes possible. (p. 68)

To educate for ethical existence, then, means to help release the joyful life energy, which draws us close to others through love and appreciation of the wonder of life and existence. The erotic impulse is the antithesis of the will to dominate or oppress others. As Bell Hooks has recently noted (2000), "domination cannot exist in any social situation when love prevails. . . .when love is present, the desire to dominate and exercise power cannot rule the day. All the great social movements for freedom and justice in our society have promoted a love ethic" (p. 98).

Hooks adds, however, that to live our lives based on the principles of a love ethic—showing care, respect, and the will to cooperate—means we have to be courageous. Learning how to face our fears, she says, is one way to embrace love.

How does this view of humanity match what we practice today? What are its implications for education? We need not look far. I wish to start with our bodies—that most vulnerable of sites that signifies the ethics that penetrate and shape our actions. Hunger, homelessness, domestic violence, loss of limbs from land mines, torture—all exemplify ways in which the human body is vulnerable and ways in which it can be systematically harmed. The suffering and pain of the human body extends beyond the boundaries of nationality, race, ethnicity, gender, social class, or sexual or religious preference—all the ways of marking ourselves off from others. Here, in physical suffering, in the commonality of the body, is a place of deeper, shared understanding. It is also a place, paradoxically, of transcendent possibility— the possibility of a more aware and more compassionate public. Media images, transmitted globally, used to support or deter particular political interests, have already proven their power of evoking a general empathy and compassion. Etched in our memories of these images are those of the severed body parts of children who have stepped on land mines; citizens of Serbia dodging sniper bullets; images of women raped; the collapsing towers of the World Trade Center. These images are experienced not as abstractions but as the way we come face to face with our own humanity. Pain, as the Dalai Lama (2000) reminds us, makes it possible for us to conceive of the general experience of suffering that can act as a unifying force that connects us with others. In this sense the tormented body becomes a powerful force in educating us toward the horrors of human brutality, violence, and degradation. The suffering body transcends the particularity of human existence and becomes a potent means of generating a sense of shared humanity. This most human part of us, the vulnerability to pain and the capability of suffering, is what also prepares us to be compassionate. Thus attending to our own capacity to suffer, writes Rachel Remen (2000, p. 205), "we can uncover a simple and profound connection between our own vulnerability and the vulnerability of others." She continues:

> Ours is not a culture that respects the sick or the old or the vulnerable. We strive for independence, competence, mastery. In embracing such frontier values, we may become intolerant of human wholeness, contemptuous of anything in ourselves and in others that has needs or is capable of suffering. The denial of a common vulnerability is the ultimate barrier to compassion.

Though Remen is speaking about the culture of the United States, her analysis is one that speaks to much of our larger world. The suffering body can provide a potent reminder of humanity's shared fragility and need for care. An education that sensitizes us to the collective body becomes the vehicle for humanity's need for healing.

To engage in the transformational process required of peace education means that we must attend to the realm of the emotional, the sensual, and the relational especially as these are harmed and hurt in the maelstrom of human conflict and war. Pedagogically we may begin with the body—the body understood as at once the public and the most intimate material inscribed by cultural values and experiences, *and* the vehicle for transcending our limited social identities to a wider sense of shared experience. Such a pedagogical practice challenges forms of existence that dehumanize the other. It implies an attending and listening to the pain of others (rather than controlling and telling); a willingness to hear and to face our most shared vulnerability and fragility, the body which is also the site of our common humanity. "Those who find the courage to share a common humanity," Remen suggests, "may find they can bless anyone, anywhere" (p. 105).

## A CRITICAL PEDAGOGY OF THE BODY

Most of us who work in the field of education have had little or no formal experiences in embodied pedagogy. (Indeed, even reading the proposals for such an education made in this chapter may come as quite a surprise.) The process discussed here was developed out of my own work in critical pedagogy, philosophy of education, and dance. I began to question how education could be connected to the process of human liberation. Knowing that the need for liberation is always the consequence of oppression meant that I would need to confront or face the realities of conflicting desires among different groups. Whatever the origin of these conflicts—ethnic, racial, religious, national, or ideological—many of them are, I have come to believe, rooted in our bodies. It is in and through our bodies that particular life experiences have shaped how we perceive others and ourselves. Human subjectivity depends, in the final analysis, on a sense of identity that is grounded in memory. Indeed, without memory there is no human consciousness. The body memories that are central to my pedagogy are a record of the felt world of self and other in all of its sensuous and relational qualities. These memories carry not only traces of life's struggles and pain but are also the grounds of the desire for a different kind of world—one with less suffering and more compassion, love, and justice. In my teaching work I am constantly reminded of just how much the body–subject draws energy and courage from the individual experience of both suffering and pleasure. Remembering our embodied lives may evoke passionate feelings of hateful destructiveness, as well as tender compassion toward self and others.

In this regard let me share with you here some of the work I have been doing over the past 10 years. I teach at a small private liberal arts college for women in North Carolina in the United States. Though here I describe a process I have created for dance, it is by no means only for dance, or only for the arts. Throughout my educational work I seek to engage students in critically examining the social construction of their identities so that they might better understand the particular cultural values they have embodied and, further, be able to critically examine how this has affected their own lives and the lives of others. My pedagogic intention is explicit. I believe that education does inevitably transmit cultural values. As such it should do so in a way that is committed to creating a more caring, loving, and just world. However, this kind of transformative education requires a methodology of embodied praxis that can expose the silent and often unnamed realities of human existence and experience.

I provide one example of how a critically reflective embodied process can engage and encourage students to question issues of identity and otherness and lead to more compassionate and ethically responsible behavior. This particular process centered on the biblical story of the relationship between Hagar and Sarah. The story lends itself to raising issues of power, jealousy, exclusion of the stranger (in this case Hagar), and the need for compassion. Students read the chapters in Genesis pertaining to the story of Sarah and Hagar (not as a religious text but as a story of human relationships) and shared their interpretations of this story. They then wrote a reflection about an experience in their own lives similar to Hagar's in which they were made to feel as *other*. Each student wrote about experiences that she remembered. There was no hesitation in writing about and reflecting upon how those experiences made her feel. This reflective process acknowledges students' own feelings so deeply insinuated in their bodies, and it values these deeply embedded experiences as a way of knowing the world. It also teaches them how to connect remembered experiences to feelings that they continue to act and react upon. Such an embodied pedagogy can be described in a three-part process. As seen in the Hagar and Sarah story, students must first become aware of their own held memories. It is the deeply embedded, emotional traces of these experiences, long after the events themselves, that continue to structure how individuals see themselves, perceive and act toward others, and interpret experience. The pain of exclusion and separation stemming from the long-ago events in their lives continues to evoke powerful feelings of desire, anger, love, and justice. The second part of the process depends on connecting these embodied memories to a cognitive map that enables students to understand how their own particular lives reflect larger social, cultural, and historical forms of relationships. Not only does this help students to understand the social construction of identity as influenced by culture and how that is sedimented within their emotional being, but it allows them to place their feelings and ideas within a larger context for critical understanding. The third part of the process is one that focuses on bringing to form their felt life-world within the context of a shared community. Here I use movement. Using movement of the body is a particularly powerful way of recovering deeply held feelings and provides a way for students to discover the intensity of these experiences. For example, after students had read about, interpreted, and written a personal story about their own experiences of being treated as *other*, they select three or four sentences from their writing that held, for them, the most resonant felt memories. After their selection, they create movement from those felt memories, calling upon their bodies to guide them in re-creating the forms of that oppression. *Re-moving* felt memories offers a way of giving form, with more clarity, to the bodily held structures of being. Expressing embodied cultural values and personal experiences through movement provides students with something more tangible to grasp as they try to make sense of their felt world. Sharing these forms with others provides a place for dialogue to begin. Not only is moving their own stories pedagogically valuable, but moving them for others allows students to share their personal pain, anguish, embarrassments, hates, or joys. It is a process that requires intention, courage, and trust from the mover, and attention, respect, and sensitivity from the observer. Creating this safe space for embodied dialogue serves in developing a compassionate community. Students come to see others as humans who too can suffer, as well as come to understand the commonly shared reasons for the creation of human contexts in which suffering and oppression take place.

Students shared with each other movements representing stories of times they had been shunned, unable to become part of groups they so desperately wanted to be in, of times families separated, and of times they did not possess the right characteristics, making them feel less than others. These felt memories provided a starting point for understanding the constructed realities of their life-worlds, providing both a mapping for their own behaviors and a compass for a deeper understanding of how they relate to others. From their memories they created movements that expressed their life stories, reflecting the pain, the humiliation, and the sorrow.

After reflecting on times they had made been made to feel excluded or discriminated against, they then remembered times they had made others to feel like the outcast—the stranger. At first they said they did not remember times they had done this. Their ability to engage in deconstructing their own behaviors was hindered by their need to emotionally protect themselves. They were unable to examine without assistance the larger social structures such as religious beliefs, national or regional ideologies, or institutional prejudices. Everyday prejudices around choices of roommates or fear of Black men were also difficult to discuss or uncover, for that would mean confronting their own place of privilege as White, middle-class women. Yet, they did remember. They had to acknowledge their own participation, whether through action or nonaction, experiences in which they too were intolerant, prejudiced, or callous. One discussion about people receiving welfare assistance led to a student defending her position by stating that "if they would just work hard enough or wanted it enough they could have what I have." As one student noted, "They don't deserve what I have or they would have it." Such statements exemplify ways in which a human being constructs stories to defend one's power and privilege by demonizing the other. The young women I work with would describe themselves as Christians who are caring and generous—who have big hearts. They are indeed caring and compassionate individuals who can often lack the critical ability to uncover their own social, economic, religious, or racial narratives. Without such a critical rendering, they are unable to change thoughts, feelings, or actions. Again, after writing their own stories, sharing with others, and discussing their experiences within the larger questions about who deserves to live well, they re-created their stories through movement.

I need to say here that in order to have the students enter into their feelings is to do more than talk about them. I use the modality of movement and the body as both the critical and creative tool to form the connections between what they know but have yet to name. Talking, as we often do in education, is not enough to address people's feelings. Here the arts can offer a powerful pedagogy, though too often the arts are thought about only in ways that relate to performance, technical virtuosity, or as something beautiful in the traditional sense of the aesthetic. Using movement as a pedagogic method, as I do, allows students to focus on their bodies, not as objects to be trained, but rather as potential active subjects of their world. Indeed without this sense of agency and power there can be no talk of emancipation and possibility. Students learn how to express the world as they experience it and through that ability become able to see themselves in others. Or as Zygmunt Bauman suggests, they can reach a place where they may "grasp hold of the self and to awaken it as an active moral agent disposed to care for the Other" (Smith, 1999, p. 181).

In my final question to students, I referred back to Sarah when she hears God speaking to Abraham about her pregnancy to come. I asked them to reflect on a time that something happened to them, as it did to Sarah, where they were surprised by something that they thought could not possibly happen. My expectation was that they would name joyous memories. Instead, each one told stories of pain and sorrow—a father's suicide, a mother's mental illness and family breakdown, a rape by a teacher, an affair that led to the end of a marriage and the beginning of another. They cried, they mourned, and they told things that shamed them. They did what they are not allowed to do in schools. They shared the things that make them most human, their erotic selves. They integrated themselves into the world of feeling, and of common humanity, capturing the transformative possibility of education. This is not an approach to teaching that should be viewed as either the simply affective or cognitive, but rather one that transcends this duality. Martin Heidegger, it is worth remembering, argued "reason is the perception of what is, which always means also what can be and ought to be" (1968, p. 41). It is an understanding of reason that concerns itself with possibility grounded in sensate-lived experience, and made sense of through critical understanding and ethical responsibility. Through a process of sensual reasoning, students might be enabled to actively engage in re-fusing the mind and body, the particular and the universal, the self and the stranger (Shapiro, 1999). Through this critical or pedagogic process, they (the students) have named their own oppressions and ways in which they have oppressed others. They recognized that their bodies hold knowledge of their world and they learned the meaning of the body as the materiality of existence. They came to know themselves as body–subjects exploring and examining the connections between inner sensibilities and outer context. *Re-membering* themselves in this sense becomes the act of reidentifying the self in all of its creative, critical, and ethical dimensions; it becomes the process of finding a home in this torn and afflicted world. It is *Tikkun olam*—the repair and healing of the world.

No longer can we suggest that the ability to rationally apprehend a situation is enough. The overemphasis on the cognitive in education has left us with people who can build smart bombs, efficient gas chambers, and supply us with many obedient soldiers. Let us not forget the moral challenge posed by the solitary individual when confronted by the stranger. What responsibility do I feel for the *other*? Our challenge as educators, especially those concerned with peace, must be to go beyond the traditional ways of educating the mind to envelop the wisdom of the body. It is in that wisdom in which we find the possibility of discerning our common existence, glimmers of compassionate connection, and the desire to live in a humane world.

## CONCLUSION

Perhaps what is most significant in this process of embodied pedagogy is the belief that to effectively teach for peace education, the deeply embedded structures of human feelings must be recognized, respected, elicited, and acknowledged. The quest is not to deny rationally but rather to acknowledge and find ways to value the powerful, inner structures of feelings *and* infuse them with intelligence and insight. What is most needed when seeking to radically change a direction of thought or belief is not another idea but the ability to touch another human being in his or her place of intimacy, in memories of pain and suffering, as well as in the joyful remembrance of connection and community. Rather than seeking to win the argument for our own privileged or particular place in the world, we must seek to embrace the commonality of human needs and desires. In this sense, peace education must seek to remind individuals of what we as humans share in common—nothing can bring us closer to this than our recognition of the body as the frail, vulnerable, but irreplaceable vessel for that mysterious presence we call life.

## REFERENCES

Bordo, S. (1993). *Unbearable weight*. Los Angeles: University of California Press.
Eagleton, T. (1990). *The ideology of the aesthetic*. Cambridge: Basil Blackwell.
Farley, W. (1996). *Eros for other: Retaining truth in a pluralistic world*. University Park, PA: The Pennsylvania State University Press.
Freire, P. (1988). *Pedagogy of the oppressed*. New York: Continuum.
Heidegger, M. (1968). *What is called thinking* (F. Wieck & J. Gray, Trans.). New York: Harper & Row.
Hooks, B. (2000). *All about love*. New York: Morrow.
Lama, D., & Cutler, H. (1998). *The art of happiness*. New York: Riverhead Books.
Remen, R. (2000). *My grandfather's blessings*. New York: Riverhead Books.
Smith, D. (1999). *Zygmunt Bauman: Prophet of postmodernity*. Oxford: Blackwell.
Shapiro, S. (1999). *Pedagogy and the politics of the body: A critical praxis*. New York: Garland.
Shapiro, S., & Shapiro, S. (1995). Silent voices: Bodies of knowledge: Towards a critical pedagogy of the body. *Journal for Curriculum & Theorizing, (1)*, 49–72.

# 13

# Memory Work and the Remaking of the Future: A Critical Look at the Pedagogical Value of the Truth and Reconciliation Commission for Peace

## Crain Soudien
### *University of Cape Town*

In the wake of over 50 years of racial separation, hostility, and struggle, the South African government has initiated a large number of public interventions seeking to achieve the twin aims of reconciliation and the building of a single nation, on the one hand, and redress and redistribution, on the other. These interventions have involved significant sectors of the South African public, have been made the subject of media debate, and have, on occasion, resulted in the adoption of legislation and public policy. A key role in these interventions has been played by the Truth and Reconciliation Commission (TRC). The brief of the TRC was shaped in public debate and was crafted as a particular instrument for the purpose of building reconciliation. In this chapter I look at the pedagogical significance of the TRC and ask, specifically, how the TRC operates as a medium for teaching peace.

Public events, in a Foucaultian sense, are intensely pedagogical. They encapsulate and seek to mediate particular kinds of truths. They are sites for the construction of verities, which are for subjects beyond dispute. How these events are staged, however, in their selection of critical truths and in their contextualization of these truths is always problematic. The argument that I make here is that "truth," as Colin Bundy (1999) in a recent talk said, is hardly out there awaiting discovery. "The way," he says, "the story is told, changes over the years." Mundane as the characterization might be, contained in it is the argument that truth exists in a realm of intersubjective meaning and is invariably always partial and impossible to understand outside of the history that surrounds it.

The TRC was conceived in the climate of political compromise and negotiation that brought a formal end to decades of political turmoil and social and economic division and inequality. Its brief was defined in the cut and thrust of the negotiated settlement in which the apartheid order was unable to maintain its hegemony and the liberation movement was unable to seize power. Like the South African Constitution (in both its transitional and final forms, viz. 1993 and 1996), the TRC has been characterized as an important element in the peace pact reached between the "minority, apartheid forces and the disenfranchised, marginalised majority lead by the ANC" (De Lange 2000, p. 21). Beginning as a *putsch* by the African National Congress (ANC) to hold the apartheid government to account, the initiative was modified to become a truth *and* reconciliation commission by members of the former ruling party, the National Party, who stressed the importance of reconciliation. These founding moments did much to influence the outcome of the truth and reconciliation process.

As many commentators (Bundy, 1999; Gerloff, 1998; Krog, 1998; Natrass, 1999; Newham, 1995; and Villa-Vicencio & Verwoerd, 2000) have noted, the TRC was an immensely important moment in the recent, South African experience. Relentlessly relayed in the audiovisual media, images such as that of Jeff Benzien, a police torturer demonstrating his wet-bag technique, and the exhuming of grave after grave of anti-apartheid activists who had disappeared in the 1980s burned deeply into the South African consciousness and brought South Africans face to face with the extreme depravity spawned by racial domination. The achievement of the TRC was to make public the trauma to which many South Africans had been subjected.

And yet, as I try to argue in this paper, as a pedagogical model for teaching peace, the TRC is somewhat deficient. This deficiency is shaped by the very conditions of its birth. Truth commissions have the capacity to help broken and traumatized people reckon with their dark psyches. They have the ability to bring to the surface the unspoken and the unsaid and to open up for discussion that which is taboo. Gerloff (1998, p. 26), for example, talks of how the Nuremberg Trials served to make universal the idea that mass murder was a crime against the whole of humanity. In this respect, the Nuremberg Trials, and the TRC, serve as forceful reminders, as teaching moments in the most public sense, of the lesson that humanity will not tolerate the systematic abuse of some people by others.

The lesson as it is presented is, however, flawed. In assessing how the TRC might work both as a spontaneous or natural opportunity for peace education and as a systematic intervention, there are essentially two areas of difficulty to which we can look. The first is a question of definition and relates to how lessons are framed. The TRC presents itself as a classic case of what Bernstein (1990) refers to as *framing*. Framing refers to the "principle regulating the communicative practices of the social relations within the reproduction of discursive resources, that is, between transmitters and acquirers" (p. 36). The second is less definitional and more procedural and relates to how one understands justice.

## FRAMING THE TRC

As Gerloff (1998) continues to say, critical voices were raised against the procedures used in the Nuremberg Trial. She cites the criticism of George Bell, who argued that Nuremberg was a trial of the victors over the vanquished and that it did not, among other things, lay the foundation for a law that made racism, aggressive war, war crimes, and crimes against humanity universally recognized criminal actions. On trial were people and not the ideas that gave rise to the actions of the individuals. In Germany, the trials targeted the top officials. In South Africa, the process focused on the gruesome details and singled out the *foot soldiers* and left unpunished the planners and the politicians who authored and authorized the evils. In Germany, the trials left unresolved the question of the involvement and the complicity of the populace. In South Africa, the leaders were allowed to escape the attention of the courts. Racism was not declared a crime.

In both contexts, Germany and South Africa, in the absence of a rigorous understanding of how power works as a social force in its deployment of popular consent, its incorporation of the person in the street into the stratagems of domination, and its insidious access to the media through which processes of demonization and othering are accomplished, the process of building peace is inevitably subsumed within the limited, political discourse of the day. In South Africa, the TRC did not have recourse to international precedent that provided it with the means to confront the whole of the beast of apartheid. It was, as a result, constrained within a discourse that sent it looking for deviant individuals. The TRC was not *permitted* to entertain the possibility of putting apartheid on trial. Instead, it was left with having to identify apartheid's most heinous henchmen and to subject these agents to a process of public scrutiny.

It is against this background that the focal lens of the TRC came to be framed, in its terms of reference, on abuses that were committed within the legal ambit of apartheid. Apartheid itself fell within the bounds of legality, but the torture, detention, and murder that characterized it were not. As Mamdani (1997, p. 25) says, the "victims of apartheid [were] now narrowly defined as those militants victimised as they struggled against apartheid, not those whose lives were mutilated in the day-to-day web of regulations that was apartheid."

The TRC operates as a framing device in this instance in so far as it serves to regulate the distinguishing features of the interactional and locational principles that constitute the communicative context. As Bernstein (1990, p. 36) says, "where framing is strong, the transmitter explicitly regulates [these] distinguishing features." We can argue that the production of the TRC involves tight control over the selection, organization, and pacing criteria of the communication and the position, posture, and dress of the communicants and, also, conscious control over the location of the process. These features are abundantly evident in the staging of the TRC hearings, as the transcripts (see TRC transcripts for Hearings, undated, involving the medical profession; see also Krog, 1998, p. 5) show. Krog for example, prefaces her discussion on the TRC as ritual by using an extract of the transcript of the hearings that involved the testimony of "the blind Lucas Baba Sikwepere." In this a commissioner, Ms. Gobodo-Madikizela, explains to the blind Sikwepere what he cannot see:

> I am going to explain to you how this hall is arranged. On your right is the hall. You are now seated on a platform. There are approximately 200 to 250 people in the hall. The tables in front of us are arranged in the shape of a horseshoe. Seated in the middle of the horseshoe is Bishop Tutu, next to him is Dr. Boraine, and I am at the extreme end of the horshoe. I am seated directly across from you, and we are facing each other. We are now going to start to talk to each other, Baba (*father*). (p. 5)

In these events the process is structured to realize the production of victimhood. The person entering the discursive space of the TRC is positioned to announce his or her victim status. Archbishop Tutu, in thanking two women who testified during the Health Sector hearings, makes the following comment:

> I just want to express again a very deep, deep appreciation to yourselves, but particularly I want to pay a very warm tribute, it is inadequate but it is from the heart . . . for the incredible resilience that you demonstrated. I have said before that the freedom that we gained would almost certainly have been impossible without the quite remarkable contribution of our women folk, and we have had here testimony again of just what wonderful people you and other women who suffered and paid a very, very heavy price. (p. 5)

The point is not to minimize the suffering to which Tutu points but to lay emphasis on the framing that the example illustrates as a lesson. Taken as a lesson in either its spontaneous form or in the formal ways it which it might be used in the classroom, the event cannot but lead to a consideration of depravity. It is human depravity or deviance that is offered for scrutiny in the story Tutu was told by the two women. The women recount the tale of a diabetic, fellow detainee who was willfully denied access to her insulin regimen by the doctors who were treating her. As Mamdani (1997, p. 25) says, with this approach, "(w)e arrive at a world in which reparations are for militants, those who suffered jail or exile, but not for those who suffered only forced labour and broken homes."

This approach has consequences for the kind of reconciliation that is possible in South Africa. It has the effect of shifting victims from being in the majority to being a small minority of the population and of leaving unaddressed the hurts and the injustices experienced by the majority of South Africans; it risks turning their disappointment into frustration and outrage. Framed as the TRC is, in its limited address, it offers, therefore, a compromised lesson for how peace might be transacted. Peace in this framing is a limited peace, enacted between a small segment of the people of South Africa, a peace that, as Yazir Henry (2000, p. 166) regrets, "trivialised the lived experience of oppression and exploitation."

## CONSTITUTING THE LESSON

The second issue I take up is that which relates to how the actual lesson of the TRC is constituted after its framing. I want to argue, as have others (see Villa-Vincencio, 2000, p. 68), that an important objective of a truth commission is, first, to prevent the recurrence of abuses of human rights. The second is to effect some form of reparation for the damages that were caused. I argued earlier that the victims of the TRC were framed so as to exclude the majority of South Africans. Beyond this, I add that the TRC was constrained to define justice within the political chemistry of the transitional process playing itself out in the country. In deciding what the modalities would be for reparation or justice, the TRC was repeatedly placed under the burden of facilitating the emergence of the new order in South Africa. Perpetrators, said Chief Justice Ismail Mohamed, for example, should be provided with opportunities for reentering society as "active, full, and creative members of the new order." The implications of this approach, involving acknowledgment, reparation, and reconciliation, amount to what Villa-Vincencio (2000, p. 73) has called restorative justice, the justice of making "things right." In discussing restorative justice, Villa-Vicencio refers to it as embodying a set of "optimal ideals in the difficult pursuit of peace" (p. 73). It involves commitment to transformation that extends beyond any one judicial procedure or political initiative.

As a number of commentators (see Bundy, 1999; Holiday, 1998; Mamdani, 1997) have remarked, the TRC straddled a particular tension between its quasi-judicial style in searching for objective and forensically informed truth and its needs to fulfill the requirements of reconciliation. Within this tension a prescription for making peace was delivered that was not without its difficulties. At the heart of this process was, as Holiday (1998) describes,

> a kind of public confessional (at which . . . Tutu was to serve as a confessor in chief . . .) [and] this made up only half of the TRC's duty. The other half of its mandate was to grant indemnity from prosecution in the courts of law to the perpetrators of crimes committed by both the champions and by the enemies of apartheid, in exchange, not for their contrition, but only for their full confession of the evils they had committed or authorised. (p. 46)

The first part of the TRC's brief was to be fulfilled by listening to historical facts and the second was by dispensing reconciliation in the form of indemnities. Much discussion of this bind or constraint has taken place. Briefly, the quarrel with the process has been that it profoundly obscures and diminishes the significance of the deep, psychic processes that accompany remorse and contrition. Holiday (1998, p. 53) makes the valuable point that judicial processes allow courts to determine guilt or innocence, but they do not dispense forgiveness. Confession, he argues, is an intensely private matter. Its expression and scrutiny involve a degree of intimacy that is not possible in the glare of the courtroom. In the TRC process, I argue, there is what one might mildly refer to as conceptual confusion in how one proceeds from the reading of evidence to the assessment of the degree of remorse or contrition manifest in a perpetrator. In the process the perpetrators were required to acknowledge the wrongness of their deeds. But what if, as Mamdani (1997, p. 25) reminds, this repentance is a charade, if confession and conversion are not forthcoming? Repentance, he argues, is a voluntary act that cannot be forced out of an adversary.

It is at this point that the process becomes important for its pedagogical value. It is at this point too that a debate may be engaged. Moosa (2000), in a deeply interesting review of the TRC, refers to it as a "performance." A performance is when the actors have already configured the "purpose of the play and there is a hope that other participants and viewers will also understand its message" (p. 114). There are many elements of Moosa's argument that open up important lines of conversation, not least of all his thesis that the TRC as justice is a moment of destabilization of accepted conventions of both what is accepted as justice and what is accepted as confession. Justice in this reading is a theoretical impossibility. It is forever, following Derrida, a "process of reinvention." More pertinent for our reading here is Moosa's argument that "truth" in the TRC came not from "without" but from "within." The "truth was what the 'party' (parties) said it was. The truth was not measured, but manufactured. To be charitable we can say the truth was negotiated" (Moosa, 2000, p. 116). "It was this same truth," he carries on to say, "that rescued South Africa from a revolutionary abyss. It is also the very same truth that will hover as a spectral figure over the country's uncertain future" (p. 116).

It is this truth that is parlayed in the TRC process that constitutes the substance of a lesson that we as teachers have to engage. It is at this juncture that the TRC as a pedagogical package is enmeshed within the same coils of much that passes for multicultural education. The content it provides for the learner insufficiently explains how one moves from the particular forms of confession to the particular forms of absolution that are dispensed. In between lurks a mystery—the miracle of the new South Africa—that viewers and participants are expected to accept on faith. Much of multiculturalism, one might argue, operates on the same principles. Learners are invited into the performance of prescribed plays in which *others* are codified, even stereotyped around essentialized characteristics that they are invited to tolerate.

## CONCLUSION

Peace education in these forms, I wish to argue, offers learners only limited opportunities for exploring the thickets of truth and what it is that divides human beings and makes them into enemies of each other. Discovery is preempted by the prepackaging of truths that young people are permitted to explore. Their exploration is thus always and only that which their teachers wish for them.

Within the process are *nonpermissable* moments that are beyond the reach of investigation. Learners are not able to explore the way in which the peace process is framed, and equally important, the mysteries of confession and absolution are placed in a space that they are not allowed to enter.

## REFERENCES

Bernstein, B. (1990). *The structure of pedagogic discourse: Class codes and control, Vol. IV.* New York: Routledge.

Bundy, C. (1999, September). *The TRC Report as History.* Paper presented at the University of Cape Town.

De Lange, J. (2000). The historical context, legal origins and philosophical foundation of the South African Truth and Reconciliation Commission. In C. Villa-Vincencio & W. Verwoerd (Eds.), *Looking back, reaching forward: Reflections on the Truth and Reconciliation Commission of South Africa.* Cape Town: University of Cape Town Press and Zed Books.

Gerloff, R. (1998). Truth, a new society and reconciliation: The Truth and Reconciliation Commission in South Africa from a German perspective. *Missionalia, 26*(1), 17–53.

Holiday, A. (1998). Forgiving and forgetting: The Truth and Reconciliation Commission. In S. Nuttall & C. Coetzee (Eds.), *Negotiating the past: The making of memory in South Africa.* Cape Town: Oxford University Press.

Henry, Y. (2000). Where healing begins. In C. Villa-Vincencio & W. Verwoerd (Eds.), In *Looking back, reaching forward: Reflections on the Truth and Reconciliation Commission of South Africa.* Cape Town: University of Cape Town Press and Zed Books.

Krog, A. (1998). The Truth and Reconciliation Commission—a national ritual? *Missionalia, 26*(1), 5–16.

Mamdani, M. (1997). Reconciliation without justice. *Southern Review, 10*(6), 22–25.

Moosa, E. (2000). Truth and reconciliation as performance: Spectres of eucharistic redemption. In C. Villa-Vincencio & W. Verwoerd (Eds.). *Looking back, reaching forward: Reflections on the Truth and Reconciliation Commission of South Africa.* Cape Town: University of Cape Town Press and Zed Books.

Nattrass, N. (1999). The Truth and Reconciliation Commission on business and Apartheid: A critical evaluation. *African Affairs, 98*, 373–391.

Newham, G. (1995). Truth and reconciliation: Realising the ideals. *Indicator SA, 12*(4), 7–12.

TRC Transcripts for Hearings (undated).

Villa-Vincencio, C. (2000). Restorative justice: Dealing with the past differently. In C. Villa-Vincencio & W. Verwoerd (Eds.), *Looking back, reaching forward: Reflections on the Truth and Reconciliation Commission of South Africa.* Cape Town: University of Cape Town Press and Zed Books.

Villa-Vicencio, C., & Verwoerd, W. (2000). Introduction. In C. Villa-Vincencio & W. Verwoerd (Eds.), *Looking back, reaching forward: Reflections on the Truth and Reconciliation Commission of South Africa.* Cape Town: University of Cape Town Press and Zed Books.

# III

# The Practice

# 14

# Belgium: The Triangle of Peace—Education, Legislation, Mediation

## Johan Leman
### Catholic University of Leuven

Based on my practical experience with multicultural education and antiracism training in Brussels, this chapter inquires into how these programs may be enriched by peace education and how peace education may find some support in them for its rationale. However, above all, I attempt to show that this practical experience demonstrates primarily that when one cultivates mutual understanding on a long-term basis, it is interesting to develop a triangle consisting of education, mediation, and legislation as a frame of reference. This applies not only to multicultural education and antiracism training but also to peace education.

However, before I go on to this and in order for the reader to better grasp the experiences described, I first briefly describe the Belgian interethnic and political situation.

## THE BELGIAN INTERETHNIC AND POLITICAL SITUATION

Belgium is a federal state comprising three communities, those speaking Flemish, those speaking French, and those speaking German; and three regions, Flanders, Wallonia, and Brussels. Flanders consists only of citizens from the Flemish

165

Community. Wallonia consists primarily of a French-speaking community but also has a small German-speaking community. Brussels, also the capital of Belgium, is largely made up of a French-speaking community (85%) but contains a small number of citizens of the Flemish community as well (15%). Nonetheless, the Dutch-speaking Flemish citizens constitute 60% of the Belgian population. In addition, approximately 10% of the Belgian population do not possess Belgian citizenship (immigrants and expatriates). Most of these people live in Brussels. In contrast, Belgium is known to have a procedure for citizenship acquisition that is both lenient and rapid and recognizes dual citizenship. This means that, in reality, the number of inhabitants of foreign origin is, in fact, much larger than one would suspect from the total number of foreigners, especially for Brussels.

In spite of all this, however, it is important to understand that the immigration of non-Europeans to Belgium is of a recent nature, dating from the 1960s continuing till today. Nevertheless, until the 1990s the colonial relationship between Belgium and the former Belgian Congo never resulted in large numbers of Congolese people coming to Belgium.

With regard to the institutional and political aspects important to our subject, Belgium is ruled by a federal government, within whose authority lie the official recognition of religions, antiracist legislation, and the decision whether or not to grant the right to vote in municipal elections.

However, there are two areas important to us, over which the federal government is not authorized: education, which belongs to the language communities, specifically the Flemish and French, and employment, which is in the hands of the regional government.

The programs discussed in this chapter take place in the Brussels' Capital Region. Multicultural education comes under the jurisdiction of the Flemish community in Brussels (albeit quantitatively, more education is provided for the French community of Brussels), whereas police training for dealing with antiracism is a matter for the federal government. Moreover, since 1990, Belgium has had an Inter-Ministerial Committee on Immigrant Policy. This is a forum in which the various approaches to integration by the federal, regional, and the community governments are coordinated.

On the streets of Brussels, for the most part, one hears French spoken, although English does predominate in some neighborhoods and districts. However, Dutch, the language of the majority of Belgians, also has its place in Brussels. In economic and geographical terms, the capital region is oriented more toward Flanders than toward the southern part of the country. In Brussels, the labor market demands, as the norm, multilingualism (primarily French and Dutch) of employees.

Also typical of the streets of Brussels are the twilight zones, characterized by the large presence of low-skilled North African and Turkish foreigners (and recently also illegal aliens and newcomers from Africa and Eastern Europe), primarily residing in the center of town (and not on the outskirts as in other European metropolitans). The relatively strong presence of poorly educated, unemployed, and unmarried young men led to certain kinds of street crime, which, for a while, in turn led to an increased police involvement. This resulted in a mutually negative conceptualization by ethnic minority youths and the police.

It is in this setting that the two kinds of projects presented here are situated. For one thing, they try to convey a positive, multicultural attitude through education, and for another, they attempt to teach antiracism through specific training. It is our intention to examine these two programs from the angle of peace education.

## MULTICULTURAL EDUCATION PROGRAMS FOR CHILDREN

In 1981, Flemish kindergartens and the primary school education system in Brussels, under the auspices of the Foyer, a Flemish Regional Minorities Integration Centre for Brussels, set up trilingual, bicultural education projects (Byram & Leman, 1990). Today, there are still seven schools that are actively and successfully involved in these projects. Three of the projects work mainly with Turkish children, two with Spanish, and a further two with Italian children. In each case, Belgian children from both the French-speaking and Flemish communities, as well as some Moroccan children, are involved. The projects are called bicultural, but nevertheless the intercultural dimension plays a fundamental role. Specific to these projects, but less important in the context of a discussion on multicultural issues, is the trilingual dimension (Leman, 1999a).

Thirty percent of the instruction in kindergarten and during the first 2 years of primary school is given in the child's mother tongue. Then, in the years that follow, children are increasingly taught in the schools' dominant teaching language (Dutch) and several hours per week in the dominant language of the street in Brussels (French).

The social–ethnic profile of the schools involved shows that the following categories of pupils can be distinguished: autochthonous Dutch speakers, autochthonous French speakers, autochthonous pupils from mixed-language families (French and Dutch), allochthonous French speakers, and depending on the school, also Turks, Italians, and Spaniards who speak or wish to learn their mother tongue.

The aim of the directors of this project is that the immigrant children from ethnic minorities have a relatively good trilingual command by the end of their primary school education, above all with a good academic knowledge of Dutch (because this is the language they will be using in their secondary school education), a reasonable conversational knowledge of the first language (or the so-called mother tongue), and an acceptable knowledge of written French for their age (a language that they will still often use as a lingua franca for interethnic contacts in Brussels).

For the development of an intercultural perspective, Foyer has divided the curriculum into five categories: language use, the strictly academic courses (mathematics and sciences), the world-orientation courses (history, geography, religion, and ethics), physical education, and the more artistic courses. In practice, the trend is to acquire the intercultural education by means of an adequate allocation of elements from the five areas: a hidden curriculum through the presence and the contents of mother-tongue education, an introduction to the world-orientation course in an intercultural perspective, though not limited to the cultures of the children present in the class, and a certain consideration for emotional and artistic enrichment by means of elements of several cultures. The differentiating approach to language is a way to perceive knowledge of group markers.

This chapter does not seek to discuss the success or the possible failings of this method. Important evaluation studies were made in the school year 1986–1987; evaluations were published in Danesi (1989), Fernandez de Rota, and del Pilar Irimia Fernandez (1989), Byram and Leman (1990), and Leman (1991), and they were later repeated, as late as in 1998 (see Leman, 1999a, 1999b). The aims of the evaluations were, among other things, to examine the change in the school culture from monoculturalism to multiculturalism, the position of parents of minority children, the processes of hybridization, and so on.

Assessments that were made, and which are probably also of consequence to peace education programs, concern the parents' positions and those of the minority teachers in these multicultural projects. Non-Belgian and Belgian parents alike are affirmed in the important role they play generally and in running the school and, in particular, in their responsibility for the educational success of their children. As for the teachers, the vast teaching staff is always designed to include some minority colleagues. In multicultural, education programs designed for children, the status of parents and teachers of minority groups, not to mention that of other significant parties (such as peers), can determine the effectiveness of the program (Marchi 1991, pp. 201–207; 1999b, pp. 127–134). When minority teachers do not enjoy the same status in a school as their "native" colleagues, the difference will soon be felt by both pupils and parents and a social–ethnic hierarchy is created (Smeekens, 1990).

However, peace education is also achieved by concretizing the multicultural perspective. The members of staff are encouraged, through various programs, to get to know their pupils' social communities better. There are also courses, either integrated into the teaching curriculum or running adjacent to them, on specific topics, such as using humor as a weapon against racism or intercultural language considerations. The intercultural study of language is a moment of reflection (Ali, 1999). Visits to a children's center, called "Normal-Foreign Palace," are used as a teaching aid in addition to the more general approaches to diversity and difference. The aim of these programs is to teach both children and parents about creating a positive image of allochthonous and other minority groups. Some of the participants of the projects voluntarily attend language holidays, which are organized between children of the majority language group (not necessarily in the homes of parents who have children in the school) and children of the minority groups.

From these data, we may conclude that at this moment in these multicultural education programs, there are, in fact, various elements that are applicable to peace education and, as such, there are elements of actual peace education already present. An important research topic for 2002 and 2003 will show how this mutual relationship can be further explored and optimized. An additional question that is dealt with later is if programs of education and training are sufficient or if something more is needed, such as legislation and mediation to attain mutual understanding on a more constant basis.

## ANTIRACISM TRAINING PROGRAMS FOR LAW ENFORCERS

Since 1989, the predecessor of the Centre for Equal Opportunities and Opposition to Racism (CEOOR; from 1989 to 1993, a Royal Commissariat for Migrant Policy existed, and in 1993 this evolved into the CEOOR) has organized and carried out police training. At first, this type of training focused on aspects of antiracism. Currently this type of training is evolving into diversity training.

In antiracism training, which is still monitored, police officers voluntarily partake in a 4-day course containing, among other things, role playing and discussions on topics such as handling diversity and reflection on our own prejudices. In general, the officers do not come into daily contact with minorities themselves through this training, but the vast majority of trainers are allochthonous CEOOR personnel, and at least 1 day is programmed in which the police meet different minority people and their organizations.

Nevertheless, after the first riots in Brussels, in 1991, between Moroccan youth and the police, a number of training sessions were programmed for the police to try to encourage a better understanding between the two specific groups, the Brussels' police and the Moroccan youth, in order to avoid new riots in the future.

The first step was to attempt to gain a better understanding of the mutual prejudices, and of how the different groups explained these empirically. From the results, it appeared that the main prejudice Moroccans had about the police was that "they are racist." The reason they gave for this statement was that "they check our passports time and again just because we are easily recognised as Moroccans."

As for the police, their prejudices about Moroccan youth were expressed as follows: "they don't let us to carry out a normal passport control; and when they are faced with one, they immediately call upon their peers for support; they won't accept a normal police presence in their neighborhood and want to keep the police from entering certain areas; they enjoy provoking us." The reason given for this statement is that "it's impossible to do a passport control without immediately being surrounded by a large number of their peers, who insult us."

Bearing this in mind, the police developed and implemented a twofold strategy. First, they initiated soccer games between Moroccan children (younger than those involved in the riots); in addition, school visits were arranged involving the police and Moroccan youngsters, as well as visits to the police stables, to organizations for immigrant women, and to mosques. These positive encounters between police and minority groups were frequently covered by the press and commented on. Alongside these encounters, a second track was designed involving voluntary training sessions for the police. Small groups were set up, and the sessions were carried out in the presence of a representative of the local police headquarters. Here the emphasis of the training was not culture, but the problems the police were encountering throughout their work (including their relationships with their superiors, the quality of the workplace, etc.).

At a further stage, contacts were made between the police and some of the more problematic segments of the Moroccan youngsters (but not the hardest core). Both were able to speak freely about the other group (their mutual frustrations, their criticisms) in the presence of a mediator who was able to ask targeted questions and, in a sense, represented the absent group. Both groups knew the meeting would be recorded on video and shown to the other group for comments. So, in a sense, the first physical contact with the antagonistic other was made indirectly by means of the video. Later, both groups were brought together for face-to-face discussions.

For the last step of this program, open campaigns were set up, aimed at both these and other youngsters to encourage them to join the police. Special preentry training programs were organized and, gradually, more and more youngsters began a career in police work. And the riots? After the 1991 riots, there were riots in 1994 and again in 1997, provoked by the death of a young Moroccan drug dealer who was in conflict with the police. However, the positive outcome is that the police no longer have a problem with entering any Brussels district freely; moreover, youngsters have begun careers as policemen and complaints about racism in the police force are decreasing. It seems that riots do not flare up as easily as before.

A number of conclusions might also be important to peace education. First, exponents of the antagonistic groups are brought together in a more relaxed environment, even if these specific people are not actually in conflict with each other. Second, those people who are in a difficult situation and are themselves mixed up in the conflict are able to discuss the whole of their problems existentially with a mediator. Finally, a kind of practice moment, a buffer moment, is afforded (as you can see on the video), allowing for the communication of their problems to one other.

Here, as is demonstrated by the buffer moment, we can speak once again of peace education. After this buffer moment, the people involved can possibly be brought in contact with each other in a common setting. Later on, an appeal might be made to the members of the minority group to encourage them to partake in the structure of the majority group, in this case the police. To this end, preentry training is organized.

There was no strict evaluation of the programs themselves. However, although by no means equal to an evaluation, a relative success can, indirectly, be deduced from the fact that request for such training has grown considerably and, along with this, the relationship between the police and the youth certainly has not deteriorated. However, other explanations can be provided that may likewise account for this development. For one thing, a certain number of ethnic minority people have already joined the police and are visible on the streets; for another, systematic control of documents belonging to minority youths has ceased.

## REFLECTIONS ON SOME BASIC
## DIFFERENCES AND SIMILARITIES
## IN BOTH PROGRAMS

Different emphases exist in the education and training programs. In the schools, children are taught "not to do but to know," whereas in the training courses the police are taught "how to do (better and differently) and not, in first instance, to know" (Martin & Savary, 1996, p. 21). In a multicultural education program there is, of course, work on attitude forming, but the accent, nevertheless, lies on knowledge, whereas in antiracism training, the intention is that through a limited period of attitude forming, there will be some change in actions.

This difference in emphasis aside, both programs work with a limited number of schools, services, or personnel on the basis of an implicit and voluntary commitment, by the parents, teachers, or police officers and an acceptance that the multiethnic group markers play a role. Here, too, there are certain important differences. Specifically, the group markers in multicultural education are not problematic and the approach is not action oriented, whereas with antiracism training among the police, the opposite is true. Moreover, in multicultural education, there is an equal emphasis in both groups on qualitative and quantitative aspects of the composition, and the groups have to interact with each other as an integral part of school and class life. This is hardly ever the case with antiracism training in which the groups are not continuously confronted, and the most antagonistic individuals from these groups are even rarely brought together.

To the extent that within both of these programs, contact—in the sense of the contact hypothesis (Allport, 1954; Amir, 1969; Pettigrew, 1998)—is a precursor to success, multicultural education should be more effective in the long run. But, of course, the programs cannot replace each other. In the first place, multicultural education deals with children and young people, most of whom are in a situation in which there are prejudices, but conflict has not yet got out of hand. In the second case, that is, the antiracism training, we are dealing with adults, most of whom are often in a situation that *has* got out of hand, even if they do not have a long, traumatic history in which troubled relations have caused a completely explosive and antagonistic situation (as is mostly the case with peace education).

# WHAT CAN WE DEDUCE AT THIS STAGE FROM BOTH PROGRAMS FOR PEACE EDUCATION?

In comparison with the multicultural and antiracism training programs, the specific characteristic of peace education seems mainly to lie in the fact that the participants are antagonists, often with a long history of mutual antagonism. This discordant history motivates the participants emotionally and intellectually, and it is precisely this that serves as the focus for educators who try to phase out the antagonisms and even influence participants positively. Thus, it is reasonable to assume that methods and techniques that were found to be effective in multicultural and in antiracism programs may also be functional in peace education.

The prime contributory factors to the effectiveness of the multicultural and antiracism programs described in this chapter, besides those mentioned specifically previously, can be listed as follows.

1. There must be an open, mutual exchange of information. The exchange of information must take place in a framework in which traditional perceptions of each other can be acceptably discarded. However, it is totally insufficient to limit an education program to an exchange of information between the carriers of culture (Kloosterman, 1984).
2. The program must be carried by organizations that integrate into their structure elements of diversity, or exponents of antagonism.
3. The participants of the programs must be rated at their level as part of the middle group, or at the very least, a significant number of participants from this middle group should be present.
4. It is best to incorporate various elements of training and education in which people become interdependent. A concept of action should be designed for contact between groups and should generate up-to-date experiences that contradict the generalized, cultural pattern (Cohen, Lockhead, & Lohman, 1976; Farley, 1982), so that a situation is created in which members of the two groups become dependent on and cooperate with one another (Sherif, Harvey, White, Hood, & Sherif, 1961; Farley, 1982).
5. A basic minimum of necessary, institutional *establishment* support is required to achieve a minimum of goals.

These five components conform to research findings on the conditions necessary for positive effects in an intergroup context, as they highlight the need for contact to be personal, to be conducted on an equal footing, to be cooperative, and to be supported by the authorities (cf. Pettigrew, 1998).

However, in the multicultural education and antiracism training cases just discussed, additional conclusions can be made that can, undoubtedly, also be useful to peace education programs, and both of which depend on a strengthening of the condition that such projects be supported by the authorities. The first conclusion deals with the place legislation holds in this, and the second conclusion regards creating an institutionally born function of mediation.

Both for the project of multicultural education, as for the antiracism training for the police, there are the explicit, institutional support and the goodwill of the political majority fostering these programs on a permanent basis, even if the participants partake voluntarily. In the case of multicultural education, the legislation was specifically altered in this way, granting official status to this type of project. As for the antiracism training, there was the explicit decision of the Minister of the Interior to entrust this type of project to an organization, founded by law to fight racism and able to do so with the help of antiracism legislation.

However (as was evident throughout the antiracism training), when necessary, an appeal can be made to certain bodies that have the right to mediate between the antagonistic groups when the conflict comes to a head, enabling difficult points of difference to gradually be settled by discussion. A more or less comparable role is taken up by the minority teachers on the condition that they are considered as an integral part of the teachers' pool, in the case of the multicultural education programs discussed earlier. Furthermore, as seen later, something similar is actually institutionalized in the multicultural education sector in order to help solve any matter of conflict with a multiethnic nature.

This leads us to the fundamental thesis of this chapter that, when we want to ensure mutual understanding on a permanent basis, education and training programs, respectively, will have to be designed as a triangle in which education and training are supplemented by the dimensions of mediation and legislation. These in turn must both be the actual interpretation of what "the support of authorities, law or custom" (Pettigrew, 1998) should be. Indeed, the mediating body should possess complete statutory autonomy over the authorities that might, at any time, themselves be a compromised party in the conflict; moreover, if possible, this body must be composed of people from the incompatible groups.

## LEGISLATION AND MEDIATION: COMPLEMENTARY REALITIES

Still, educational–training programs do have their limitations. Stormy, emotional encounters can render them ineffective or even impossible for a greater or lesser period of time. This is why it is desirable to try to place the programs within an institutional environment if the political environment is favorable. This kind of support can help restrain otherwise uncontrollable, violent emotions, or at least provide buffer zones where such emotions can be gradually managed when they arise.

Such institutional support can be grounded at two levels: first, at the level of the optimal goals that are striven for; and second, at the minimum, acceptable level whose boundaries should never be crossed, that is, which the aggression must never exceed. The institutional support does not undermine the role that educational and training programs must play. On the contrary, it protects it; moreover, the educational and training programs are a condition absolutely necessary to ensure regular achievement of the minimal goals and the ongoing struggle for the optimal goals.

In order to safeguard movement toward these optimal goals, a monitoring and mediation committee can be set up, composed of members of high public standing who represent the relevant parties and oversee compliance with the goals. An example of this is the way the Assessment and Mediation Committee in the Flemish Council of Education has, since 1993, overseen the achievement of a number of goals in the education system of the Flemish Community in Belgium (Leman, 1999b).

So that society does not fall below the minimal goals, legislation is required— when racial tensions are concerned, an antiracism law should be passed and there should be an antidiscrimination law for more general cases of discrimination. Experience in the Netherlands (The National Bureau For the Fight Against Racism), in Great Britain (The Commission for Racial Equality), and in Belgium (CEOOR) clearly demonstrates that an organization should be set up by law to work alongside the legislative bodies with the aim of safeguarding compliance with the minimal goals of the laws invoked.

When the optimal goal of multiculturalism, a harmonious and peaceful society, is aimed for, the public encouragement of a constructive, mutually enriching acceptance is crucial. Similarly, when the bottom line of a humane approach that must never be crossed is safeguarded, the institutional protection of a minimal level of passive tolerance is, for the most part, necessary.

Under a broader institutional framework, educational–training programs can gain in social status because of the institutional protection they enjoy, and this will more readily guarantee them a place of importance at the center of life in society.

In order to apply such a Triangle of Peace (education and training–legislation– mediation) to different countries, we must take account of the historical and social– political specificity of each country. For example, contacts between the Belgian Federal CEOOR and the Provincial Government of the South African Free State led to the establishment of a specific law instituting a Centre for Citizenship, Education and Conflict Resolution (law of the Free State of South Africa, 27.09.1996). Under the law, in this specific case, the education programs and mediation functions (with regard to both the minimal tolerance and the optimal acceptance) were entrusted to the one Centre and the network around it, something somewhat different from the Belgian situation. However, although it is absolutely correct that the context should define the approach, still whatever the context, "the support of authorities, law, or custom" (Pettigrew, 1998) is crucial; this means that legislation and mediation are called for.

# RESEARCH QUESTIONS
# AND CONCLUSIONS

Several questions arise out of what has been written here. From the perspective of peace education, is multicultural education seen as effective as its organizers believe it to be? The number of parents who place their children in this type of program is growing all the time, but is this absolute proof of its efficacy? Again, we can consider the facts and conclude that results in the schools under the multicultural curriculum are quite satisfactory and the children enjoy going to school. But is this sufficient? Moreover, it would also be useful to have evidence of the most effective aspects of the various intercultural and peace educational initiatives underlying this type of program. Does the use of multilingual teaching practices on an equal level give a positive incentive to the mutual acceptance of group markers? Is the equal status of all members of a multicultural teaching staff a *conditio sine qua non*? Is this also the case for the participation of all parents on an equal footing? Does intercultural reflection on the different status of the use of languages in society bring about a greater, mutual acceptance by the students?

Maybe these aspects cannot be weighed against each other, but it is surely instructive to see the effectiveness of each and also to study them with regard to a possible application to other more explicit forms of peace education.

Yet another series of questions concerns the lessons taught. Should we be paying more attention to lesson content, for example, or to giving the children of the opponent (in the event that the other is an *opponent*) the opportunity to learn in their own language within the context of the school of the majority? Or should we be delving deeper into a study of structural aspects, such as the composition of the teaching staff or the school management? Or is it, in fact, rather the antagonistic reality among the young people involved, which will provide us with more answers? Is this so for multicultural education, and, if so, can this be generalised to all peace education?

In the same way, certain specific questions can be asked about antiracism training. What is the difference in effectiveness between training courses in which both antagonistic groups are explicitly physically present (at first by means of video) and training courses in which the antagonistic groups are physically absent most of the time? What is the impact of *training*, both on learning how to deal with antagonistic groups and in practice in reality? Does the training make it easier, or not? What role can the audiovisual media and new technology play in multicultural and peace education programs?

What is clear, however, is that we can derive two angles from this chapter that take precedence over the questions presented here. First, we must focus on research into what multicultural education and peace education can mutually impart to each. Second, we need to research the impact of legislation and mediation (as described herein) as authority reinforcement on the effectiveness and durability of peace education.

# REFERENCES

Ali, M. (1999). Moedertaal en taalbeschouwing in intercultureel onderwijs. In J. Leman, (Ed.), *Moedertaalonderwijs bij allochtonen* (pp. 119–126). Leuven/Amersfoort: Acco.

Allport, G. W. (1954). *The nature of prejudice*. Reading, MA: Addison-Wesley.

Amir, Y. (1969). Contact hypothesis. *Psychological Bulletin, 71*, 319–342.

Byram, M., & Leman, J. (Eds). (1990). *Bicultural and trilingual education*. Clevedon: Multilingual Matters.

Cohen, E., Lockhead, M. F., & Lohman, M. R. (1976). The center for international cooperation: A field experiment, *Sociology of Education, 49*, 47–58.

Danesi, M. (1989). L'uso della lingua madre in ambito scolastico straniero: Esperienze belghe e canadesi. *Italian Canadiana, 5*, 39–48.

Farley, J. E. (1982). *Majority–minority relations*. Englewood Cliffs, NJ: Prentice-Hall.

Fernandez de Rota, J. A., & del Pilar Irimia Fernandez. (1989). Identités et culture dans l'expérience Foyer pour élèves espagnols. *Les Cahiers Internationaux de Psychologie Sociale, 2–3*, 141–174.

Kloosterman, A. (1984). Intercultureel onderwijs: Hoe komen ze d'r aan, d'r af, of d'r uit [Intercultural education: Success or failure]? *Samenwijs, 5*(3), 91–96.

Leman, J. (Ed.). (1991). *Intégrité, intégration: Innovation pédagogique et pluralité culturelle*. Brussels: De Boeck Université.

Leman, J. (Ed.). (1999a). Education, ethnic homogenization and cultural hybridization. *International Journal of Educational Research, 31*(4), 257–353.

Leman, J. (Ed.). (1999b). *Moedertaalonderwijs bij allochtonen*. Leuven/Amersfoort: Acco.

Marchi, L. (1991). Faisons aussi jouer l'interculturel aux parents! In J. Leman (Ed.), *Intégrité, intégration: Innovation pédagogique et pluralité culturelle* (pp. 201–207). Brussels: De Boeck Université.

Marchi, L. (1999). Voor meer begrip tussen de allochtone ouders en de school. In J. Leman (Ed.), *Moedertaalonderwijs bij allochtonen* (pp. 127–134). Leuven/Amersfoort: Acco.

Martin, J. P., & Savary, E. (1996). *Formateur d'adultes*. Lyon: Chronique Sociale.

Pettigrew, T. F. (1998). Intergroup contact theory. *Annual Review of Psychology, 49*, 65–85.

Sherif, M., Harvey, O. J., White, B. J., Hood, W. R., & Sherif, C. W. (1961). *Intergroup conflict and cooperation: The Robber's Cave experiment*. Norman, Ok: University of Oklahoma Press.

Smeekens, L. (1990). Structural change: from monocultural to bicultural schools. In M. Byram & J. Leman (Eds.), *Bicultural and trilingual education* (pp. 136–146). Clevedon: Multilingual Matters.

# 15

# Croatia: For Peace Education in New Democracies

## Dinka Čorkalo
### University of Zagreb

Contemporary society has witnessed two parallel processes as a consequence of the end of cold war era. On the one hand, there has been a process of globalization and cooperation among countries, thereby establishing new rules for peaceful coexistence; on the other hand, in many hot spots around the world, crises have erupted.

The collapse of Communist regimes in Eastern Europe brought to light suppressed national identities and religious, ethnic, and minority issues. In these countries there were no history and practice of looking at conflict as a potential for social change. Conflict was always defined as unacceptable and in most of the former so-called Communist countries, ethnic and minority issues were forbidden themes, transformed into matters of class struggle. If one takes these facts into account, then it becomes clear that the goals of peace education in emerging new democracies are twofold: (1) to develop a climate of acceptance of conflict as a potential for social change, and to promote active and constructive ways of solving it; and (2) to promote the right to diversity as a common interest in order to enable various national, ethnic, and religious groups to live together peacefully.

My point of view is that the tasks facing programs for peace education in its narrower meaning are too demanding and almost impossible to accomplish if such programs are isolated from the wider societal context and directed toward only specific groups of people (e.g., mental health professionals, teachers, or children from different backgrounds).[1] I strongly believe that the process of establishing peace, and creating tolerance and cooperation among different groups as social norms in a community at the microlevel, should be paralleled by the same process on the broader, societal or national macrolevel. Peace education can be effective only if its efforts are made on both these levels.

In the postconflict, new democracies, these two levels of peace education correspond to two basic approaches, the bottom-up approach and top-down approach. With the bottom-up approach, on a microlevel, several stages of a peace education process should be developed. These stages should include trauma healing; education for nonviolent conflict resolution; education for mutual interdependence, tolerance, and respect for diversity; education for social justice and human rights; and education for democracy and civil rights. With the top-down approach, on the more macrolevel, strong institutional support for all stages of peace education should be secured and policy strategies from above that foster peace and coexistence should be established. This kind of convergent action could accomplish the ultimate goal of peace education—more global and enduring changes in people's ways of thinking.

I first explain what I propose as the stages of a bottom-up approach as applied to peace education.

## TRAUMA HEALING AND DEALING WITH THE PAST

Many so-called new democracies bear the burden of past traumas that were forbidden issues during the Communist era: for example, state crimes in Siberia in the former Soviet Union, persecution of political opponents in the former USSR and in other Communist countries as well, and violation of human rights and other forms of institutional violence by Communist regimes. In some countries, unresolved traumas from the period of the Second World War have constituted serious obstacles for building an enduring peace. Former Yugoslavia and Croatia, in particular, are good examples of how unhealed traumas from the past could be misused as fertile ground for incitement of chauvinism and national hatred. The Serbian myth

---

[1] However, one should not underestimate the usefulness of programs aiming to bring together small groups of people from different backgrounds. Sometimes, these groups of professionals, teachers, mental health workers, and local and middle-range leaders are people who have enough willingness and strength to initiate dialogue and to bridge the gap within even protracted conflict settings. One could object that this kind of small-scale intervention cannot contribute to the peace process to any great extent. I agree partially. However, I very much agree with Lederach's (1997) notion that relationship is the keystone of both the conflict and its long-term solution. What we, as professionals, can do is to empower these people to handle and resist group pressure within their communities and support their willingness to work together in creating a more favorable social climate.

of the battle of Kosovo is the most recent example (Anzulovic, 1999). Moreover, many scholars consider unhealed trauma as the determining contributing factor in the outbreak of the war in the former Yugoslavia. Although it was clear from the very beginning that the primary motivation of Milošević's army was to take over as much territory as possible, unresolved traumas from the past contributed to the intensity of the conflict and shaped it in many ways. What is unique, however, is the fact that some collective traumas were taboo subjects, something one was not supposed to talk about. This was not the voluntary conspiracy of silence, so well known among third-generation Holocaust survivors (Ajduković, 1997). Instead, the silence was imposed by repression. Trauma psychology teaches us that traumatic events often cannot be put behind or forgotten. Although the traumatized person might try to suppress it, this would not eliminate its negative consequences, at least not in the long run. Mental health professionals claim that unhealed traumatic experience could shape the whole life of a traumatized person, so that it could become the central issue of his or her daily life. A similar process could be observed with traumatizing events experienced by communities or nations. The memories of suffering and trauma become a part of history later transformed into national myths and transmitted from one generation to the next (Volkan, 1998).

In the former Yugoslavia, for example, there were several collective traumas that contributed significantly to the nature of the war: state crimes committed by the pro-Nazi regime against the Serbs during the Second World War in Croatia, and mass executions of Croatian soldiers and civilians committed by the new Communist rulers after the Second World War, to mention only two of the most severe ones. Indeed, the dark deeds of the Pro-Nazi regime in Croatia during the period of Second World War found their place in the textbooks, thus shaping the historical perceptions of the youth, sometimes imposing feelings of collective guilt. At the same time, there was no mention of crimes committed by the other side, neither in textbooks nor elsewhere. These stories nevertheless were secretly passed on, with fear and bitterness, among the Croatians, within the family and community.

After the first democratic elections in Croatia, every symbol of Croatian independence was perceived by the Serbian minority as a sign of reviving the times of the past. Instead of trying to shape a new Croatian identity with a firm commitment to democracy and a determined resolve to leave history to the historians, the new Croatian political elite tried to reconcile the irreconcilable—a strong antifascist movement and the pro-Nazi regime ruling Croatia during the Second World War. Like most European countries that had experienced fascist rule, so too had Croatia. During the Communist regime, neither Croatian historians nor the nation as a whole had the opportunity to confront objectively and constructively this episode from their past. The new political elite during Tudjman's era made things worse, allowing the past to present itself as a real political option for the present.

Although peace education does not deal with individual traumas, or it does not do that primarily, it must deal with collective traumas for several reasons. In order to reshape group stereotypes and to decrease the intensity of prejudice and mutual distrust between groups with a history of conflict, one has to take into account all the relevant phenomena that form community and group identities. Collective traumas, with their symbolism and emotional tension, certainly shape our group identity but determine the others' perception of *us* as well. In this respect, a thorough study of collective traumas, community and national myths, narratives, and stories should be an important part in peace research bound to have impact on peace education.

This is especially important in new democracies that have to face their own histories, so often traumatic ones. Some empirical data confirm the importance of history in Eastern European countries. Research carried out in 27 European countries about the attitudes of young people toward history showed increased interest in historical events among young people in Croatia and Russia, compared with youth from Western European countries (Šiber, 1996). Results from the same study also show the stronger importance of nationality and national identity issues among the youth from Croatia and several other former Communist countries compared with youth from countries with a longer democratic tradition and with no current conflict (Angvik & von Borries, 1997).

## REDEFINITION OF CONFLICT AND SKILLS BUILDING FOR NONVIOLENT CONFLICT RESOLUTION

Any social reality is specific to the countries going through the process of transition both in the way they define conflict and in their perception of the role the conflict could have for social change. Rubenstein (1992) argues that conflicts and conflict resolution are culturally constrained terms that can be understood differently in different cultures. Whereas the older democracies of North America and Western Europe have cultivated the role of conflict in maintaining social stability and social change, this kind of work has only just begun in the new democracies. During the Communist regime, conflict was seen as class struggle and the ethnic division was considered as irrelevant, preventing the "working class" from accomplishing its time interests. Moreover, conflict was seen as unacceptable tool with potential to damage the unity of the "society of equals" (see Shonholtz, 1998). This definition of conflict was reinforced by the idea of complete unacceptability of interest representation of various social groups, something that makes impossible the participation in power outside of the ruling party. However, with the collapse of the Communist regime, the opportunity for building a new political culture was present. Now conflict could be redefined as the collision of interests in which every interest group would have the right to articulate its particular interests, to do so publicly, and to fulfill them in accordance with the interests and needs of other groups within society. In the same way, redefinition of the concepts of conflict and conflict management should be an indispensable and integral part of peace education in post-Communist countries. Psychologically speaking, this redefinition of conflict from complete unacceptance to that of something neither good nor bad, but carrying the potential for change, implies the learning of new skills of conflict management and conflict resolution as well.[2] This is especially true for those countries that, in addition to suffering a collapse of their political regime and underlying value system, underwent a period of ethnopolitical violence or war (e.g., those countries that were part of the former Yugoslavia and USSR). Lasting for several years, ethnopolitical clashes brought a *culture of violence* in which violence became a usual tool for conflict resolution and a norm for social functioning. The impact, on the young, of this "culture" is particularly lethal. Because they were raised in a violent environment, educating them for peace assumes reshaping their worldview from that of a culture of violence to one of peace. It was with this intention that the National Board For Human Rights Education in Croatia introduced its program in 1999, designed for all levels of education from preschool through high school. An integral part of this program is peace education, and its implementation in the school system is in its experimental phase.

## EDUCATION FOR MUTUAL INTERDEPENDENCE, TOLERANCE, AND RESPECT FOR DIVERSITY

This type of education should be regarded as the third challenge for peace education in countries in transition and understood as *conditio sine qua non* of any serious and well-formulated peace education program. Most of the people in the countries under discussion have had the experience of living in multiethnic communities. However, in the process of political transition, many of them went through serious interethnic conflicts, with some of these conflicts developing into wars, motivated by the attempts of minorities to fulfill their rights to self-determination. After the first free elections in Croatia, the definition of the state was changed. The state now became, by Constitution, the "national state of the Croatian nation and the state of the members of other nations and national minorities ... who are its citizens ... who are guaranteed equality with the citizens

---

[2] One should be cautious about bringing under one roof all former Communist countries. Some of them, although under even stronger ideological pressure than Croatia, succeeded in managing conflicts peacefully. The former Czechoslovakia is a good example, with its famous Velvet Revolution and the peaceful split between the Czech and Slovak Federal Republic (for a more elaborate analysis, see Klicperova-Baker, 1999).

of Croatian nationality. . . ." In this constitutional definition, *nation* has a meaning of *demos* and not *ethnos*. However, this was not how the largest minority within Croatia, that is, Serbs, perceived it. They became a *new*[3] minority with equal rights to those of the other minorities, but the issue of the determination of the status of the Croatian Serbs escalated into an open conflict between authorities and a segment of the Croatian Serbs. Like any other minority, all the Croatian Serbs have to do is learn how to regulate their status in accordance with the majority group and the other minorities. This is, by no means, the obligation of minorities only; the role of the majority group is to regulate the status of minorities and to provide every opportunity for their full development within the state. The changed status of the minorities, especially the Serbs, was additionally complicated by the war, for a substantial segment of Croatian Serbs participated actively in the rebellion against Croatia, many of them leaving Croatia, whether voluntarily or as the result of real or perceived pressure to do so.[4] Further, migrations caused by war have changed the demographic picture in many areas, especially in those most affected by the war. With all aforementioned facts taken into account, peace education should necessarily include education for tolerance and respect for diversity and multiculturality as well. It is evident that in the presence of social change, crisis, or actual conflict between groups, ethnocentrism could facilitate structuring an uncertain environment, simplifying one's view of the situation by a division between *them* and *us*. This tendency applies not only to the group we are in conflict with, but also to any group we perceive as different from ourselves (Held, 1993; Corkalo & Kamenov, 1993). Ingroup homogenization and ethnocentrism lead to an unwillingness and an inability to understand the beliefs, values, culture, religion, and customs of other groups. This tendency is even stronger in the postconflict societies, where conflict originated in issues of nationality and self-determination. Moreover, conflict was defined as an issue of national survival. In such an atmosphere, in which the nation and its defense are so glorified, the (national) group becomes the basic source of identification and other sources of individual identity are often suspended or forgotten (Stern, 1995). Group pressure of being "with us or against us" is not easy to overcome, and in the transition of a postconflict society the right to be different must be relearned. This relearning process implies learning that my identity, whether national, religious, linguistic, or cultural, is not endangered by someone else's identity that is different from mine. In sum, peace education should include education for tolerance, respect for diversity, and mutual interdependence in order to create prerequisites for building a peaceful society (see Lederach, 1997).

---

[3]According to the Constitution of the former Yugoslavia, six nations (Serbs, Croats, Slovenians, Muslims, Macedonians, and Montenegrins) were treated as constitutive nations of the state.

[4]Today's proportion of the Serbian minority is between 4% and 5% of the Croatian population, compared with approximately 12% before the war.

# EDUCATION FOR SOCIAL JUSTICE AND HUMAN RIGHTS

Peace education takes as its operating assumption respect for the rights of the individual. Without social justice and respect for individual freedom and basic human rights, peace within society is unattainable. This assumption is included in the very definition of peace itself, according to which peace means the absence of both physical and structural violence (Dugan & Carey, 1996). In many postwar countries, the absence of physical and direct violence does at the same time mean the absence of structural violence. This is especially true for the aftermath of the war. In the case of Croatia, that means that there should be equal rights in the resettlement process for both Croats and Serbs as well as equal rights for job opportunities, education, and fair treatment. These are basic to the achievement of social justice within society. This kind of education is especially important in the countries that altogether lack a democratic tradition. Here the first step in the period of transition should be the creation of the political institutions basic to a new democratic system as well as the rules necessary for shaping the political behavior of citizens, organizations, and the ruling elite (Pusić, 1999). With the pursuit of individual rights, that is, human rights, and social justice in general, along with the practice of personal responsibility and democratic procedure in all segments of social life, countries in the transition process can aspire to a modicum of democratic consolidation, that is, legitimization of democratic institutions and a wider acceptance of the basic democratic norms.

Why do we consider education for democracy and human rights as an integral part of peace education, at least in so-called new democracies? The reason is not just in the easily observable fact that the presence of democratic institutions and civil political culture correlate with the presence of peace and their absence or elimination are often accompanied by violence and war (Gleditsch, 1998; Salomon & Nevo, 1999). Moreover, war conditions or the presence of intergroup violence often serve as an excuse for suspension of democratic institutions and their replacement by autocratic regimes with the usurpation of authority over various aspects of social life. Croatia, for example, underwent this in its transition period during the first few years of its existence. Some scholars label this kind of government a "dictatorship with democratic legitimization" (Pusić, 1999). However, their only democratic legitimacy is the fact that the governing party was elected in the free elections. This is not, however, what democracy is all about. The rule of the majority or of *demos* is only a translation of the concept of democracy. Procedurally speaking, democracy is not the unconditional and unrestricted rule of the majority. Democracy means, regardless of how we define minority, allowing minorities the right to articulate their own political will and interests. With regard to the issue of ethnic minorities, the protection of human rights and social justice are particularly important. If and only if minorities feel that their collective as well as individual rights are protected and that society enables them to develop their full potential can the state count on their peacefulness and loyalty.

An additional reason for promoting the principle of human rights within peace education in former Communist counties lies in the fact that the concept itself was absent during the rule of communists; instead, blatant violation of basic human rights was everyday practice. In contrast, the establishment of a democratic system introduces human rights as basic to the democratic procedure. To transform one value system into another cannot be done overnight; this is a process of socialization in which peace education has a role to play. We see this in the education and development of the self-confident and competent individual, knowledgeable and fully aware of his or her rights and obligations, as well as of the rights of others. This is one possible way of building interpersonal trust among citizens, who are able to cooperate with each other, as individuals and groups, and with the public institutions, in creating a civic political culture, democratic stability, and enduring peace (see Almond & Verba, 1989).

## CONCLUDING REMARKS

The guiding principle in this approach to peace education has been the parallel between the principles of bottom up and top down. My basic assumption has been that learning principles of tolerance and mutual cooperation in daily life on the local scene can lead to the establishment of these norms as basic to social functioning. That is, although contemporary, democratic societies declare allegiance to principles of tolerance, equal opportunity, and mutual cooperation, a disregard of these principles is found almost exclusively on the local level. Local leadership can help in promoting a basic, democratic way of life. Their role, however, is by no means exclusive. Principles of peacebuilding and peace education should be included in every segment of everyday life. They should be introduced at all levels of the educational system, private organizations, professional associations, and so forth. In this process the cooperation between governmental and nongovernmental sectors is of special importance in order to establish and develop controlling mechanisms for the stable functioning of the society.

When society has just begun its democratic development and lacks the meaningful support of public institutions to implement the aforementioned principles, the process of building a multicultural, tolerant, and peaceful society is very slow. This is why I believe that in societies that have undergone ethnopolitical conflict or serious clashes in the political system, or value system, the process of establishing the social norms of tolerance and cooperation on the level of institutional support and the process of pursuing them on lower, local levels should be parallel.

Where lies the basic connection between peace education and the overall democratization of society? First and foremost, we see this parallelism in the fact that peace education could hardly accomplish its goal were it treated only as another school subject. The educational system is not aimed only at teaching specific subjects; it also transmits beliefs, ways of life, values, and social norms operating in society. Learning about tolerance, cooperation, mutual interdependence, and social justice in schools, without implementing these principles in everyday social life, may perhaps produce an educated individual, but not necessarily one with a sense of personal responsibility for pursuing these principles actively.[5] Discordance between various levels of the system leaves room for a *principle–implementation gap*, a phenomenon studied in conjunction with modern racism theories. Namely, there is an apparent contradiction between the public support by White Americans for racial equality and at the same time their consistent opposition to the implementation of policies that might put principle into practice (Schuman, Steeh, & Bobo, 1985).

Is there anything unique to peace education in *new democracies*? Or should there be anything unique? The answer is not easy and certainly not unambiguous. If there is anything unique, it is the simultaneous struggle for social stability and social change. As history has taught us, democracy is not an ironclad guarantee for the absence of conflict and war. Yet, with all its flaws, it is still the best kind of social organization available to human beings.

# REFERENCES

Ajduković, D. (1997). Challenges to training for trauma recovery. In D. Ajduković (Ed.), *Trauma recovery training: Lessons learned* (pp. 27–37). Zagreb: Society for Psychological Assistance.

Almond, G. A., & Verba, S. (1989). *The civic culture. Political attitudes and democracy in five nations.* Newbury Park: Sage.

Angvik, M., & von Borries, B. (Eds.). (1997). *Youth and history: A comparative European survey on historical consciousness and political attitudes among adolescents.* Hamburg: Koerber-Stiftung

Anzulovic, B. (1999). *Heavenly Serbia: From myth to genocide.* New York: New York University Press.

Corkalo, D., & Kamenov, Z. (1993). Perspektive suživota: Očekivanja glede povratka i etnički stavovi prognanika. U: D. Ajduković (Pr.), *Psihološke dimenzije progonstva* [Perspectives of co-existence: Expectations and ethnic attitudes of internally displaced persons. In D. Ajduković (Ed.), *Psychological dimensions of banishment*]. Zagreb: Alinea. (in Croatian)

Dugan, M. A., & Carey, D. (1996). Toward a definition of peace studies. In R. J. Burns & R. Aspeslagh (Eds.), *Three decades of peace education around the world: An anthology* (pp. 79–96). New York: Garland.

---

[5]During one of my visits to Vukovar, a city practically completely destroyed in the war, I met a mother, a returnee to the city. Her son, a child in elementary school, participates in peace workshops organized at his school. Her reactions illustrate the difference between the formal system and the real everyday life the child encounters after school (and who knows how many other children as well?). The mother told me: "Let them teach in school whatever *they have to*. But I shall tell him *the truth* at home. I am not ready for reconciliation and I very much doubt that I ever will be." I stress this example as an indicator of how important it is to adopt a multilevel approach to peace education, going simultaneously from individual to system and the reverse.

Gleditsch, N. P. (1998). Democracy and peace. In L. Kurtz (Ed.), *Encyclopedia of violence, peace, and conflict*. New York: Academic.

Held, J. (1993). *Democracy and right-wing politics in Eastern Europe in the 1990s*. New York: East European Monographs, Columbia University Press.

Klicperova-Baker, M. (Ed). (1999). *Ready for democracy? Civic culture and civility with a focus on Czech society*. Prague: Institute of Psychology, Academy of Sciences of the Czech Republic.

Lederach, J. P. (1997). *Building peace: Sustainable reconciliation in divided societies*. Washington, DC: United States Institute of Peace Press.

Pusić, V. (1999). *Demokracije i diktature: Politička tranzicija u Hrvatskoj i jugoistočnoj Evropi* [*Democracies and dictatorships: Political transition in Croatia and Southeast Europe*]. Zagreb: Durieux. (in Croatian)

Rubenstein, R. E. (1992). Dispute resolution on the Eastern frontier: Some questions for modern missionaries. *Negotiation Journal, 8*, 205–213.

Salomon, G., & Nevo, B. (1999). *Peace education: An active field in need for research*. Unpublished manuscript.

Schuman, H., Steeh, C., & Bobo, L. (1985). *Racial attitudes in America: Trends and interpretations*. Cambridge, MA: Harvard University Press.

Shonholtz, R. (1998). Conflict resolution moves east: How the emerging democracies of Central and Eastern Europe are facing interethnic conflict. In E. Weiner (Ed.), *The handbook of interethnic coexistence* (pp. 359–381). New York: The Abraham Fund.

Šiber, I. (1996). Mladi i povijest. Odnos prema povijesti i povijesna svijest. *Politička misao* [Young people and history: Historical awareness and the attitude towards history. *Croatian Political Science Review*] *33*(1), 29–148. (in Croatian)

Stern, P. C. (1995). Why do people sacrifice for their nation? *Political Psychology, 16*, 217–235.

Volkan, V. D. (1998). The tree model: Psychopolitical dialogues and the promotion of coexistence. In E. Weiner (Ed.), *The handbook of Interethnic coexistence* (pp. 343–358). New York: The Abraham Fund.

# 16

# Israel: An Integrative Peace Education in an NGO—The Case of the Jewish–Arab Center for Peace at Givat Haviva

Sarah Ozacky-Lazar

*The Jewish–Arab Center for Peace at Givat Haviva*

In Israel, the official, educational system only started to prepare itself for peace in the past decade, and even these efforts have not been comprehensive or intensive enough. Grassroots groups and Non-Governmental Organizations (NGOs) that have developed various philosophies and methodologies to cope with the violent warlike reality have done work over the years that is important but not far reaching enough. One of these organizations, perhaps the oldest of its kind, is The Jewish–Arab Center for Peace at Givat Haviva (JACP), located in the heart of the Wadi 'Ara region—an area characterized by a mosaic of an ethnically mixed population.

The JACP integrates projects of instruction, education, research, and community involvement with diverse populations in Israel. It helps design programs suited to different target groups and sectors in accordance with their wishes, needs, and level of comprehension. Its members constantly explore new ways to deal with the changing reality in Israel and in the Middle East and to meet the various needs of the participants of its programs.

## AIMS AND OBJECTIVES OF THE JACP:
## AN OVERVIEW

The JACP was established in 1963 at the Givat Haviva, Kibbutz Artzi Educational Center. Its aims are to foster closer relations between Jews and Arabs in Israel, to educate for mutual understanding, and to promote partnership between the two communities.

The Center works in a variety of ways in an effort to create true equality among all the citizens of the state. This is accomplished through constant, critical examination of reality as it stands, and by striving for renewal and change.

The Center functions within the spirit of humanism, in the belief that all human beings are entitled to be regarded of equal worth and treated with equal dignity. It strives to lead the way to attaining a greater degree of democracy and equality of civil rights between the Jewish and Palestinian citizens of Israel; to create social and cultural pluralism in the country; and to achieve reconciliation and peace among the nations in the region.

The Center initiates innovative models for the advancement of its educational and social aims, and it operates by way of encounters, dialogue, partnership, study, and research.

Each of the departments of the JACP engages in a particular area of specialization: education, language instruction, research, counseling, and community work. The Center reaches out to many sectors of society and works with children, teens, and adults. Its professional, dedicated staff consists of approximately 25 educators and various freelance facilitators. Each year, well over 25,000 people, mostly from Israel but some from abroad, participate in the programming. At the same time, senior staff members attend programs, conferences, and workshops in Israel and abroad, delivering the Center's message worldwide and returning with newfound insights.

At its Peace Library and Information Center, there is a large collection of books, periodicals, and documents that serves scholars, students, researchers, and academics from Israel and around the world.

## THE DEPARTMENT FOR REGIONAL
## COOPERATION

The main focus of the Department for Regional Cooperation is the development of cooperative, dialogue programming between Israelis and Palestinians. When possible, other regional partners are included. Workshops are designed with full input from all parties and cover such topics as democracy, women's issues, language studies, and youth leadership. The department also provides a training ground for binational groups interested in dialogue development. All programming is based on personal contact with a view to encouraging personal engagement and involvement.

The primary aim is to inculcate the present generation with new ideas, perspectives, and views. Based on ongoing contact, a number of well-grounded alliances have already been established between Givat Haviva and Palestinian organizations. High school and university students, teachers, and administrative government staff all partake in programming of this kind. Overall, the department aims to promote and support the following:

- the Palestinians' quest for democracy
- programming for peace education
- ongoing dialogue between communities

In 1999 a Palestinian–Israeli–Jordanian youth magazine (in English) called *Crossing Borders* was launched, operated by youngsters from all three nations. This bimonthly magazine serves as a vehicle for dialogue and self-expression for the youth of the region. The young journalists meet regularly in the region or in Denmark (the sponsoring country) and work together on the paper. Despite the violent events of 2000–2001, the magazine has been published regularly and the dialogue between its participants has been conducted through the Internet when they could not meet in person.

## THE ABED AL-AZIZ ZU'BI INSTITUTE FOR ARABIC STUDIES

This Institute for Arabic Studies offers a number of comprehensive, Arabic language programs at various campus locations throughout Israel. One of them is an intensive, 9 month, annual course covering Arabic language, culture, and history and including special exchanges with Israeli–Arab communities as well as a study trip to Egypt. The idea behind the Institute is that learning the language and getting to know the culture of one's neighbors (and rivals) help ease the alienation and create bridges of understanding and empathy. The Institute emphasizes the common roots and similar values of the Hebrew and the Arab cultures and languages, and it brings together students and teachers from both side for cultural exchange.

## THE DEPARTMENT OF EDUCATION

The Department of Education at the JACP has as its focus both Arab and Hebrew schools. Teachers and trainers develop creative techniques in an effort to highlight the concept of equality and common Israeli citizenship, tolerance, and acceptance of "the other"—all this, regardless of race, religion, or gender and despite the deep ethnic division in Israeli society.

There are a number of major projects that the Center promotes. One is *Children Teaching Children* (CTC). This project is based on the recognition of several key principles, among them the profound influence of the Jewish–Arab conflict on all Israeli citizens, its complexity, and the need to learn to live with the conflict even if it is not resolved; and the concept of citizenship as a partnership shared by two equal communities.

The main objective of CTC is to help students and teachers develop the skills required to cope with the Jewish–Arab conflict in Israel, for here Arab and Jewish participants have a unique opportunity to engage in dialogue with the other side in a supportive environment that facilitates personal change and growth. The 2-year CTC program runs simultaneously in pairs of neighboring schools, as part of the official curriculum. In the uninational meetings, the Jewish and Arab classes separately examine their national identity. In the binational meetings, the issue of a common citizenship is emphasized, as is the need to achieve equality between the two national groups.

## FACE TO FACE

For high school or university students, Face to Face is a Jewish–Arab encounter experience in which participants confront stereotypical perceptions and deal with the difficulties of accepting people who are different. The project explores several important areas, and it makes use of facilitators to assist participants in processing their experiences in the light of the following: a mutual understanding of Arab and Jewish society in Israel; the nature of citizens' rights; equality between men and women; democracy and personal freedom; and minority–majority issues in Israel. A separate program, specifically for Arab youth, helps individuals to use their personal skills to deal in a progressive fashion with the notion of being a Palestinian–Arab minority in the Jewish State.

## THE COUNSELING CENTER
## FOR PEACE EDUCATION

This Center runs programs that deal with a cross-section of subjects: peace, democracy, conflict management, pluralism, divisions within Israeli society, freedom of expression, forms of protest, and Arab–Jewish relations. The Center counsels other institutions in creating their own peace education programming, and it organizes international seminars for overseas delegations. Additional projects and activities include annual teacher-training seminars and teacher retraining programs; human rights' seminars and workshops for high school students; enrichment programs for elementary and high school educators; people-to-people forums for

Israeli and Palestinian educators; and specialized programs on leadership training for youth movements.

## THE INSTITUTE FOR PEACE RESEARCH

At the Institute for Peace Research, Jewish and Arab scholars jointly explore different aspects of the Jewish–Arab relationship in Israel. Research activity is designed to provide relevant, up-to-date data for leading scholars and decision makers. The Institute examines Jewish–Arab relations in the State of Israel, the issue of Palestinian nationality, and the more generic issues of peace and coexistence. To date, the Institute has published over 70 publications and conducts regular surveys and public opinion polls on these issues. On a more regular and ongoing basis, two series of publications are produced. The first is Surveys on the Arabs in Israel. It is an overview of the variety of social, political, and cultural issues that relate to the Arab citizens living in the country. The second is Palestinian Studies. It is a series of research papers reflecting different facets of Palestinian social, cultural, and political life in the Palestinian Authority.

## THE DEPARTMENT OF WOMEN'S AND GENDER STUDIES

This fairly new department at the JACP offers special programs for the empowerment of women. One of the leading programs is Women in the Community, which consists of groups of Arab and Jewish social workers or community workers who jointly design projects for women in their communities. The participants go through an individual process of inner growth and increasing awareness of women's issues and then return to their communities with practical projects to help other women.

## SUMMARY

We at the center believe that no political agreement in the region can survive if it is not accompanied by changing the way people think and behave toward each other. Perhaps one of the reasons for the recent collapse of the peace process is the lack of support from the ordinary "man in the street," which is a result of the lack of cultivation of the heart and mind of a significant part of the population.

There is an urgent need to integrate peace education into the regular school curriculum and to train teachers and educators to implement it in their daily work. The authorities who design such a curriculum should use the cumulative knowledge and experience that exist among NGOs and grassroots groups. Special programs for peace education should be also implemented in the community at large, for adults and decision makers and not only within the school system. The media could be used to convey messages of peace education and so could literature, art, and theater. Educators in Israel and in the Arab countries should lead the way to change instead of themselves being led by a violent and hostile reality. We call for the creation of a regional "Forum of Educators" to discuss these issues together.

# 17

# Cyprus: A Partnership Between Conflict Resolution and Peace Education

## Maria Hadjipavlou
### *University of Cyprus*

## THE GENERALIZED MYTHS

As a child I felt not only that Cyprus was altogether Turkish but that it was part of Anatolia, a literal translation of whose name, Anatolu, is "full of mother." Symbolically, Turkey was the mother and Cyprus its child.... Parents often spoke of Turkey and passed along to their children a sense of identity with the mainland country, which seemed a land of promise.... I can still remember what we learned in elementary school on Cyprus: "Cyprus was once connected with Anatolia, but it sank into the sea. It rose only to sink again. When it rose for the third time after its third submersion, it was alas, no longer connected with Anatolia."[1] (Volkan, 1979, p. 190)

---

[1]After World War II, the Greek Cypriots viewed Cyprus as part of the Greek national territory; the Turkish Cypriots viewed it as British territory, and later (mid-1950s) as non-Greek. To the Greek Cypriot nationalists, denial of enosis meant denial of their Helleno-Christian cultural heritage; to the Turkish Cypriot, enosis meant subjugation to a Christian rule and gradual cultural annihilation; thus they supported the status quo—either return of Cyprus to Turkey, or partition. The divergent outlooks of the two communities were reinforced by cultivated myths and upbringing both at home and in the schools. In the 1950s the schools played an active part in organizing demonstrations and boycotts against the British. The development of symbolic myths in both communities along with the noted practices of childrearing helped develop psychological distancing and fighting over the same object for the realization of different historical memories (see Hadjipavlou-Trigeorgis, 1987 and Volkan, 1979).

Similarly, the Greek Cypriot children learned of Cyprus as "the young, sad, and unprotected daughter awaiting the mother's (Greece's) embrace." They are taught that Cyprus has always been a Hellenic island and will remain so forever, despite the fact that there are many remnants of other civilizations on the island, as it is at the crossroads of three continents. The call was to stay faithful believers in the "ideals and values of the Hellenic Ethnos and to Orthodoxy. This is the only way to safeguard our national consciousness and our identity. Have we not been for 3,000 years inhaling and exhaling Greece?" (*Simerini*, April 12, 1992). A recent analysis of the Greek Cypriot history textbooks demonstrates how emphasis is laid on the Hellenization of the island in the 12th century B.C. and the construction of an unbroken Hellenic continuity starting in the 12th century B.C. up to the present. In contrast, the history textbooks of the Turkish Cypriot children present the island as being Turkish for 400 years and they present the Greeks who lived on the island as *Rums* (*Romoi, Romans*), which implies that they were a mixed race; they thus challenge the Greekness of the island. Thus, two nations, which according to the official narratives have been mortal enemies for centuries, have had claims on Cyprus and still continue to do so to this day.

Thus, the cultivated, mythic desire of each Cypriot ethnic group was to fight for its ethnic origin and purity in a concerted effort to save the child from some mythological outside evil. Both images call for reconnection of the child to its mother. This was the prevailing situation before Cyprus' independence in 1960, and still is to this day, albeit in a more subtle form. On the other hand, the Greek Cypriot official position in the 1990s has been to promote full membership of the Republic of Cyprus to the European Union, thus pointing to a new European identity. In case this is realized, the Turkish and Turkish Cypriot officials threaten to annex the northern part of the island to Turkey.

Similarly, the national ideology, cultivated in the Greek Cypriot schools, stresses, among other issues, the historical heroism and sacrifice of those who died to liberate the island from its many conquerors, especially from the Ottoman and the British Empires. The youth is often given the example of how a handful of young idealists put up a fight against an entire Empire! Nowadays, also the enslaved lands occupied by the Turkish barbarian boot in 1974 call upon the young generation not to forget and prepare to honor the heroic deeds of Greek fighters and thus liberate the land from the foreign army. In the words of some Greek and Turkish Cypriot educationists at one of the conflict resolution workshops in 1992, "schools are in part institutions used to promote nationalism and militarism through activities like celebrating national motherlands' days, naming schools after military heroes, showing pictures of atrocities and holding competitions in poetry and essay-writing, based on nationalistic themes or 'past glories' of each nation."[2]

---

[2]In the latest bicommunal Educators *Conflict Resolution* Workshop held in Cambridge, Massachusetts, in August 1996, 30 high-level educators participated. I served as a resource person and member of the workshop design team. This was one of the most intense learning experiences

Three years after Cyprus' independence (1963), interethnic fighting broke out, and renewed violence in 1967 created economic hardship for the Turkish Cypriots and psychological distancing together with geographic divisions, giving dialogue a limited space and a poor chance to develop. The majority of Turkish Cypriots experienced the period (1963–1974) as a time of exclusion and deprivation of their citizens' rights. For them the constitution was dead and the partnership republic had come to an end. In addition, closer ties were being developed with mother-land, Turkey. At the same period, the Greek Cypriots experienced prosperity and international recognition.

Cyprus was partitioned de facto in 1974, following a Greek junta-engineered coup and the Turkish invasions of July 15 and July 20, respectively. The northern part (or the self-declared Turkish Republic of Northern Cyprus, recognized only by Turkey), which consists of 37% of the territory, is controlled by Turkish Cypriots and the 35,000 Turkish military. Two percent constitutes the buffer zone manned by the United Nations Peacekeeping Force. The remaining 60% of the Republic is run by the Greek Cypriot government, which is internationally recognized. There is no free movement between the two parts and no trade cooperation or direct communication. The Greek Cypriots constitute 80% of the total population (700,000), the Turkish Cypriots 18%, and the Armenians, Maronites, and Latins the remaining 2%.

This chapter addresses the following questions. First, what are the main ideological underpinnings of the educational systems in each Cypriot community? What kind of information, belief systems, and images about the other are transmitted (or not transmitted) to the respective school populations? Second, how can the young generation be educated in a way that both respects the other's cultural identity and prepares them for citizenship in a future, democratic, federal, and multi-cultural Cyprus? Reference is made to the recommendations Cypriot educationists and students jointly put forward in conflict resolution training workshops.

## THEORETICAL FRAMEWORK

Theories of international relations often treat states as unitary actors. The societies they represent, however, are far from being monolithic entities. In intercommunal or international conflicts, internal divisions can either contribute to the mainte-nance of the conflict and impose constraints on the leadership or they can provide opportunities for change. As Kelman (1996) states:

---

(2 continued)

because during that week violence broke out along the demarcation line back in Cyprus. This incident brought home to the participants the urgent need to reinforce their efforts for peace education both in the classroom and in the community.

such divisions challenge the monolithic image of the enemy that parties in conflict tend to hold and enable them to deal with each other in a more differentiated way. They can come to recognize that even in a community mobilized to engage actively in a violent conflict, there may be elements amenable to an alternative approach who are potential partners for negotiation. (p. 12)

The assumption here is that an international conflict is multilayered and it is both an interstate and intersocietal phenomenon that concerns not only the efforts undertaken at the official and diplomatic levels but also the societies themselves. Thus the individual or the group (in this case, educators) is assigned a role in the process of conflict prevention and peaceful conflict resolution.

Viewing conflict as an intersocietal process with an interactive dynamic, according to Kelman (1996), immediately prompts us to examine what is happening within and across each society and how the microlevel can be mobilized to contribute to a redefinition of the adversarial relationship. The kind of relationship that will develop between the two parties will determine the level of reconciliation, attitude change, and the recognition of interdependence between the groups. A positive relationship would encourage cooperation and a mutually enriching influence, and it would focus on future development. The institution of education is in a dialectical relationship with society, for what prevails on the outside affects what happens inside the schools.

Intercommunal and international conflict is a process driven not only by objective factors, such as national and strategic interests on the part of political decision makers, but also by collective needs, historical grievances, traumas, and fears (Burton, 1987; Fisher, 1972, 1990; Kelman, 1979, 1993, 1996; Mitchell, 1990; Montville, 1987; Volkan, 1979, 1991). When these basic human needs of identity, security, recognition, autonomy, participation, self-esteem, and a sense of justice continue to be frustrated and remain unfulfilled, then fears of the other (often exaggerated) and a culture of separation would prevail, facilitating the *us versus them* mindset, which is then instituted in curricula and behaviors. In the case of Cyprus, the identity and security issues have been at the core of much of the conflict and continue to this day to remain unsettled. Both fear that their Greekness or Turkishness is being threatened. The Greek Cypriots fear Turkification of the northern part and Turkish expansionism constitute threats to their identity. The Turkish Cypriots believe that *enosis* (union with Greece) or accession of the Republic of Cyprus to the EU will eliminate their identity. The failure to develop loyalty to common Cypriot values and a strong sense of citizenship led to a polarized view of each other and to antagonistic educational systems.

Another assumption in conflict resolution is that change is possible, provided the conflicting parties identify such opportunities and construct a narrative, school curricula and institutional structures that would fulfill all groups' fundamental needs and build reassurances for mutual benefits.

# PRESENT REALITIES:
# THE PREVAILING PARADIGM

I now turn to the question of what kind of socialization each community's educational system promotes in view of the other—what information, beliefs, and images about the other are transmitted to the young generation of Cypriots? What kind of paradigm emerges? I base my discussion on data and reports from bicommunal educators and student conflict resolution training workshops held during the period from 1989 to 1996, during which time 300 educators and some university students participated and I was either a trainer–facilitator or a participant observer.

In each community the discourse on education—its philosophical and ideological underpinnings—has always been intense in view of its political and historical role in creating the national self and other. There has always been a tension between espoused theory and practice. For instance, the 1992–1994 National Report on Education in Cyprus of the Greek Cypriot Ministry of Education spelled out that one of its objectives was "The creation of democratic citizens and the promotion of friendship and cooperation between the various communities of the country . . . and respect for the dignity and uniqueness of each individual. . . ." In the summer of 1996, however, there appeared, in some of the Greek Cypriot press, a seething attack on those Greek Cypriot teachers and pupils who dared correspond with the youth from across the dividing line in order to start building levels of communication, understanding, and perhaps friendships and thus implement the stated objective. Reconciliation activities at the unofficial level among Greek Cypriot citizens are often criticized by nationalist groups because they are interpreted as reaching out to the enemy and thus delegitimizing the international nature of the Cyprus problem.

There were also newspaper editorials urging the Ministry of Education to "stop such dangerous projects like *Writing to the Other Side* because they constitute a threat to our identity and national cause." Similar was the reaction across the dividing line, labeling the teachers and students "traitors" and "pawns in the hands of the Greeks."

Such attitudes and perceptions promote the consolidation of the status quo and the promotion of the culture of separation. The model that emerges is easily built on the blame–defend mindset and the polarized view of us versus them and the enemy image fed by a monofocal interpretation of historical events. For instance, the event of July 20, 1974, constitutes for the Greek Cypriots an invasion by a barbaric, expansionist nation, that is, Turkey, which brought about economic catastrophe, upheaval, and death of loved ones. The Turkish Cypriots experienced the same barbaric event as a peace operation that liberated them from the domination of the Greeks and thus celebrate it as a victory.

The international community has also shown concern about the state of affairs in the island's education system and curricula. For instance, the United Nations Secretary-General, in his report to the Security Council in 1993, made ample mention of the importance of education and bicommunal contacts in conflict prevention and resolution. He noted, among other issues, that neither teaches the other's language in its schools, that Turkish Cypriot authorities discourage and prevent citizens from having contacts and dealings with Greek Cypriots and vice versa, and that school textbooks are not exempt from that campaign (UN Report, November 1993).

In 1994 a delegation from the European Inter-Parliamentary Union (IPU), having studied the conflict experience in the two communities, wrote a report in which they commented on education and the lack of sustained contacts and communication between the two communities. They noted that since 1974 education tended to build up a negative vision of the other community in the minds of children and students, and they recommended an urgent revision of textbooks to prepare the young generation for peace, tolerance, and mutual respect (IPU Report, 1994). These reports confirmed those experiences of educators and students who have been advocating such changes.

## Building a Culture of Violence and Exclusion of the Other

Often the constructed myths originating in the Greek and Turkish histories are taught in the context of primitive, rough memories and dramatization of historical events, in such a way as to leave a frightening and indelible mark on the very young minds of children who know about the other in a mediated way. As Yashin (1989) states:

> These myths, based on events such as wars and slaughter in history, are the source whereby both communities derive their views about each other. Literature made them popular by using them. The Greek Cypriots, having been given all the characteristics of 'barbarians,' 'kafirs,' 'cowards,' 'hypocrites,' 'buffoons,' 'treacherous,' 'enemy,' 'sneaky,' etc., were excluded from being human beings like us. (Yashin, p. 59).

A consequence of the reconstruction of the past is that memories of suffering in the hands of past oppressors are transferred to the younger generations while the experiences of the other ethnic group are ignored. This promotes the impression that it is only *us* who suffered, a notion that gives rise to historic wrongs and latent feelings of revenge (Papadakis, 1993) and keeps the nationalistic agenda alive. School visits by the Turkish Cypriot children to the Museum of Barbarism in southern Nicosia, which is filled with enlarged pictures of "mass graves and atrocities, and expulsion of Turkish Cypriots from their homes in the south during the 1963–1974 dark period. "We teach them to be afraid of Greeks and hate them. In the end these children have nightmares. I am twenty-two and I still have nightmares" (Turkish Cypriot student's experience, 1993). Thus school visits to national museums contribute significantly to meeting with the enemy. The story of violence and inhumanity of the evil other become alive in such places. Thus historic enemies are constructed and the heroes of one group become the villains of the other.

Similarly, the Greek Cypriot children are taken to the Museum of National Struggle to learn and experience the brutality of the British against the E.O.K.A fighters and are encouraged to admire their heroism and sacrifice. Students are also socialized in the educational–ideological campaign of I Do Not Forget, I Will Struggle (i.e., to liberate the occupied lands), and they are given free time to protest in the streets, along the dividing line, against Turkey's occupation of the Greek Cypriot lands since 1974. Special readers on I Do Not Forget are compiled for such a purpose. There are weekly radio programs entitled I Don't Forget inviting older refugees to talk about their occupied villages and reminisce about "the good old days" (Boutzouvi, 1998–1999). Pupils are instructed in what to forget and what to remember.

## BICOMMUNAL CYPRIOT EDUCATORS' EVALUATION OF THE PREVAILING EDUCATIONAL SYSTEMS

Since 1989, over 40 conflict resolution training and dialogue workshops with educators and students from both communities have taken place either in Cyprus or abroad. The main principle underlying these meetings was the contact theory (Allport, 1954) and intergroup relations theory. These meetings have a dual purpose, one being educational (constructing a new mindset) and the other political, as the intention is to transmit the change to society and the decision makers. Some of the main issues—the concerns and fears and the needs and hopes, as expressed jointly by the participants—are given as follows.

### The System

Both Greek and Turkish Cypriot educators, representing the different levels of education, agree that the structure of the educational system is centralized, patriarchal, hierarchical, and syllabus oriented, leaving little space for relationship building, critical thinking, and human development. The system lacks flexibility and the teachers have little motivation to be creative and cannot introduce new material without the central authority's approval. Teachers, as a group, are considered as "generally holding conservative attitudes" (Fisher, 1991), more so in the secondary schools. The underlying philosophy is ethnocentric and utilitarian at the expense of humanistic and universal values. The Greek Orthodox Church still influences education more in the Greek Cypriot community than does religion for the Turkish Cypriots (although lately, Islamic fundamentalism affects some groups). There is almost no space for trying out new ideas and the bureaucratic mindset prevails. The way promotions and teacher evaluation are carried out encourages nepotism and functionalism. Teachers, on the whole, do not feel part of the decision-making process on issues of curriculum, philosophy of education, and innovation. Many Turkish Cypriot teachers have lately lost their jobs or been forced into early retirement because they expressed views contrary to official, educational policies and demanded more Cypriocentric curriculum instead of the Turcocentric.

## The Curriculum

There is consensus among the bicommunal educator groups that the general spirit of education is nationalistic, chauvinistic, and built on the "chosen glories and chosen traumas." The teaching of history is selective and each side ignores the plight and grievances of the other. No loyalty to a common homeland is promoted, nor is Cypriotism as a shared citizenship. For instance, in a recent conflict resolution training workshop (1996), as an exercise, the 30 Cypriot educators were asked to "Walk Through History" (Montville, 1993). They worked in monocommunal groups and were asked to go as far back as they each chose and beyond the 1990s. They each had to choose the most important events and talk about how these events were presented in their classrooms. Both groups struggled a great deal over objective and subjective truths of history and between lived experiences and imagined ones. Both groups used the same timeline but chose different significant events and came up with different significant dates. The Greek Cypriots went as far back as 6,000 B.C., up to the 1990s, and produced 37 historical periods, whereas the Turkish Cypriots started their timeline *from 1191* (the Byzantine Period) up until 1990s, and produced 26 events. When each group was asked to take a specific event and tell the other what is formally taught in its respective schools, it was noted that they each gave a monodimensional story completely excluding the other's perspective or interpretation.

For instance, November 15, 1983 is taught to Turkish Cypriot children as a great national day, for on that day they acquired their own state, the Turkish Republic of Northern Cyprus (TRNC), thus acquiring their own flag, government, and parliament. People came out into the streets and celebrated. Although they were forced to declare their own separate state unilaterally because of the intransigent Greeks, their ultimate goal is peace and security.

The Greek Cypriot pupils learn that the declaration of a so-called TRNC is illegal and it is a pseudo-state recognized only by Turkey and having no legitimacy. Since then their economy has become worse because of absolute dependency on Turkey, and many Turkish Cypriots leave the occupied northern part. The international community has condemned the illegal state. The Greek Cypriot refugees felt grief and despair because they saw this event as making it more difficult for their right to return.

Since then, every year, November 15 is a day of celebration and military marches for the Turkish Cypriot community, whereas for the Greek Cypriots it is a day of protest, mourning, and indignation. This is but one illustration of a series of historical events that express different and antagonistic interpretations. Thus, much work is needed in the joint conflict resolution workshops to deconstruct this socialization and reconstruct a much more complex one.

## A NEW INTEGRATIVE PLURALISTIC PARADIGM: THE UNDERLYING PRINCIPLES

Let us now consider the question as to how the new generations can be educated in a way that enables both to respect each other's cultural identity and prepares them for citizenship in a future, democratic, hopefully federal, multicultural Cyprus. As mentioned earlier, there is ample evidence (there are nowadays over 50 such cross-ethnic groups with over 60 members in each) that the willingness exists to change the adversarial mindset and institute a process for reconciliation despite political and militaristic obstacles. What are the principles and structures that would help us build new attitudes and mutual acceptance toward a culture of peace education? What I present here is based on the views and recommendations expressed by hundreds of Cypriots in bicommunal dialogues, structured meetings, and conflict resolution workshops. There exists by now a support core group of citizens, educators, students, and other professionals who are ready to commit to a new way of thinking in order to socialize citizens in the values of democracy, pluralism, and multiculturalism. The proposed paradigm is characterized by (a) inclusion (a big shift from the either–or mode that currently prevails); (b) flexibility, which is enlarging the curriculum to give recognition to the part that each side has been excluding, something that will lead to both self-understanding and other understanding; (c) openness to dialogue, which means diversity of interpretations and worldviews and constant, critical assessment of one's social, educational, and political system so as to keep both the system alive and democracy dynamic; (d) mutual humanization, which means acknowledging mutual hurts and being sensitive to each side's historical grievances, traumas, and values; and (e) mutual awareness of the requirements of future coexistence, cooperation, and interdependence. In other words, the challenge is how to educate the Cypriot citizen of tomorrow in a democratic multicultural Cyprus. What are the values and attitudes that would help create a culture of peace, and growth for all?

It would help both communities to keep their cultural identity separate from their political one, which means shifting political loyalties from their referent nations

(Greece and Turkey) to the future Cypriot, federal, and democratic state, so as to be able to share interethnic interests in a progressive, open society. And when Cyprus becomes a member of the European Union then the reference point will be enlarged even more. Historically, politicization of cultural–ethnic loyalty has been a threat to common citizenship. Sound, social criticism and serious reflection on social values relevant to the needs of a conflict-ridden society are fundamental. It is important to free the future Cypriot citizens from having to choose between different parts of their identity. The new citizenship should be built on relatedness and in conversation with rather than competition with and domination of one group over the other. Ultimately, what is involved in multicultural education is much the same as what is involved in the development of a democratic public. Pupils must learn how to listen and how to discourse about differences, where the rules of discourse are part of the process of understanding their own culture, which is just as complex as is the process of understanding the other's culture. This means viewing one's own activity and behavior as a cultural product and avoiding defining it as modeling cultural norms, as has been the case of dominant cultures in a multiethnic society. Thus, a major task for education in a democratic, multicultural society is coming to terms with *otherness*. As Feinberg (1995) states:

> Ultimately, knowledge of the other culture enables the student to see her own position as contingent and subject to reflexive development and change. To be educated in a multicultural way means to understand the nature of this contingency and the possibilities for development and change that it provides. Hence, regardless of one's cultural foundation there is something that all people who are educated in this way have in common: the recognition of a constructed contingent self whose understanding depends upon an acknowledgment of otherness. (p. 215)

Teaching children to view their own identities (standards, norms, and ways of life) as a cultural product (not a sacred, undisputed, eternal symbol) implicitly teaches them to respect people with other identities. Children need to learn that identities are not static but continually evolving.

## Shared Curriculum

The introduction of a common civics curriculum would help foster the Cypriots' understanding of citizenship responsibilities and promote the principles of pluralism and the need to be taught something about the other fellow citizen's culture, way of life, and creative expression. Students would be able to develop a knowledge and understanding of the similarities and differences between the cultural traditions and historical experiences that influence people in their country. Greek Cypriot students should also learn about the Turkish Cypriot culture (language, religion, customs) and traditions, and the Armenian, Latin, and Maronite ways of life, without fearing that this threatens their uniqueness as Greeks and Cypriots. The same applies to all other ethnic groups. It would also be educationally enriching to produce television and radio programs about the different cultures and their symbiosis on the island, as well as a multicultural journal in which creative minds from all Cypriot communities can publish their different experiences emanating from the same homeland. Using technology, a new series of public education courses can begin introducing the different societies to the complexity of experiences and offering space for a shared, Cypriot perspective. Gradually a new language and positive images will be created from these new concepts, ensuring that different identities can coexist and that Cypriot citizenship unifies them all.

Another common curriculum topic should aim to expose all Cypriot students to the system of democracy and its ideals, its different kinds and its various tensions and strains. This curriculum should also raise consciousness against any form of discrimination and promote every support for human rights. After all, democracy is a way of life and cannot be the exclusive possession of any ethnic group, or social class, or any subgroup of a body of citizens. I believe this is crucially important for Cyprus because what we often witness are the resignation of citizens and their passive detachment from politics.

For those living in a patriarchal and hierarchical society, it is appropriate to introduce early on gender studies and human relations so as to sensitize students to alternative worldviews and the consequences of the social construction of gender. Related to this is the teaching and practice of conflict resolution skills, problem solving, and communication skills.

Such ideas can be realized by expanding teacher education and training. Teachers should be exposed to new resources (programs for skill training—communication, mediation, negotiations, joint student projects on social studies, and local history issues), building partnerships across ethnic lines. Thus, the institution of education would become a support system for conflict prevention and resolution.

## Joint Recommendations

The ideas presented here and are expanded upon all derive from cross-ethnic dialogues and workshops. Educators and students have expressed the need for increased and open communication and face-to-face contacts, especially among the new generation. They want to build trust and get rid of the mutual fears; emphasize commonalities and shared, past experiences; institute a process to heal old wounds and get rid of the enemy image; and build strong, democratic, civil, and political institutions and bicommunal organizations. They want to be open to new ideas and assume responsibility as citizens to do something for peace, to respect each other's religious and social beliefs and historical monuments, to voice publicly the desire for peace, and influence politicians to come together toward that end.

With regard to undertaking activities and joint projects, educators and students have proposed the organization of peace camps for youth from both communities.

They have recommended establishing a Cypriot publishing house to publish new, joint materials and books (e.g., Cypriot fairy tales, oral histories, local customs) and disseminating these new resources in all schools. They suggest organizing a series of bicommunal Peace Seminars and inviting speakers from other conflict-ridden societies to share experiences and knowledge of what other societies do toward reconciliation. They wish to establish a multicultural research center where interested scholars from all Cypriot communities can engage in joint research projects (hopefully funded by EU); hold joint art exhibitions, and have dance and drama groups perform and create together. They are in favor of establishing a bicommunal Language Center for teaching each other's language and literature, and organizing both bicommunal and monocommunal conflict resolution workshops for educators, students, and parents. They advocate writing, in each other's newspapers, articles supporting the ideology of rapprochement, and setting up an interethnic Peace Radio or TV Station to disseminate the new language of coexistence and cooperation. Although some of these activities are being carried out, they are often fraught with obstacles, whether political or otherwise.

## Limitations and Obstacles

The silent majority syndrome (civic fatigue, denial, and psychological resignation) often contributes to the strengthening of the resistant forces. This resistance stems from a variety of sources, both domestic and external. External factors include the constant, foreign interference from the motherlands (separation increases dependency on Greece or Turkey) or third parties in the rescuer roles. Domestically, there are historical, structural, and psychological factors—mutual fears (often exaggerated and politicized), misperceptions, mistrust, and the vocal positions of authorities, such as political and church leaders speaking out against the perceived intentions of the other, which reinforces mutual suspicion. Furthermore, extremist groups who feel left out of the process and whose leadership lacks sufficient political will often freeze or escalate conflictual relationships.

In the Turkish Cypriot community, the authorities are against contacts and rapprochement because such a process violates their professed political position that the two nations cannot live together, having being historical enemies for centuries. They prevent contacts by not granting permission to the Turkish Cypriots or by screening who is to attend and who is not. Also depending on the political ideology of the Minister of Education and the level of his commitment to motherland Turkey, the nationalistic and chauvinistic tone is at times subdued and other times intensified. Dissenting opinions are not tolerated for long. Children are asked to forget the places their parents and grandparents lived in the south of Cyprus and to feel proud of their newly established state. New generations grow up acquiring a distorted view of the other.

In contrast, in the Greek Cypriot community, tradition is such that the schools have been the places where nationalist and religious leaders have acquired political legitimacy. Some teachers still study in their respective, motherland universities and return imbued with a romanticized view of history and of the superiority of their culture over the other's; this is subsequently channeled into the schools. Many of them are thus threatened by new concepts such as multiculturalism, pluralism, and social construction of identity or concepts of muliple identities. The local status of many of these educationalists and intellectuals is high because they represent the values of the Greek nation and Orthodoxy as traditionally defined and understood. Some of them are still in positions of making educational policies and determining the context of the curriculum. The establishment of a State Cyprus University (which is by law bi-communal) has a role to play in promoting social change and the values of a pluralistic multicultural democracy as forces to reconnect the multi-ethnic fabric of Cyprus.

## CONCLUDING REMARKS

For historical and political reasons, the prevalent education paradigm (which is a representation of the political culture) in the two communities has been mainly based on the us versus them dichotomy, and students have been educated and socialized in the conflict. Yet, the psychological and geographic separation of teachers and students has been challenged. This has been done through the systematic use of conflict resolution training workshops and interethnic encounters that expose citizens to alternative ways of viewing each other and history of the conflict, and that provides opportunities and a safe space to address underlying fears, concerns, and the basic needs of each community. This has led to a desire for a renewed relationship based on mutual understanding, respect, and mutual trust. There is today a group of educators who themselves have become trainers and organize educator and student workshops that hopefully will contribute to the development of a peace culture and an environment of mutual appreciation.

The proposed integrative, pluralistic educational paradigm calls for abandoning the competitive and antagonistic approach to addressing differences, replacing it with a new, joint problem-solving-oriented paradigm that promotes the building of a new, social, and political culture based on the principles of democracy, pluralism, and multiculturalism. Education can thus function as a healing platform for past mutual grievances and develop joint responsibility toward a shared common future. A new, inclusive, and more complex narrative should thus be born out of this educational vision in a new Cyprus, where education is linked very appropriately to the greater peacebuilding efforts on the island.

The enlightened intellectuals together with grass root Non-Governmental Organizations (NGOs) can exert pressure on the leadership in both Cypriot communities and on other interested third parties so that they listen to the encouraging messages that the youth of both communities are projecting. Their message is one of nostalgia for a normal life, for peace, and for reconciliation. However, although the desire for change exists, it has to manifest itself more profoundly and openly. Thus, the role of intellectuals in both Cypriot communities who are able to imagine a new Cyprus is dual. First, they wish to promote further research in both communities and produce data on the current realities, using scientific analysis for informing policymakers; second, they wish to engage in an alternative, social discourse in which self-criticism becomes a tool for enlarging the prevailing mental map. The call for a change in attitudes and mindsets cannot wait until the political settlement; it must precede and continue during and after a mutually acceptable agreement. The UN Secretary-General, in his last report to the Security Council of December 1996 (UN Report, December 1996), stressed once again the importance of the creation of an atmosphere of confidence and reconciliation between the two communities for any future success to occur in the formal negotiations. He calls on the leaders to shift the polemics in their public statements and proposes a number of measures such as those put forward by many conflict resolution groups: This is an example when the voice of civil society groups are taken into account and promoted by the International community. It remains up to the local decision-makers to implement and the pressure groups to continue their efforts.

> Messages of reconciliation and tolerance from both leaders and their communities are long overdue. Both sides should also implement goodwill measures that give tangible indications of their good intentions and help create an atmosphere of confidence. Such measures could include the following: crossing with minimal formality by members of both communities at the Ledra Palace checkpoints; facilitating bicommunal contacts, cooperation and joint projects in areas of intercommunal concern such as the environment, water, health, education (including the elimination of biased and negative representations of each other) and the restoration of historic sites; youth and student exchanges; bicommunal sports events; elimination of provocative emblems and slogans; island-wide telephone communications; and bicommunal commercial activities and trade. I call on both leaders to take such measures. (p. 5)

This challenge remains on both official and unofficial levels.

# REFERENCES

Allport, G. W. (1954). *The nature of prejudice*. Reading, MA: Addison-Wesley.

Boutzouvi, A. (1999). Events, Selective Organization of Memory—I do not forget. In *Sychrona Themata* (Greek) Vol. 68–70 (July 1998–March 1999) pp. 147–155.

Burton, W. J. (1987). *Resolving deep-rooted conflict: A handbook*. Lanham, MD: University Press of America.

European Inter-Parliamentary Union (1994). IPU Report. European Union Publications, Brussels, Belgium.

Fisher, R. J. (1972). Third party consultation: A method for the study and resolution of conflict. *Journal of Conflict Resolution, 16,* 67–94.

Fisher, R. J. (1991). *Conflict analysis workshop on Cyprus: Final report.* Ottawa: Canadian Institute for International Peace and Security.

Fisher, R. J. (1997). *Interactive conflict resolution.* Syracuse, New York: Syracuse University Press.

Hadjipavlou-Trigeorgis, M. (1987). *Identity conflict in divided societies: The case of Cyprus.* Unpublished doctoral dissertation, Boston University, Boston.

Kelman, H. C. (1979). An interactional approach to conflict resolution and its application to Israeli Palestinian relations. *International Interactions, 6,* 99–122.

Kelman, H. C. (1993). Coalitions cross conflict lines: The interplay of conflicts within and between the Israeli and Palestinian communities. In J. Simpson & S. Worchel (Eds.), *Conflict between peoples and people* (pp. 236–258). Chicago: Nelson Hall.

Kelman, H. C. (1996). Negotiation as interactive problem solving. *International Negotiation, 1,* 99–123.

Mavros, L. (1996). "Tis Epanaprosenpisis." The Rapprochment, *Simerini,* 18 Nov., p. 20.

Mitchell, C. R. (1990). Necessitous man and conflict resolution: More basic questions about basic human needs theory. In W. J. Burton (Ed.), *Conflict human needs theory* (pp. 149–176). New York: St. Martin's Press.

Montville, V. J. (1987). The arrow and olive branch: A case of track two diplomacy. In J. McDonald & D. Bendahmane (Eds.), *Conflict resolution: Track II diplomacy.* Washington, DC: U.S. Government Printing Office.

Montville, V. J. (1993). The healing function in political conflict resolution. In J. D. Sandole & H. van de Merwe (Eds.), *Conflict resolution: Theory and practice* (pp. 112–128). Manchester: Manchester University Press.

Papadakis, Y. (1993). *Perceptions of history and collective identity: A study of contemporary Greek Cypriot and Turkish Cypriot nationalism.* Unpublished doctoral dissertation, University of Cambridge, Cambridge.

United Nations (1993). UN Report on Cyprus, November, paragraphs 102a–102d.

United Nations (1994). UN Report on Cyprus, December, S/1996/1055.

Volkan, V. D. (1979). *Cyprus war and adaptation: A psychoanalytic history of two ethnic groups in conflict.* Charlottesville, VA: The University Press of Virginia.

Volkan, V. D. (1991). On chosen traumas. *Mind and Human Interaction, 2,* 3–13.

# ADDITIONAL RESOURCES

Azar, E. E. (1985). Protracted social conflict: Ten propositions. *International Interactions, 12,* 59–70.

Azar, E. E. (1990). *The management of protracted social conflict.* Aldershot, Hampshire, UK: Gower Publishing.

Bar-Tal, D. (2000). From intractable conflict through conflict resolution to reconciliation: Psychological analysis. *Political Psychology, 21*(2), 351–365.

Burton, W. J. (1979). *Deviance, terrorism and war: The process of solving unsolved social and political problems.* New York: St. Martin's Press.

Burton, W. J. (1993). Conflict resolution as a political system. In D. Sandole & H. van der Merwe (Eds.), *Conflict resolution theory and practice* (pp. 55–65). Manchester: Manchester University Press.

Diamond, L., & McDonald, J. (1991). Multi-Track diplomacy: A systems guide and analysis. Occasional Paper 3, Grinnell, IA: Iowa Peace Institute.

Hadjipavlou-Trigeorgis, M. (1989). Conflict resolution mechanisms: A comparative study of four societies. *The Cyprus Review, 1*(1), 67–92.

Hadjipavlou-Trigeorgis, M. (1993). Cyprus—an evolutionary approach. *Journal of Conflict Resolution, 37*( 2), 340–360.

Hadjipavlou-Trigeorgis, M. (1998). Different relationships to the land: Personal narratives, political implications and future possibilities. In V. Calotychos (Ed.), *Cyprus and its people, nation, identity, and experience in an unimaginable community 1955–1997* (pp. 251–277). Westview Press.

Hadjipavlou, M. (in press). Conflict resolution in Cyprus: A critical appraisal. In A. Ackerman (Ed.), *Reconciliation in international conflict*. Baltimore, MD: John Hopkins University Press.

Kelman, H. C. (1976). The problem-solving workshop: A social-psychological contribution to the resolution of international conflicts. *Journal of Peace Research, 13,* 79–90.

Kitromilides, M. P. (1977). From coexistence to confrontation: The dynamics of ethnic conflict in Cyprus. In M. Attalides (Ed.), *Cyprus reviewed*. Nicosia: The Jus Cypris Association.

Papadakis, Y. (2000). Memories of walls, walls of memories. In Y. Ioannou, F. Metral, & M. Yon (Eds.), *Chypre et la Mediterranee Orientale. Travaux de la Maison de l'Orient Mediterraneen* (No. 31, pp. 231–241). Lyon: University Lumiere-Lyon 2.

Pollis, A. (1973). Intergroup conflict and British colonial policy: The case of Cyprus. *Comparative Politics, 5*(4), 575–599.

Rouhana, N. N., & Kelman, H. C. (1994). Promoting joint thinking in international conflicts: An Israeli Palestinian continuing workshop. *Journal of Social Issues, 50,* 157–178.

Rouhana, N. N., & Korper, S. (1996). Dealing with power asymmetry: Dilemmas of intervention in asymmetrical intergroup conflict. *Negotiation Journal, 12,* 315–328.

Rouhana, N. N., & Bar-Tal, D. (1998). Psychological dynamics of intractable ethnonational conflicts— the Israeli-Palestinian case. *American Psychologist, 53*(7), 761–770.

Salem, N. (1992). *Cyprus: A regional conflict and its resolution*. London: St. Martin's Press.

Saunders, H. H. (1991). Officials and citizens in international relations. In V. Julius, A. D. Montville, & V. D. Volkan (Eds.), *The psychodynamics of international relations: Unofficial diplomacy at work* (Vol. II., pp. 41–71). Lexington, MA: Lexington Books.

Van den Broek, H. (1997). Bicommunal cooperation: The path to mutual trust and reconciliation. Speech delivered at the Ledra Palace, Nicosia, December 2.

Volkan, V. D., & Itzkowitz, N. (1994). *Turks and Greeks: Neighbors in conflict*. Hunghton, Campbs: Eothen Press.

Yashin, M. (1990). The question of identity and its social historical basis in Turkish Cypriot literature. In M. A. Aydidn (Ed.), *Turkish Cypriot identity in literature* (pp. 33–62). London: Fatal Publication.

# 18

# Israel: Empowering Arab and Jew—School Leadership in Acre

## Rachel Hertz-Lazarowitz
*Haifa University*

## Devorah Eden
*Western Galilee College*

The focus for this chapter is a citywide project, a long-term and large-scale program, aimed at improving the educational system in Acre, a mixed Arab and Jewish city. This chapter describes the background of Acre, the meaning of coexistence and partnership, and the community project conducted there, in the course of which many Arab–Jewish partnerships were formed. The chapter also describes the Schools' Forum of Principals and its contribution to coexistence and partnership between Jews and Arabs in the city of Acre from 1995 to 2000, the years in which the program took place.

Acre can be regarded as representative of the potential for peaceful coexistence within Israel. A community-based model such as the one described here can serve as a working model for peace and coexistence building in conflicted communities. In light of the current political uprising and the unrest in Israel, since October 2000, we returned for follow-up interviews in Acre in April 2001, 2 years after the citywide project was over. Despite the troubles, it seems that impact of the Forum of Principals on the community is still holding. Day to day life takes place in this city on a relatively peaceful basis. However, the question still arises as to whether Acre can maintain the spirit of community, coexistence, democracy, and peace, and if so, how (see Fig 1.).

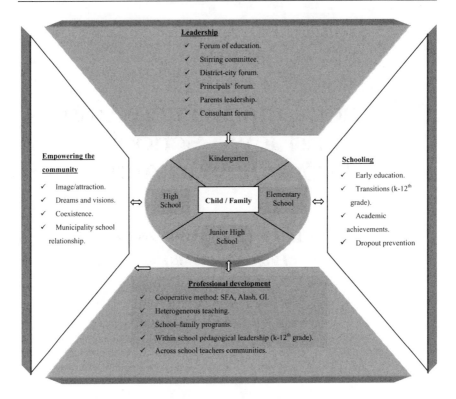

FIG. 18.1.   The Investigation Task Force (ITF): A community approach.

## ACRE'S BACKGROUND

Acre is a city in the north of Israel with a population of 45,000 people, of whom two thirds are Jews and one third is Arabs. Demographically, the Jewish population consists of two groups: one is the old-established population, some of whom are educated and well off, and the other is that of newcomers (immigrants) from the Asian republics of the former Soviet Union and from Ethiopia. Members of the second group are mostly of low, socioeconomic status (SES) and have special needs that demand large, financial allocations. The Arab population is mostly Muslim and partly Christian. There is a large percentage of low SES, Arab families in the city, mainly in the old city, as evident in data on income and unemployment. However, the city also has a notable group of elite Arabs, active in a variety of religious, cultural, and educational associations and community centers.

The composition of the population has been changing because of Arab expansion as a result of natural increase, concurrent with the decrease in the number of Jews. The municipality, unable to collect taxes from low SES citizens, has become bankrupt as a result of these changes. In addition, in the early 1990s the

government froze its funding to the city amid allegations of ineffectual administration and as a result the city was, for a period of time, paralyzed (*North 1*,
December 23, 1994, p. 20).

Acre faces many problems, of which the most relevant to this chapter are three:
The flight of high SES, Jewish families from Acre to other cities; the flight of Arab
children to a private, secondary school in a neighboring village; and the drastic
impoverishment of the city.

## THE MEANING OF COEXISTENCE
## AND PARTNERSHIP IN ACRE

Acre is a city in which Arabs and Jews live in the greatest proximity and are for the
most part integrated. As one Jewish principal of a local school said: "Here we do
not need programs for coexistence because here coexistence is a fact of daily life;
just take a look at the names on the postboxes in any building in the city." In the
past 50 years the city has experienced many changes. Up until 1948 the city had a
majority of Arabs, although Jews had been living in the city all along (Luria, 2000).
The different waves of immigration brought Jews to the city, but in recent years,
as mentioned earlier, the Arabs have been becoming more influential in the city.

Demography effects coexistence. The housing, especially for middle and high
SES, is more integrated than in any other city in Israel. Schooling, segregated into
sectors by state law (Al-Haj, 1998; Elboim-Dror, 1981), is becoming integrated
in preschool education, as families send their children to the kindergarten on the
street where they live, and this trend is beginning to be felt in elementary schools.
Arab political power as representatives in the municipality is significant, as it is
hard to form coalition without them.

Yet there are many voices that express distress, fear of the other, and discrimination in Acre. Listening and talking to people, one hears what some Jews have
to say: "This is going to be an Arab city within 10 years. . . . We are on the losing
end. . . . My heart breaks that I have to leave. . . . There is no future for me in this
city. . . . How come the government is not helping us more?"

In contrasts, Arabs can be heard to say: "In the old city, there is terrible
crowding and housing conditions are appalling. . . . We are losing the younger
generation to drugs and crime. . . . Nobody really cares about us. . . . Look at our
schools, 1,300 children are crowded into one building that does not abide by the
security regulations. . . . The Jews, by comparison, have a fine school for every
300 students. . . . For more than 20 years we have not been able to get the land for
building a school. . . . In this city there is discrimination against Arabs. . . . We are
treated as second rate citizens."

Both Arabs and Jews feel trapped, attributing their predicament to national and
local politics, to certain personages, and to the fact that the two national groups do
not cooperate with each other. Yet many have faith in the city and are devoted to

it. They say: "This is a beautiful city with great potential. . . . Some prince should come along and awaken the sleeping princess. . . . This is a stubborn city, and the people are strong. Acre has resisted many emperors and overcome many battles. We can do this again, but we need the leadership."

## THE ACRE COMMUNITY PROJECT: 1995–2000

In 1994 the Israeli Ministry of Education initiated the operation of the 36-Settlement Project in order to strengthen the local educational systems that had potential for improvement (Gordon, 1996). Included in the program were Arab and Jewish communities, including Acre, all of which received additional funds. With the program calling for cooperation and participation of the two national groups, 13 forums comprising Arab and Jewish members were established. The leadership by the school principals and the parents (not reported here) was emphasized, inspiring coexistence and partnership. The description of this program is detailed in Hertz-Lazarowitz (1999), and the full story of the Forum of School Principals is presented elsewhere (Hertz-Lazarowitz & Eden, 2001).

## SCHOOL PRINCIPALS: FROM "I SWIM YOU SINK," TO "WE SWIM OR SINK TOGETHER"

The Forum of School Principals included all 22 of Acre's school principals, both Arab and Jewish, whether secular or religious, coming from state or private, regular or special education schools from first grade to twelfth grade. This forum met on the average once a month, over the 5 years in which the program operated. An organizational consultant facilitated the functioning of the forum, which worked in coordination with members of a Steering Committee constituting the city's governing body of the program (Kidron et al., 1996; Schonberg, 1997). Progress beyond the orientation of competition to one of cooperation and interdependence evolved in three stages, ultimately transforming the school principals from mere individuals into an organized, critically thinking, and politically engaged group of leaders.

### First Stage: Professional Development for School Principals

The school principals were first convened for instrumental purposes, to help them become better and more efficient at their job. But with time, it soon became evident that the moment was ripe for enterprise beyond the limits of professional duties.

It was what Kingdon (1984) spoke of as a rare moment, a window of opportunity opening up in which the problems, the solutions, and the decision makers merge. Because the entrepreneur is there to seize the moment and to act, a policy is born that meets the challenge of the time. Social and political change followed as a consequence of the involvement of school principals in the community project.

Very early on, in the meetings, the principals realized that they shared a common obstacle in their work; in their words; "We have to change our mode of communication with the municipality so that information that we need and demand will be available and accurate." The city's economic straits had had ramifications for the schools. The municipality owed large debts to the schools because it had withheld money received for the schools from the Ministry of Education. Hence financial policy was being concealed from the school administrators. Without such vital information but more to the point, without the actual funds, the educational system in Acre could not fulfill its potential to do good work.

It was while the school principals were meeting and discussing professional issues that they found out that information and policies regarding important municipal issues were being concealed from them. These included mainly knowledge about demographic changes, and the municipality's policies in regard to those changes. It was commonly known that the growth of the Arab population led to high classroom density in the schools, yet there were no plans for additional construction of classrooms. This situation was perceived as unjustified and the principals were determined to find ways to address this problem in the Arab sector. However, the most obvious possibility, namely to hand over a Jewish school to the Arabs, was extremely difficult for psychological and ideological reasons, as it indicated loss of territory and public validation for Acre becoming less Jewish.

The decrease in the Jewish population also caused competition between the Jewish principals in attracting students, something that served to arouse suspicion and hostility among them, deepening the already prevailing rivalry, segregation, and mistrust. Thus it became clear that interdependence between Arabs and Jews was actually the key issue for the city and its schools. Consequently, the principals shifted the focus of the forum from one of individual and professional development to a task force that addresses citywide problems. This goal was achieved merely by bringing the principals together in contact with each other, legitimizing professional exchange of thoughts and sharing of hardships: "We saw that we could connect [Jewish with Arab schools] to each other to establish a forum."

## Second Stage: Becoming an Interest Group

After establishing the forum and gaining recognition for this, all of which took about a year, the principals saw the need to act as a public, educational body like that which existed in local communities other than Acre. Hence, they formed a private interest group continuing to work as a task force in the 2 years following.

# Third Stage: Becoming an Avant-garde Community Group

Redefining their role, the principals transformed themselves from educational leaders into political leaders. They desired to become active agents of change in the city. This reached its peak when in November of 1998 the former principal of the city's comprehensive school was elected to be the new mayor of Acre.

These three stages were defined as conceptually separate stages, although some of the events occurred simultaneously.

The achievements of the Forum for Principals with its focus on Arab–Jewish issues is now summarized. The principals saw their greatest achievements in the following areas.

*Collecting Debts.*    Under pressure from the forum, the municipality paid the arrears it owed the schools that had accumulated over 8 years.

*Information Access.*    Following the establishment of the forum, schools obtained information about their financial situation and future demographic trends. They could now foresee what the expenses would be whether in educational or in school renovation costs, and they could have control over those significant issues in their school.

*Support for Schools.*    The forum backed individual schools faced with their unique problems. It supported the principal of an Arab high school that had gone on strike (organized by parents). The forum also agreed to transfer special funds to that school as an affirmative-action practice.

*Mediating Between Disputing Principals.*    Occasionally the forum would intervene in professional matters of a personal nature. One school principal published a stinging criticism of a colleague in the local newspaper. The forum discussed this at its meeting and concluded by asking the offending party to publish an apology in the newspaper. In this way, the forum created a more civilized atmosphere for public debate.

*The Big Strike.*    A completely citywide strike took place at the beginning of September 1997. It was organized and led by the city's Arab and Jewish Parents' Association (PA), and by local businessmen, following the government's decision to revoke the city's "Development A" status, something that threatened to exacerbate the flight of residents from the city. The principals supported the strike, albeit in a private capacity because they were not allowed to close their schools, but the PA consulted with them unofficially. The strike included blocking the entrance roads leading into the city and demonstrating outside government offices and the Knesset in Jerusalem. In the end, the government finally restored to Acre its "Development A" status, which represented a great gain for all Acre citizens.

In addition to the sense of empowerment experienced, the forum also gained cohesion never experienced before. "The municipality understood that the leadership of the principals that had come to the fore would not yield nor conform." This empowerment was enjoyed by all equally, as the words of the principal of the Arab secondary school attest: "I am proud to have true friends who understand my problems and address them. We did not have this before. Now everybody in town knows about the special problems of the Arab sector."

Now, the struggles of the forum made education the most important issue on the local, political agenda. The principal of the comprehensive school competed with the former director of education on the city council for the position of mayor. Both candidates had declared that education would be their "baby," and they would handle it personally. However, they differed on the Arab agenda, as the principal supported equality for the Arabs, whereas the other candidate was against it.

The principal, who was a very active force behind the strike, won the election and became the mayor. He subsequently formed a political coalition with the Arab parties and, from 1998 until today, he has been making every effort to improve the condition of education in general and that of Arab education in particular. Some of the forum members are of the opinion that it was on the forum that he attained his political savvy and training. He has denied this, but he did admit that he had decided to run for the position following the strike and in response to the request of his school PA. Today, the new mayor works in cooperation with the Steering Committee and the Forum of School Principals.

At the time of our follow-up (April 1999) on the community project, it was in the stage of closure, yet the forum remained strong and active. It has also survived a large-scale manpower turnover caused by the retirement of several of the city's school principals and their replacement by new people. Indeed, the forum helped these new administrators become partners in their work. In a recent follow-up (April 2001), the Forum of School Principals is all the while holding strong, and meetings of the Arab and Jewish principals are still held regularly. Yet, the scars of the painful events of the uprising of October 2000 and the killing of 13 Arabs by the Israeli police cast a dark shadow over the city. Some people say, "Now we have to work harder on coexistence then we did before, "but, for others," there are wounds that have first to heal."

At this stage, the forum, with the strong support of the mayor, is a proactive group, seeking to improve the way things are by working for inclusion and voicing the need for equality for all the schools. The forum belongs to those organizations that control funds and wield influence, such as the city Steering Committee, Project Renewal (renewal of low-SES neighborhoods), the citywide PA, and the ruling committees in the municipality.

In sum, the school principals of Acre have shown that educators can free themselves from the technical-objective thinking conferred on them by their training, and instead view education as a political matter that is part and parcel of the power structure of society (Eden, 1998). However, their liberation is not yet complete. It will only be so when the relationship achieved moves beyond functional co-operation and is transformed. In the ultimate relationship all people should be emancipated from cultural and national boundaries that cause hostility among them, and they should be treated as part of the community and not as "others" with whom the community is obliged to cooperate to save the city. Power is a requisite of social change, but emancipation calls for a different view of human relations, one that the forum has yet to attain.

# REFERENCES

Al-Haj, M. (1998). *Education among the Arabs in Israel: Control and change.* Jerusalem: Magnes Press, Hebrew University & Floersheimer Institute for Policy Studies.

Eden, D. (1998). The paradox of school leadership. *Journal of Educational Administration, 36*(3), 249–261.

Elboim-Dror, R. (1981). Conflict and consensus in educational policy making. *International Journal of Political Education, 4,* 219–232.

Gordon, D. (1996). *Restructuring and holism as principles of systemic change: The case of the 36-Settlement Project in Israel.* Jerusalem: Ministry of Education, Culture and Sports. (in Hebrew)

Hertz-Lazarowitz, R. (1999). Cooperative learning and group investigation in Israel's Jewish-Arab schools: A community approach. *Theory into Practice, 38*(2), 105–113.

Hertz-Lazarowitz, R., & Eden, D. (2001). The political power of principals in Northville. *Studies in Organization and Management in Education, 24,* 73–100. (in Hebrew)

Kidron, O., Hertz-Lazarowitz, R., Warshuwski, B., Ashkar T., Kerem, R., Shperling, Z., & Mula, W. (1995, March). *The model of Community Group Investigation (CGI) in Acre.* Presentation to Acre forums.

Kingdon, J. W. (1984). *Agendas, alternatives, and public policies.* Boston: Little, Brown.

Luria, J. (2000). *Acre: The city of walls.* Tel Aviv: Yron Golan. (in Hebrew)

*North One,* a weekly local newspaper (1994, December 23, p. 20).

Schonberg, A. (1997, April). What we are not talking about: *Some issues in the Forum of School Principals in a mixed Arab-Jewish town.* Paper presented at the conference on Holism in Education, Mikveh Israel.

# 19

# Northern Ireland: The Impact of Peacemaking in Northern Ireland on Intergroup Behavior

### Ed Cairns
*University of Ulster*

### Miles Hewstone
*University of Oxford*

"Fall in cross-community activity in bomb wake." This headline ("Fall," 2000), in a recent Northern Irish newspaper, was significant because it was referring to data from the period following August, 1998, the date of Northern Ireland's worst terrorist atrocity when 29 men, women, and children were killed in a bomb blast on the main street of the small market town of Omagh. According to the local educational authorities for the Omagh area, cross-community contact between Catholic and Protestant schools fell, in the subsequent year, from 90% to 66% for secondary schools and from 71% to 57% for elementary schools.

Was this merely a temporary blip on the community relations' map? Alternatively, is this worrying evidence that some 25 years and millions of pounds of investment in peace education work in Northern Ireland has had such a superficial effect, that it can be thrown off course, just at the time when one might suggest it was needed most? After some introductory material, this chapter examines evidence concerning naturally occurring intergroup contact in Northern Ireland and the efforts that have been made to enhance this contact. Following this overview, the possible impact contact may have had on intergroup behavior is reviewed.

## CONFLICT IN NORTHERN IRELAND

The conflict in Northern Ireland has been basically a struggle between those who wish to see Northern Ireland remain part of the United Kingdom (Protestants–Unionists–Loyalists) and those (Catholics–Nationalists–Republicans) who wish to see the unification of the island of Ireland. This conflict is underpinned by historical, religious, political, economic, and psychological elements. These lie behind the violence that has spanned the past 30 years, led to death, injury, and increased community divisions, and has affected mental health (Cairns & Darby, 1998).

## CONTACT IN NORTHERN IRELAND

### Informal Contact

Today the Protestant population of Northern Ireland is estimated at 50%, the Catholic, 38% with those not wishing to state a denomination comprising the greater part of the remainder. Perhaps because both communities are relatively large, they are able to maintain their own political, social, cultural, and educational infrastructure. For example, over 90% of children in Northern Ireland attend either a Catholic school or a Protestant school at both elementary and secondary level. This in turn means that there are, for example, separate teacher-training colleges.

In spite of this separation, total residential segregation does not exist in Northern Ireland. As a result, unlike some other apparently intractable conflicts, the potential for contact between members of the two communities exists in many areas (Cairns & Darby, 1998; Trew, 1986). Even in the cities, where working-class housing areas in particular are more highly segregated, people often travel out of their own area to work, thus increasing the potential for contact. Data to bear this out come from a survey (Templegrove, 1996) in a very segregated district (94% Catholic) in a predominantly Catholic city (92% Catholic). Despite these levels of segregation, some 35% of respondents claimed that up to half of the people they "socialize" with came from the other denominational group.

### Formal Contact

In an attempt to transform the conflict, various policy initiatives have been pursued, including attempts to improve community relations. This policy has been implemented since 1987 by means of the Central Community Relations' Unit (CCRU), whose importance can be gauged by the fact that in 1995–1996 it received £5.3m out of a total government spending for Northern Ireland on community relations of £8.4m (Knox & Hughes, 1997). As these authors note, CCRU has funded a wide range of community relations' projects, which have ranged from Cultural Traditions workshops that focus on cultural awareness to reconciliation groups and groups set up in response to some particular act of political violence (Hughes, 1997). In addition, the educational authorities in Northern Ireland have funded peace education (see Dunn & Morgan, 1999) through encouraging contact between Catholic and Protestant schools, and more recently through the development of planned, integrated schools. Although specific goals for all these projects have been framed in generic terms, they have concentrated principally on making contact between Catholics and Protestants possible (Knox & Hughes, 1997).

## HAS CONTACT MADE A DIFFERENCE?

Here an attempt is made to review empirical data in order to determine if these policies have been effective in Northern Ireland. For the purposes of this chapter it is assumed that the goal of policymakers in attempting to implement cross-community contact was ultimately to achieve a melting pot situation in Northern Ireland leading to the virtual integration of the two communities in terms of social behavior.

Whether this goal was achieved will be decided by examining archival data in Northern Ireland. Fortunately, baseline data exist against which comparisons can be made with present-day statistics. These data come from a random, sample survey of the Northern Irish population carried out in 1968 and reported in Rose (1971). The year 1968 is significant because it is the last year of peace before the political violence, which was to last for the next 30 years, erupted. It is also fortunate that since that first survey was carried out, a series of similar surveys has been carried out at approximately 10-year intervals, which have repeated many of the questions originally asked by Rose in 1968 (1971). This means that this chapter does not simply ask, Are things improving in Northern Ireland? Instead, it addresses the more taxing question, Have intergroup relations reached levels comparable with those of the 1968, preconflict era? In addition, rather than focusing on attitude change, this chapter examines what could be regarded as harder data, such as levels of segregation in housing, schooling, data related to voting patterns, and the extent of cross-denominational marriage.

## HOUSING PATTERNS

In 1968 Rose (1971) reported that Northern Ireland was a fairly segregated society. Since then, one might expect geographical patterns to have changed because of government policies favoring greater intergroup mixing. In particular, given the change in attitudes toward greater segregation in housing noted earlier, one would expect to find a corresponding change in actual behavior. However, according to the available survey data (Table 19.1), there has been little change since 1968, up to the present day (1998), with, if anything, people reporting that their neighborhoods are perhaps slightly more segregated since the political violence began.

**TABLE 19.1**

Proportion of Respondents Reporting That All or Most of Their Neighbors
Are of the Same Religion as Themselves

| Year | Catholic (%) | Protestant (%) | Source |
|------|--------------|----------------|--------|
| 1968 | 57 | 68 | Rose (1971) |
| 1978 | 61 | 75 | Moxon-Browne (1983) |
| 1989 | 62 | 67 | Gallagher & Dunn (1991) |
| 1998 | 64* | 75* | Cairns & Hewstone (1999) |

*Original question "different religion from you": responses reversed scored.

**TABLE 19.2**

Proportion of Respondents Reporting That All or Most of Their Friends Are
of the Same Religion as Themselves

| Year | Catholic (%) | Protestant (%) | Source |
|------|--------------|----------------|--------|
| 1968 | 57 | 78 | Rose (1971) |
| 1978 | 56 | 75 | Moxon-Browne (1983) |
| 1989 | 63 | 72 | Gallagher & Dunn (1991) |
| 1998 | 55* | 68* | Cairns & Hewstone (1999) |

*Original question "different religion from you": responses reversed scored.

## CROSS-GROUP FRIENDSHIPS PATTERNS

Given the absence of mass desegregation in housing, it is perhaps not surprising
that when one examines data related to cross-group friendships there is also little
evidence for change, with approximately 55% of Protestants and 75% of Catholics
reporting that "all or most" of their friends are of the same religion as themselves.
Given that there is always a certain amount of error associated with sampling in
this way, it could be argued that patterns of intergroup friendships have remained
virtually constant from 1968 to 1998 (Table 19.2).

## MIXED MARRIAGES

A sterner test of the development of intergroup friendship is to look at the pattern of
intergroup marriages—what are known in Northern Ireland as "mixed marriages."
Rose (1971) in his 1968 survey found that only 5% of marriages crossed the
communal divide; 10 years later, Moxon-Browne (1983) found the proportion to
be exactly the same, and in the 1989 Northern Ireland Social Attitudes Survey the
figure was just slightly less (4%).

However, the most recent survey to collect data on this question (Northern Ireland Life and Times, 1998), which this time asked, "Is your spouse/partner the same religion?" reports an increase to 9.2%. This increase could, however, be due as much to changing attitudes to religion in general as to changing attitudes to "mixed marriages" per se. Whatever the level of intermarriage in Northern Ireland, however, there is the suspicion that when intermarriage does occur, "it bridged no gaps, for usually the husband cut off all ties with his own kin" (Whyte, 1986, p. 230). Paradoxically, it appears that attitudes toward mixed marriages are not improving, at least among those not directly involved in them. Several surveys have asked people if they think that "most" people would not mind a close relative entering a mixed marriage. In 1989, 43% of Catholics and only 18% of Protestants thought that most people would not mind, and in 1998 these figures were 37% and 17%, respectively.

## INTEGRATED EDUCATION

Educational segregation in Northern Ireland is virtually complete. In fact it has been noted that educational segregation is much more common than residential segregation (Poole, 1982). Further, this segregation is entirely voluntary. Catholic parents choose to send their children to Catholic schools and Protestant parents choose to send their children to Protestant schools, even in residentially integrated neighborhoods.

The 1980s, however, heralded the most dramatic development in education in Northern Ireland for some 20 years with the development of integrated schools (Smith, 1995). These schools share a common aim of reflecting both communities in the governing body, and in pupil and staff composition. In addition they aspire to reflect cultural pluralism in the curriculum.

By the early 1990s there were 10 such schools and today, aided by educational reforms that provided financial support to the integrated sector, there are 37 operational, of which 24 are elementary and 13 postelementary. However, despite this rapid development, today the integrated sector in Northern Ireland is still relatively small and only educates less than 10% of Northern Ireland's school-age children. One reason for this, according to the integrated school movement, is that the existing integrated schools are oversubscribed, which means that every year children have to be turned away. For example, in 1999 it was claimed that almost 1,000 children were refused a place in an integrated school because of lack of space. Nevertheless, it would appear that the target, set by the founders of the integrated school movement, of one third of all of Belfast's children being educated in integrated schools by the year 2000 (Frazer & Fitzduff, 1986) is unlikely to be met for some years. Part of the problem is, as the integrated school movement would claim, lack of resources, but part is also due to lack of public support, with integrated schools today still not receiving official support from all of the churches and often opening to a background of protest from existing (segregated) schools, their teachers, and parents. Once again, it is difficult to see in the support given to integrated schools any evidence for a dramatic desire on the part of Northern Irish people to abandon their segregated ways.

## VOTING BEHAVIOR

According to Stewart (1977), people in Northern Ireland simply assume the political attitudes of the faith into which they were born. As a result, in Northern Ireland the relationship between religious denomination and political party loyalty is uniquely close (Whyte, 1991). However, as Whyte (1991) also notes, this relationship is not perfect for several reasons. The main one is that since the 1970s there has been a centrist grouping known as the Alliance party that attracts both Catholic and Protestant voters. Given the existence of this centrist party, one might imagine that an improvement in intergroup relations in Northern Ireland would be reflected in an increase in the number of people voting for the Alliance party.

However, examination of the voting record of the Alliance party, in the local elections from 1973 to 1997, reveals that in this period the Alliance party has suffered a downturn in electoral support. In the 1970s approximately 14% of the electorate supported the Alliance party, but this fell to around 7% in the late 1980s and has remained at this level at least up until 1997. Therefore, as Hughes and Carmichael (1998) have noted, there is a paradox in that, despite some signs that public, intergroup attitudes may be becoming more liberal over the past 20 years, electoral behavior is becoming increasingly polarized. The available evidence therefore appears to support the hypothesis entertained by Cairns in 1987, that "generations of voters coming of age in the year 2000 in Northern Ireland might be expected to faithfully reproduce voting patterns which have their roots in the experience of earlier generations in the violence of the 1970's" (p. 146).

## CONCLUSIONS

The evidence reviewed herein would appear to suggest that massive changes in social behavior in Northern Ireland have not been brought about as a result of the policies designed to implement the contact hypothesis over the past 20 or so years. In fact, the evidence can be interpreted as suggesting that Northern Ireland remains a deeply segregated society at all levels. This is not to suggest that Northern Irish society has not changed at all over this period. According to Hughes and Carmichael (1998), who have reviewed this area extensively, there is evidence from surveys over the period 1989–1996 that "offers cautious grounds for optimism" because they reveal an improvement in attitudes toward community relations. And of course there have been ground-breaking political changes following on from

**TABLE 19.3**

Changes in Optimism Levels About Community Relations in Northern Ireland
1968–1999

| | Catholic | | | Protestant | | |
|---|---|---|---|---|---|---|
| Year | Better (%) | About the Same (%) | Worse (%) | Better (%) | About the Same (%) | Worse (%) |
| 1968 | 65 | 27 | 4 | 56 | 35 | 7 |
| 1986 | 9 | 45 | 46 | 11 | 41 | 47 |
| 1989 | 23 | 44 | 31 | 20 | 50 | 26 |
| 1991 | 31 | 50 | 16 | 28 | 53 | 15 |
| 1999 | 60 | 33 | 4 | 42 | 46 | 10 |

the signing of the Good Friday agreement. In turn these are reflected in a downturn in political violence. The result is a "social and institutional environment, which is seen to be conducive to greater mutual understanding" on the one hand, and on the other hand, "ongoing sectarian conflict" (Hughes, 1999, p. 26). In other words, despite a major investment of time and money in promoting greater contact, a major divide still exists between the Catholics and Protestants of Northern Ireland. This conclusion, that cross-community relations have not improved beyond 1968 levels, is reinforced not just by the data noted earlier, or the views of expert commentators, but also by the views of the Northern Irish public. Survey data over the period 1968–1999 indicate that although public levels of optimism about the future of cross-community relations have been improving, they still have not moved beyond the point they had reached in 1968 before the *troubles* began, and before the policy of encouraging cross-community contact was implemented (see Table 19.3).

## WHY HAS CONTACT NOT LED
## TO GREATER CHANGES?

A combination of factors may have contributed to the fact that contact between the two communities in Northern Ireland has not led to greater behavioral change. For example, it may be that, in the main, contact schemes were preaching to the converted. That is, those who held more liberal attitudes and who were already in contact with the other community were more likely to be involved in contact schemes. Another possibility is that although some contact schemes have been successful, this success has been negated by the impact of selective migration, with those whose behavior had been changed more likely to leave Northern Ireland and its ancient quarrels and settle elsewhere. In particular, it can be argued that intergroup contact has almost certainly not led to greater changes because, in the main, intergroup contact in Northern Ireland has been rather superficial. Certainly, this is the pattern in everyday contact and there is both qualitative and quantitative evidence to substantiate this.

Cairns, Dunn, and Gallagher (1993) took advantage of the fact that Northern Ireland's universities are desegregated (unlike the majority of primary and secondary level educational institutions) to carry out a series of individual interviews with university students. What they reported was that many of the students interviewed expressed concern, even anxiety about the possibility of making cross-community contacts. As a result, although mixing does occur at university, for the most part, it is relatively cursory, consisting of casual rather than intimate contact.

This ensures that on a day-to-day basis, people from the two groups interact peaceably. This is achieved, however, by Catholic and Protestant students avoiding divisive topics of conversation such as politics and religion when they do meet—guided, as the poet Seamus Heaney has put it, by the motto "whatever you say, say nothing." People in Northern Ireland can do so because they are socially competent at recognising ingroup and outgroup members (Cairns, 1987) and use this skill to ensure that they do not enter into divisive communications with members of the outgroup.

The casual nature of cross-community contact in Northern Ireland is borne out in data from a recent survey carried out in 1998 (Cairns & Hewstone, 1999). This included not only questions about how many outgroup friends and neighbors people had, but, for the first time, also questions about the amount of actual contact in different contexts. What this survey revealed is that the majority of Catholics (68%) and Protestants (59%) "very often" enjoy casual conversations with members of the outgroup. In contrast, contact that could be considered as more intimate, such as home visits or meeting at local events, were only experienced "very often" by 20% of Catholics and 15% of Protestants.


## CONTACT HYPOTHESIS: PRACTICE AND THEORY

### Practice

Little is known, in detail, about the way the contact hypothesis has been implemented in community relations' schemes in Northern Ireland except, as noted earlier, that contact was usually involved at some level. Of course, as McCartney (1990) also noted, some schemes did have a well worked out philosophy, but many others simply operated on a "gut feeling" that what they were doing was right. It seems fair to say, therefore, to paraphrase McCartney (1990), that for most, the contact hypothesis was more a hope than a strategy. As a result, many regarded it as a measure of success that "planned, cross-community, contact programmes between young people in contemporary Northern Ireland take place at all" (Robinson & Brown, 1991, p. 354).

Further, there is also anecdotal evidence that the defensive patterns of behavior, used when Catholics and Protestants come into contact in Northern Ireland in everyday life, are carried over into more formal contact situations, including those arranged to promote community relations (Cornell, 1994; Robinson & Brown, 1991). That is, there is evidence that even when contact activities are seen as the main aim of a cross-community scheme, contact still remains relatively superficial. For example, in the course of Cairns et al.'s (1993) study, one university student recalled her school based, cross-community contacts as involving "competitions and things like that but we didn't mix with them. We maybe said 'hello' but there was no mixing." Another gave a more graphic account of intergroup contacts in the form of soccer matches where "We were cheering on our boys and they were cheering on their boys and it was a real hate thing, well it wouldn't have been hate, it was only children but we didn't like them and they didn't like us and that was obvious." Even when competition was not involved the results were not particularly encouraging, as another student recalled: "In sixth year we had 1 day when some of the Protestant schools came over. It was supposed to be like... mixing, but there was very little mixing. It wasn't because we didn't want to; it was just really awkward type of thing." As a result of all of this, some commentators have claimed that people in Northern Ireland do not want "to hold hands" with members of the outgroup, but instead have settled for "benign apartheid" (O'Connor, 1993).

## Theory

The contact hypothesis was never conceived of as a simple solution to intergroup conflict (Allport, 1954). Nevertheless, this is the way that practitioners have tended to interpret it. However, regardless of how one views early attempts at theorizing in this area, it is clear that recent work has now become much more sophisticated.

This is because current work in this area has moved away from the simple question of Does the contact hypothesis work? Now the question is, When does it work? and Why has it worked? This line of research has led to three highly contrasted models, which focus either on decategorization, categorization, or recategorization (for a review, see Hewstone & Cairns, 2001).

The decategorization model (Brewer & Miller, 1984) places most emphasis on contact taking place between individuals, endorsing the belief that for contact to be most effective, group salience should be low. Hewstone and Brown (1986), in contrast, have been insistent that only when intergroup contact takes place, that is, only when group membership is salient, will positive effects generalize to the outgroup as a whole. Finally, there is a school of thought that believes that only when contact leads people to think of themselves as being members of a larger, superordinate group will contact be effective (Gaertner, Dovidio, Anastasio, Bachman, & Rust, 1993). This approach is often referred to as the Common Ingroup

Identity Model because it emphasizes the importance of recategorization's is taking place.

Recently Pettigrew (1998) attempted to integrate these three models of intergroup contact by suggesting that all three of the processes (decategorization, categorization, and recategorization) are necessary for contact to be effective, but that they must occur in a particular sequence. He suggests, therefore, that first people should get to know each other as friends, that they should then understand that they come from two opposing groups, and finally that an attempt should be made to forge a common identity.

Of course, as Pettigrew (1998) notes, situational factors prior to contact and, indeed, individual differences among the participants will play a role. In this latter context, it is interesting to note that Hewstone and Lord (1998) have suggested that contact will be more effective if it takes place between (among other things) people who are typical of their group, and who can be seen as representing their group in some way and so cannot be easily dismissed as forming a "subtype."

## RESEARCH IMPLICATIONS

Before discussing what new research is needed in this area, we must consider a vitally important question posed by Whyte (1991, p. 246). He is perhaps the only commentator to consider the question, Why has research on the Northern Ireland problem not been more effective? Of the answers he suggests, two are of particular relevance to future research related to the implementation of the contact hypothesis in Northern Ireland (and indeed in other societies). First, there is the possibility that people (here we could perhaps substitute "practitioners" for "people") simply do not read research. Second, as Whyte (1991) has pointed out, even if they do read it, some people find it too painful to accept research "which runs counter to their psychological needs." If we include in those psychological needs the need to feel that one's pet theory is correct, then this allows an insight into what has been happening in the community relations' field in Northern Ireland.

Research in Northern Ireland, therefore, has to look more closely at the actual practitioners who are charged with implementing the contact hypothesis. In particular, it has to examine practitioners' understanding of the contact hypothesis, in detail, and how they put what they understand into practice. Research such as this should examine the working models used by practitioners in Northern Ireland. It is no secret that some contact schemes have been more successful than others. What we do not know is why. Practitioners in Northern Ireland have a wealth of knowledge about the practicalities of applying the contact hypothesis. Unfortunately, successful practitioners have not always been willing to share the secrets of their success with others. Yet this is valuable knowledge, because it involves not simply implementing contact in a laboratory situation, or as the result of some short-term conflict. What is special about the conflict in Northern Ireland is that it is a life or death conflict that has gone on for generations.

Allied to this, more research has to be done to persuade practitioners to pay attention to research. Northern Ireland is a very well researched part of the world and the contact hypothesis is, some would say, an overresearched area, internationally. Despite this, the available research has had a limited impact on peace education practice in Northern Ireland.

In addition, research is also needed that looks in detail at what happens when contact actually occurs—both when such contact is spontaneous and when it takes place in more formal, cross-community settings. This would require gathering more information from those taking part in such contact situations regarding the nature of the interactions they are involved in, and the impact, if any, it is having on them.

Finally, there is the unresearched question of timing; that is, at what stage in a conflict should one attempt to implement the contact hypothesis? Conflicts such as those in Northern Ireland are often cyclical in nature, reappearing long after they have apparently been settled. For example, as political stability draws nearer in Northern Ireland, it is now being recognized that politics alone will not provide a final solution (Dunn, 1999). One possibility, therefore, is that the contact hypothesis, although it may not play a major role in ending conflict, may play a crucial part in bringing to an end the cycles of revenge that tend to haunt ethnic conflicts, even after a political settlement has been reached. In other words, it may be that "a political settlement in Northern Ireland [is] a beginning to a solution of the problem, not an end to it" (Heskin, 1980, p. 153). Hopefully, if research on these and other, related topics can be implemented in Northern Ireland, or in societies with similar conflicts, it will lead to theoretical developments that will not simply fill academic journals but that will have an impact on practice and in turn lead to long-term peace in divided societies.

# REFERENCES

Allport, G. W. (1954). *The nature of prejudice*. New York: Addison-Wesley.

Brewer, M. B., & Miller, N. (1984). Contact and cooperation: When do they work? In P. Katz & D. Taylor (Eds.), *Eliminating racism: Means and controversies* (pp. 315–326). New York: Plenum.

Cairns, E. (1987). *Caught in crossfire: Children in Northern Ireland*. Belfast and Syracuse, NY: Appletree Press and Syracuse University Press.

Cairns, E., & Darby, J. (1998). The conflict in Northern Ireland—causes, consequences and controls. *American Psychologist, 53*(7), 754–760.

Cairns, E., & Hewstone, M. (1999). [Templeton Intergroup Forgiveness Project]. Unpublished raw data.

Cairns, E., Dunn, S., & Gallagher, A. (1993). *Intergroup contact in a Northern Irish university setting: A report to the Central Community Relations Unit*. Coleraine: Centre for the Study of Conflict.

Cornell, J. C. (1994). Prejudice reduction through intergroup contact in Northern Ireland: A social-psychological critique. *Conflict Quarterly, 14*(1), 30–46.

Dunn, S. (1999). Northern Ireland: A promising or partisan peace. *Journal of International Affairs, 52*(2), 719–733.

Dunn, S., & Morgan, V. (1999). A fraught path—education as a basis for developing community relations in Northern Ireland. *Oxford Review of Education, 25*(1–2), 141–153.

Fall in cross-community activity in bomb wake. (2000, January 19). *Belfast Telegraph*, p. 6.

Frazer, H., & Fitzduff, M. (1986). *Improving community relations*. Paper prepared for the Standing Advisory Commission on Human Rights. Belfast, North Ireland.

Gallagher, A. M., & Dunn, S. (1991). Community relations in Northern Ireland: Attitudes to contact and integration. In P. Stringer & G. Robinson (Eds.), *Social attitudes in Northern Ireland: The first report* (pp. 7–22). Belfast: Blackstaff Press.

Gaertner, S. L., Dovidio, J. F., Anastasio, P. A., Bachman, B. A., & Rust, M. C. (1993). The common ingroup identity model: Recategorization and the reduction of intergroup bias. *European Review of Social Psychology, 4*, 1–26.

Heskin, K. (1980). *Northern Ireland: A psychological analysis*. Dublin: Gill & Macmillan.

Hewstone, M., & Brown, R. (Eds.). (1986). *Contact and conflict in inter-group encounters*. Oxford, England: Basil Backwell.

Hewstone, M., & Cairns, E. (2001). Social psychology and intergroup conflict. In D. Chirot & M. E. P. Seligman (Eds.), *Ethnopolitical warfare: Causes, consequences and possible solutions* (pp. 319–342). Washington, DC: American Psychological Association.

Hewstone, M., & Lord, C. G. (1998). Changing intergroup cognitions and intergroup behaviour: The role of typicality. In C. Sedikides, J. Schopler, & C. Insko (Eds.), *Intergroup cognition and inter-group behaviour* (pp. 367–392). Hillsdale, NJ: Lawrence Erlbaum Associates.

Hughes, J. (1999). Bridging the gap: Community relations' policy in Northern Ireland. *Ulster Papers in Public Policy and Management*, No. 87. Belfast: University of Ulster.

Hughes, J., & Carmichael, P. (1998). Community relations in Northern Ireland: Attitudes to contact and integration. In G. Robinson, D. Heenan, A. M. Gray, & K. Thompson (Eds.), *Social attitudes in Northern Ireland: The seventh report* (p . 8). Hants: Ashgate Publishing.

Hughes, J. (1997). Rerouting community relations in the wake of Drumcree. *Ulster Papers in Public Policy and Management*, No. 69. Belfast: University of Ulster.

Knox, C., & Hughes, J. (1997). *Ten years wasted effort? An overview of community relations in N. Ireland*. Jordanstown: School of Public Policy, Economics and Law, University of Ulster.

Moxon-Browne, E. (1983). *Nation, class and creed in Northern Ireland*. Aldershot: Gower.

Northern Ireland Life and Times (1998). htttp://www.qub.ac.uk/ss/csr/nilt

McCartney, C. (1990). *Making ripples: An evaluation of the inter-community contact grant scheme of the Northern Ireland Voluntary Trust*. Coleraine: Centre for the Study of Conflict.

O'Connor, F. (1993). *In search of a state: Catholics in Northern Ireland*. Belfast: Blackstaff Press.

Pettigrew, T. F. (1998). Inter-group contact theory. *Annual Review of Psychology, 47*, 65–85.

Poole, M. A. (1982). Religious residential segregation in urban Northern Ireland. In F. W. Boal & J. H. N. Douglas (Eds.), *Integration and division: Geographic perspectives on the Northern Ireland Problem* (pp. 281–308). London: Academic.

Robinson, A., & Brown, J. (1991). Northern Ireland children and cross-community holiday projects. *Children & Society, 5*(4), 347–356.

Rose, R. (1971). *Governing without consensus: An Irish perspective*. London: Faber & Faber.

Smith, A. (1995). Education and the conflict in Northern Ireland. In S. Dunn (Ed.), *Facets of the conflict in Northern Ireland* (pp. 168–186). New York: St. Martin's Press.

Stewart, A. T. Q. (1977). *The narrow ground: Aspects of Ulster, 1609–1969*. London: Faber & Faber.

Trew, K. (1986). Catholic-Protestant contact in Northern Ireland. In M. Hewstone & R. Brown (Eds.), *Contact and conflict in intergroup encounters* (pp. 93–106). London: Blackwell.

Templegrove Action Research Limited (1996). http://cain.ulst.ac.uk/issues/segregated/temple/chap3.htm

Whyte, J. (1991). *Interpreting Northern Ireland*. Oxford: Clarendon Press.

Whyte, J. (1986). How is the boundary maintained between the two communities in Northern Ireland? *Ethnic and Racial Studies, 9*(2), 219–234.

# 20

# Rwanda: Attaining and Sustaining Peace

*East Africa Agency for Cooperation
and Research in Development*

Humanity is confronted with the challenge of countering the unprecedented violence in Rwanda that has resulted in unending streams of refugees and in widespread killing. There has been widespread physical destruction as well as general deterioration of the social fabric, for visible destruction has been accompanied by hatred arising between different groups, social exclusion and injustice, unequal distribution of resources, and political manipulation. In order for these related and complex problems to be tackled, it is imperative that a culture of peace replace the culture of war and violence.

## HISTORICAL BACKGROUND

Rwanda is a small, landlocked country with a population of about 8,000,000 million people in an area of 26,238 square kilometers. More than 90% of the Rwandese people depend on agriculture, but with unequal distribution of arable land. This hunger for land is believed to be one of the crucial problems that have fueled violence. In the course of the past half-century, this violence culminated in genocide that took more than 1 million lives and sent more than 2 million into exile within a period of only 3 months, between April and July 1994.

Rwandese people are divided into three ethnic groups: Hutu, Tutsi, and Twa. Historically Tutsi and Hutu identities have been inseparable. Indeed, the terms *Tutsi* and *Hutu* appear to have originally been flexible terms; the proof of this is that a man could be Tutsi in relation to his clients or inferiors and Hutu in relation to his own patrons or superiors. (Lemarchand, 1996, pp. 9–10). Moreover, it was possible for people born Hutu or Twa to be ennobled and to hold elite positions as a consequence. Intermarriage also took place between Hutu men and Tutsi women. There are many people of mixed blood, and identity categories in Rwanda have changed over time.

Notions of *Tutsi, Hutu,* and *Twa* were then sharply redefined by colonial and missionary policies as well as through Rwanda government policies. When the Belgians introduced identity cards in 1931, for example, they could not decide who was Tutsi and who was Hutu. They therefore decided to use strictly economic parameters for identification. Anyone with more than 10 cows at that time was classified as a Tutsi, and so were all his children, grandchildren, and so on. Anyone with fewer than 10 cows became Hutu or Twa. Later on, after independence, the government used these same identity cards to specify ethnic origins. Most importantly, they were used to identify victims during the genocide at roadblocks, in churches, hospitals, schools, and municipal offices.

During the 19th and early 20th centuries, the country was ruled by a Tutsi elite under the auspices of European colonial rule. The regime was characterized by pronounced, hierarchical relationships that were maintained between the elite and the majority of the population, bound together by "a chain of client/master relations between the central and the local elites." (Lemarchand, 1970, p. 477) Many of the colonial practices of forced labor, taxation, and absolute control over the peasantry were continued by the Tutsi. In particular, Chiefs continued to exercise almost total control over the movement of people, their farming activities, educational levels, and working lives.

Racial theories, provided by colonial powers to justify their choice of the Tutsi as their collaborators in administration, fed into preexisting myths to give the Tutsi a feeling of almost unquestioned superiority, and the Hutu a feeling of their own unworthiness in comparison. After independence, the Hutu elite fashioned a reversal of this myth, in which the only honest, hardworking, and really authentic inhabitants of Rwanda were the Hutu. The Tutsi came to be seen as unwelcome interlopers, invaders from the North, who had to be gotten rid of. Later, after independence in 1962, the ruling party, which sought to take power by instituting and legalizing exclusion, expulsion, segregation, and eventually extermination, claimed itself to be a victim (Guillaumin, 1990, p. 9).

In 1959, when the Hutu had overthrown the Tutsi, a conflict between the elite from both groups led to the flight of large numbers of Tutsi, who settled in neighboring countries. This was a destabilizing influence for the country for many years, as groups of armed Tutsi staged attacks in a bid to return home and to power. From then on, a series of killings was organized in retaliation, leading to renewed streams of Tutsi refugees.

On every flight of the Tutsi, their land that was used as pasture or farm was immediately taken over by their Hutu neighbors. This provided new space for the Hutu remaining behind, relieving pressure on their limited resources. Whereas strife was a way for politicians to remain in power, it gave to poor peasants the opportunity to acquire more land. Whenever the Tutsi refugees voiced their claim to return, this land was successfully used as a manipulative tool for the masses: extremists deliberately fueled fear among the peaceful peasants that the land would be reclaimed and given back to the returning Tutsi. One can thus comprehend the anger of the impoverished peasants, who saw their chances of eking out a living coming under threat.

The so-called Social Revolution of 1959 was taken as the starting point for any Hutu position, and the Hutu elite introduced a policy of excluding the Tutsi from direct access to political positions. In reality, that Social Revolution of 1959 benefited the Hutu elite only, not the poorer Hutu whose largely social and class-based grievances were overlooked by the elite. The overall outcome was less a social revolution than the substitution of one elite group by another, in which nothing much changed for ordinary Rwandans, whether Hutu or Tutsi: "The governing elite borrowed from the past the tools to shape the future." (Lemarchand, 1970, p. 492). For the majority of poor Rwandese, life was characterized by a gradual reduction of the opportunity to acquire an education and make a living. More than 90% of the national resources were controlled by a handful of people in power. A quota system was introduced whereby access to education, state employment, military positions, and bank loans was reserved primarily for the Hutu from the north and only after for the Hutu from the south, and then lastly for Tutsi. This policy reflected part of the institutional structure of power.

Thus, it should not surprise us that the majority of those killed in Rwanda in the 1994 genocide were poor, rural Tutsi, who were in no way different from their Hutu neighbors. They were identical in language, in religion, almost identical in educational and income level, in the number of cows they owned and acres of land they farmed, and in the size of their families. Indeed, both in 1959 and in the prodemocracy agitation of the 1990s, what motivated popular unrest was a sense of frustration at the system's inability to ensure most people a reasonable living standard. Thus, ethnic identities were not the cause of conflict but rather a result of political division within the state and of the long-standing structural violence that followed from it.

## STRUCTURAL VIOLENCE IN RWANDA

Structural violence can be defined as the institutionalization of inequality of opportunity and its implementation against a particular group. Such inequality, characterized by discrimination, injustice, and exclusion, damages the physical, social, and psychological well-being of the target group. By this definition, even without outright, physical violence, Rwandese society suffers from violence.

In Rwanda, the regimes in power have been characterized by politics of duplicity: officially, the regime is fighting for national unity and against poverty, whereas in reality it practices the politics of exclusion and of physical elimination of those who hold different views. The refusal to share power and wealth has meant the exclusion of the majority of the population. State-operated terror, along with established prejudices and widespread poverty, left their mark on a population that felt vulnerable, haunted by fear, and susceptible to manipulation. In a word, the refusal to share power has been the fundamental cause of conflict in Rwanda.

## UNEQUAL DISTRIBUTION OF ECONOMIC RESOURCES

One aspect of structural violence is the unequal distribution of economic resources. More than 90% of the population of Rwanda make their living from agriculture, but the basic capital, which is land, does not belong to them. Already in 1994, 57% of rural households owned less than one hectare of land, and 25% owned less than half a hectare. Instead, the land belongs to the high-ranking officials who do not need it for a living and who consequently do not invest in its development.

In a survey carried out before the April 1994 genocide, the Ministry of Agriculture observed that 45% of the rural dwellers (estimated to constitute 92% of the total population of Rwanda) were unemployed, landless peasants. This was an alarming situation if one was to add to it the urban unemployed and an ever-increasing rural exodus to the cities. It is true that the country is densely populated in terms of available arable land, but the inequality in the distribution of the land is worse than the demographic pressure itself. There is a minority that has accumulated all the resources for itself, and a majority with no future. There can be no question that with such landowning politics operating, economic insecurity and the struggle for survival contributed to the tragedy that befell Rwanda in 1994. The government, unable to address the issue of land redistribution without a consequent loss of the land by the ruling elite, used land scarcity as a tool for political manipulation and incitement to hatred.

## THE INSTITUTION OF A DOMESTIC SPYING SYSTEM

The existing, internal security system was strongly boosted in human and material resources to spy on and report any person likely to criticize the government. This was state terrorism characterized by the disappearance of civilians, arbitrary detention, assassinations, poisoning, and motor vehicle "accidents." Newspapers were closed down and politicians mysteriously died in such car "accidents"; in addition, fully equipped places for torture were operated. While all of this was going on, the majority of the population preferred to keep silent and to tell lies and flatter the authorities in order to survive. The government, on its part, had to surround itself with trusty people, confining strategic positions to those ready to defend their own interests, and excluding anyone likely to betray it.

## MOBILIZATION OF
## GOVERNMENT SUPPORT

The most successful example of the self-protection strategy practiced by the people in power was the creation of the Interahamwe militia. Whereas for the ruling class, it was a strategy to keep itself in power, for the militia, who were essentially young desperados, lawless, and lacking any moral values, it was an opportunity to get rich through the looting of other people's property, thus improving their economic standing. They were taught how to use firearms and they received favors that they could never have hoped for during normal times. Tired of the endless, political wrangling and having no future to look forward to, they were easily manipulated. The ruling elite recruited their followers among "half schooled youths, without any sense of direction and easily lured by money, alcohol and Indian hemp" (Liberation Journal, 1994). Perhaps, for the youths, it was their revenge against an oppressive system. Unfortunately, their energies were directed against a scapegoat, the Tutsi, who themselves had always been victims of the system.

## PREJUDICE AGAINST
## THE RURAL POPULATION

The poor Rwandan population, like that everywhere else in Africa, is considered immature, unintelligent, and incapable of reasoning and of undertaking any responsible action. So there is always the administration, the political authorities and intellectuals, to speak on their behalf and show them what to do. According to Kabiligi (1997), "lack of popular opinion constitutes a strong potential for violence. When people are not able to express themselves either in words, or in acts in a society, because there are always intellectuals to do it for them and tell them what to do, it is normal that they accumulate resentment and dissatisfaction that end up exploding in an uncontrollable manner as soon as there is an opportunity."

The ethnic prejudice maintained by the political regimes for a long time was used to justify their use of power, to divert the attention of civilians from the true causes of the national malaise, and especially to cover up a second prejudice that was in operation. In the words of Peter Uvin (1998, pp. 128–129): "Besides ethnic prejudice, there exists another very pronounced prejudice that is never mentioned among the Rwandan society, because it is accepted as normal, the prejudice of the so-called "évolués," the city people, the educated, developed, civilized against their rural counterparts, who are uneducated, under-developed." The poor are considered as backward and treated as such. This can be observed everywhere from government office and courtroom, to medical clinic and even taxicab.

## HUMILIATION AND LOSS OF SELF-ESTEEM

These politics of exclusion, of discrimination against the majority of the population, and the rejection of their fundamental rights have created among these people feelings of frustration, inhibition, and humiliation, for the intellectuals show contempt for their thinking capacity, and their work as farmers. Indeed, the term peasant "umuturage" in the national language has acquired a pejorative connotation meaning an ignoramus, someone uncouth and without education.

Quite understandably, feelings of inferiority vis-à-vis the évolués have been strongly internalized by the rural poor who feel small before them, do not think of contradicting them, and, worse still, try to reject their own values to emulate the lifestyle of the évolués. In humble submission to their power, they confess their ignorance before the authorities and the intellectuals. They have lost pride in themselves and look to the city-dwellers and intellectuals as models for their own lives. The social norms no longer have anything to do with personal values of dignity and self-esteem, of respect for commitment; what matters instead is the level of formal education, the job that one has, and the material possessions one owns, irrespective of the way they were acquired. In this way the human values that constituted the individual and social equilibrium have been seriously eroded.

In the light of what has been said here, structural violence against the poor majority by the rich, powerful minority is the root cause of civil war and the terrible massacres in Rwanda. Peace education therefore has to bring about a radical change in structure and power relations in order to replace the culture of violence by the culture of peace.

## A CULTURE OF PEACE AND PEACE EDUCATION

Many organizations working in Rwanda are convinced that peace education is a crucial element for building a culture of peace and further that in order to achieve significant results, peace education has to address the social and political imbalance between those in power and the rest of the people. There has to be a persistent process of changing relationships, behaviors, and attitudes. Indeed, peace education differs from classical education in the sense that it goes beyond the acquisition of knowledge to actively transforming one's surroundings, thus representing action taken to transform systems of inequality into power sharing and more democratic structures. Peace education represents an attitude that aims at eradicating prejudice among individuals, promoting tolerance and solidarity. Peace education represents a socializing process, through which children acquire values of democracy, freedom, and self-determination and learn to live in a multicultural society that acknowledges the value of different cultures.

The following is an example of a peace activity carried out by ACORD (Agency for Cooperation and Research in Development) in the Great Lakes Region (Rwanda, Burundi, and Congo). The project aimed to:

- Reduce prejudice and stereotyping in different ethnic groups
- Support local peace initiatives
- Promote dialogue and reconciliation between different groups
- Support coalitions and strategic alliances to challenge government rule

The project, comprising a variety of activities at the national and regional levels, has been based on working with ten people from each of the following three countries, Rwanda, Burundi, and Congo, selected on the basis of a number of criteria: their interest in and commitment to peacebuilding, while differing in ethnic and political background; their capacity to influence public policy and their community; and their capacity to carry out peace projects in their respective countries.

Training provides the knowledge and skills to enable members of the group to handle conflict situations. Groups that have undergone training include: 10 members from 10 other organizations; 75 people from human rights; school clubs (60 students and 15 teachers); as well as 30 leaders from a local institution, Abashingantahe, dealing with the internal peace process in Burundi; and a group of 30 Muslim women. Youth organizations for peacebuilding in the community have been founded, as well as women's committees.

Sports, traditional dances, work camps, and open debates afford participants the opportunity to become acquainted and form solid ties in a mixed, ethnic environment. There is use of the media, posters, drama, and video to campaign for peace: A videotape on prejudice was widely broadcast on national television and radio and has been a valuable tool for public education. The project has offered the Hutu and Tutsi an opportunity to discuss sensitive issues freely and to share feelings about the conflict, in a forum that was safe for both ethnic groups. A lot of work has been done behind doors and has been very effective in transforming people's attitudes and feelings.

# CONCLUSION

Attaining and sustaining peace in Rwanda can be achieved. However, we have to bear in mind that more than half a century of violence and incitement to ethnic hatred have become deeply entrenched in the national psyche and cannot be done away with overnight. The people of Rwanda have suffered at the hands of those in power for more than 50 years, from poverty, subjection to humiliation, prejudice, and institutionalized violence that have culminated in genocide of unprecedented magnitude on the African continent.

We believe that there is an urgent need for positive change and that this role can be played by peace education. Just like other people, the people of Rwanda need peace. They need to live as a free society, devoid of all forms of prejudice, exploitation, manipulation, and fear. They need to live a decent life, to recover their cultural and moral values; mostly they need to recover their humanity.

Peacebuilding is a long and arduous process, but a sustained effort and support can achieve a culture of peace. Peace education is a step in the right direction for Rwanda and its people, and there are already some signs in the way of positive changes of attitudes and feelings among people that have come into contact with the project. As the Chinese saying goes, a journey of one thousand miles begins with one step. The culture of war and violence that has been the hallmark of Rwandese society for more than half a century must give way to the culture of peace. This is an imperative that can be achieved through the implementation of this project.

# REFERENCES

Banque, M. (1998). *Etude actualisée de la pauvreté au Rwanda.*

Chambers, R. (1997). Whose Reality Counts? London: UK Intermediate Technology Publications.

Chrétien, J. P. (1994). Journal Libération du 26/04/1994

Guillaumin, C. (1990). L'idéologie Raciste: Institut d'études et de recherches Interethniques et culturelles. The Hague, Netherlands: Mouton de Gruyter.

Kabiligi, L. (1997, June). *The Great Lakes sub-region: A world in need of rethinking?* Paper presented at Regional Conference on Peace, Burundi.

Kabiligi, L., (1994, June). *Génocide au Rwanda: Une honte pour l'humanité. Reflexions d'un responsable d'une ONG sous-régionale.* Paper presented at regional NGO's meeting Bujumbura.

Lemarchand, R. (1970). *Burundi and Rwanda.* New York: Praeger

Lemarchand, R. (1996). Power and Stratification in Rwanda: A Reconsideration. Cahiers d'Etudes Africaines 24, 6:592–610.

Uvin, P. (1998). Aiding violence: The development enterprise in Rwanda. Bloomfield, CT: Kumarian Press.

# 21

# South Africa: The Truth and Reconciliation Commission as a Model of Peace Education

## Penny Enslin
*School of Education,*
*University of Witwatersrand*

How can the work of South Africa's Truth and Reconciliation Commission (TRC) be taken up as a model of peace education? In considering this question, both in the context of South Africa and more broadly, I reflect on Gabi Solomon's account of features of peace education (1999), showing both the ways in which the TRC exemplifies peace education and considering the extent to which it does actually constitute such a model.[1]

## THE TRC: AIMS, PROCESS, AND FINDINGS

The term *peace education* is not widely used in South Africa, but there are good grounds for claiming that our TRC constitutes a definitive moment in the transition from the old Apartheid order to a new and more peaceful one. One respected commentator has described the TRC as "destined for a place in history. Certainly

---

[1]The account in this chapter of the work and findings of the TRC draws on "Citizenship, identity and myth" (Enslin, 2000). The central argument in that article is against citizenship education aimed at developing national identity through myth making and does not address the theme of peace education.

it is the most important political testament to emerge from South Africa and I suspect that to describe it as one of the most important documents of the 20th century is to judge conservatively" (Beresford, 1998, p. 22). Interest in the TRC by the international academic community suggests that part of its significance lies in its potential as an example to be followed in other, similar contexts of transition from oppression to democracy.

Several societies in transition to democracy, such as Chile and South Africa, have established truth and reconciliation commissions as a way of dealing with a painful past and fostering a new order.

The objectives of the Commission were to conduct inquiries into "gross human rights violations" between 1960 and the transition to democracy in 1994, establishing the identity of persons, organizations, and institutions involved in these violations, whether or not they were the result of deliberate planning, and inquiring into who was accountable for them—that is, to come to terms with our history and to deal with its legacy. The most conspicuous part of the Commission's work was conducted by the Human Rights Violations Committee, which heard the accounts of victims and conducted investigations. Over a period of $2\frac{1}{2}$ years, the Commission conducted hearings across the country. Its findings draw on over 21,000 statements on human rights' violations, as well as other documents such as applications for amnesty. The latter, especially from a large number of security policemen, provided information that proved difficult to obtain by other means. As a process, the Commission was a compelling and unique spectacle. Over months of public hearings, with comprehensive and often disturbing coverage in the media, the victims of human rights' violations, or their relations, told their stories, as did some of the perpetrators. In some of the TRC's more dramatic moments, the victims were able to confront their former torturers.

In its aims and general features, the TRC is clearly an exercise in peace education. As Salomon (1999) points out, one of the distinguishing features of peace education is that it deals with conflict between groups based on a combination of ethnic hostilities and historical inequities. It also sets out to deal with deep divisions and addresses narratives that have "a traumatic, painful, historical dimension to them" (p. 5). By involving many ordinary people who spoke at and attended the hearings, as well as by enabling members of the public to follow them through the print and electronic media, the hearings became a process of public education.

The Report of the TRC observes that "the Apartheid system was maintained through repressive means, depriving the majority of South Africans of the most basic human rights, including civil, political, social and economic rights" (Independent Newspapers, 1998b, p. 2). The consequences of this general deprivation of rights were many: economic deprivation and poor living conditions, physical and psychological trauma resulting from conflict between the state and its opponents, arrests, abductions, detention, restrictions, exile, loss of breadwinners, physical injuries and disabilities, and homelessness caused by the destruction of homes and the displacement of families in intracommunity violence (ibid., p. 3).

The main focus of the Commission's work was gross violations of human rights, which it found "were perpetrated and facilitated by all the major role-players in the conflicts of the mandate era" (ibid., p. 6), including the state and its security and law-enforcement agencies, homeland governments, conservative surrogate organizations, White right-wing organizations, liberation movements, and nonstate paramilitary formations.

Most of the major participants are criticized not only for their actions but also for their response to the attempts by the Commission to establish responsibility for the injustices of the past. Leaders of the former state lacked an appreciation of the extent of both the violations and the massive suffering they caused. The former state had the active and passive support of the White electorate. Although it was critical of most organizations to varying degrees—including the African National Congress and its internal allies—the Commission's primary finding was that "The predominant portion of gross violations of human rights was committed by the former State through its security and law-enforcement agencies" (ibid., p. 6).

In arguing that the main responsibly for human rights' violations rests with the former state and its associates, the Commission distinguished between the conduct of the state and the liberation movements, arguing that Apartheid was a crime against humanity, that it had been the state that had engendered violent conflict, and that its actions should be assessed against higher standards of conduct because it was the legally constituted government. Rejecting the arguments of some members of the liberation movements, it recognized the notion of a just war in appraising their conduct but found that "a just war does not exempt an organization from pursuing its goals through just means" (ibid., p. 6).

The Commission established the truth about many events of the Apartheid years; unanswered questions about prominent political murders and disappearances were answered. Victims and perpetrators told their stories, the latter with varying degrees of honesty. Although the Report states that its task was not to write the history of the country, it was quite successful in its efforts "to expose the violations of all parties in an attempt to lay the basis for a culture in which human rights are respected and not violated" (Independent Newspapers, 1998c, p. 2). Compiling an accurate account of events was seen as a crucial prerequisite for reconciliation: "there can be no genuine, lasting reconciliation without truth" (ibid., p. 6). A driving motive of the Commission's work was to acknowledge suffering and allocate responsibility for it.

## TRUTH AND RECONCILIATION?

Did the TRC succeed in revealing the truth and has it fostered reconciliation? There is disagreement on both issues. The Commission has been criticized for its reliance on unverified statements made in applications for amnesty and on unsubstantiated statements made by victims, few of them given under oath and few tested under cross-examination (Jeffrey, 1999). Some have responded that such criticism of the TRC misses the point: The value of the Commission's work lies in the process that it oversaw, of the telling of stories by survivors or their families, and of the resulting shift in Whites' perceptions of the past (Du Preez, 1999).

The debate about whether and in what sense the Commission revealed the truth is set to continue. So too will the controversy about whether the TRC has produced reconciliation. For some it did. The Report presents the telling of their stories by victims of violations as a process of healing through truth telling. Such a story is that of Lukas Baba Sikwepere, shot in the face and blinded in a settlement near Cape Town and later tortured by the police: "I feel that what has been making me sick all the time is the fact that I couldn't tell my story. But now it feels like I got my sight back by coming here and telling you the story" (Independent Newspapers, 1998c, p. 6).

Hennie Smit's 8-year-old son was killed by a bomb planted at a shopping center in Amanzimtoti. Smit said: "We buried him in Pretoria. I told newspapers that I thought my son was a hero because he died for freedom for people. . . . He died in the cause of the oppressed people. A lot of people criticized me for this. They said that I was a traitor, and they condemned me, but I still feel that way today. . . ." (ibid., pp. 7–8). Smit reported to the Commission his relief, on meeting the parents of the boy who had planted the bomb, that he bore them no grudge.

In a more complex tale, former political detainee, Alwinu Mralasi, told the Commission how he encountered by chance, after 5 years, the man who had given false testimony against him. Set on revenge and with his knife ready, he planned to kill his accuser, but found him changed and unable to speak: "And I asked my wife to take out one pound and give it to this man so that he could buy food for himself. And that was the last I saw of him. He never went back to his house. He went to the hospital and that was the end of his life" (Independent Newspapers, 1998c, p. 7).

## MATERIAL FOR PEACE EDUCATION

Stories like these present compelling evidence of reconciliation. Even alone, they provide powerful material for peace education. Gabi Salomon argues (1999, p. 6) that in its best form, peace education sets out to change people's attitudes and behaviors toward the *other*. The four kinds of closely interrelated outcomes of peace education identified by Salomon are strongly evident in the TRC's work. First, a willingness to accept the narrative provided by the other as well as its implications is manifest in the shift in Whites' perception of the past, as claimed by Du Preez (1999). It is also apparent in Hennie Smit's story of how he came to see the loss of his son as a contribution to the cause of the oppressed, a cause of which he had not until then been so aware. Second, in the narratives of both Smit and Mralasi, empathy is achieved against the odds—between Smit and the parents of his son's killer, and on Mralasi's part toward his betrayer. Third, if Du Preez is right, the TRC accomplished, through a shift in Whites' attitudes, a willingness to acknowledge the culpability of the state that most Whites had supported. Such a shift was also expressed in the actions of those perpetrators of violations who showed remorse for their actions. Fourth, the TRC's insistence that all the major players, though primarily and emphatically the Apartheid state, should take some responsibility for violation of human rights during the mandate period reflects a determination to see the conflict and the actions of its various participants in what Salomon calls relativistic rather than absolute terms.

One possible approach that peace education could take in the wake of the TRC would be to try to remove the very attitudes to the *other* that led to the human rights' abuses investigated by the TRC. This could be undertaken, it might be argued, by basing peace education on the development of a common identity based on a national myth. However, such myth making would not be a defensible approach to otherness. First, given the degree of falsification it would require in a society still so divided, it would be likely to undermine the teaching of autonomy and critical thinking (see Enslin, 2000). Second, Aletta Norval (1998) argues that the exercise of understanding the memory work of the TRC, "[i]n contrast to the usual constructions of memories of a nation's past... has no *singular* past and commemorates no one *unified* nationhood" (1998, p. 258, emphasis in original). Instead, she observes: "This memory work... contains the seeds of a relation to the past and to memory which may lead South Africa to a *post-national* conception of identity; a conception of identity characterised by the distance it takes from that which was exemplary in the identitarian conception that informed Apartheid" (Norval, 1998, p. 259, emphasis in original).

Another sense in which the TRC exemplifies peace education is in the way the process followed by the TRC involved people by allowing their voices to be heard, enacting a communicative model of democracy (Young, 1996) that was inclusive and attentive to difference. Its didactic value lies thus in its commitment to deliberation rather than violence. South Africa is now a far less militarized society than it was.

A corrective orientation to the future (Salomon, 1999, p. 15) is evident in the TRC's recommendations. The Report observes that for reconciliation to be achieved, extensive healing and social and political reconstruction is required at every level of society. Although conceding that reconciliation will be a complex and long-term process, it recommends a number of steps that are necessary for its achievement. One is that if reconciliation is to have a chance of succeeding, a human rights' culture will have to be developed and ought to be included in the formal education curriculum (Independent Newspapers, 1998c, p. 2). Another is that all the Commission's records be preserved and made available to the public, including on a Web site and at decentralized *centers of memory* (p. 2).

The Commission recommends the following measures to foster reconciliation: The alleviation of poverty, closing the gap between the advantaged and the disadvantaged, and allowing those who have benefited from past exploitation to contribute. This will require the creation of job opportunities. There must be a commitment to transformation in both the corporate sphere and government structures like prisons, health care, the justice system, and the security forces. Assistance should be extended to victims and survivors, in the form of reparations and rehabilitation as well as apologies for human rights' abuses, including those committed by the liberation movements. Rehabilitation should include those falsely accused of being informers and collaborators that were ostracized from their communities.

# THE TRC AS A MODEL
# OF PEACE EDUCATION

In asking how the work of the TRC in South Africa can be taken up as a model for peace education, two subquestions are raised: its significance for peace education within South Africa, and its applicability in pursuit of peace education to other societies.

As far as the question of the TRC as a model for peace education in South Africa itself goes, the discussion so far has indicated a number of ways in which it has indeed been a powerful model for peace education, even as an event in itself. This constitutes both its great strength and a drawback. For the powerful impact of the TRC lies to a considerable extent in the event itself as it unfolded. Where it provided actual contact between perpetrators and victims, especially where forgiveness was possible, it was a symbolic moment in the cause of fostering peace. But for most of the population, the country's demography dictates that regular contact with the other remains as uncommon as before. For those who were not part of the process, even allowing for creative ways in which the school curriculum can potentially use the stories of the TRC to telling effect, the likely future impact of the TRC is less clear.

For learners in schools, many of the issues raised by the TRC are morally very complex, and an effective peace education program in schools would also need strong emphasis on civic competence and life skills in general. A further difficulty in relating the TRC to peace education as part of the school curriculum lies in the state of many of our schools, which are still so dysfunctional that peace education may have a better chance of succeeding through less formal initiatives, especially the mass media.

It is also important to bear in mind that factors that continue to undermine peace and have no obvious link with the TRC remain a serious obstacle to peace education. South African society is still prey to endemic violence and crime, including in many of its schools. Domestic violence is common and so conceptually remote from the TRC in people's perceptions that it has to be tackled in a campaign of its own. We have not succeeded in addressing the problem of racism. There is a long road ahead in addressing a number of issues whose solution cannot come by means of the TRC and its impact.

Finally, is South Africa's TRC a model for peace education in other societies similarly plagued by violence and deep division? Peace education is an imperative in all societies similarly prone to structural and other forms of violence. But distinctive of South Africa's TRC was its context—that of a negotiated transition to democracy, reflecting the need for a profound change in the prevailing power relationships. For other divided societies contemplating possible lessons of this TRC, it could be observed that such a model of peace education is not transferable in the absence of similar major changes in the power relations between diverse groups in conflict with one another.

# REFERENCES

Beresford, D. (1998, November 6–12). How could they try to gag history? *Mail & Guardian*, Johannesburg.

Du Preez, M. (1999, July 29). TRC healed and opened eyes. *The Star*.

Enslin, P. (2000). Citizenship, identity and myth: Educational implications of South Africa's Truth and Reconciliation Commission. *Change: Transformations in Education, 3*(1), 80–90.

Independent Newspapers and the Institute for Democracy in South Africa. (1998a). *Truth and Reconciliation Report Extract, 1*, Johannesburg, 2 November.

Independent Newspapers and the Institute for Democracy in South Africa. (1998b). *Truth and Reconciliation Report Extract, 4*, Johannesburg, 5 November.

Independent Newspapers and the Institute for Democracy in South Africa. (1998c). *Truth and Reconciliation Report Extract, 5*, Johannesburg, 6 November.

Ismail, S., & Grossman, J. (1998). Liberation now! Education later! Militants of the Bonteheuwel Military Wing reflect on aspects of their struggle. In J. van der Vyver (Ed.), *Facing the Millennium: Education at/on the edge. Selected papers from the joint Kenton Association/Southern African Society for Education Conference* (pp. 173–189). Kei Mouth.

Jeffrey, A. (1999). *The truth about the Truth Commission*. Johannesburg: South African Institute of Race Relations.

Norval, A. (1998). Memory, identity and the (im)possibility of reconciliation: The work of the Truth and Reconciliation Commission in South Africa. *Constellations, 5*(2), 250–256.

Salomon, G. (1999, May). *Research on peace education: Provocative questions, challenging criteria*. Paper presented at the NCPRC meeting, Phoenix, AZ.

Young, I. M. (1996). Communication and the other: Beyond deliberative democracy. In S. Benhabib (Ed.), *Democracy and difference: Contesting the boundaries of the political* (pp. 120–135). Princeton: Princeton University Press.

# IV

# The Research

# 22

# Head-first versus Feet-first in Peace Education

## Clark McCauley
### *Bryn Mawr College*

Peace education is a broad conception, linking individual and group goals that may include personal and spiritual growth, interpersonal and intergroup conflict resolution, and even political and cultural transformation. A large part of what actually goes on in peace education, however, may be much narrower than the sweep of conceptualizations might suggest. It appears that the most common form of peace education, both in and out of schools, is some variety of small-group workshop. This paper reflects on the surprising fact that such workshops aim to change hearts and minds of participants, but typically offer little support for behavior change.

## DIVERSITY WORKSHOPS

In the United States, the most common form of peace education is a small-group intervention that brings members of different ethnic groups together for a period of a few hours or, at most, a few days. These interventions are usually called diversity training or diversity workshops but may also be referred to as anti-bias training or multicultural training. In 1998 a national survey found that about two thirds of U.S. 4-year colleges and universities were offering or requiring some form of diversity workshop for their students (McCauley, Wright, & Harris, 2000). Similar workshops are increasingly popular in primary and secondary schools and in corporate settings (McCauley & Wright, 1999). It appears that diversity workshops may be the fastest growing innovation in the history of U.S. education.

In their campus survey, McCauley et al. (2000) found that the most commonly reported workshop activities were as follows: Participants sharing stories of their own experiences with bias or discrimination (reported by 92% of campuses using diversity workshops), group exercises for exploring ethnic differences (87%), written information on handouts (86%), personal contact with minority participants (82%), lectures (75%), discussion of actual campus incidents (73%), role playing or behavioral training (71%), videos (68%), and skits (67%). Notable in this list of workshop activities is the relatively small emphasis given to behavior; role playing or behavioral training is number seven in the top ten activities. In contrast, the number one activity focuses on affective learning in sharing of stories of bias and discrimination. The goal of the workshops, judged by the list of activities, is to change the feelings and beliefs of the participants, both about individual outgroup members participating in the workshop and about the outgroup as a whole.

Workshop effectiveness is currently unknown. McCauley et al. (2000) did not find any college or university conducting research on the impact of their workshops, although participants are often asked whether they liked the workshop or thought it worthwhile. McCauley and Wright (1999) found only one published experiment assessing the impact of a diversity workshop for undergraduate participants, and the results showed no difference between the workshop group and a control group (Neville & Furlong, 1994). Two correlational studies of U.S. undergraduates found small tendencies for workshop participants to be more positive about ethnic minorities than nonparticipants (Astin, 1993; Pascarella, Edison, Nora, Hagedorn, & Terenzini, 1996), but the observed correlations may be a result of self-selection such that students more positive about minorities are more likely to participate in a workshop. McCauley and Wright concluded that there is no evidence that diversity workshops are having any effect on the beliefs, attitudes, or behaviors of the millions of workshop participants.

Diversity workshops are not just an American idiosyncrasy. The Haifa Conference brought reports from Belgium (Johan Leman), Croatia (Dinka Corkalo), Northern Ireland (Edward Cairns), South Africa (Merle Friedman), and Israel (Daniel Bar-On, Sarah Ozacky, Marwan Darweish, Ifat Maoz, and Baruch Nevo) about peace education programs that are similarly based on bringing small groups of individuals together from two groups in conflict. In these programs, as in the United States, the focus is on changing perceptions of and feelings about the outgroup by developing personal relationships between ingroup and outgroup participants in the workshop. As Allport (1954) put it, the contact is designed to develop perceptions of shared humanity among participants.

# TWO ASSUMPTIONS OF DIVERSITY WORKSHOPS

Given the popularity of diversity workshops in the United States and in many other countries, and given that the effectiveness of these workshops is currently unknown, it is worth examining some of the premises of this innovative form of peace education.

## The Problem Is Hostility to the Outgroup

The first assumption is that the crucial obstacle to improving relations between groups is the sum of individuals' negative beliefs and feelings about outgroup members. These are what the workshops aim to change.

A contrary perspective is that the crucial support of group conflict is devotion to the ingroup. As long as individuals are in the position of choosing between the welfare of the ingroup and the welfare of the outgroup, conflict may be inevitable. This is a perspective that comes directly from recent research on minimal groups, such as can be created by flipping a coin to assign group membership. The theoretical developments from minimal groups' research, Social Identity Theory and Social Categorization Theory, focus particularly on the ingroup implications of the boundary between ingroup and outgroup (Brewer & Brown, 1998). The same focus on the ingroup comes from research on men in combat, who, in relation to minimal groups, may be thought of as maximal groups. Soldiers fight and kill less because of hatred for the enemy than because of attachment to their own group, especially attachment to the small group of buddies in their squad or fire team (Stouffer et al., 1949).

For both minimal and maximal groups, then, it appears that conflict arises more from perceived threat to the ingroup than from perceived, negative qualities of the outgroup. The implication for peace education is that learning about the positive qualities of outgroup individuals may do little to reduce group conflict. Rather it is the perception and the reality of mutual threat that must be addressed.

## The Solution Is Increased Contact

If negative perceptions of the outgroup are what has to be changed, the next assumption is that more contact with members of the outgroup is the best means of effecting the desired change. This is the essence of Allport's (1954) contact hypothesis. Research has made clear that, for contact to improve relations between groups, the contact must be personal, equal status, cooperative, and authority supported. Probably most important is the requirement that contact should include cooperation for common goals; unfortunately, this is also the condition most difficult to arrange for an ad hoc group such as a workshop with a lifetime of only a few hours or a few days.

Even these four conditions are probably not enough. Stephan (1985) reviews research indicating that the necessary conditions for effective contact must be extended to 13 or more, including equal numbers of each group in the contact situation, equal status outside as well as inside the contact situation, and success in attaining the common goal sought by cooperation. Although there is some evidence suggesting that intergroup friendships can improve intergroup attitudes (Pettigrew, 1998), it is not clear that contact situations as brief as a few hours or even a few days can support the development of such friendships. Thus research on the contact hypothesis does not offer much support for the idea that intergroup contact in brief workshops will reduce group conflict.

## WINNING HEARTS AND MINDS

Although the two assumptions of diversity workshops can be questioned, they are consistent and mutually reinforcing in that they are both cast at the level of the individual. If group conflict is just individual beliefs and feelings writ large, then the solution to group conflict is interpersonal contact under circumstances that will change individual beliefs and feelings. Taken together, the two assumptions lead to workshops aimed at winning the minds and hearts of participants. In this section I examine the mechanics of changing hearts and minds—the theory of persuasion that I believe lies behind many of the exercises in diversity workshops, at least in the United States and perhaps elsewhere as well.

In brief, the theory that can be discerned in diversity workshops is this: New information changes beliefs, new beliefs change attitudes, and new attitudes change behavior. In a workshop, getting to know individuals from the outgroup will change beliefs (stereotypes) about these individuals and their group; the new beliefs will change feelings (attitudes) toward these individuals and their group; and the new feelings will change behaviors toward these individuals and their group. Unfortunately, this "hearts and minds" pathway has long been recognized as unreliable (Abelson, 1972), and it may be obstructed by special problems in the context of diversity workshops.

## Information May Not Compel Belief Change

Stereotypes are beliefs about group characteristics. Although they were originally theorized as pictures in our heads that apply to every member of a stereotyped group, stereotypes are almost never held as 100% generalizations. Today stereotypes are theorized as probabilistic predictions about group differences (McCauley,

Stitt, & Segal, 1980). Once the picture metaphor is gone, there is no reason to expect that meeting a few outgroup members who do not fit the stereotype will lead to revision of the stereotype. A few exceptions only "prove" the rule, when the rule is probabilistic. Indeed, revising a population prediction on the basis of a small nonrandom sample is the kind of mistake that Kahneman and Tversky (1973) have ridiculed as the Law of Small Numbers—treating small sample results as if they are as informative as large sample results. One way people dodge this error is by creating a new subtype for outgroup members who do not fit the stereotype: A grandmother wearing tennis shoes and driving a muscle car can be categorized as a little old lady from Pasadena, leaving untouched the Whistler's mother stereotype of a grandmother as a gray-haired lady of somber dress reposed in a rocking chair.

Of course stereotypes do change, notably as a result of changes in intergroup relations, as, for instance, World War II changed U.S. stereotypes of Japanese and Germans for a while (Gilbert, 1951; Karlins, Coffman, & Walters, 1969; Katz & Braly, 1933). But stereotype change resulting from brief or even extended personal experience with members of the stereotyped group has not been easy to find (Schwartzwald, Amir, & Crain, 1992; Triandis & Vassiliou, 1967). It may be that changing stereotypes is about as difficult as Kahneman and Tversky could hope.

In diversity workshops, the difficulty of changing stereotypes arises as an issue of generalizability. If workshop participants develop new perceptions of the outgroup members in their workshop, does this learning generalize to perceptions of the outgroup as a whole? The obvious alternative is that the new perceptions are limited to the new acquaintances within the workshop. Another possibility is that participants protect larger outgroup stereotypes by creating new subtypes: Workshops in Israel, for instance, may lead to distinguishing moderate Palestinians from Palestinians and liberal Jews from Jews. The Law of Small Numbers may not be very powerful when it comes to changing stereotypes.

## Belief Change May Not Compel Attitude Change

Starting with studies of World War II propaganda, there are many persuasion studies that show strong effects on belief but weak or nonsignificant effects on attitude. In a classic of this genre, Hovland, Lumsdaine, and Sheffield (1949) found that the "Battle of Britain" (a film in Frank Capra's "Why We Fight" series for U.S. troops) had strong effects on soldiers' knowledge about the facts of Royal Air Force heroism but no effect on attitude toward the British as allies. Similarly, Patterson and McClure (1976), in their landmark study of political advertising, found that television advertisements gave less-involved voters new beliefs about candidates' positions on issues (e.g., for or against decreased military spending) but did not change voters' attitudes on these issues (decreased military spending seen as good or bad). Especially for familiar attitude objects, change in just a few of the many beliefs held about an object cannot be expected to lead to large changes in attitude (Ajzen, 1988). Recent research on more and less effortful reaction to new information further emphasizes the complex relations between new beliefs and changes in attitude (Petty & Wegener, 1998).

In diversity workshops, even if the outgroup comes to be seen as more similar to the ingroup—seen as sharing a common humanity, with common needs, fears, and aspirations—attitude toward the outgroup may remain negative. Realistic group conflict theory (Sherif, Harvey, White, Hood, & Sherif, 1961) can predict hostility between groups even when the groups perceive themselves as similar. Indeed, realistic group conflict may be exacerbated by perceived similarity. "They are more similar to us than I thought," workshop participants may think; "they want what we want—in fact they want what we have!" Just as Sherif et al. moved two experimentally matched groups of boys to conflict by means of competition in a tournament, so similarity is no guarantee against hostility and conflict when groups see themselves in competition for significant resources.

## Changed Attitudes May Not Compel Changed Behavior

In diversity workshops, new perceptions of and more positive attitudes toward the outgroup may have little or no effect on intergroup behavior because of countervailing pressures from other determinants of behavior. These factors notably include habits, perceived norms, and perceived control—how we are used to behaving, how the people we care about want us to behave, and whether we feel capable of behavior consistent with our beliefs and attitudes (Ajzen, 1988; Sabini, 1995, chap. 17). A smoker, for instance, may believe that smoking is unhealthful, may feel negatively toward smoking, and may even be surrounded by family and friends who want the smoker to stop. However, if the smoker sees herself as unable to control her behavior, physically unable to stop smoking, then she will not even try to stop.

As already noted, the behavioral component of persuasion tends to get relatively little attention in diversity workshops. Workshops sometimes include role playing of intergroup relations, but even this may focus more on high-profile incidents than on everyday, campus behaviors.

Suppose a majority individual after a campus diversity workshop is persuaded that he should make more of an effort to interact with minority members. He comes off the end of the lunch line one day with his tray in his hand and thinks about joining an all-minority table. What should he say in approaching the table? How can he join this foreign subculture without appearing a condescending idiot? If the workshop does not prepare him with answers to these questions, does not give him practice with the new behavior, he will be as helpless as the smoker who would like to quit but does not know how.

My brief summary of persuasion research should not leave the conclusion that there is no causal path from belief to feeling to behavior, but only that this path is not the royal road to changing behavior. Particularly in the context of diversity workshops, with groups facing real differences that both sides care about, the progression from perceived similarity to liking to cooperation may be far from certain.

## FEET-FIRST PERSUASION

The hearts and minds approach to reducing intergroup conflict may seem so obvious that it is difficult to imagine an alternative. Nevertheless there is an alternative: A *feet-first* path, which depends on the fact that small steps in a particular direction can be the cause of more and larger steps in the same direction and the development of beliefs and attitudes consistent with these steps (Cialdini, 1993).

## Dissonance

Evidence for the feet-first path begins with the well-studied phenomena of dissonance theory. When we act in a way that is inconsistent with our attitudes and values, we are likely to change our beliefs to rationalize the new behaviors. The motivation for the change is to avoid looking stupid or sleazy, to ourselves or others (Sabini, 1995). Dissonance results depend on some perception of choice; there is no need to rationalize a counterattitudinal behavior that is undertaken for large payment or under duress. The big money or the big threat is sufficient to justify the behavior, and no further rationalization is needed.

Although dissonance research has focused on changed attitudes following upon behavioral commitment, there is good reason to believe that dissonance can also lead from behavioral commitment to more behavior in the same direction. One variation of Milgram's famous obedience study, for instance, had a supposed other subject rather than the experimenter come up with the idea of increasing the shock level each time the "learner" made a mistake. In this variation, shock giving was less than the 60% level found in the standard Milgram paradigm, but still 20% of subjects continued raising the shock level all the way to the maximum 450 volts "XXX-Dangerous-Strong-Shock." In this variation, the authority of the experimenter cannot explain the shock giving; rather it appears to be the graded escalation of shock that is the explanation. There is no reason not to give the first few, low-level shocks, and the levels are so close together (15-volt increments) that each shock given becomes a reason to give the next shock. The subject is on a slippery slope where refusing to give the next level of shock must imply at least something stupid or sleazy about having given the last, similar, level of shock. This is a psychology of escalating commitment, with dissonance lurking beneath the staircase (McCauley & Segal, 1987).

## Foot in the Door

Possibly related to dissonance theory is the "foot in the door" (FITD) approach
to behavior change. In its original demonstration (Freedman & Fraser, 1966), the
FITD effect was obtained by sending an experimenter door to door in a suburban
neighborhood, asking a sample of homeowners to display in their windows a
$3 \times 3$ inch sign that said "Be A Safe Driver." All accepted the small sign. A
week or two later another experimenter went to the same homes, and, showing
a photograph of a large clumsily lettered sign saying "Drive Carefully," asked
homeowners if he could stake a sign like this into their front yard. A remarkable
76% said yes, whereas a random control group who were approached only with
the large-sign request produced only 17% agreement.

In this experiment, random assignment to groups allows a clear conclusion
that saying yes to the first small request was a cause of saying yes to the later
large request. Similar experiments have shown that accepting a pin advertising a
cause, or signing a petition for a cause, can cause increased money donation to the
cause at a later time (Pliner, Hart, Kohl, & Saari, 1974; Schwartzwald, Bizman,
& Moshe, 1983). The power of the FITD is such that Cialdini (1993), a leading
persuasion expert, tries to avoid even signing a petition for any cause he is not
ready to support more fulsomely.

## Reciprocity

Finally, the power of the "reciprocity rule" makes it a prime source of behavioral
escalations for both positive and negative behaviors (Cialdini, 1993). In cultures
around the world, people expect, get, and naturalize the return of good for good
and harm for harm. Krishnas pressing gifts into the hands of travelers in airports,
cold-calling salesmen who mail you a crisp dollar bill a few days before they
call, individuals seeking revenge, and clans waging vendetta—all are expressing
their confidence in the demand for reciprocity. If observation were not enough
on this point, there are experiments. Regan (1971), for instance, brought pairs
of undergraduates into the lab for a survey study. While on break, one "subject"
(experimental confederate) went out for a soda and brought back two, giving one,
unsolicited, to the real subject. Later the same confederate asked the subject if
he would buy a raffle ticket for a charity. Compared with the subject of a control
condition in which no soda was gifted, the gifted subject bought on average one
more raffle ticket. Because the tickets were 25 cents each and the sodas 10 cents
each, the average profit from the reciprocity rule was 15 cents; that is, reciprocity
returned more than double the value of the gift.

The conclusion from this fast look at the feet-first approach is that past behavior
can become a reason for and a cause of future behavior. Studies of dissonance,
FITD, and reciprocity all point to the power of small steps to motivate larger steps in
the same direction. The implication for diversity workshops is that behavior toward

outgroup members in the contact situation can become a reason for similar behavior toward outgroup members after workshop participants return home. New behaviors that can be practiced in the home environment should be particularly powerful in moving participants to more positive behavior toward outgroup members. Feet-first persuasion may be worth considering as an alternative to the minds-and-hearts road to improving intergroup relations.

# IMPLICATIONS FOR PRACTICE AND RESEARCH

Organizers of diversity workshops commonly recognize a reentry problem: the difficulty workshop participants face in putting their new feelings and beliefs into practice once they leave the workshop and return to their homes. This problem has several dimensions. Already noted is the question of whether the positive relations with outgroup individuals in the workshop will generalize to positive beliefs and feelings about outgroup members generally. If there is generalization, what opportunities for expressing the new relation to the outgroup are available on return to the home community? If there are opportunities, what new behaviors are participants competent to perform?

For groups in conflict, or even for groups marked by strong cultural differences, the home environment usually offers little contact with members of the outgroup. This indeed is why the workshops are seen as necessary. The rare opportunities for contact usually offer little support for positive behavior toward the outgroup; indeed, the norms and habits of the home community are likely to support antagonistic behavior toward the outgroup.

At the Haifa Conference, Ed Cairns told a story both amusing and illuminating. At the end of a peace education workshop in a city in Northern Ireland, Protestant and Catholic boys together are being returned to their home neighborhoods by bus. At one stop, a boy's friends run up to greet him as he descends from the bus. This whole group, including the boy who just stepped off the bus, then turns to shout ethnic slurs and throw stones at the bus as it pulls away. This boy *is* the reentry problem, and he solves it in the only way that leaves him a chance of behaving more positively another day.

The weakness of the behavioral component of diversity workshops is a substantial part of the reentry problem. A new heart and a new mind will not change behavior without some support and practice for the new behavior. I am suggesting that no workshop is complete without an effort to prepare participants to behave differently once they return to home and ingroup. At a minimum, workshops should encourage small, behavioral commitments to a more positive relation with the outgroup; Givat Haviva, for instance, asks children to make drawings of their conception of peace. More ambitiously, workshop participants might analyze their own behavior in the workshop as a practicum and microcosm of the world they will return to after the workshop (Maoz, 2000).

Another implication of the feet-first approach is that participants in peace education might better be recruited as pairs or small groups of friends or coworkers, rather than as individuals (Lippitt, 1949). Recruiting work teams from an office or production line is relatively easy (Rynes & Rosen, 1995), and recruiting from existing groups in trade unions, church groups, and schools is possible in many circumstances (Maoz, 2000; Mulvihill & Ross, 1999). Nevertheless, many peace education programs, including diversity workshops on U.S. campuses (McCauley et al., 2000), recruit participants as individuals. This issue is important because participants recruited as individuals return to their communities as individuals, where each is likely to feel isolated and helpless as a minority of one facing a majority committed to conflict.

In contrast, participants recruited as a group of friends or coworkers will return to their home community as a nucleus of support for more tolerant views and behaviors. Experimental research on conformity (Asch, 1956) indicates that the power of a unanimous majority is largely broken when the minority individual has even one partner who agrees with her. As Jesus sent apostles out into the world, not singly but two by two, so graduates of peace education might profit by some assurance of social support after their conversion.

Finally, it is worth noting that the feet-first approach to persuasion recognizes the importance of social norms and social structures for understanding intergroup relations. Government and its reward powers in education and the workplace; the judicial system and its punishment powers; corporations, unions, churches, and other private organizations and their power to mediate between individual and state; cultural norms and their determinants of honor and status—these structures sharply constrain the space available for individual action based on individual beliefs and feelings. At the individual level, these structures are normative influences that make some intergroup behaviors easier, some more difficult, and some inconceivable. At the group level, these structures are the expression and organization of ingroup power for violence against the outgroup and—often overlooked in discussions of intergroup conflict—for punishing deviates from ingroup norms. I agree with those at the Haifa Conference who emphasized the need for more attention to group-level issues of law and power; indeed, I have tried to suggest some of the difficulties of diversity workshops focused exclusively at the level of individual beliefs and feelings.

The importance of social structures means that peace education reserved for the individual level must remain an education for people of exceptional strength of character. Heroism is required for an individual with a peaceful heart and peace-willed mind to alone create new behaviors and new norms in a home environment where social norms and social structures are committed to intergroup violence. Heroism is what would have been required for the boy in Northern Ireland to stand back from his friends' stoning his bus from the peace workshop;

heroism to the point of martyrdom would have been required for him to try to stop them.

Peace education must succeed with those of us who do not aspire to heroism.

## ACKNOWLEDGMENTS

Thanks to David Perkins for the "feet-first versus head-first" title, although he should not be held accountable for what I have written beneath his headline. Thanks also to the United States Agency for International Development and to the Solomon Asch Center for Study of Ethnopolitical Conflict for supporting my participation in the Haifa Conference.

## REFERENCES

Abelson, R. (1972). Are attitudes necessary? In B. King & E. McGinnies (Eds.), *Attitudes, conflict, and social change* (pp. 19–32). New York: Academic.

Allport, G. W. (1954). *The nature of prejudice.* Cambridge, MA: Addison-Wesley.

Ajzen, I. (1988). *Attitudes, personality and behavior.* Chicago: Dorsey.

Asch, S. (1956). Studies of independence and conformity: A minority of one against a unanimous majority. *Psychological Monographs, 70* (Whole No. 416).

Astin, A. W. (1993). Diversity and multiculturalism on the campus: How are students affected? *Change, March/April.*

Brewer, M., & Brown, R. J. (1998). Intergroup relations. In D. T. Gilbert, S. T. Fiske, & G. Lindzey (Eds.), *The handbook of social psychology* (4th ed., Vol. 2, pp. 554–594). New York: McGraw-Hill.

Cialdini, R. (1993). *Influence: Science and practice* (3rd ed.). New York: Harper Collins.

Freedman, J. L., & Fraser, S. C. (1966). Compliance without pressure: The foot-in-the-door technique. *Journal of Personality and Social Psychology, 4,* 195–202.

Gilbert, G. M. (1951). Stereotype persistence and change among college students. *Journal of Abnormal and Social Psychology, 46,* 245–254.

Hovland, C. I., Lumsdaine, A. A., & Sheffield, F. D. (1949). *Experiments on mass communication.* Princeton: Princeton University Press.

Kahneman, D., & Tversky, A. (1973). On the psychology of prediction. *Psychological Review, 80,* 237–251.

Karlins, M., Coffman, T. L., & Walters, G. (1969). On the fading of social stereotypes: Studies on three generations of college students. *Journal of Personality and Social Psychology, 13,* 1–16.

Katz, D., & Braly, K. W. (1933). Racial stereotypes of one hundred college students. *Journal of Abnormal and Social Psychology, 28,* 280–290.

Lippitt, R. (1949). *Training in community relations.* New York: Harper.

Maoz, I. (2000). Multiple conflicts and competing agendas: A framework for conceptualizing structured encounters between groups in conflict—The case of a coexistence project of Jews and Palestinians in Israel. *Peace and Conflict: Journal of Peace Psychology, 6,* 135–156.

McCauley, C., Stitt, C. L., & Segal, M. (1980). Stereotyping: From prejudice to prediction. *Psychological Bulletin, 87,* 195–208.

McCauley, C., & Segal, M. (1987). Social psychology of terrorist groups. In C. Hendrick (Ed.), *Review of Personality and Social Psychology* (Vol. 9, pp. 231–256). Beverly Hills, CA: Sage.

McCauley, C., & Wright, M. (1999). Diversity training workshops on campus: A review of recent models and relevant research. Unpublished manuscript.

McCauley, C., Wright, M., & Harris, M. (2000). Diversity workshops on campus: A survey of current practice at U.S. colleges and universities. *College Student Journal, 34,* 100–114.

Mulvihill, R., & Ross, M. H. (1999). Understanding the pluralistic objectives of conflict resolution interventions in Northern Ireland. In M. H. Ross, & J. Rothman (Eds.), *Theory and practice in ethnic conflict management: Theorizing success and failure* (pp. 143–160). London: MacMillan.

Neville, H., & Furlong, M. (1994). The impact of participation in a cultural awareness program on the racial attitudes and social behaviors of first-year college students. *Journal of College Student Development, (35),* 371–377.

Pascarella, E. T., Edison, M., Nora, A., Hagedorn, L. S., & Terenzini, P. T. (1996). Influences on students' openness to diversity and challenge in the first year of college. *Journal of Higher Education, 67*(2), 174–195.

Patterson, T. E., & McClure, R. D. (1976). *The unseeing eye: The myth of television power in national elections.* New York: Putnam.

Pettigrew, T. F. (1998). Intergroup contact theory. *Annual Review of Psychology, 49,* 65–85.

Petty, R. E., & Wegener, D. T. (1998). Attitude change: Multiple roles for persuasion variables. In D. T. Gilbert, S. T. Fiske, & G. Lindzey (Eds.), *The handbook of social psychology* (4th ed., Vol. 1., pp. 323–390). New York: McGraw-Hill.

Pliner, P. H., Hart, H., Kohl, J., & Saari, D. (1974). Compliance without pressure: Some further data on the foot-in-the-door technique. *Journal of Experimental Social Psychology, 10,* 17–22.

Regan, D. T. (1971). Effects of a favor and liking on compliance. *Journal of Experimental Social Psychology, 7,* 627–639.

Rynes, S., & Rosen, B. (1995). A field study of factors affecting the adoption and perceived success of diversity training. *Personnel Psychology, 48,* 247–270.

Sabini, J. (1995). *Social psychology* (2nd ed.). New York: Norton.

Schwartzwald, J., Bizman, A., & Moshe, R. (1983). The foot-in-the-door paradigm: Effects of second request size on donation probability and donor generosity. *Personality and Social Psychology Bulletin, 9,* 181–196.

Schwartzwald, J., Amir, Y., & Crain, R. L. (1992). Long-term effects of school desegregation experiences on interpersonal relations in the Israeli Defense Forces. *Personality and Social Psychology Bulletin, 18,* 357–368.

Sherif, M., Harvey, O. J., White, B. J., Hood, W. R., & Sherif, C. (1961). *Intergroup conflict and cooperation: The Robbers' Cave experiment.* Norman, OK: Oklahoma Book Exchange.

Stephan, W. G. (1985). Intergroup Relations. In G. Lindzey, & E. Aronson (Eds.), *The handbook of social psychology* (Vol. 2, pp. 599–658). New York: Random House.

Stouffer, S. A., Lumsdaine, A. A., Lumsdaine, M. H., Williams, R. M. Jr., Smith, W. B., Jauis, I. L., Starr, S. A., & Cottrell, L. S. Jr. (1949). *The American soldier: conflict and its aftermath.* Princeton: Princeton University Press.

Triandis, H., & Vassiliou, V. (1967). Frequency of contact and stereotyping. *Journal of Personality and Social Psychology, 7,* 316–328.

# 23

# Conceptual Mapping and Evaluation of Peace Education Programs: The Case of Education for Coexistence Through Intergroup Encounters Between Jews and Arabs In Israel

Ifat Maoz

*The Hebrew University of Jerusalem*

## AN OVERVIEW

The goals of this study are twofold—first, to identify basic categories for the conceptual mapping and classification of peace education programs, and second, to define criteria for evaluating what a good peace or coexistence education project is. This study is based on an evaluation research of 47 peace education encounter programs that were conducted in Israel in 1999–2000.

# CONTEXT OF STUDY

Before I begin to describe this study, it is important to define the specific context in which it was done, within the more general domain of peace education. This study concerns education for coexistence through intergroup encounters. This is a specific category of peace education, which is implemented through encounters between two ethnic or national groups. Certainly in Israel this is a very prevalent form of peace education that receives a large if not the major share of the funding for peace education programs.[1]

When looking at peace education through encounters in the context of Jews and Arabs in Israel, it is important to consider the sociopolitical context in which these interventions are done (Bar & Bargal, 1995). Generally, we are dealing with two national groups that live together, side by side, in the same territory, in a situation of conflict over shared resources and of power asymmetry in which one group (the Jewish majority) gets more of these resources.

In this context, peace education encounter programs are somewhat paradoxical endeavors that aim to create a microreality of cooperation and some symmetry in a still prevailing macroreality of conflict and asymmetry. Given this sociopolitical context in which Israeli peace education encounter programs are embedded, it is important to consider, when investigating these programs, issues such as the power relations between the sides, and symmetry and asymmetry in status and participation in the intergroup interaction.

# RESEARCH GOALS

This study had two linked goals: (1) to perform conceptual mapping and classification of models of Jewish–Arab coexistence and peace education implemented by various institutions and organizations in Israel; and (2) to define criteria for evaluating coexistence and peace education activities.

# RESEARCH POPULATION

The research population included some 47 different programs and activities of coexistence-aimed encounters between Jews and Arabs conducted in Israel in the years 1999–2000.[2] The analysis was also informed by a previous study of a decade of encounters between Jewish and Arab teachers (encounters conducted

---

[1] For an earlier comprehensive and key evaluation study conducted on Jewish-Arab encounters see Bar and Bargal, 1995.

[2] These programs were supported by the Abraham Fund.

in the Jerusalem Van Leer Institute between 1983 and 1993; Maoz, 2000a), and by a study of a yearlong, encounter process of Jewish and Arab students led by facilitators from the School of Peace in Neveh Shalom in the framework of an academic course conducted by the author (1998–1999).

Typically, and also in the cases investigated here, coexistence programs include a series of intergroup encounters (conducted at a frequency of once a week to once a month) that go on for a period of at least 3 or 4 months to 1 year. These encounters typically include 5–15 participants from each national group and are facilitated by an Arab and by a Jewish facilitator.

## METHODOLOGY

The methodology used was based on the following: (1) interviews with directors, organizers, facilitators and participants of coexistence encounter activities; (2) observations of encounter activities and analysis of interaction; (3) analysis of documents describing these activities (organizational reports, plans, and grant proposals).

## MAJOR CATEGORIES FOR CLASSIFYING MODELS OF PEACE EDUCATION THROUGH ENCOUNTERS

The following major categories were found as meaningful for classifying peace or coexistence education models.

### Goals of Activity and the Ideology Upon Which It Is Based

A major dimension that was found as meaningful in mapping peace education or coexistence activities was the goals of the activity and its ideology as defined by the directors and implementers of the project. Generally we find two major approaches to peace or coexistence education through encounters. At one end of the continuum, we find traditional, coexistence models that are aimed at getting to know each other, fostering tolerance, reducing stereotypes, and improving intergroup relations and other goals in the spirit of the contact hypothesis (Allport, 1954; Pettigrew, 1998). Whereas these models emphasize, through various devices such as working toward a common goal (Sherif, 1966), themes of togetherness and similarity, we find, at the other end of the continuum, confrontational models that emphasize the conflict between the sides. These models aim at changing the

construction of identities of majority and minority group members, at making the
Jewish majority members more aware of the asymmetric relations and of their role
as oppressors, and empowering the Arab minority members through their direct
confrontation with the Jews (Sonnenschein, Halabi, & Friedman, 1998; Suleiman,
1997).

The first category of activities can easily be traced to theories in intergroup
relations and represents a major model of coexistence or peace education that we
find internationally in several conflict sites (Salomon, 1999). However, the second,
confrontational model exemplifies a dynamic we often see in social or educational
interventions, in which theory lags after practice. We find this model operating in
several, large, coexistence or peace education programs in Israel, but it does not
appear in scientific peace education literature or in descriptions of interventions
done in other conflict sites in the world.

Several conceptual issues can be raised regarding the aforementioned models
of encounters: Should confrontational models be included in the domain of peace
education and on what grounds would we choose to include or not to include
them? What are the advantages and problems of each of the two models? What
scientific theories can we point to that can help us understand and conceptualize
the confrontational model? Finally, which criteria would we use to evaluate the
effectiveness of the confrontational model?

The confrontational model evidently arose from the needs and dynamics of the
field, and it was initially presented by Arab facilitators and participants (Suleiman,
1997) who were later joined by some of their Jewish counterparts (Maoz, 2000a,
2000b). Currently, it occupies a central role in the arena of coexistence activities
in Israel. Given that, it is important to try to conceptualize it better and analyze its
relation to the domain of peace education.

A third mixed model, that includes both coexistence and confrontational
elements, is a model of working through conflict through sharing personal, life
stories of members of one's own group and of members of the other group
(Bar-On, 1999). This model is aimed at deepening the understanding of others
and of the complexity of the relations with them and through that, enabling more
meaningful communication that combines both the interpersonal and the intergroup dimension. This model of encounters has yet to be looked at more closely,
in terms of its effectiveness and in terms of its relation to the two major models
defined earlier.

*Distribution of Activities by Ideological Approach.*    Most of the activities investigated (60% of them) were based on an ideological approach of coexistence. Some 21% of the activities presented a mixed ideological approach that
included both components of coexistence and of confrontation. A small part of the
activities (13% of them) that were all targeted for high school youth or for adults
presented a confrontational ideological approach.

## Age Groups

Another important category for classifying peace education programs is the age group for which they are targeted. In this study, the following, major, target age groups were identified: (1) preschool, (2) first to fourth grade, (3) fifth to eight grade, (4) youth, ninth to twelfth grade, and (5) adults (the last category included mainly teachers, student teachers, and women groups).

*Distribution of Activities Among Age Groups.* The distribution of activities among age groups was as follows: 8.5% of the activities were targeted for preschool children, 10.6% of the activities were targeted for first to fourth grade children, 25.5% of the activities were targeted for fifth to eighth graders, another 25.5% of the activities included high school youth, and the remaining 29.9% of the activities were targeted for adults. In terms of wider age categories, most of the activities (70% of them) were targeted for pupils (including preschool, elementary school, and high school), and the remaining activities involved adults (these adults were mostly in-service teachers or student teachers that were trained to transmit peace education activities to their classes now or in the future).

## Types of Activity

Another meaningful classification category is the content and type of activity conducted. The following major types of activities were identified in this study: (1) dialogue, either political, or interpersonal, or both; (2) social activities, including social games and social events; and (3) arts and creative activities.

It is important to note that these are ideal types and that many actual programs combine two or three of the types of activity that are often enacted at different stages of the project. For instance, a dialogue can lead to social activities and arts activities can be used to prepare the stage for a dialogue.

*Distribution of Contents and Types of Activities.* The most prevalent type of activity was social activity, which was included in 66% of the investigated, encounter programs.[3] Dialogue activities were included in 38% of the encounter programs and arts activities were included in 26% of the programs.

It was further found that programs targeted for preschool children or for children in the first to the eighth grade did not include components of dialogue. However, most of the programs involving adults and youth (75% of the programs involving high school youth and 64% of the programs involving adults) did include such components.

---

[3] A type of activity was considered as included in a program if at least one third of the meeting time was dedicated to this component.

# CRITERIA FOR EVALUATING PEACE EDUCATION PROGRAMS: PROCESS-ORIENTED APPROACHES

The second goal of this study was, as stated before, to define criteria for evaluating the effectiveness of coexistence or peace education encounters. The most common approach to evaluating the effectiveness of intergroup contact is based on measurements of before–after changes in attitudes, perceptions, and emotions of participants. Though they provide important evaluation criteria, there are also problems and limitations to the use of such measurements (for interesting discussions on the limitations of before–after attitude-change measurements in evaluating effectiveness of peace education programs, see Salomon, 1999; McCauley, chap. 22, this volume).

Here I present two additional approaches that focus on the here and now of the encounter. These process-oriented approaches could be useful to employ in combination with the more traditional, outcome focused, attitude-change measurements.

## The Basic Functioning Approach

This approach involves looking at the basic functioning of the project. Major evaluation questions to be asked within this approach are as follows: Is the project functioning reasonably? Are meetings held regularly? Are participants from both sides arriving at the meetings? Are the activities that were planned carried out in these meetings? Are the actual contents of the meetings somehow related to peace education?

The main assumption used here is that in order to be effective, a coexistence program must fulfill the basic conditions of functioning. That is, there should be a series of meetings between the groups; once or even twice is not enough. Meetings should also not be too far apart; a gap of 3 weeks or more may disrupt the continuity of the process. These may seem very basic standards of evaluation, yet a survey of the field of Jewish–Arab coexistence activities over the years shows that these are not trivial demands. Typically, we find that part of these activities are not carried out as planned, not carried out at all, or only partly implemented because of what can be generally named *technical problems*. These include programs that begin to operate much later than planned, programs that begin operating and then suddenly stop, or programs in which there are very large intervals between the meetings (Maoz, 2000b). It is important to note though that in the present research population, of encounter activities conducted in the year 1999–2000, a relatively high percentage of activities (more than 90% of them) were carried out as planned in terms of number and frequency of meetings.

Technical problems often reflect problems in recruiting staff or participants from one or both sides, or problems inside the organizations themselves (financial, personnel). Technical problems can also reflect ambivalence of the organizers or the participants in regard to the project. Finally, such problems often signify a lack of infrastructure, or a lack of knowledge on part of the organizers on how to carry out the planned activity in a way that is responsive to the needs, preferences, and limitations of the participants. These problems may tend to characterize more often novice or smaller organizations that have not clearly defined to themselves what they want to do about peace education or how.

Given the above predictors or correlates of technical problems in encounter programs, it is possible to diagnose, in advance, programs that are at high risk for technical problems in their functioning. Such a diagnosis could guide policies of funding and investment in peace education programs. In addition, it could also enable the use of preventive measures that might help strengthen, ahead of time, some of the weaker areas of functioning in the organization.

## The Quality of Interaction Approach

Another approach to evaluating peace education encounters centers on the quality of the interaction between the participants in the encounter. The basic assumption used here is that we would expect some minimal, behavioral learning to occur after participating for some time in such an intergroup activity. That is, we would generally expect to observe individuals from both groups participating in the activity, interacting with each other, relating to each other, and so on.

Thus, we evaluate peace education or coexistence activities by looking at behavioral indicators such as degree of participation or involvement in intergroup interaction. Evaluation questions that can be asked within this approach are as follows: Are people interacting with each other in these meetings? Do people from both sides participate in the interaction? Do these interactions fulfill our minimal expectations of learning to relate to each other?

One important criterion for interaction quality, proposed here, is symmetry in participation. As described earlier, Jewish–Arab encounters in Israel are embedded in a sociopolitical reality of asymmetrical power relations between the Jewish majority and the Arab minority. Peace education encounters that replicate this asymmetry through dominance in the encounter of Jewish participants can help perpetuate the existing negative attitudes and stereotypes that stem from the asymmetry in power.

Therefore, an important aspect of the quality of the intergroup interaction in peace education encounters is symmetry in participation. Specifically, this parameter relates to the degree to which participants from both groups take an equal part in speaking, in bringing up ideas, and in determining and initiating topics of conversations and directions of activity.

Participating in an intergroup interaction in which both groups take an equal part or close to an equal part, may help individuals to unlearn previous asymmetrical patterns of majority–minority interaction (in which the majority group members dominate the interaction). It may enable them to experience a different option of interacting with the other group that they may not have sufficiently encountered before and outside of the intervention.

Though these interaction expectations may seem low, again, their fulfillment within the encounter is not trivial. Clearly, if we want higher aims of attitude change or inclusion of the other within the self to be reached, this more minimal goal of interaction between the groups has to be achieved.

The process-oriented criteria outlined in this section can be used to differentiate between successful and effective peace education models and less effective ones. Effective programs would be, according to the basic standards presented here, those that function regularly and that involve their participants in a symmetrical or close to symmetrical intergroup interaction. These requirements are fundamental in the sense that higher goals of attitude change and reduction of stereotypes are not likely to be achieved if the program does not fulfil these basic standards.

The next step that can be taken, after we have identified our basic criteria for evaluating the effectiveness of intergroup, contact interventions, is to see what characterizes effective programs. Here, one would look for the attributes that differentiate between effective and less effective encounters, for the principles or guidelines that could be suggested, on the basis of observations in the field, for forming an effective model of peace education through encounters. Observing the field suggests that in order to conduct a peace education encounter project that could be minimally effective in reaching its goals, one has to take into consideration a series of necessary (though not sufficient) conditions for the *good enough* peace education model (Ross, 2000). Basically these conditions refer to a model that should be responsive to the needs and interests of the participants, so they would be motivated to take part and to participate in it.

In the next section, I outline some of these major conditions for effective projects—the attributes that were found in this study as differentiating between effective peace education encounter programs and less effective ones.

## CONDITIONS FOR CONDUCTING EFFECTIVE PEACE EDUCATION ENCOUNTER PROGRAMS

The conceptual mapping and evaluation of the different peace education encounter-programs reveals a number of major principles or necessary conditions for conducting an effective peace education encounter intervention. Some of these are presented below.

- **Goals:** Organizations doing peace education encounter programs must clearly define their goals, and specify the practices they use to achieve these goals.

- **Suitability:** Peace education encounter programs must suit the needs of target populations that may differ as a function of age, gender, degree of religiosity or other characterstics of that population.
- **Role Models:** People organizing peace education encounter programs must themselves be knowledgeable and experienced in the field of peace education through encounters and be committed to peace education work. Facilitators of these activities should know, based on their own experience, how to deal with dynamics of contradicting emotions that may rise both within and between the groups.
- **Symmetry:** An organization conducting peace education through intergroup encounters must have some degree of symmetry (equality) in the proportion of members of both groups in its staff and management.
- An activity of peace education through intergroup encounters must have one facilitator from each group and a similar number of participants from each participating group.
- **Preparation:** Some participants, especially children who have not met the other side before, may need preparation before the encounter. Theoretical learning about the relations between the sides may not be enough. Discussions of feelings and expectations may be needed.
- **Forms of Activity:** In order to create sustained contacts and lasting results a few conditions must be filled in terms of quantity and frequency of meetings between the two groups:
  - There must be enough meetings between the groups. Once or even twice is not enough. At least four to eight meetings may be needed to create lasting contacts.
  - Meetings of both groups must not be too far apart. A gap of three weeks or more may disrupt the continuity of the process.
  - In case of unavoidable gaps between meetings of the two groups, it is advisable to preserve continuity by conducting relevant discussions and activities of each national group alone. These single-group meetings can be used to discuss the last intergroup meeting and to prepare toward the coming one.

## CONCLUSION AND PRACTICAL IMPLICATIONS

In this paper I have outlined basic categories that can be used to classify peace education encounters, such as the ideological approach, and the age target group. The second step after defining the basic building blocks of the peace education encounter was to propose criteria for evaluating the effectiveness of these interventions. The criteria suggested here are focused on the here and now and on the process of the activity.

This process-oriented evaluation approach, when taken together with the more outcome-oriented approach of attitude-change measurements, can provide a comprehensive paradigm for assessing effectiveness of peace education interventions. In addition, the process-oriented evaluation proposed here can be used as an online, formative, evaluation mechanism. This mechanism can provide the organizers of the program and its facilitators with feedback that can help them make changes and improvements in the quality of the intergroup interaction or in the functioning of the project, while it is still going on, thus increasing the chances for its effectiveness.

Returning to the previously defined categories of peace education encounter programs, I believe it could also be useful to examine the relation between the category the program belongs to and its effectiveness in terms of interaction quality, basic functioning, and attitude change. Do we find, for instance, that programs involving youth show lower interaction quality than those involving children or adults? Are confrontational models more or less effective in attitude change than the traditional coexistence ones? Do programs targeted at adults function better than those targeted at school children and youth? Examining these questions in relation to ongoing activities can help organizers and funders of peace education programs determine the cost effectiveness of different categories of interventions and can, thus, provide guidelines for the future planning of their peace education policy.

## ACKNOWLEDGMENTS

This study is part of larger research project sponsored by the Abraham Fund, that supports a major part of the coexistence activities in Israel. The results presented here are preliminary and represent part of the findings at the present stage of research. I wish to express my appreciation to the Abraham Fund for enabling and supporting this research. For a summary evaluation report of this research, see Maoz (2001).

## REFERENCES

Allport, G. (1954). *The nature of prejudice*. Reading, MA: Addison-Wesley.
Bar, H., & Bargal, D. (1995). *Living with the conflict: Encounters between Jewish and Palestinian Israeli Youth*. Jerusalem: The Jerusalem Institute for Israel Studies (Hebrew).
Bar-On, D. (1999, November). *Beyond victimhood: Some contradictions in the concept of coexistence*. Paper presented at the University of Haifa Faculty of Education & the Abraham Fund Conference, Interethnic Coexistence: Educating for an Emerging Global Field. Israel, Haifa, University of Haifa.
Maoz, I. (2000a). Power relations in intergroup encounters: A case study of Jewish-Arab encounters: In Israel *International Journal of Intercultural Relations, 24*(4), 259–277.
Maoz, I. (2000b). Multiple conflicts and competing agendas: A framework for conceptualizing structured encounters between groups in conflict—a case of a coexistence project between Jews and Palestinians in Israel. *Journal of Peace Psychology, 6*(2), 135–156.

Maoz, I. (2001, February). *Evaluation of Jewish-Arab coexistence activities in Israel, 1999–2000—A summary evaluation report*. Submitted to the Abraham Fund, Jerusalem, Israel. (in Hebrew)

Pettigrew, T. (1998). Intergroup contact theory. *Annual Review of Psychology, 49*, 65–85.

Sherif, M. (1966). *Group conflict and cooperation*. London: Routledge & Kegan Paul.

Salomon, G. (1999, November). *Reexamination of peace education principles in interethnic conflict context*. Paper presented at the University of Haifa Faculty of Education & the Abraham Fund Conference, Interethnic Coexistence: Educating for an Emerging Global Field. Israel, Haifa, University of Haifa.

Sonnenschein, N., Halabi, R., & Friedman, A. (1998). Legitimization of national identity and the change in power relationships in workshops dealing with the Israeli/Palestinian conflict. In E. Weiner (Ed.), *The handbook of interethnic coexistence*. New York: Abraham Fund.

Suleiman, R. (1997). The planned encounter between Israeli Jews and Palestinians as a microcosm: A social-psychological perspective, *Iyunim Bechinuch, 1*(2), 71–85. (in Hebrew)

Ross, M. (2000). "Good-enough" isn't so bad: Thinking about success and failure in ethnic conflict management. *Journal of Peace Psychology, 6*(1), 27–47.

# 24

# Peace Education Programs and The Evaluation of their Effectiveness

Baruch Nevo and Iris Brem

*University of Haifa*

The purpose of this chapter is to summarize, conceptually as well as quantitatively, the body of research that has been published in the past 20 years in which an attempt was made to evaluate the effectiveness of a Peace Education (PE) program. During the period 1981–2000, close to 1,000 articles, chapters in books, institutional reports, and convention–symposium presentations that dealt with the broadly defined topic of PE were published (based on a search of PsyLit, Eric, and numerous peace-focused Web sites). Approximately 30% of these items referred to a particular PE intervention program.

Before advancing any further in the issue of effectiveness evaluation (of these programs), let us first propose a conceptual framework that organizes all or most PE programs into a comprehensive model. This framework is a facetlike taxonomy. Facet models were suggested by Louis Guttman as being most appropriate for describing and analyzing complete, behavioral universes.[1]

Each PE program can be classified by any one of the facets. A specific PE program is characterized by a *facet profile* (or "structuple" in Guttman's terminology).

---

[1] The best source for Guttman's ideas is a posthumous collection of Guttman's writings edited by Shlomit Levy, his student and colleague (see Levy, 1994). Facet theory is treated in many of the chapters, especially chaps. 1, 5, 7, and 9.

# ORIENTATION MAP FOR PE PROGRAMS

The following are the major proposed facets. Evaluation methodology is integrated within the taxonomy.

## Facet A: Purpose of the Program

A1: The enhancement of:
- $a_{1.1}$ conflict resolution skills
- $a_{1.2}$ prosocial skills orientation
- $a_{1.3}$ political efficacy
- $a_{1.4}$ value-oriented attitudes
- $a_{1.5}$ tolerance toward diversity; multiculturalism
- $a_{1.6}$ coexistence; cooperation
- $a_{1.7}$ respect for the other; sense of equality
- $a_{1.8}$ reconciliation, forgiveness, empathy
- $a_{1.9}$ enrichment of information about the *other*
- $a_{1.10}$ democratic beliefs
- $a_{1.11}$ good interpersonal relations

A2: The reduction of:
- $a_{2.1}$ aggression
- $a_{2.2}$ violence
- $a_{2.3}$ delinquency
- $a_{2.4}$ prejudice; stereotype
- $a_{2.5}$ ethnocentrism

## Facet B: Age of Participants

Most PE programs aim at students who are in the following:

- $b_1$ primary school (8–12 years)
- $b_2$ junior high school (13–15 years)
- $b_3$ senior high school (16–18 years)
- $b_4$ college students (18–25 years)

## Facet C: Major Didactic Approach Used in the Program

- $c_1$ lectures given by teachers tutors
- $c_2$ lectures given by students
- $c_3$ watching videos, films, listening to tapes that present relevant materials; reading relevant materials
- $c_4$ writing essays
- $c_5$ mixed group sessions (with the *other*); open discussions
- $c_6$ mixed group sessions (with the *other*); structured meetings

$c_7$ conducting a joint project that is related unrelated to peace processes
$c_8$ simulations (of conflicts, negotiations, etc.)

## Facet D: Duration of the Program

$d_1$ several hours
$d_2$ several weeks/months
$d_3$ school year
$d_4$ several years

## Facet E: Research Design That Is Used by the Researcher (in Order To Measure Effectiveness)

E1: PE intervention with a control:  E2: Without control group:
   (No treatment) group.     $e_{2.1}$ posttest only
   For both groups:     $e_{2.2}$ pretest and posttest
$e_{1.1}$ posttest only     $e_{2.3}$ pretest, posttest, and delayed
$e_{1.2}$ pretest and posttest       posttest
$e_{1.3}$ pretest, posttest, and delayed
   posttest

Most researchers agree that the optimal design for the study of effectiveness of educational intervention programs is $e_{1.3}$.

## Facet F: Method of Measurement (Operational)

$f_1$ self-report questionnaires
$f_2$ structured observations (by teachers, parents, and researchers)
$f_3$ essays analysis
$f_4$ self-reported behaviors
$f_5$ official statistics (i.e., rate of violent incidents; rate of mixed marriages)
$f_6$ knowledge mastery tests
$f_7$ structured interviews

As an explanation of how the model works, an example is provided here. Roush and Hall (1993) conducted a PE program in which the emphasis was on teaching conflict resolution techniques to elementary and junior high school students. Here is the abstract of the article in which Roush and Hall reported their study:

> Conflict is a regular occurrence in school. The study described here was designed to evaluate the effects of teaching students peaceful conflict resolution skills and

training mediators. At the elementary school level, conflict resolution lessons were taught to fourth, fifth, and sixth graders. At the junior high level, an elective course was taught in conflict resolution. Mediators were trained at both levels. It was theorized that students would increase significantly their knowledge in conflict resolution, mediators' self-esteem would improve significantly, and conflicts would decrease significantly on the elementary school playground. (p. 185)

For the sake of simplicity, we refer here to the elementary school program only. The purpose of the program was the enhancement of conflict resolution skills ($a_{1.1}$) and reduction of violence ($a_{2.2}$). Age of participants was elementary school ($b_2$). Major didactic approaches adopted by the teachers were lectures given by teachers ($c_1$) and training for mediators by simulations ($c_8$). Duration of the program was one semester ($d_2$). The research design that was applied was postintervention versus preintervention comparison, with no control group ($e_{2.2}$). The effects of the PE program were measured by official statistics ($f_5$) and knowledge test ($f_6$).

The facet structuple of Roush and Hall study is, in sum:

$$[a_{1.1}; a_{2.2}/b_2/c_1; c_8/d_2/e_{2.2}/f_5; f_6]$$

## WHAT'S MISSING?

After this descriptive map is reviewed, a more critical approach can follow. It might be worthwhile to look again at the various facets and elements and at the same time at the variety of PE programs and point to missing parts, that is, elements that are rare among actual PE programs traced in our survey. The major points are as follows.

Facet A:
- Not enough attention is given to behavior. Only a few programs aimed at this goal.
- Theoretically, it is possible that while an intervention program enhances a certain skill or attitude, at the same time, *other* skills or attitudes are reduced or weakened. For instance, PE may enhance tolerance for the *other* and yet at the same time it may reduce one's sense of identity with a particular collective.

Facet B:
- What about PE for adults? Only a few PE programs aimed at adults.

Facet C:
- The majority of PE programs appeal to rationality; only a few relate to emotional aspects.

Facet D:
- Very few PE programs continue operating with same participants for more than 1 year.

Facet E:
- Delayed posttest is important; nevertheless, it is very rare in PE research.
- Generalizability of the program onto related individuals (i.e., parents or siblings) was hardly studied.

# EVALUATION

Out of the approximately 300 items that referred to a 1981–2000 literature survey and described a PE program, one third (about 100) had in them elements of effectiveness evaluation. This figure by itself is a testimony to the relative scarcity of evaluation studies in PE. It is quite clear that hundreds of PE programs are initiated and operated around the globe, at any particular period, without being subjected to any act of empirical validation.

The reasons for the lack of accompanying evaluation phase in many PE interventions are hypothesized to be the low level of awareness regarding the importance and usefulness of that phase; a lack of expertise in evaluation methodology; budgetary considerations; and avoidance tactics.

The list of the 104 articles, chapters in books, institutional reports, and convention presentations constitute Appendix A.

Some of these manuscripts provide details regarding two or even three evaluation studies. In contrast, for many items the information provided by the document did not allow for classification of program effectiveness. Here we also included items for which we had failed to trace the full-text manuscript or even its abstract. Some 29 items belong to this no-information category.

In all, 79 evaluation studies created the body for this analysis.

For each study we asked only one question: Was the intervention effective? Studies were grouped into three categories:

- The intervention was found to be statistically effective.
- No effectiveness was proved.
- Findings regarding the intervention effectiveness were unclear. Some criteria variables were significant; others were not (partially effective).

The following table summarizes our review:

Effectiveness of Peace Education Programs

| Program Success | No. of Studies |
| --- | --- |
| Effective | 51 |
| Partially effective | 18 |
| Noneffective | 10 |
| Total | 79 |

The general impression regarding PE programs seems to be positive: Out of 79 studies, the majority of programs were found to be effective (51) or partially effective (18). This is certainly an encouraging picture.

## CAUTIONARY REMARKS

First, this summary is based on the authors' judgment of the studies' findings. Some of these judgments, especially those related to the intermediate category, (Partially Effective) are subjective by their nature. Second, this summary is not a formal meta-analysis. A formal meta-analysis necessitates the calculation of $d$ (the measure of intervention effect in terms of criterion change) for each study; characterizing the studies on the basis of their methodological strength; weighing each study's contribution by its sample size; and so on. We lack the resources required for such an undertaking. Third, it is not unreasonable to assume that the impact of PE is somewhat less encouraging than what is reflected in the table here. There might be a positive correlation between the PE programs' effectiveness and the willingness of the program leader to expose it to an evaluation process and his or her willingness to report the findings. In other words, it is quite possible that some of the failures in this area (zero or negative effect) were never reported publicly.

The next step in this line of analysis was an attempt to compare the effective PE interventions with the noneffective ones and study the particular characteristics that differentiate between them. The orientation map was used. Some interesting characteristics were identified.

The following are some of the profile characteristics of the noneffective programs (as compared with the effective ones): more noneffective than effective programs attempted to reduce actual violence; more noneffective programs focused on junior high schools; more noneffective programs lasted more than 1 year; fewer noneffective programs used simulations as a didactic tool; more noneffective programs used official statistics as a measurement device. Some of these findings are contraintuitive. For instance, in this comparison there is an indication that long-range programs are *less* effective than shorter programs. This is exactly the kind of information a researcher or a practitioner would like to receive. This is why we need evaluation studies. Here also, a methodological comment is in place: The noneffective group consisted of 10 studies only. Any index based on such a small sample might be inconsistent.

## CONCLUSION

In spite of some methodological reservations, it seems that, in general, PE programs do have a positive effect. An analysis of 79 such studies revealed that 80%–90% of the programs are effective or at least partially effective. This is a very encouraging picture.

# REFERENCES

Levy, S. (1994). *Louis Guttman on theory and methodology*. Hampshire, U.K.: Dartmouth.

Roush, G., & Hall, E. (1993). Teaching peaceful conflict resolution. *Mediation Quarterly, 11*(2), 185–191.

## List of Papers Reporting on PE Effectiveness (1985–2000)

Aber, L. J., Brown, J. L., & Henrich, C. C. (1999). *Teaching conflict resolution: An effective school-based approach to violence*. New York: Columbia University.

Aber, J. L., Jones, S. M., Brown, J. L., Chaudry, N., & Samples, F. (1998). Resolving conflict creatively: Evaluating the developmental effects of a school-based violence prevention program in neighborhood and classroom context. *Development and Psychopathology, 10*(2), 187–213.

Aitken, C. J. (1995). *Using a classroom approach to teach peer mediation to grades 3 and 4 by developing a peacebuster manual* (Practicum Report). Nova Southeastern University.

Araki, C. T., Takeshita, C., & Kadomoto, L. (1989). *Research results and final report for the Dispute Management in the Schools Project*. Honolulu, HI: University of Hawaii. (ERIC Document Reproduction Service No. ED 312 750)

Argyris, P., Kaiser, R., Storm, S., Swartz, E., & Voss, S. (1994). *Improving Conflict Resolution Skills of Primary Students through Curriculum Adaptation and Teacher Interventions*. Master's Thesis, Saint Xavier University, Wheeling Illinois. (ERIC Document Reproduction Service No. ED 374 377)

Bar, H., & Bargal, D. (1985). *The school for peace at Neve Shalom: Description and analysis of an action research*. Jerusalem: The Israel Institute of Applied Social Research.

Bar, H., Bargal, D., & Asaqla, J. (1989). *The School for Peace at Neve-Shalom 1985–1989: A preliminary integrative summary of the findings of an evaluation and action research*. Jerusalem: The Israel Institute of Applied Social Research.

Bar, H. & Bargal, D. (1992). *Development of an intervention model for management of intergroup conflict among groups of Arabs and Jews: An action research perspective*. Paper presented at the 4th annual Kurt Lewin Conference, Philadelphia.

Bargal, D. (1992). Conflict management workshops for Palestinian and Jewish youth: A framework for planning, intervention and evaluation. *Social Work with Groups, 15*(1), 51–68.

Beetham, S., McLennan, C., & Witucke, C. (1998). *Improving social competencies through the use of conflict resolution and cooperative learning*. Action Research Project, Saint Xavier University, Chicago, Illinois. (ERIC Document Reproduction Service No. ED 421 271)

Bell, M., Dawson, D., Nelson, J., & Savdie, C. (1997). *Improving primary level interpersonal skills through conflict resolution, cooperative learning and children's literature*. Master's Action Research Project, Saint Xavier University, Braidwood, Illinois. (ERIC Document Reproduction Service No. ED 410 059)

Bergman, A. B. (1989). *Results of Conflict Resolution Goal at Maugham School: A report*. Tenafly Public Schools.

Berlowitz, M. J., & Kmitta, D. M. (1993). *Pilot project research on conflict resolution training in an urban school setting*. Paper presented at the American Educational Studies Association Convention, Chicago.

Bjerstedt, A. (1988). Preparedness for peace: A research and development project in process. *Didakometry and Sociometry, 20*(1–2).

Bodine, R. J., & Crawford, D. K. (1998). *The handbook of conflict resolution education: A guide to building quality programs in schools*. San Francisco: Jossey-Bass.

Brown, R. S., Soudack, A., Edwards, C., Kearns, T., & Harris, K. (1995). *An evaluation of the conflict resolution programs at the secondary level at the Toronto Board of Education 1993–94.* Toronto: Board of Education. Master's Thesis, Saint Xavier University, Illinois. (ERIC Document Reproduction Service No. ED 380 730)

Carter, S. (1990). *Evaluation report on New Mexico mediation in schools: 1989–90.* Albuquerque, NM: University of New Mexico.

Christie, D. J. (1991, August). *The measurement of psychological constructs in peace education.* Paper presented at the 98th annual meeting of the American Psychological Association, Boston.

Crary, D. (1992). Community benefits from mediation: A test of the "peace virus Hypothesis." *Mediation Quarterly, 9,* 241–252.

CRU Institute (1999). *Sealth high school 1998–1999 training project evaluation outcomes.* Bellevue, WA: CRU Institute.

Darom, D. (1998). Peace education in Israel—encounter and dialogue. *Mediterranean Journal of Educational Studies, 3*(1), 129–139.

Deutsch, M., Khattri, N., Mitchell, M., Tepavac, L., Zhang, Q., Weitzman, E. A., & Lynch, R. (1992). *The effects of training in conflict resolution and cooperative learning in an alternative high school.* New York: Columbia University.

Dudley, B. S., Johnson, D. W., & Johnson, R. (1996). Conflict-resolution training and middle-school students' integrative negotiation behavior. *Journal of Applied Social Psychology, 26,* 2038–2052.

Eckhardt, W. (1984). Peace studies and attitude change: A value theory of peace studies. *Peace and Change, 4*(1), 79–85.

Epstein, E. B. (1996). Evaluation of an elementary school conflict resolution peer mediation program. *Dissertation Abstracts International Section A: Humanities and Social Sciences, 57*(6-A), 2370.

Fuller, R. M., Kimsey, W. D., & Mckinney, B. C. (1993). *School-based dispute systems design: Communication training in tolerance of other ethnic groups.* Paper presented at the National Conference on Peacemaking and Conflict Resolution, Portland, OR.

Garibaldi, A., Blanchard, L., & Brooks, S. (1998). Conflict resolution training, teacher effectiveness and student suspension: The impact of a health and safety initiative in the New Orleans public schools. *Journal of Negro Education, 65*(4), 408–413.

Gentry, B., & Benenson, W. (1993). School-to-home transfer of conflict management skills among school-age children. *Families in Society, 74,* 67–73.

Graham, B. C., & Pulvino, C. (2000). Multicultural conflict resolution: Development, implementation and assessment of a program for third graders. *Professional School Counseling, 3*(3), 172–179.

Grossman, D. C., Neckerman, J. J., & Koepsell, T. D. (1997). The effectiveness of a violence prevention curriculum among children in elementary school: A randomized controlled trial. *Journal of the American Medical Association, 277*(20), 1605–1611.

Halpert, J. A. (1990, August). *Evaluation of a peace education program: Results, problems, and needs.* Paper presented at the 98th Annual Convention of the American Psychological Association, Boston. (ERIC Document Reproduction Service No. ED 339 665)

Hanson, M. K. (1996). *Evaluation of project PROUD (Peacefully Resolving Our Unsettled Differences)* (Final Report, 1992–93 through 1994–95). Dade County Public Schools' Office of Educational Accountability.

Harder Company Community Research (1997). *Whole schools Conflict Resolution Project.* San Francisco: San Francisco Peer Resources, Community Board Program.

Harris, I. M. (1990). *Peace studies in the United States at the university and college level.* (ERIC Document Reproduction Service No. ED 322 046)

Harris, I. M. (1992). The challenge of peace education: Do our efforts make a difference? *Educational Foundations, 6*(4), 75–98.

Harris, I. M., & Callender, A. (1995). Comparative study of peace education approaches and their effectiveness, *NAMTA Journal, 20*(2), 133–144.

Harris, I. M., Glowinski, J., & Perleberg, N. (1998). *Factors that promote implementation of peace education training* (Peace Education Miniprints No. 94). Sweden: Lund University. (ERIC Document Reproduction Service No. ED 429 898)

Harris, I. M., Jeffries, R., & Opels, R. (1997). Assessing the effectiveness of the University of Wisconsin—Milwaukee Summer Institute on Nonviolence. *Viewpoints on war, peace, and global cooperation* (pp. 26–41).

Hay, I., Byrne, M., & Butler, C. (2000). Evaluation of a conflict resolution and problem-solving programme to enhance adolescents' self-concept. *British Journal of Guidance & Counseling, 28*(1), 2000.

Hogan, L. (1993). A *Delphi study of effective characteristics of conflict mediation/resolution training programs for students in Washington schools*. Unpublished doctoral dissertation, Seattle University, Seattle.

Jenkins, J., & Smith, M. (1987). *Mediation in the schools 1986–87: Program Evaluation*. Albuquerque, NM: University of New Mexico.

Johnson, E. A., Thomas, D., & Krochak, D. (1998). Effects of peer mediation training in junior high school on mediators' conflict resolution attitudes and abilities in high school. *The Alberta Journal of Educational Research, 44*(3), 339–341.

Johnson, C. E., & Tempelton, R. A. (1998). *Promoting peace in a place called school*. Paper presented at the Annual Meeting of the American Educational Research Association, San Diego, CA. (ERIC Document Reproduction Service No. ED 422 648)

Johnson, D. W., & Johnson, R. T. (1995). Why violence prevention programs don't work and what does. *Educational Leadership, 52*(5), 63–68.

Johnson, D. W., & Johnson, R. T. (1995). Teaching students to be peacemakers: Results of five years of research. *Peace and Conflict: Journal of Peace Psychology, 1*, 417–438.

Johnson, D. W., & Johnson, R. T. (1996). Conflict resolution and peer mediation programs in elementary and secondary schools: A review of the research. *Review of Educational Research, 66*(4), 459–506.

Johnson, D. W., & Johnson, R. T. (1998). Teaching all students how to manage conflicts constructively: The Peacemakers Program. *Journal of Negro Education, 65*(3), 322–335.

Johnson, D. W., Johnson, R., Cotten, B., Harris, D., & Louison, S. (1995). Using conflict managers to mediate conflicts in an elementary school. *Mediation Quarterly, 12*(4), 379–390.

Johnson, D. W., Johnson, R. T., & Dudley, D. (1992). Effects of peer mediation training on elementary school students. *Mediation Quarterly, 10*, 89–99.

Johnson, D. W., Johnson, R. T., Dudley, B., & Acikgoz, K. (1994). Effects of conflict resolution training on elementary school students. *Journal of Social Psychology, 134*, 803–817.

Johnson, D. W., Johnson, R., Dudley, B., Mitchell, J., & Fredrickson, J. (1997). The impact of conflict resolution training on middle school students. *Journal of Social Psychology, 137*(1), 11–21.

Johnson, D. W., Johnson, R. T., Dudley, D., & Magnuson, D. (1995). Training of elementary school students to manage conflict. *Journal of Social Psychology, 135*(6), 673–686.

Johnson, D. W., Johnson, R. T., Dudley, D., Ward, M., & Magnuson, D. (1995). Impact of peer mediation training on the management of school and home conflicts. *American Educational Research Journal, 32*, 829–844.

Johnson, D. W., Johnson, R., Mitchell, J., Cotten, B., Harris, D., & Louison, S. (1996). Effectiveness of conflict managers in an inner-city elementary school. *Journal of Educational Research, 89*(5), 280–285.

Johnson, J., & Reed, F. (1996). Improving student's ability to resolve conflict. Master's Action Research Project, Saint Xavier University, Illinois. (ERIC Document Reproduction Service No. ED 400 074)

Jones, T. (1998, March–April). Research supports effectiveness of peer mediation. *The Fourth R* (CREnet), 82, 1, 10–12, 18, 21, 25, 27.

Jones, T. (1997). *Comprehensive peer mediation evaluation project: Preliminary final report*. William and Flora Hewlett Foundation, Surdna Foundation.

Kalmakoff, S., & Shaw, J. (1987). *Final report of the school peacemakers education project.*

Karneboge, L., Smith, S. B., Vandeschraaf, C., Wiegardt, C. G., & Wormer, G. (1999). Improving elementary and middle school students' abilities to manage conflict. Master's Action Research Project, Saint Xavier University, Illinois. (ERIC Document Reproduction Service No. ED 434 752)

Kemp, A. (1987). The impact of peace studies course on attitudes. *Journal of Peace Research, 19*(1), 11–18.

Kenneth, P. E., Muir-McClain, L., & Halasyamani, L. (1995). A review of selected school-based conflict resolution and peer mediation projects. *The Journal of School Health, 65*(10), 426–431.

Kinasewitz, T. M. (1996). *Reducing aggression in a high school setting through a conflict resolution and peer mediation program* (Practicum Report). Danbury, CT: Nova Southeastern University. (ERIC Document Reproduction Service No. ED 400 495)

Kmitta, D. M. (1997). *Peaceful possibilities: Three years of evaluative research of school-based conflict resolution programs.* Unpublished master's thesis, University of Cincinnati.

Kmitta, D. M., & Berlowitz, M. (1993). *Evaluation of the Center for Peace education programs 1992–1993: Final report.* Cincinnati, OH: University of Cincinnati. (ERIC Document Reproduction Service No. ED 405 390)

Kolan, K. (1999). An analysis of the short-term impact of peer mediation on high school disputants in an ethnically diverse suburban school system. Unpublished doctoral dissertation, George Washington University, Washington, DC. (ERIC Document Reproduction Service No. ED 430 168)

Korpi, M., Kaplan, G., & Arons, S. (1990). *Menlo-Atherton mediation program first-year evaluation report.*

Lam, J. (1989). *The impact of conflict resolution programs on schools: A review and synthesis of the evidence.* Amherst, MA: National Association for Mediation in Education. (ERIC Document Reproduction Service No. ED 358535)

Lanham, K., & Baker, D. (1997). Improving student behaviors through the use of conflict resolution in fifth and eighth grades. Master's Action Research Project, Saint Xavier University, Illinois.

LeBlanc, P., Lacey, C. H., & Mulder R. Jr. (1998). Conflict resolution. A case study of one high school class's experience. *Journal for a Just and Caring Education, 4*(2), 224–244.

Leonard, K. M. (1995). *Improving the social skills of kindergarten students in their multicultural setting through a peacemaking program* (Practicum Report). Absecon, NJ: Nova Southeastern University. (ERIC Document Reproduction Service No. ED 384 422)

Lindsay, P. (1998). Conflict resolution and peer mediation in public schools: What works? *Mediation Quarterly, 16*(1), 85–99.

Long, J. J., Fabricius, W. V., Musheno, M., & Palumbo, D. (1998). Exploring the cognitive and affective capacities of child mediators in a "successful" inner-city peer mediation program. *Mediation Quarterly, 15*(4), 289–300.

Mantovani, K. D. (1999). *Seventh-grade students attitudes toward conflict before and after applying a conflict resolution curriculum.* (ERIC Document Reproduction Service No. ED 430 974)

Maoz, Y. (1999). *Israeli-Palestinian youth encounter workshops in the framework of the IPCRI Educational Peace Project: Basic summary of research findings.*

Maoz, Y. (2000). Multiple conflicts and competing agendas: A framework for conceptualizing structured encounters between groups in conflict—The case of a coexistence project of Jews and Palestinians in Israel. *Peace and Conflict: Journal of Peace Psychology, 6*(2), 135–156.

Maoz, Y. (2000). An experiment in peace: Reconciliation-aimed workshops of Jewish-Israeli and Palestinian youth. *Journal of Peace Research, 37*(6), 721–736.

Mathur, S. R., & Rutherford, R. D. (1991). Peer-mediated interventions promoting social skills of children and youth with behavioral disorders. *Education and Treatment of Children, 14*(3), 227–242.

McCormick, M. (1988). *Evaluating school-based peer mediation programs.* Paper presented at the National Conference on Conflict Resolution in the Schools, Santa Fe, NM.

Metis Associates. (1998). *Atlanta Public Schools Resolving Conflict Creatively Program: Summary of the Final Evaluation Report 1996–1997.* Atlanta, GA: Metis.

Metis Associates. (1990). *The Resolving Conflict Creatively Program 1988–89: Summary of significant findings.* Atlanta, GA: Metis. (ERIC Document Reproduction Service No. ED 348 422)

Nakkula, M., & Nikitopoulous, C. (1998). *Program for young negotiators independent evaluation report.* Cambridge, MA: Harvard University.

Nakkula, M., & Nikitopoulous, C. (1996). *Preliminary evaluation findings for the fall 1995 implementation of the program for young negotiators.* Cambridge, MA: Harvard University.

Nelson, H. L. (1996). The impact of the student conflict resolution program in Dallas Public Schools. *Dissertation Abstracts International Section A: Humanities and Social Sciences, 56*(9-A), 3458.

O'Donnell, H. (1999). From the eyes of the students: An in-depth study of a fourth grade peer mediation class. *Dissertation Abstracts International Section A: Humanities and Social Sciences, 60*(2-A), 341.

Orpinas, P., Kelder, S., Frankowski, R., Murray, N., Zhang, Q., & McAlister, A. (2000). Outcome evaluation of a multi-component violence-prevention program for middle schools: The Students for Peace Project. *Health Education Research, 15*(1), 45–58.

Roderick, T. (1998). Evaluating the resolving conflict creatively program. *The Fourth R* (CRENet), 82, 3.

Rogers, P. (1991). *Education for peace in the classroom curriculum development strategies and materials: A case study from Ireland* (Peace Education Miniprints No. 24). (ERIC Document Reproduction Service No. ED 369 693)

Roush, G., & Hall, E.(1993). Teaching peaceful conflict resolution. *Mediation Quarterly, 11*(2), 185–191.

Salazar, M. L. (1995). *Peace education in the Denver public schools. A study of social studies classes in grade 7* (Peace Education Miniprints No. 78). Lund University, Sweden. (ERIC Document Reproduction Service No. ED 387 378)

Sherrod, M. (1995). Student peer conflict management in California high schools: A survey of programs and their efficacy as perceived by disciplinarians. *The Peer Facilitator Quarterly, 12*(4), 12–14.

Smith, M. W. (1981). *Improving intergroup relations: The impact of two types of small group encounters between Israeli Arab and Jewish youth.* Unpublished doctoral dissertation, Temple University, Philadelphia.

Soutter, A., & Mckenzie, A. (1998). Evaluation of the dispute resolution project in Australian secondary schools. *School Psychology International, 19*(4), 307–316.

Speirs, R. (1994). *Decreasing suspensions in grades nine through twelve through the implementation of a peace curriculum* (Practicum Report). Sanford, FL: Nova University. (ERIC Document Reproduction Service No. ED 378090)

Stevahn, L., Johnson, D. W., Johnson, R. T., & Real, R. (1996). The impact of a cooperative or individualistic context on the effectiveness of conflict resolution training. *American Educational Research Journal, 33*, 801–823.

Stevahn, L., Johnson, D. W., Johnson, R. T., Green, K., & Laginski, A. M. (1997). Effects on high school students of conflict resolution training integrated into English literature. *Journal of Social Psychology, 137*(3), 302–315.

Stevahn, L., Johnson, D. W., Johnson, R. T., Laginski, A. M., & O'Coin, I. (1996). Effects on high school students of integrating conflict resolution and peer mediation training into an academic unit. *Mediation Quarterly, 14*(1), 21–36.

Stevahn, L., Johnson, D. W., Johnson, R. T., Oberle, K., & Wahl, L. (2000). Effects of conflict resolution training into a kindergarten curriculum. *Child Development, 71*(3), 772–784.

Terry, B. L., & Gerber, S. (1997). *An evaluation of a high school peer mediation Program.* (ERIC Document Reproduction Service No. ED 415 455)

Tillman, Y. (1995). *Improving social skills in second graders through the implementation of a peace education/conflict resolution skills curriculum* (Practicum Report). Nova Southeastern University. (ERIC Document Reproduction Service No. ED 387 238)

Tolson, E., McDonald, S., & Moriarty, A. (1992). Peer mediation among high school students: A test of effectiveness. *Social Work in Education, 14*(2), 86–93.

Van Slyck, M., & Stern, M. (1991). Conflict resolution in educational settings: Assessing the impact of peer mediation programs. In K. G. Duffy, J. W. Grosch, & P. V. Olczak (Eds.), *The art and science of community mediation: A handbook for practitioners and researchers* (pp. 257–274). New York: Guilford.

Van Slyck, M., Stern, M., & Wulfert, E. (1998). *Understanding, enhancing and assessing peace education: An attitude change approach.* Paper presented at the meeting of the American Psychological Association, San Francisco.

Webster, D. W. (1993). The unconvincing case for school-based conflict resolution programs for adolescents. *Health Affairs Journal, 12*, 127–141.

Yvetta, G. (1995, November). *Effect of peaceful solutions peer mediation training on knowledge and skills of elementary students.* Paper presented during a training session at the Annual Conference of the Mid-South Educational Research Association, Biloxi, MS. (ERIC Document Reproduction Service No. ED 392 553)

# Author Index

# Subject Index